VIRTUAL REALMS & BEYOND: A METAVERSE RESEARCH ODYSSEY

EXPLORATION OF DIGITAL REALITIES IN THE METAVERSE ENVIRONMENT

DEVYANSH ARORA

Contents

The Metaverse is not just about creating a digital world to retreat to but also a digital world to augment, expand, and improve our reality.

Preface

Welcome to the Metaverse,

In recent years, the concept of the metaverse has captured the imaginations of millions around the globe. This virtual realm, teeming with endless possibilities and boundless creativity, has emerged as the next frontier in human interaction and innovation. From immersive virtual worlds to augmented reality experiences, the metaverse promises to revolutionise how we live, work, and play.

As an enthusiast and observer of this burgeoning phenomenon, I was inspired to delve deeper into the intricacies of the metaverse and its potential impact on society.

Despite its fanbase's genuine enthusiasm and its creators' determined efforts, the metaverse has challenges. In these pages, we will confront the myriad issues that must be addressed before the metaverse can be fully embraced. From concerns about privacy and security to questions of accessibility and inclusivity, significant barriers must be overcome to realise the full potential of this virtual realm.

But amidst these challenges, there is also cause for optimism. The metaverse represents a blank canvas upon which we can paint new worlds, forge new connections, and redefine the boundaries of human experience. By tackling the issues head-on and engaging in thoughtful dialogue, we can pave the way for a genuinely transformative, empowering, and equitable metaverse for all.

In writing this book, my aim is to inform and educate, spark conversation, and inspire action.

Thank you for embarking on this adventure with me.

Devyansh Arora

Acknowledgements

Writing a book is never a solitary endeavour; it is the culmination of support, guidance, and inspiration from countless individuals and experiences. I am deeply grateful to every person who has played a role in creating this book on the metaverse.

First and foremost, I extend my heartfelt thanks to my mentor, Ms. Richa Yadav, whose unwavering support and invaluable insights guided me through every step of this journey. Ms. Richa's dedication to refining the content, scrutinising the research, and enhancing the book's quality has been instrumental in its development.

To my father, whose unconventional teaching methods have profoundly shaped my perspective, I owe a debt of gratitude that words alone cannot express. His constant encouragement and belief in my abilities have strengthened and motivated me throughout this process. Making him proud remains my ultimate aspiration.

I am equally indebted to my mother, whose unwavering emotional support and understanding helped me navigate the challenges inherent in completing this book.

Special thanks are also due to Ms. Khushi, whose constant encouragement and motivation played a pivotal role in transforming this book from a mere idea into a tangible reality. Her unwavering support served as a constant reminder of the importance of perseverance and determination.

I am also immensely grateful to my friend, Mr. Pavun Singh, for his unwavering support and encouragement. Pavun has been a steadfast companion, always ready to lend an ear and offer support no matter how absurd my ideas may sound. His friendship and loyalty have been a constant source of strength and reassurance throughout this journey.

With sincere gratitude,

Devyansh Arora

CHAPTER I

Governance Models in Virtual Worlds: Legal and Economic Perspectives

INTRODUCTION

Virtual worlds, digital environments designed to replicate real-life experiences and interactions, have evolved beyond their initial purpose as entertainment platforms and have developed into intricate ecosystems with diverse governing structures. These models encompass complex frameworks that establish the guidelines, regulations, and systems that control these dynamic digital environments' interactions, transactions, and behaviours. Examining governance models in virtual worlds entails investigating the complex equilibrium between regulatory structures and individual autonomy that serves as the foundation for these digital environments.

The Evolution of Virtual worlds has experienced a significant transformation, progressing from their first text-based forms in the past to the graphically immersive and interactive environments that exist today. The range of these settings is extensive, encompassing many forms such as massively multiplayer online games, social networks, virtual reality simulations, and augmented reality experiences. The governance of virtual worlds becomes increasingly intricate as the underlying technology progresses. The importance of management is evident in virtual worlds, as it significantly influences the experiences and interactions of its inhabitants. These models significantly impact various aspects, including the generation and exchange of virtual assets, the formation of social norms, and the resolution of conflicts. Effective governance is crucial in maintaining a unified and peaceful atmosphere, whereas insufficient administration can result in disorder and disputes.

Achieving a harmonious equilibrium between user autonomy and essential regulatory measures is a significant obstacle in developing governance frameworks for virtual environments. Excessive regulation has the potential to impede innovation and impede the development of organic societies, whilst little regulation can lead to anarchy and exploitation. Attaining this intricate balance necessitates deeply comprehending the distinct dynamics inherent in virtual environments. The legal dimensions of governance structures in virtual worlds are of significant interest. There is a proliferation of inquiries about intellectual property rights, ownership of virtual property, and user agreements. As content generation, digital asset acquisition, and transactional engagement by users increase, it becomes imperative for legal frameworks to evolve to offer clarity and safeguarding measures.

The emergence of virtual economies has significant economic implications. Individuals engage in financial endeavours, including acquiring, exchanging, and disposing virtual commodities, frequently facilitated by virtual currency. The examination of governance models encompasses analysing economic issues, specifically focusing on the emergence and prosperity of economic systems inside digital settings. The scope and objectives of this study involved examining the governance models employed in virtual worlds to comprehend the intricate layers of complexity that regulate these dynamic digital ecosystems. This study offers insights into the design, implementation, and impact of different governance models by examining case studies, theoretical frameworks, and practical examples. In essence, the grasp of these models not only increases our understanding of virtual worlds but also provides vital insights into the broader intersections of technology, society, and regulation.

BACKGROUND

The inception of virtual worlds can be traced back to the nascent stages of computer technology, characterised by the emergence of text-based adventures and simulations. Over time, the progression of technology has resulted in the development of visually captivating three-dimensional virtual environments. These environments facilitate various activities, encompassing social interaction, recreational pursuits, discovery, and commercial exchanges. The increasing complexity of virtual worlds has underscored the necessity for efficient governance to regulate their wide range of activities effectively.

The evolution of governance in virtual worlds has occurred in parallel with the growth and development of these digital environments. In the nascent stages of virtual worlds, creators frequently depended on basic regulations to govern the functioning of these digital environments. Nevertheless, increasingly complex governance models began to develop with the proliferation of user-generated content, social connections, and economic activity. These models are influenced by legal, economic, and social frameworks observed in the real world and are further tailored to suit the distinct attributes of virtual worlds.

SIGNIFICANCE

Implementing governance models ensures that virtual worlds offer a favourable and captivating user experience while fostering community building. They play a vital role in establishing guidelines for behaviour, hence promoting the development of dynamic and all-encompassing online communities.

The emergence of virtual worlds has given rise to robust economies characterised by user participation in the acquisition, exchange, and commerce of virtual assets. Governance models are crucial in establishing structured frameworks for economic transactions and facilitating the growth of innovation, entrepreneurship, and virtual marketplaces.

The governance structures handle the ownership of virtual assets and intellectual property, considered crucial aspects of digital rights. These approaches effectively address the intricate challenges associated with copyright, trademark, and patent matters in the digital domain. The impact of governance models on social dynamics and identity is seen in their ability to mitigate harassment, cyberbullying, and other detrimental behaviours. Furthermore, they also contribute to the identity management process by facilitating users' expression within the boundaries of community standards.

The utilisation of virtual worlds has been observed in education and training. Governance models serve as the framework for facilitating immersive learning experiences, simulations, and collaborative environments. Legal and ethical considerations emerge as virtual worlds progressively intertwine with the physical realm. Governance models encompass various aspects such as jurisdictional considerations, user agreements, data protection, and the ethical utilisation of technology. There is a growing recognition among policymakers and regulators of the societal implications of virtual worlds. The presence of effective governance models plays a significant role in facilitating informed policy decisions that strike a balance between technical innovation and the overall welfare of society.

VIRTUAL WORLDS: AN OVERVIEW

Definition

The definition and purpose of governance models in virtual worlds involve a multifaceted system of policies, regulations, and guidelines that form the structural foundation for user behaviour, interactions, and activities within digital environments. Similar to how laws and institutions are essential for maintaining order in real-world civilisations, governance models in virtual worlds fulfil a comparable function by establishing a structured setting where users can participate, generate content, and conduct transactions in a regulated and orderly fashion.

Characteristics and Components

1. Rule Formulation and Clarity: Governance models encompass formulating and effectively communicating specific rules and norms that users must adhere to. The regulations above encompass a broad spectrum of behaviours, encompassing proper communication protocols, standards for generating information, and the suitable utilisation of virtual resources. The framing of rules with clarity is essential in mitigating misunderstandings and promoting consistent enforcement.

2. Flexibility and Adaptability: Effective governance models aim to strike a harmonious equilibrium between the imperative for organisational structure and acknowledge virtual realms' inherent dynamism and perpetual transformation. These entities are specifically engineered to accommodate technological progress, evolving user inclinations, and rising societal standards.

3. Enforcement Mechanisms: Enforcement mechanisms are established inside governance frameworks to ensure compliance with rules and address instances of infractions. This process may encompass the utilisation of automated technologies, human moderation, and the inclusion of reporting functionalities that empower people to identify and report information or behaviour that is deemed improper. User involvement and participation are frequently encouraged in governance models as a means to involve users in the process of creating rules. Virtual world communities often incorporate various tools that enable users to suggest modifications to existing laws, offer comments, and actively participate in the formulation of community principles.

4. Dispute Resolution Procedures: Implementing dispute resolution procedures is an essential element within governance models, as conflicts are bound to occur inside virtual environments. Efficient models offer well-defined strategies for resolving disputes, encompassing mediation, arbitration, or specific assistance channels.

5. Privacy and Data Management: Privacy and data management in virtual worlds are addressed by establishing governance models that delineate rules about data privacy, user permission, and data utilisation. The concerns above are of utmost importance in ensuring the protection of user information and adherence to pertinent data protection legislation.

Evolution and growth

The creation and growth of virtual worlds have been impressive as they have transitioned from basic text-based simulations to complex and visually engaging digital landscapes. Technological improvements, alterations in user tastes, and the rise of novel platforms have propelled the shift above. The progression of virtual worlds demonstrates human ingenuity, advancement, and the continuously broadening potential of digital encounters.

The inception of virtual worlds can be attributed to the nascent era of computing, during which the establishment of text-based adventures and simulations served as the fundamental building blocks. Individuals interacted with these rudimentary surroundings using textual instructions, thereby navigating around virtual realms shown using ASCII characters. Although possessing modest visual fidelity, these initial virtual worlds ignited users' creativity and alluded to the possibilities of immersive digital encounters. The advent of graphical interfaces was a pivotal milestone in the progression of virtual environments. The advancement of graphics technology has led to virtual environments that exhibit enhanced levels of detail and visual aesthetics. The transition from text-based to graphical interfaces facilitated users navigating and engaging with two-dimensional (2D) and three-dimensional (3D) environments, establishing the foundation for increasingly immersive experiences.

The emergence of the internet and the availability of broadband access have had a significant role in facilitating the growth and popularity of massively multiplayer online games (MMOs). These games enabled the convergence of numerous players within permanent virtual environments, allowing for instantaneous interactions and cooperative endeavours. Massively multiplayer online games (MMOs) such as "World of Warcraft" and "Second Life" have provided players with the opportunity to engage in shared virtual environments, enabling them to interact with others, embark on diverse missions, and partake in a range of activities. The development of virtual worlds has led to their transformation from conventional gaming environments to including social networks and user-generated content. Virtual platforms such as "Second Life" allowed users to generate and mould their virtual worlds, cultivating a sense of proprietorship and stimulating creative expression. This development represented a notable transition towards virtual experiences characterised by more openness and collaboration, allowing users to actively participate in defining the virtual environment.

The convergence of virtual reality (VR) and augmented reality (AR) technology has significantly advanced the development of virtual environments. Virtual Reality (VR) provides users with a comprehensive and immersive experience, enabling them to engage with virtual settings through specialised hardware. In contrast, augmented reality (AR) superimposes digital features onto the physical environment, augmenting ordinary encounters. The advent of these technologies has significantly broadened the scope of interactive storytelling, education, training, and entertainment within virtual environments. The emergence of metaverse concepts has garnered attention in recent years, as it proposes the creation of a virtual shared environment beyond the boundaries of distinct virtual worlds. The metaverse concept signifies the completion of the progressive development of virtual worlds when interconnected digital spaces merge to create an expansive and interconnected digital cosmos. The concept above has incited deliberations about interoperability, identity, and the amalgamation of tangible and virtual encounters.

The global impact and prospects of virtual worlds on several sectors of contemporary life, including entertainment, education, trade, and social interaction, can be attributed to their evolution and growth. In the foreseeable future, the progression of virtual worlds is expected to undergo further development, propelled by advancements in technology such as artificial intelligence, blockchain, and spatial computing. As the progression of these technologies persists, the distinction between the virtual realm and physical reality is anticipated to diminish progressively.

ECONOMIC IMPACT AND VIRTUAL ECONOMIES

Virtual worlds have evolved beyond being simple digital platforms for escapism. Instead, they have developed into complex ecosystems with substantial economic ramifications, both within the virtual environment and in the larger real-world context. The financial implications of virtual worlds extend beyond digital representations and virtual characters, encompassing various aspects such as revenue production, employment opportunities, trade, and the ability to shape consumer behaviour. These digital landscapes have undergone significant transformations and become complex economic entities requiring comprehensive examination.

Virtual worlds have been identified as highly profitable undertakings in terms of their economic impact. The influx of cash into virtual platforms has been facilitated by user subscriptions, in-game purchases, and the sale of virtual currency, thereby establishing a novel revenue model. The virtual nature of these money inflows notwithstanding, they have discernible impacts on the concrete economy of platform operators and developers in the real world. This exemplifies the potential of virtual interactions to generate tangible economic benefits in the physical world.

Furthermore, the emergence of virtual worlds has led to the creation of employment prospects in diverse industries. Virtual platforms require a workforce to maintain and enhance the user experience, encompassing various roles such as software development, customer service, and community administration. The contemporary labour market is being enriched by the rise of virtual entrepreneurs, who actively develop, produce, and exchange virtual commodities, augmenting the employment landscape. The dynamic relationship between virtual and real-world employment highlights the multifaceted economic consequences of virtual worlds.

The virtual economies that flourish within virtual worlds play a pivotal role in the economic dynamics of these environments. Digital marketplaces replicate their real-world counterparts, encompassing various commodities, currencies, and trade systems. Individuals participate in transactions involving virtual products surrounding digital fashion articles, accessories, and virtual properties. Digital currency users support the virtual economy by acquiring, utilising, and trading, frequently blurring the boundary between virtual and real-world financial frameworks.

Virtual economies demonstrate similarities to conventional economies since they adhere to fundamental principles such as supply and demand, scarcity, and inflation, which remain significant. Users fulfil various economic functions, including consumers, producers, merchants, and entrepreneurs. Virtual entrepreneurs serve as a prime illustration of the intersection between the virtual and tangible economic domains. Individuals utilise their acquired abilities to develop virtual goods for commercial purposes, transforming their online pursuits into natural sources of financial gain.

The reciprocal relationship between virtual and real-world economies allows for mutual influence and impact. The exchange of virtual cash for tangible currency significantly influences foreign exchange rates, emphasising the interdependence between these seemingly distinct realms. Furthermore, examining behavioural patterns witnessed in virtual economies can serve as a reflection of broader socioeconomic trends and consumer preferences, providing significant insights into the decision-making processes of individuals and the dynamics of markets.

Nevertheless, with the proliferation of virtual economies, concerns about regulation and governance come to the forefront. The simultaneous presence of virtual and real-world economic activity has prompted deliberations over taxation, legal structures, and the obligations of virtual platform operators. Governments and regulatory entities have the complex task of incorporating these innovative economic systems within established legal and fiscal frameworks.

LEGAL PERSPECTIVES ON GOVERNANCE IN VIRTUAL WORLDS

Jurisdictional challenges and conflicts

The advent of the digital era has given rise to virtual realms surpassing physical limitations, providing users unparalleled prospects for engagement, innovation, and economic transactions. Nevertheless, the absence of borders in virtual environments presents complex jurisdictional issues and disputes that encompass legal, ethical, and regulatory aspects. Addressing these matters becomes significant, given the increasing overlap between virtual and tangible activity, which complicates the delineation of governance and responsibility.

Virtual worlds exist in a realm that surpasses the limitations imposed by geographical boundaries, allowing for unrestricted operation. Individuals from many regions worldwide come together in everyday virtual environments, engaging in actions that yield tangible effects in the physical realm. The absence of borders poses difficulties in ascertaining the applicable laws and regulations governing virtual exchanges, transactions, and conflicts.

One of the main obstacles involves the identification of a suitable legal jurisdiction for operations conducted in virtual worlds. The potential for conflicting legal jurisdictions arises from the disparity in physical locations among the user, the server hosting the virtual world, and the virtual entity or platform. This intricate network of locations can give rise to a complex legal landscape. This situation may give rise to legal ambiguity, causing users to doubt the applicable legal framework that controls their conduct.

Intellectual property and digital assets frequently include the generation and transaction of digital entities, including but not limited to virtual properties, virtual commodities, and digital artistic creations within virtual environments. Nevertheless, ascertaining ownership, copyright, and intellectual property rights inside these digital domains can be complex. Individuals have the potential to generate, exchange, and duplicate virtual assets, which raises inquiries regarding the relevance and suitability of intellectual property legislation in the physical realm.

User Behaviour and Regulation invirtual environments encompass diverse user behaviours, from interpersonal engagements and creative endeavours to economic transactions and financial exchanges. The complexity of regulating user behaviour and content arises when considering the wide range of cultural standards, the principle of freedom of expression, and the possibility of offensive or destructive behaviour. Developing protocols and processes to enforce suitable conduct while simultaneously upholding users' rights presents a formidable undertaking.

The taxes and regulation of economic activity in virtual worlds, such as virtual commerce and virtual currency transactions, give rise to financial rules and taxation inquiries. The difficulty of ascertaining the taxability of virtual trades and the jurisdiction responsible for imposing such taxes is a matter of considerable complexity. More clearly defined legal frameworks may give rise to the possibility of tax evasion or unanticipated repercussions.

The resolution of disputes that develop within virtual environments is a distinctive challenge. Traditional legal systems may need more tools and mechanisms to effectively address virtual problems, whereas online platforms frequently employ internal methods for resolving conflicts. The absence of defined procedures for resolving disputes in various virtual environments further exacerbates the situation.

The emergence of self-government has been observed in certain virtual worlds as a response to the issues above. In these virtual environments, users actively formulate rules and resolve disputes, thereby collectively contributing to the governance of the community. The concept of self-governance confers authority and autonomy to a community, although it also engenders inquiries on the principles of responsibility, representation, and the possibility of disparate influence.

THE PATH TOWARDS PROGRESS: ACHIEVING A BALANCE BETWEEN REALITIES

The requirement to handle jurisdictional difficulties and conflicts becomes increasingly significant as virtual worlds expand and become more intertwined with real-world activity. The implementation of globally acknowledged standards and guidelines tailored to virtual environments, the promotion of cooperation among governments, virtual platform operators, and legal professionals, and the utilisation of emerging technologies such as blockchain for transparent record-keeping are measures that can facilitate navigation within this intricate domain. The future trajectory of virtual worlds will be determined by the delicate equilibrium between their capacity for innovation and the imperative for legal and ethical oversight.

USER RIGHTS AND VIRTUAL PROPERTY

Navigating the Complex Digital Landscape

Within the expansive and continuously growing domain of virtual worlds and online settings, a novel aspect of rights and ownership has surfaced, specifically concerning user rights and virtual property. As individuals engage extensively in these dynamic digital environments, inquiries about ownership, control, and the limitations of digital interactions have emerged as prominent concerns. Exploring the sophisticated framework of user rights inside virtual property unveils a terrain with many obstacles, intricacies, and prospects.

The narrative surrounding user rights in virtual worlds has experienced a notable progression, characterised by transforming these digital environments from basic text-based simulations to fully immersive 3D realities. The concept of user rights has also undergone a metamorphosis with this development. User rights have expanded beyond the physical domain, encompassing various factors like personal autonomy, expression, and the complexities of virtual property ownership.

The discussion's central focus on user rights concerns virtual property, which digitally represents physical goods in the actual world. The concept of virtual property comprises a diverse range of digital entities, creations, and assets that people get, personalise, or engage with within virtual settings. The content of virtual property, encompassing virtual real estate, avatars' apparel, intricate virtual art, and in-game money, reflects extensive user interactions.

Exploring user rights in the realm of virtual property

Upon delving into the complexities surrounding user rights in virtual property, many crucial factors come to light. Ownership extends beyond tangible assets, as virtual property challenges the traditional distinction between the tangible and intangible domains. Individuals allocate time, exertion, and substantial resources to obtain and enhance virtual assets. Therefore, it is crucial to prioritise establishing clear and indisputable ownership rights to cultivate a feeling of control and emotional connection.

The appeal of virtual economies stems from their potential to facilitate dynamic trade and business. Establishing guidelines for the proper transfer of virtual assets, whether it involves sales, exchanges, or gifts, requires a careful balance between user autonomy and the marketplace dynamics.

The concept of creative autonomy and modification is essential to the flourishing of virtual worlds, as these digital environments heavily rely on user-driven innovation. Allowing users to alter, adapt, and create distinct virtual objects fosters heightened involvement and individualisation.

Safeguarding Against Unlawful Use is the establishment of measures to prevent unlawful copying, replication, or misuse of virtual property, which constitutes a fundamental aspect of user entitlements. Implementing this protective measure maintains the authenticity and reliability of digital assets and fosters a climate of confidence and reliance.

The complexities of virtual economies arise from the intricate relationship between virtual property and user rights, introducing additional intricacy levels. These economies comprise a vibrant ecosystem characterised by user-driven commerce, entrepreneurial activities, and trade. Achieving equilibrium between user rights and the economic factors inherent in virtual economies necessitates a nuanced comprehension of the intricate interdependence between individual ownership and communal success.

The crucial role of platform operators is seen in the ongoing discourse surrounding user rights and virtual property. These operators play a vital role in managing and organising the virtual environment, influencing the regulations governing interactions, the boundaries of ownership, and the structure of virtual economies. Achieving a state of equilibrium that encompasses the protection of user rights, the long-term viability of platforms, and the intricacies of economic forces requires a multifaceted and cooperative strategy.

Choosing a Course of Action andAddressing user rights in the context of virtual property requires a multifaceted approach. Collaboration among platform owners, legal professionals, user groups, and regulatory organisations becomes crucial. Establishing thorough guidelines, open governance structures, and solid dispute-resolution procedures gives users a sense of security and confidence in the digital space.

INTELLECTUAL PROPERTY ISSUES

The present study aims to examine the complex landscape of intellectual property concerns within virtual worlds. By delving into several dimensions of this topic, we seek to comprehensively analyse the challenges and considerations associated with intellectual property in virtual environments.

Virtual worlds have brought about a new era of complexity in intellectual property (IP), where creativity, economics, and community intersect inside dynamic digital landscapes. Within these vast and extensive environments, individuals create, cooperate, and interact with diverse digital materials, giving birth to complex intellectual property (IP) issues encompassing several areas, such as copyright, trademark, and patent law. In light of the increasing convergence between the virtual and the real, it is crucial to undertake a more thorough exploration of these intricacies to achieve a comprehensive comprehension.

The virtual realms exemplify the boundless creative potential of human expression, unrestricted by the limitations imposed by the physical world. Users engage in the creation of elaborate narratives, the production of visually captivating virtual art, the composition of original musical pieces, and the development of immersive virtual worlds. The manifestation of artistic expression, a defining characteristic of virtual environments, establishes the fundamental basis for a dynamic digital culture. However, it additionally establishes the foundation for a comprehensive examination of intellectual property concerns.

The intricacies surrounding copyright in virtual worlds present novel challenges to the legal framework for safeguarding unique creative works. Users create a broad spectrum of content, encompassing derivative works that draw inspiration from pre-existing intellectual assets and transformative masterpieces that exhibit originality and innovation. The delineation of the limits between fair use, derivative works, and clear-cut infringement poses a significant and pressing obstacle.

The phenomenon of trademark challenges and branding in virtual realms is common as virtual worlds frequently replicate real-world environments, encompassing a wide array of branded products and services. However, the coexistence of user-generated content alongside virtual trademarks raises concerns over the weakening of brand identity, potential misunderstanding among consumers, and the possibility of infringing upon established trademarks. Navigating the delicate balance between protecting the rights of trademark owners and fostering the organic creativity of users is challenging.

Virtual worlds encompass more than just artistic expressions; they also encompass virtual real estate, architectural wonders, and intricate algorithms. These components raise issues around ownership, architectural rights, and intellectual property (IP) within the foundational code. Delineating intellectual property rights within these complex realms is a distinctive problem specific to the digital domain.

Utilising virtual worlds extends beyond their role as creative environments, as they serve as platforms for developing innovative technologies such as virtual reality (VR), augmented reality (AR), and blockchain. Patents serve as a means of safeguarding these innovative developments. However, the convergence of these technologies with user-generated material introduces unique intellectual property (IP) complexities, particularly within collaborative settings.

The phenomenon of user-generated content and the dynamics of ownership inside virtual environments highlight the active role of users as creators rather than passive consumers. They create digital art, the composition of storylines, and the formation of virtual landscapes. Ensuring unambiguous ownership and licensing conditions for user-generated content is of utmost importance in safeguarding the rights of creators while sustaining a flourishing digital environment.

Collaborative endeavours and collective creations are frequently observed within virtual environments when individuals combine their skills and abilities to generate a collective output surpassing individual contributions. The allocation of intellectual property rights in these enterprises necessitates the examination of issues about authorship, contribution, and group ownership.

The Intersection of Legal Jurisdictions and Ethical Considerations:

Virtual worlds possess a lack of geographical boundaries, hence drawing in individuals from various regions worldwide. The presence of international diversity raises inquiries regarding the jurisdictional scope of intellectual property laws and the ethical considerations about the development and utilisation of material. Navigating the intricate interplay between legal and ethical boundaries introduces a multifaceted dimension of intricacy.

TERMS OF SERVICE AND USER AGREEMENTS IN VIRTUAL WORLDS: GUIDANCE FOR DIGITAL INTERACTION AND LEGAL STRUCTURES

Virtual worlds, vast and complex digital environments, are regulated by a crucial but frequently undervalued element known as the Terms of Service (ToS) and User Agreements (UAs). The legal documents are guiding instruments that navigate the intricate landscape of user interactions, establishing the entitlements, responsibilities, and boundaries inside these immersive environments. This investigation comprehensively examines Terms of Service (ToS) and User Agreements (UAs). We recognise their fundamental significance in influencing user encounters and setting legal and ethical foundations for digital environments.

The Importance of Terms of Service and User Agreements:

The Terms of Service (ToS) and User Agreements (UAs) are fundamental texts establishing users' and platform operators' regulations, entitlements, and obligations in virtual environments. They fulfil diverse and complex functions:

The legal framework encompasses the agreements that establish the legal foundation, clarifying the complex interplay between users and platform operators. The topics covered encompass a wide range of concerns, including the ownership of virtual assets and the establishment of mechanisms for dispute resolution, thereby establishing a comprehensive legal framework for the virtual realm.

> **User Protections:** Terms of Service (ToS) and User Agreements (UAs) serve a dual purpose by addressing legal matters and preserving user rights and protections. The authors clarify users' rights regarding privacy, freedom of speech, and fair treatment, guaranteeing that users' encounters are marked by impartiality and courtesy. The rights of platform operators encompass granting authority to oversee and regulate the virtual realm. This includes the tasks of content moderation, the implementation of community norms, and the authority to suspend or cancel user accounts as required to uphold a secure and pleasant online environment.

Content policies, such as Terms of Service (ToS) and User Agreements (UAs), commonly include guidelines that outline the regulations about content users create. These policies establish the fundamental principles for creating a safe and balanced online environment, including addressing issues such as hate speech, harassment, and adherence to copyright regulations. The intricate components of Terms of Service (ToS) and User Agreements (UAs):

The structure and terminology employed in Terms of Service (ToS) and User Agreements (UAs) can be complex, incorporating various components that necessitate meticulous scrutiny.

> **Legal jargon:** The use of legal terminology in these documents renders them challenging for the average individual to comprehend in their entirety. The continuous problem revolves around ensuring that consumers can understand the words. The topic of discussion pertains to privacy policies. In the contemporary era characterised by data-centric interactions, virtual environments frequently amass user data. Privacy policies incorporated into terms of service (ToS) and user agreements (UAs) clarify how data is collected, utilised, and safeguarded to protect user information.

> **Guidelines for Content Creation:** User-generated material is crucial in virtual environments. However, it is imperative to establish explicit guidelines. Terms of Service (ToS) and User Agreements (UAs) frequently define the parameters of permissible material, encompassing matters such as hate speech, harassment, and the protection of intellectual property rights.

Dispute resolution agreements encompass provisions that delineate the techniques employed to address conflicts, encompassing various methods such as arbitration, mediation, or alternative approaches. These tools provide users with opportunities to address their issues within the legal framework of the virtual world. The concept of informed consent is of utmost importance, despite users generally consenting to Terms of Service (ToS) and User Agreements (UAs) when creating accounts or entering virtual worlds. It is imperative for users to fully understand the ramifications of these agreements, encompassing aspects such as data utilisation, retention of rights, and mechanisms for resolving disputes.

> **Evolution and Adaptation:** Terms of Service (ToS) and User Agreements (UAs) are subject to continuous modification to meet technological changes, user behaviours, and regulatory regulations. It is crucial to ensure transparency and fairness by ensuring that users are aware of these changes and offering them the option to provide consent or choose not to participate.

The engagement of users and their education on Terms of Service (ToS) and User Agreements (UAs) are crucial aspects of effective communication. This encompasses the provision of concise summaries or explanations in plain language for important terminology and updates, allowing user enquiries, and cultivating a culture that promotes responsible digital citizenship.

ECONOMIC PERSPECTIVES ON VIRTUAL WORLD GOVERNANCE

The Digital Economy: Market Dynamics and Virtual Currency in Virtual Worlds

Virtual worlds have transformed from solely recreational environments to dynamic digital ecosystems encompassing their economic systems. Central to these digital domains resides virtual currency, which serves as a digital manifestation of worth, propelling an intricate web of financial transactions. Understanding the complex interplay between market dynamics and virtual currency is crucial for appreciating the complicated economic complexities of virtual environments.

The Significance of Virtual Currency in Contemporary Contexts

Virtual currency, commonly called in-game currency or virtual credits, is the primary economic mechanism within virtual worlds. The platform facilitates transactions, enabling individuals to purchase, sell, and exchange various virtual commodities and services. Digital coins or credits are the foundation for various economic transactions within virtual environments. These transactions include acquiring virtual real estate, personalising avatars, and participating in virtual commerce.

Market Dynamics in the Digital Realm

The fundamental concepts of supply and demand govern Virtual economies. Virtual objects that are rare or in high demand sometimes have higher pricing, leading to a market dynamic that resembles consumer behaviour in the real world.

Economic agents in virtual worlds undertake roles equivalent to those assumed by individuals in the real-world economy. Individuals in society fulfil multiple roles, including consumers, producers, traders, and entrepreneurs. Through their various actions and decisions, these individuals significantly influence economic relationships and ultimately determine the consequences of these interactions.

The emergence of virtual entrepreneurship is a defining characteristic of virtual worlds. Individuals can generate and trade virtual commodities and services, converting their online activities into tangible sources of financial gain. The presence of an entrepreneurial spirit contributes a distinct aspect to virtual economies.

Market platforms are commonly seen in virtual worlds, serving as virtual marketplaces or auction houses where users use virtual currency transactions. These platforms facilitate commercial transactions, establish effective pricing systems, and enhance market liquidity.

The interplay between virtual and real economies is a complex and varied interaction.

Real-money transactions (RMT) refer to the practice observed in certain virtual worlds where users can convert virtual currency into actual monetary value using external markets. The phenomenon referred to as real-money transactions (RMT) has significant economic consequences in the real world, affecting several aspects such as foreign exchange rates, taxation, and individuals' livelihoods.

Examining behavioural patterns inside virtual economies might provide valuable insights into broader socioeconomic trends and consumer preferences. Gaining insight into how users distribute their virtual resources can provide valuable insights into decision-making mechanisms in the physical realm.

Regulation and Administration Problematic Situations:

As virtual economies flourish, regulatory and administrative issues arise:

1. Taxation: The taxation of virtual transactions and Real Money Trading (RMT) presents significant issues for governmental entities and regulatory authorities. The need for established standardised frameworks requires the exploration and creation of novel ways for taxation within the digital domain.

2. Legal Structures: The presence of both virtual and real-world economic activity has sparked debates over legal frameworks, consumer safeguards, and the obligations of platform operators within virtual environments. The task of achieving harmony between different legal spheres is multifaceted and intricate.

Changing Markets and Technological Developments:

Virtual worlds are constantly evolving, dynamic environments:

Emerging technologies, such as blockchain technology, have the potential to significantly transform virtual economies by establishing transparent and decentralised mechanisms for the management of virtual assets. These technologies can augment security measures, facilitate traceability of transactions, and provide clear ownership rights.

Developers' introduction of novel virtual goods and services often leads to changes in market dynamics and user behaviour. The influence of events, promotions, and updates on virtual economies can be substantial, as they play a crucial role in shaping user engagement and spending behaviours.

Strategies for Consumer Behaviour and User Engagement:

Market dynamics in virtual environments are profoundly impacted by user engagement and behaviour:

1. User Demand: The influence of user preferences and aspirations is vital in shaping market dynamics. Products that align with prevailing trends, user preferences, or in-game occurrences frequently see heightened levels of demand and variations in pricing.

2. User Engagement tactics: Developers and platform operators utilise several tactics to foster user engagement, such as implementing time-limited offers, providing prizes, and organising community events, intending to promote user participation and stimulate economic activity. These strategies have an impact on user expenditure and market dynamics.

VIRTUAL ASSET TRANSACTION

Trading virtual assets is a thriving aspect of the economies of virtual worlds:

Marketplaces are commonly found in virtual worlds within the game or on other platforms. These marketplaces allow users to list, purchase, and sell virtual assets. These marketplaces serve as platforms for facilitating commercial transactions and determining market prices.

The concept of currency exchange is prevalent in numerous virtual worlds, enabling players to convert virtual currencies from one type to another or even engage in virtual currency exchange for real-world currency, sometimes called real-money trading (RMT).

Peer-to-peer trading enables users to participate in direct transactions with one another, engaging in negotiations to acquire virtual assets that are not conducted through formal marketplaces.

Difficulties and Considerations:

Virtual asset ownership and commerce present unique complexities

> The trading of virtual assets carries inherent dangers in terms of security and fraudulent activities. Users should exercise prudence and

choose trading platforms that offer robust security measures.

> The legal and fiscal aspects of the trade of virtual assets exhibit jurisdictional variations. Governments and regulatory authorities are trying to establish comprehensive frameworks for digital transactions.

> Market volatility refers to the tendency of virtual assets to experience fluctuations in value, which are influenced by factors such as market sentiment and the interplay between supply and demand. Users must be aware of the possibility of price swings.

> Intellectual property encompasses the ownership of content users contribute and the intricate nature of copyright concerns that may arise. Certain virtual worlds offer explicit guidelines and licensing alternatives.

> Blockchain technology has introduced a new paradigm in virtual asset trading, particularly with the emergence of non-fungible tokens (NFTs). These blockchain-based assets have revolutionised transparency and ownership verification in this domain. However, it is essential to acknowledge that this technology's scalability and environmental implications may pose challenges that warrant further examination.

A FRAMEWORK FOR SUSTAINABLE DIGITAL ECONOMIES: ECONOMIC POLICIES AND REGULATIONS IN VIRTUAL WORLDS

Virtual worlds have become prominent digital environments characterised by dynamic economic interactions. Within dynamic digital environments, individuals actively participate in virtual asset ownership, currency exchange, and entrepreneurial pursuits, frequently resembling financial behaviours observed in the physical world. The compelling necessity of implementing economic policies and regulations has emerged to guarantee virtual economies' fairness, security, and sustainability. This study article aims to examine the complex and diverse terrain of economic policies and regulations in virtual worlds, providing insight into their importance, difficulties, and consequences.

The Importance of Economic Strategies:

The proliferation of virtual economies necessitates the implementation of economic policies for several compelling reasons.

> Consumer protection is a crucial aspect of economic policy as it plays

a critical role in ensuring the safety of users from fraudulent activities and exploitative practices that may occur inside virtual economies. Establishing norms about secure transactions, transparent product descriptions, and effective dispute resolution methods uphold users' trust and confidence.

> The stability of virtual marketplaces is a matter of utmost importance. Policies are formulated to reduce price fluctuations and address market manipulation, fostering fairness and peace within virtual economies.

> Taxation frameworks are relevant in virtual worlds as users produce revenue and participate in transactions. These frameworks pertain to the taxes of virtual trades and the money generated from virtual entrepreneurship, potentially affecting tangible and government revenue streams.

> The proliferation of user-generated material in virtual worlds has created a pressing need to establish laws that clearly define intellectual property rights and license terms. These policies aim to achieve a nuanced equilibrium between creators' rights and platform operators' duties.

Principal Economic Policies and Rules:

A thorough examination of the economic policies and regulations governing virtual environments reveals several crucial aspects:

Consumer protections are measures implemented by economic policies that aim to safeguard consumers. These measures often include standards for ensuring secure transactions, providing clear and accurate product descriptions, and establishing effective dispute resolution methods. These protective measures enhance user trust and instil confidence in virtual marketplaces.

Anti-fraud measures encompass a set of regulations devised and executed to counter fraudulent schemes and scams that specifically target those unaware of such deceptive activities. Implementing these safeguards is crucial to uphold the integrity of virtual economies and safeguard users from potential financial detriment.

Monetary policies are frequently observed in virtual economies, wherein distinct currencies are implemented to enhance the overall functioning of these economic systems. Economic policies are crucial in governing virtual currencies' generation, circulation, and transaction, safeguarding stability and mitigating financial crises.

In response to the growing economic activity in virtual worlds, governments are formulating taxation frameworks to regulate the income derived from virtual and real-money transactions. These frameworks contain several issues, including capital gains taxes and sales taxes.

Regulations about virtual marketplaces play a vital role in shaping virtual economies. The policies regulating these markets encompass several aspects, such as listing fees, transaction fees, and item pricing, to promote openness and efficiency in commercial transactions.

In light of the extensive production of user-generated content in virtual environments, establishing regulations becomes imperative to delineate intellectual property rights and licensing agreement parameters. The rules above aim to strike a balance between the rights of those who create material and the obligations of those who operate platforms, with the ultimate goal of fostering a harmonious atmosphere for creative expression.

Difficulties in Governing Virtual Economies:

The regulation of virtual economies poses numerous problems:

1. Cross-border transactions in virtual worlds present intricate challenges due to their ability to transcend physical boundaries, resulting in complex transactional activities and regulatory coordination endeavours. The task of achieving regulatory harmonisation across a range of various jurisdictions is a significant challenge.

2. Virtual economies have dynamic characteristics and are susceptible to expansion. As the economies experience growth and development, scalability concerns will likely emerge, necessitating solid systems that can effectively manage the rising number of users and transaction volumes.

3. The emergence of blockchain technology and its application in the form of assets and non-fungible tokens (NFTs) has brought forth additional levels of intricacy. The decentralised and pseudonymous characteristics of the subject under discussion provide significant challenges in tracing ownership, taxation, and regulatory compliance.

4. Privacy difficulties arise due to the collection and exploitation of user data within virtual worlds, giving rise to substantial implications for privacy. Regulatory frameworks should aim to achieve a harmonious equilibrium between safeguarding user data and facilitating lawful data-centric commercial endeavours.

5. The swift development of virtual economies frequently surpasses existing regulatory frameworks, leading to exploitable regulatory loopholes. Policymakers must maintain high adaptability and initiative in effectively tackling emerging difficulties.

The Significance of Platform Operators in Contemporary Contexts:

Platform operators in virtual worlds significantly impact the formulation and implementation of economic policies.

1. Policy Implementation: Platform operators are responsible for adopting and enforcing economic policies and laws within virtual environments. Their responsibility involves the development of regulations, protocols, and systems to ensure adherence.

2. User Education: The imperative duty of platform operators is to provide users with knowledge about economic principles, responsible trading practices, and their rights and obligations. Users must comprehensively understand the subject matter to participate in virtual economies with safety and efficacy.

3. Security precautions: Implementing security measures is paramount in safeguarding virtual economies. Platform operators employ various security measures to protect users against fraudulent activities, frauds, and unauthorised access to sensitive data, enhancing user trust and confidence in the digital marketplace.

4. Market Observation: The responsibility for overseeing virtual marketplaces lies under the jurisdiction of platform operators. Marketplace operations are monitored by individuals who ensure that trading practices are fair and transparent.

Achieving a Harmonious Coexistence between Innovation and Regulation:

One of the primary difficulties resides in achieving a nuanced equilibrium between innovation and regulation in virtual economies. The excessive imposition of regulations can impede creativity and hinder the economy's progress, restricting the natural evolution of virtual worlds. On the other hand, insufficient regulation may subject users to various forms of exploitation and contribute to economic instability. Attaining the appropriate equilibrium is a continuous and intricate undertaking.

Supporting Digital Realms through Monetization Models and Virtual World Economies

Virtual worlds have evolved into thriving digital ecosystems with opportunities for economic interaction and expansion. Monetisation models are the financial mechanisms that sustain these digital domains, allowing platform operators to generate revenue as users engage in various activities. To fully comprehend the complex relationship between monetisation models and virtual world economies, it is essential to investigate how these models operate, their effects, and the obstacles they present.

DIVERSE VIRTUAL WORLD MONETIZATION MODELS:

Monetisation in virtual worlds incorporates a variety of models, each tailored to the preferences and experiences of individual users:

Users pay a recurring charge to access the virtual world, typically monthly or yearly. Typically, subscribers receive premium content, enhanced features, or virtual currency subsidies. This model provides platform operators with a stable income stream.

Consumers make small in-game purchases using virtual currency or real money. This could include purchasing virtual items, cosmetics, or currency bundles. Microtransactions are prevalent in free-to-play virtual environments, and they can increase user engagement. Users can buy virtual currency with real currency, which can then be used for various transactions within the virtual world. As users exchange real money for virtual purchasing power, this model bridges the divide between real and virtual economies.

As a method of monetisation, virtual environments may incorporate advertising. These advertisements may be displayed within the virtual environment, and revenue is generated based on ad impressions, clicks, or user interactions. Some virtual worlds allow users to acquire and cultivate virtual real estate. Land sales and maintenance fees generate revenue as users invest in and customise their virtual properties. Users can buy tickets to gain access to virtual events, experiences, and exclusive content releases. This model generates revenue through exclusive events and experiences.

MONETISATION MODEL'S EFFECTS ON VIRTUAL WORLD ECONOMIES:

The selection of a monetisation model can considerably affect the economic dynamics of a virtual world:

Monetisation models can influence patterns of user engagement. Microtransactions, for instance, encourage ongoing user participation because users frequently make minor purchases to enhance their experience over time. The availability of virtual currency for purchase can affect market dynamics. A monetary influx can affect prices and generate supply-and-demand dynamics.

Various monetisation models may result in economic disparities between consumers. Subscription-based business models may affect subscribers' and non-subscribers virtual wealth and content access. Monetisation models can incentivise content creators to produce high-quality virtual products, experiences, and services by allowing them to profit from their creations.

Platform administrators frequently regulate virtual marketplaces to guarantee fairness and transparency. This regulation is intended to prevent price manipulation, fraudulent activity, and unjust business practices.

Challenges and considerations about the process of monetisation:

Effectively managing monetisation strategies within virtual worlds necessitates the careful examination and resolution of several difficulties and considerations:

Achieving a harmonious equilibrium between income generation and maintaining a favourable user experience is paramount. Excessive use of commercialisation strategies can estrange people and undermine the long-term sustainability of a virtual environment. User retention is a nuanced difficulty as it necessitates striking a balance between retaining users and fostering their spending propensity. The optimisation of monetisation strategies should prioritise the augmentation of the total user experience rather than diminishing its quality.

Establishing regulations and promoting fairness is essential in guaranteeing equity within virtual marketplaces and enhancing transparency in monetisation strategies. The establishment of trust plays a crucial role in ensuring the long-term viability of virtual worlds since it fosters an environment where users perceive equitable treatment.

To maintain competitiveness, virtual worlds must alter their tactics for monetisation in response to evolving user preferences and industry trends. The ability to adapt and be flexible is crucial in maintaining relevance.

MODELS OF GOVERNANCE IN VIRTUAL WORLDS

Governance and Control in Virtual Worlds with Centralized Administration

The topic of interest pertains to centralised administration within virtual worlds, specifically focusing on the complexities associated with navigating governance and control in such environments.

Establishing centralised management is a fundamental element inside the complex framework of virtual worlds. Inside the digital technology sphere, a singular body or organisation assumes the role of wielding authority, managing a diverse range of essential responsibilities to uphold order, ensure security, and foster progress inside the virtual domain. This particular mode of governance is characterised by its capacity to implement policies efficiently, keep regulations, and oversee the technological and social framework of these ever-changing digital ecosystems.

The core of centralised administration is centred around the development and execution of regulations and policies that govern user behaviour within the digital realm. These standards play a crucial role in moulding the entire user experience, establishing the parameters of permissible behaviour, and safeguarding the integrity of the virtual community. The policies, including content creation and user interactions, manifest the principles and vision established by the administration.

The role of content filtering has become a vital aspect of centralised governance. Administrators must ensure that user-generated content conforms to community standards and legal restrictions. This process entails using automatic tools and human moderators to carefully curate and monitor the content being transmitted within the digital realm. Maintaining a delicate equilibrium necessitates constant attentiveness to mitigate the presence of unsuitable or detrimental material while safeguarding the artistic manifestation's integrity.

Preserving security and safety holds utmost importance in virtual environments, with the onus being on centralised administrators to protect users from many potential risks. This entails deploying effective strategies to prevent hacking incidents, fraudulent activities, harassment cases, and other types of wrongdoing. Establishing a secure environment is crucial in cultivating user trust and confidence, as it plays a pivotal role in ensuring user retention and the overall well-being of the virtual realm.

Economic regulation is a notable aspect of centralised administration that frequently arises within the framework of virtual economies. Within digital environments, individuals actively partake in diverse financial endeavours, encompassing the trade of virtual assets and involvement in virtual currency markets. Centralised administrators can significantly impact the establishment of exchange rates, pricing of items, and implementation of transaction procedures to promote equitable and transparent economic practices. These regulations serve the purpose of ensuring the stability and functionality of the virtual economy.

The upkeep of technical infrastructure is a core obligation of centralised administrators. Maintaining and monitoring the virtual world's servers, software, and technological architecture is essential to ensure uninterrupted functionality. Providing regular maintenance, implementing software updates, and strategically planning for scalability is necessary to effectively support the continuously expanding user bases and evolving technical requirements.

User support plays a vital role in the framework of centralised administration. Core responsibilities encompass responding to customer questions, handling technical issues, resolving disputes, and fulfilling diverse user needs. Providing efficient user support is crucial in ensuring a favourable user experience within the virtual environment, enhancing user happiness and promoting user retention.

Although centralised administration offers benefits in terms of efficient policy implementation and control, it is not exempt from encountering several problems. Apprehensions over censorship and the possibility of the misuse of authority are significant in magnitude. The issue of reconciling the preservation of a secure atmosphere with the promotion of principles related to unrestricted speech can often give rise to disagreements. In addition, the concentration of authority renders virtual environments susceptible to security threats and weaknesses, hence requiring the implementation of robust security protocols. The cultivation and preservation of user trust heavily rely on ensuring transparency in decision-making and policy enforcement.

GOVERNANCE DECENTRALIZATION IN VIRTUAL WORLDS: EMPOWERING USER COMMUNITIES

The concept of decentralised governance signifies a fundamental change in how virtual worlds are administered and managed. In contrast to centralised models, decentralised governance entails delegating decision-making authority to the user community, typically facilitated through blockchain technology and decentralised autonomous organisations (DAOs). This paradigm enables users to actively engage in the process of determining the rules, policies, and development of the virtual environment.

Decentralised governance fundamentally redefines the conventional hierarchical method of establishing rules within virtual environments. Rather than a singular centralised authority imposing policies, users are actively engaged as stakeholders in decision-making. Facilitating this transition is commonly achieved through voting mechanisms based on blockchain technology, which empowers users to actively participate in decision-making processes about a wide range of subjects, including content rules and economic policies.

The nature of content moderation in decentralised virtual worlds exhibits distinct characteristics. In contrast to the exclusive dependence on centralised administrators for content curation and regulation, decentralised models frequently adopt community-driven content moderation. Users report and vote on content breaches, and judgments are decided through a collaborative process rather than unilateral actions. This enables the community to uphold standards while mitigating issues about censorship.

Decentralised governance presents novel ideas in the domains of security and safety. The utilisation of blockchain technology, characterised by its inherent attributes of transparency and immutability, bolsters security measures by mitigating the potential for data breaches and unauthorised access through hacking. Furthermore, the decentralised structure of blockchain networks enhances their resistance against potential vulnerabilities stemming from singular points of failure, strengthening the digital realm's overall security stance.

The economic regulation observed in decentralised virtual worlds is distinguished by its emphasis on user-centricity. In contrast to centralised administrators who determine exchange rates and item prices, decentralised solutions frequently depend on market dynamics influenced by user-driven supply and demand. Smart contracts and assets based on blockchain technology can automate economic processes, guaranteeing principles of justice and transparency.

The maintenance of technical infrastructure in decentralised virtual worlds is a collective duty. Individuals engaging in the network can actively contribute to its upkeep by doing tasks such as validating transactions or operating blockchain nodes. Utilising a distributed strategy can improve scalability and dependability since it distributes the workload among a network of participants.

In decentralised governance models, user support assumes a collaborative aspect. Community members frequently take a substantial role in assisting others, particularly in technical matters, typically addressed through various platforms such as forums, chat channels, or peer-to-peer support systems. Although formal support channels may be available, decentralised governance's primary advantage is in the user community's aggregate knowledge and support.

The concept of decentralised governance poses problems to conventional understandings of control and authority in virtual environments. The system above facilitates the redistribution of authority among its users and utilises technological advancements to simplify the process of communal decision-making. Nevertheless, it is full of an array of obstacles. The speed of decision-making procedures may need to be improved due to the necessity of consensus among users. Furthermore, it is vital to carefully deliberate on the apprehensions around the possibility of abuse or manipulation inside decentralised frameworks.

Hybrid Governance Approaches in Virtual Worlds: Integrating Centralization and Decentralization

Hybrid governance approaches embody a dynamic and innovative methodology for managing virtual environments. These models aim to integrate aspects of centralised and decentralised governance to use the advantages of each paradigm while minimising their inherent drawbacks. Hybrid governance endeavours to achieve a nuanced equilibrium that empowers users while guaranteeing efficient administration and management of the virtual environment.

The fundamental characteristics of hybrid governance are as follows:

> Policy design frequently incorporates hybrid governance models that entail the active involvement of users in the decision-making process. Individuals possess the capacity to contribute to the establishment of regulations, principles, and benchmarks within the realm of virtual environments. This input can facilitate the alignment of policies with the values and expectations of the community.
> Hybrid models prioritise user empowerment. Individuals can suggest and participate in the voting process for modifications to the regulations and guidelines governing the virtual realm, thereby cultivating a feeling of ownership and engagement in the decision-making process.
> Centralised administration is a crucial aspect of hybrid governance models, as users continue to play a substantial role. The centralised entity manages technical infrastructure, ensures security measures, and oversees certain parts of content moderation to optimise efficiency and maintain a secure environment.
> The content moderation process frequently incorporates the community's active participation in reporting and resolving instances of infractions. Users are granted the capability to identify and report objectionable content, supported by established procedures for collaborative deliberation on removing such content.
> The integration of blockchain technology has the potential to boost transparency, security, and user interaction in hybrid models. Blockchain technology can offer an immutable and unalterable ledger of decisions and transactions, holding significant relevance in governance procedures.

The ramifications of hybrid governance are significant:

Policies that prioritise user input in the formulation process tend to result in the development of policies that are better aligned with the values and preferences of the community. This has the potential to increase user pleasure and foster trust.

Centralised administration facilitates the effective oversight and control of technical infrastructure, security measures, and critical operations, enhancing operational efficiency. This practice effectively mitigates bottlenecks and enables prompt resolutions to technological challenges.

The act of empowering users by their active involvement in decision-making processes has the potential to cultivate a user base that is more engaged and devoted. There is a higher probability that individuals will experience a sense of ownership and accountability towards the virtual realm.

Integrating centralised and decentralised components enables a dynamic response to changing customer demands and shifts in industry dynamics, fostering innovation and adaptability. The phenomenon achieves a harmonious equilibrium between stability and innovation.

The decision-making process in hybrid governance models is often characterised by greater complexity than that in solely centralised or decentralised forms. The attainment of consensus among users and administrators may necessitate delineated procedures.

The complexities of Hybrid Governance:

Striking a balance between centralised and decentralised aspects might present difficulties. Achieving an optimal balance necessitates meticulous strategising and thoughtful deliberation regarding the unique requirements of the virtual realm.

The decision-making process in hybrid models frequently necessitates consensus-building across various stakeholders. Reaching a consensus on policy and implementing changes can be a time-intensive endeavour.

Incorporating blockchain or other technologies into governance procedures can present significant technical complexities and necessitate specialised knowledge and substantial resources.

Transparency is a crucial factor in guaranteeing the integrity of decision-making processes and the effective implementation of policies. Achieving a harmonious equilibrium between the need for transparency and the imperative to protect privacy is a nuanced undertaking.

COMPREHENSIVE EVALUATION OF THE EFFECTIVENESS OF GOVERNANCE MODELS IN VIRTUAL WORLDS

An in-depth analysis of the efficacy of governance models in virtual worlds:

The assessment of governance models in virtual worlds is a complex undertaking that involves a comprehensive examination of the fundamental principles and practices that govern the management and operation of these digital environments. The evaluation of effectiveness is of utmost importance to ascertain the alignment between governance models and the objectives of the virtual realm, as well as to adequately cater to the needs and desires of the user community. This study thoroughly examines the fundamental criteria and methodology employed to assess the effectiveness of different governance frameworks.

User happiness is a fundamental aspect of an efficient governance scheme. Comprehending users' perceptions and engagement with the governance structure is paramount. Surveys, feedback mechanisms, and sentiment analysis methodologies can offer valuable insights into the sentiments expressed by users. Frequently, a high level of user happiness indicates the efficacy of the governance model in cultivating a favourable and cohesive virtual milieu.

The maintenance of effective governance is contingent upon the continual adherence to set regulations and procedures. The evaluation process is significantly influenced by monitoring policy infractions and the subsequent actions taken to remedy them. Monitoring the frequency and characteristics of policy violations, as well as the promptness and efficacy of enforcement measures, provides a comprehensive assessment of the efficiency of the governance framework in preserving order and adhering to community norms.

Transparency is widely recognised as a fundamental principle of efficient governance. Users must possess a comprehensive comprehension of the processes involved in decision-making, the implementation of policies, and the modification of rules. The assessment of governance transparency entails critically examining the procedures employed in making decisions, the accessibility of policy documents, and the effectiveness of communication regarding modifications to stakeholders. A governance model that effectively promotes trust is characterised by its commitment to transparency in its operations.

It should be noted that virtual worlds are not impervious to conflicts and disputes. The efficacy measurement heavily relies on the governance model's capacity to address these concerns efficiently. Metrics such as the duration of dispute resolution, user satisfaction with the results of settlement, and the proportion of effectively resolved disputes can offer valuable insights into this facet of governance.

The preservation of security is of utmost importance in virtual environments, particularly in safeguarding user data, assets, and the general integrity of the virtual world. The evaluation of security measures entails the assessment of security breaches, the strength of security protocols, and the promptness and effectiveness of responses to security incidents. Establishing a safe virtual environment fosters user confidence and enhances overall operational efficiency.

The capacity of a governance model to adjust to evolving conditions and user requirements is a fundamental determinant of its sustained efficacy. Governance institutions must possess adaptability and the capacity to grow to address emerging difficulties effectively. Adaptability evaluation entails analysing the model's response to novel challenges, integration of user feedback, and timely and pertinent policy adjustments.

The adherence to legal and ethical standards is of utmost importance in governance models. In this context, evaluation pertains to assessing the extent to which the governance model conforms to local and international legal frameworks, intellectual property rights, and ethical values. Non-adherence to established regulations and guidelines can have legal ramifications and negatively impact one's reputation.

Cost efficiency is an additional aspect of effectiveness that pertains to the optimal utilisation of resources. Assessing cost-efficiency entails examining the resources utilised in governance activities and the outcomes attained.

An economically efficient governance model aims to optimise the utilisation of resources to achieve maximum impact while eliminating inefficiencies and unnecessary expenditures.

CHAPTER II

Navigating the Intellectual Property Maze: Protecting Creators in the Metaverse

INTRODUCTION

The phrase "metaverse" refers to a unified virtual environment that integrates aspects of the physical world alongside digital, virtual, and augmented reality realms. Within the metaverse, individuals interact with one another and digital entities, typically shown as avatars, generating a durable and interconnected virtual realm. The digital domain is commonly entered using many technologies, such as virtual reality (VR), augmented reality (AR), and the internet.

THE INCREASING RELEVANCE IN CONTEMPORARY SOCIETY

The metaverse is becoming increasingly significant in contemporary life due to various factors:

Digital transformation is characterised by the increasing convergence of the physical and digital realms, propelled by ongoing technological advancements. The metaverse signifies the subsequent phase in the societal digital revolution, providing immersive and interconnected encounters. The metaverse has emerged as a rapidly expanding economic environment, offering many economic opportunities. It offers prospects for enterprises, innovators, and individuals with entrepreneurial pursuits to partake in online commerce, generate digital media, and deliver virtual services. The COVID-19 epidemic has brought attention to the significance of virtual communication, leading to the emergence of the metaverse as a novel platform for individuals to engage, interact, and cooperate inside digital environments. The metaverse is currently utilised for many purposes, such as virtual meetings, social events, and educational activities.

The entertainment and gaming sectors have substantially influenced the evolution of the metaverse. The advent of online multiplayer games, virtual worlds, and esports has facilitated the emergence of highly immersive digital experiences. The metaverse is utilised by artists, designers, and content providers to manifest their creative expressions. They engage in the creation of digital art, fashion, music, and architecture within virtual environments. Academic institutions and corporate entities are investigating the metaverse as a viable platform for facilitating immersive learning and training opportunities. Various educational methods, such as virtual classrooms, simulations, and on-the-job training, can be effectively implemented in this digital arena.

The increasing time people spend in the metaverse has led to a heightened awareness and apprehension over data privacy and security. The ethical and legal implications surrounding the gathering and utilising personal data in virtual worlds are of significant importance.

The metaverse poses intricate economic and legal obstacles encompassing concerns related to intellectual property, virtual property rights, and jurisdictional matters. The resolution of these difficulties is of utmost importance for the sustained expansion and stability of the subject matter. The metaverse development is witnessing significant investment from major players in the technology industry. This encompasses the development of virtual environments, technological apparatus, and software frameworks specifically tailored to enable metaverse encounters.

OVERVIEW OF CREATIVE POTENTIAL IN THE METAVERSE

The metaverse provides a rich environment for diverse forms of creative expression spanning multiple fields. The following is a comprehensive analysis of the creative possibilities that it provides.

1. Digital Artistry

i) Interactive works: Within the metaverse, artists can generate interactive jobs that exhibit responsiveness to the activities and movements of users. An instance of a virtual sculpture can undergo shape alterations or emit auditory stimuli in response to user engagement, thereby delivering a dynamic and immersive interactive encounter.

ii) Virtual Galleries: Virtual galleries allow artists to curate their exhibitions or collaborate to exhibit their artwork. These galleries frequently replicate physical art settings, allowing visitors to engage with art, featuring intricate 3D painting representations virtually.

2. Virtual Fashion

i) Avatar Customization: Users can customise their avatars by including virtual fashion items, fostering designers' creation of diverse clothing styles and accessories. The phenomenon above has given rise to virtual fashion boutiques, wherein individuals can engage in shopping experiences for distinctive digital garments.

ii) The Advancements in Digital Fabric Technology: The realm of digital fabric innovation enables virtual fashion designers to transcend the constraints imposed by actual textiles. One potential avenue for exploration involves using exclusively digital materials, enabling the creation of garments featuring distinctive textures, patterns, and visual effects that would otherwise be unattainable in physicality.

3. Music and Performances

i) Immersive Audiovisual Experiences: Integrating music and visual art can result in immersive experiences when musicians and visual artists cooperate to produce performances that engage many senses. Virtual reality (VR) headsets and spatial audio technology enable users to employ music in a three-dimensional space, where auditory and visual elements synergistically combine to produce a multimodal encounter.

ii) Virtual Concert Venues: Virtual music venues in the metaverse possess the capacity to be intricately crafted with elements of fantasy and otherworldliness. Musicians can partake in performances within virtual realms, which are unattainable to replicate in tangible environments. Consequently, this enables listeners to experience novel avenues of music engagement.

4. Architecture & Design

i) Virtual Prototyping: Using the metaverse enables architects to prototype and experiment quickly. Virtual models of architectural designs can be generated and evaluated in real time, facilitating the process of making necessary alterations and improvements with enhanced efficiency.

ii) Imaginative Urban Planning: The concept of innovative urban planning involves the collaborative efforts of designers in creating virtual cities, thereby expanding the frontiers of urban planning and sustainable building. These projects have the potential to investigate urban landscapes that are futuristic, environmentally sustainable, or romantic.

5. Storytelling & Narrative

i) User-Driven Stories: Within the metaverse, individuals can shape the path of the narrative by their decision-making, thus enabling user-driven stories. This interactive narrative structure gives users a heightened level of control and a more profound engagement experience.

ii) Simulations and role-playing games: Role-playing and simulation experiences in virtual environments inside the metaverse facilitate a convergence of storytelling and gaming, thereby blurring the distinction between the two. Individuals can assume virtual avatars' identities and engage in intricate narratives within the metaverse.

6. Game Development

i) Immersive Worlds: The creation of immersive virtual worlds with intricately designed environments and intricate ecosystems is a capability possessed by game developers. Players can achieve complete immersion in these virtual environments, engaging in activities such as exploration, puzzle-solving, and interactive communication with fellow players, surpassing the boundaries of conventional gaming encounters.

ii) User-Generated Content: Certain metaverse platforms allow users to generate their games and experiences, fostering a more egalitarian approach to game production. This facilitates the development of a user-generated content culture, enhancing the scope for creative exploration.

7. Virtual galleries and museums

i) Interactive Exhibitions: It offers interactive exhibitions, enabling people to engage with art beyond mere observation. This may encompass closely examining brushstrokes, acquiring knowledge about the artist's creative methodology through multimedia exhibits, or immersing oneself within a painting or sculpture.

ii) Global Accessibility: Virtual art spaces have the potential to overcome geographical limitations, hence enhancing global accessibility. Exhibitions serve as a means for art enthusiasts across the globe to access and engage with varied artistic expressions, facilitating the expansion of art appreciation to a broader audience.

8. Content Creation

i) Immersive Storytelling: The field of content creation is witnessing the emergence of immersive storytelling, wherein content creators actively develop narrative experiences that allow viewers to immerse themselves in the story entirely. The incidents above frequently incorporate narrative paths that diverge and are influenced by user decisions, enhancing engagement in consuming information.

ii) Virtual Influencers: Virtual influencers have emerged as a novel phenomenon in which content creators utilise avatars to establish influential personalities inside the metaverse, thereby constructing comprehensive digital identities. These digital avatars engage in partnerships with companies and generate material that effectively appeals to the virtual reality community.

OVERVIEW OF ECONOMIC OPPORTUNITIES IN THE METAVERSE

The economic climate within the metaverse exhibits a dynamic and varied nature, presenting a wide range of prospects for innovation and entrepreneurial endeavours. As the metaverse undergoes further expansion, its economic landscape will transform, giving rise to novel occupational fields and market opportunities. The technology possesses the capacity to fundamentally change conventional economic frameworks, offering not only monetary prospects but also a medium for worldwide cooperation and innovative manifestation.

1. Virtual Commerce:

i) Digital Goods Marketplace: Virtual commerce refers to commercial activities within virtual environments. In addition to conventional e-commerce platforms, metaverse markets allow users to buy and sell digital goods. These goods include virtual apparel, accessories, 3D models, and digital art. Digital creators can generate revenue by engaging in the sale of their digital products within these marketplaces, contributing to the growth and prosperity of the digital economy.

ii) Virtual Currency Ecosystem: The virtual currency ecosystem encompasses several metaverse systems that have developed their types of digital currencies, such as virtual coins or tokens. Individuals can acquire, exchange, and utilise these monetary units within the metaverse, generating prospects for establishing virtual currency exchange services and trading platforms.

2. Digital Advertising:

i) Virtual Billboards and Brand Integration: Utilizing virtual billboards and brand integration in the metaverse allows advertisers to strategically position and incorporate their brands into the virtual environment. This provides monetary gains and promotes user involvement through immersive branded encounters.

ii) Data-Driven Advertising: Metaverse platforms can accumulate substantial quantities of user data, facilitating the implementation of highly focused advertising strategies. Advertisers can utilise this data to customise their marketing efforts according to user preferences and behaviours.

3. Virtual Real Estate:

i) Property Development and Management: The emergence of virtual real estate as a highly desirable asset has created new prospects for individuals involved in property development and management. One of their key responsibilities is creating, advancing, and maintaining virtual assets, encompassing virtual residences, enterprises, and recreational establishments.

ii) Virtual Property Investment: Virtual property investment involves acquiring and retaining virtual real estate by investors to capitalise on prospective increases in value. The practice of virtual land speculation has emerged as a specialised sector, bearing a resemblance to the realm of real-world property investing.

4. Metaverse Employment:

i) Organisers of Virtual Events: The metaverse serves as a platform for various events, encompassing virtual conferences, concerts, and conventions. Event organisers and managers play a vital role in the strategic planning, effective promotion, and efficient execution of various events.

ii) Moderation and Security: The maintenance of a secure and pleasant metaverse experience necessitates the presence of employees dedicated to moderation and security. The individuals in question are responsible for managing user interactions, ensuring adherence to platform regulations, and implementing security protocols.

iii) Tech Support and Customer Service: Providing technical assistance, inquiry resolution, and troubleshooting services is essential for virtual platforms to support their customers effectively. This necessitates the presence of dedicated support teams. This encompasses providing VR headset support, software assistance, and comprehensive customer service.

5. Education and Training:

i) Virtual Learning Platforms: The utilisation of the metaverse for immersive learning experiences is increasingly embraced by educational institutions and enterprises. Several prospects are available for educators, instructional designers, and content providers to conceive and administer virtual courses and training programs.

ii) Edutainment Content: Edutainment content integrates educational and entertainment elements within the metaverse. Creators of edutainment content aim to develop captivating experiences that teach and delight users. This content is designed to cater to a diverse range of learners, ensuring its accessibility to a broad audience.

6. Blockchain and NFTs:

i) NFT Creation and Trading: The metaverse has emerged as a suitable environment for creating and trading non-fungible tokens (NFTs). Various stakeholders, including artists, collectors, and entrepreneurs, engage in NFT creation, trade, and management processes. The emergence of digital art and collectables has created a novel market.

ii) Blockchain Development: Blockchain development is fundamental in establishing and functioning many metaverse ecosystems. There is a high demand for blockchain engineers with the necessary skills to design and sustain blockchain networks that facilitate virtual currencies, non-fungible tokens (NFTs), and safe transactions.

7. Metaverse Infrastructure:

i) Virtual World Creation: Establishing a metaverse necessitates the involvement of entities and persons with expertise in developing virtual worlds and surroundings. These stakeholders play a crucial role in facilitating the expansion and development of the metaverse. The individuals are responsible for creating immersive landscapes and experiences that users explore.

ii) Hardware and Software Development: The advancement of hardware and software in the context of virtual reality and augmented reality, the creation of software platforms for metaverse applications and the establishment of networking infrastructure collectively contribute to the technological underpinnings of the metaverse. The emergence of the metaverse is facilitated by the collective efforts of hardware engineers, software developers, and network professionals.

8. Entertainment and Events:

i) The production of virtual events: The execution of virtual concerts, conventions, and esports events necessitates the expertise of event producers, directors, and technical personnel. These individuals are responsible for curating and organising interactive events that engage and fascinate audiences worldwide.

ii) Esports Professionals: Esports professionals actively engage in the expanding virtual competitive gaming landscape within the metaverse.

This includes the involvement of professional players, esports organisations, and event organisers, who collectively contribute to the flourishing esports industry in this digital realm.

8. Consulting and Services:

i) Metaverse Consulting: Consulting firms and industry specialists offer professional advice and assistance in developing metaverse strategies, conducting market analysis, and facilitating digital transformation. They assist businesses and individuals in navigating the many aspects of the metaverse.

ii) Legal and Intellectual Property Services: In light of the distinctive legal complexities associated with the metaverse, legal experts with expertise in safeguarding virtual property rights, intellectual property protection, and digital asset management provide essential services to protect creators and enterprises.

THE IMPERATIVE TO CONFRONT INTELLECTUAL PROPERTY (IP) CONSIDERATIONS WITHIN THE METAVERSE.

The metaverse, an emerging virtual domain that combines immersive experiences, commercial activities, and creative endeavours, is ushering in a novel epoch of human interaction and ingenuity. Within its virtual realm, individuals assume the dual role of consumers and makers of digital content, producing various forms of virtual fashion, architectural marvels, and elaborate digital artworks. Preserving intellectual property (IP) rights is of utmost importance in the ever-evolving digital landscape, as these innovations possess inherent worth. This examines the several complex factors that justify the imperative of resolving intellectual property (IP) concerns in the metaverse, emphasising its significance as a pivotal element for ensuring its long-term development and success.

Creativity and Innovation Incentive:

Within the metaverse, a realm characterised by limitless creative potential, safeguarding intellectual property is fundamental in motivating innovators to venture into uncharted territories. When individuals engaged in artistic, design, musical, and content production endeavours are assured that their digital creations are adequately protected, they tend to be more motivated to allocate their time, exertion, and creative faculties towards generating original and pioneering content. This cultivates an environment that encourages ongoing innovation and challenges the limitations of the metaverse, resulting in a vibrant and captivating virtual realm.

The Economic Basis:

The metaverse is undergoing rapid development as it transforms into a resilient economic ecosystem, facilitating virtual trade, digital asset exchange, and content monetisation for individuals, producers, and enterprises. The booming digital economy relies heavily on robust intellectual property (IP) safeguards. Creators, investors, and entrepreneurs require a sense of assurance over protecting their intellectual property (IP) rights to make informed and confident investments in the metaverse. Establishing a robust economic foundation guarantees the metaverse's sustainability and catalyses economic growth and innovation, thereby facilitating its evolution into a prosperous digital marketplace.

Virtual Property and Asset Protection:

The increasing prominence of virtual real estate, non-fungible tokens (NFTs), and other virtual assets underscores the critical importance of ensuring safe ownership and copyright protections. Valuable support and properties inhabit the digital environment of the metaverse, necessitating substantial intellectual property (IP) protections. These safeguards are necessary for conflicts about ownership and usage rights to ensure the economic dynamics of the metaverse, hence giving rise to intricate legal complexities that could compromise the integrity of the digital ecosystem.

Brand Authenticity and Consumer Confidence:

The success of businesses functioning in the metaverse, regardless of whether they are virtual entities or physical organisations with a virtual presence, is significantly influenced by their brand identification and trademarks. The unauthorised utilisation or improper handling of trademarks can undermine a brand's integrity and generate perplexity among consumers. An established intellectual property (IP) framework serves the dual purpose of safeguarding company interests and maintaining consumer trust, facilitating secure and transparent virtual commerce, and promoting online marketplace growth.

Content Protection against Infringement:

The issue of content piracy poses a significant and immediate concern within the metaverse. The proliferation of digital content replication and distribution has emerged as a substantial source of apprehension for authors and individuals holding rights to such content. Without significant intellectual property (IP) safeguards, unapproved reproductions of digital assets can inundate the metaverse, resulting in a depreciation of the original content and posing a threat to the economic sustainability of authors. Implementing robust intellectual property (IP) protection measures is a crucial defence mechanism against the unauthorised replication and distribution of digital information. This safeguard plays a pivotal role in upholding the intrinsic worth and authenticity of digital creations while also guaranteeing that creators can fully benefit from the fruits of their labour.

Content Generated by Users and Collaboration:

The metaverse flourishes through its users' content creation and collaborative efforts across multiple platforms. The ever-changing nature of this environment gives rise to intricate inquiries about ownership, licensing, and usage rights. Establishing precise and uniform intellectual property norms is crucial to delineating these rights, minimising conflicts, and promoting a more efficient and cohesive environment for collaboration. These standards play a vital role in ensuring that users can create, share, and create teamwork content with a sense of assurance, as they know their contributions are safeguarded.

Cross-Border Complicatedness:

The significance of international standards and agreements for intellectual property (IP) protection must be considered, considering the metaverse's extensive global reach and cross-border nature. These guidelines serve the purpose of ensuring the consistent enforcement of intellectual property rights across various jurisdictions. This feature empowers creators, enterprises, and users to confidently traverse the metaverse, as it guarantees the protection of their intellectual property rights, irrespective of their geographical location. Establishing a comprehensive intellectual property (IP) rights framework facilitates international cooperation and promotes advancements in various fields of knowledge and creativity.

Increasing Investment and Entrepreneurial Activity:

Establishing a secure IP environment within the metaverse is a significant driver for investment and entrepreneurial activities. Business entities and people have a higher propensity to allocate resources when they possess a sense of assurance over safeguarding their intellectual property and valuable assets. Consequently, this phenomenon contributes to the stimulation of economic expansion, fostering technological advancements and the emergence of novel services and innovations within the metaverse. Establishing substantial intellectual property (IP) safeguards fosters a conducive atmosphere for the growth and progress of startups, creators, and investors, hence facilitating the development and extension of the metaverse.

OVERVIEW OF INTELLECTUAL PROPERTY

Examining intellectual property (IP) elucidates a fundamental structure aimed at safeguarding and stimulating innovation and creativity. Intellectual property (IP) comprises diverse intangible assets important in the contemporary economy.

Patents are fundamental to safeguarding intellectual property (IP), bestowed upon innovators for their original, non-evident, and practical innovations or discoveries. Patents grant inventors the exclusive rights to regulate the utilisation and distribution of their creations for a designated duration, usually lasting 20 years. Patents are a robust motivator for research and development endeavours by guaranteeing inventors the ability to benefit from their innovative contributions.

The concept of copyright entails safeguarding intellectual property rights for works of authorship that are deemed original. This protection encompasses a wide range of creative expressions, including but not limited to literature, music, art, software, and various other forms of artistic and intellectual endeavours. Copyright protection is automatically granted to creators whenever their work is created and expressed in a physical medium. The concept of copyright encompasses the provision of exclusive privileges to reproduce, distribute, perform, and display a particular work. This framework aims to establish a harmonious equilibrium between promoting creative expression and regulating intellectual property rights.

Trademarks protect distinctive symbols, names, and slogans that differentiate various goods and services within the commercial sphere. These unique characteristics are crucial in establishing brand identification and fostering consumer confidence. The owners of trademarks are granted exclusive rights to their marks, which facilitates the establishment of their brand and guarantees that consumers can make well-informed decisions when choosing between different products or services.

Trade secrets are a form of legal protection that safeguards proprietary knowledge about business operations, including but not limited to formulas, methods, and customer lists. In contrast to patents, trade secrets necessitate proactive safeguarding and maintaining confidentiality, as they do not entail public disclosure. Non-disclosure agreements (NDAs) are frequently utilised as legal instruments to protect these valuable assets. Trade secrets motivate corporations to allocate resources towards innovation since they enable these companies to sustain a competitive advantage by maintaining confidentiality.

Industrial designs serve as a means of safeguarding the visual aesthetics and design components of valuable goods. Industrial design rights provide exclusive protection for the visual aspects of a product, encompassing a wide range of consumer goods such as consumer electronics and furniture. This practice promotes innovation in product design and improves the marketability of distinct and aesthetically pleasing items.

Plant varieties are safeguarded by plant breeders' rights, which protect newly developed plant varieties that exhibit specific characteristics, uniformity, and stability. This intellectual property framework promotes agricultural innovation by conferring breeders exclusive privileges to reproduce and commercialise their novel plant varieties. This practice guarantees that breeders can recover their investments in research and development, thereby fostering progress in agriculture.

Geographical Indications (GIs) protect items closely tied to a particular geographical location, preserving their distinct qualities, reputation, and unique attributes. Geographical indications (GIs) safeguard the cultural and commercial significance of certain products, such as wines, cheeses, and agricultural goods, by protecting their heritage and preserving their esteemed reputation associated with specific locations. Simultaneously, these initiatives serve to stimulate local economies and preserve cultural traditions while also acting as a deterrent against the unauthorised appropriation of geographical names.

The Significance of Intellectual Property to Creators and Innovators

The term "intellectual property" (IP) pertains to a legal structure that grants exclusive rights and safeguards for products of human intellect. The creations above can incorporate diverse intangible assets, such as inventions, literary and creative works, brand identities, and other similar entities. The essential significance of intellectual property (IP) rests in its function as a tool for providing incentives and protecting the endeavours of creators and innovators. This discourse explains the intellectual property (IP) concept, focusing on its profound implications for individuals fostering innovation and creativity.

Definition of Intellectual Property

Intellectual property refers to a legal construct covering a collection of unique privileges bestowed to persons or entities in recognition of their creative and inventive endeavours. The purpose of these rights is to safeguard the novelty, distinctiveness, and economic worth of intellectual contributions. The fundamental classifications of intellectual promerty encompass patents, copyrights, trademarks, trade secrets, industrial designs, plant breeders' rights, and geographical indications, with each category specifically designed to protect distinct forms of intellectual assets.

IP's Significance for Creators and Innovators

Intellectual properties (IP) significance for creators and innovators is multifaceted and profoundly ingrained in the fabric of contemporary society. IP functions as both a shield and a potent incentive, playing a crucial role in fostering innovation, fostering creativity, and facilitating economic growth. Let's delve deeper into why intellectual property is critical for those who drive progress through inventive and creative endeavours.

Protection of Investments in Intellectual Property:

IP provides a fortress of protection for intellectual investments at its foundation. For creators and innovators, whether inventors, artists, writers, or business owners, intellectual property (IP) assures that their intellectual creations, technological breakthroughs, artistic masterpieces, or innovative solutions will be protected from unauthorised use or exploitation. This protection is not merely a legal formality; the linchpin guarantees the fruits of their labour remain secure, undamaged, and under their control.

Innovation and creativity incentive:

IP is a powerful incentive that stokes the flames of innovation and creativity. It accomplishes this by assuring creators and innovators exclusive rights to their creations and the possibility of monetary gain. Individuals and organisations are encouraged to invest in research, development, and creative endeavours when they know their intellectual property will be protected. It enables them to confront complex problems, explore uncharted territory, and expand the limits of human knowledge. With intellectual property, the motor of progress and innovation would retain significant fuel.

Commercialisation and Profitability:

IP also facilitates monetisation and commercialisation, in addition to protection. Creators and innovators can utilise their intellectual property rights to derive economic value from their intellectual assets. They can transform their creations into revenue streams through licensing agreements, sales, and collaborative efforts. This rewards their creative endeavours and contributes to economic development by introducing market-ready innovations of value.

Cultural and Artistic Expression Preservation:

Copyright protection is indispensable in art, literature, music, and entertainment. It protects not only the rights of creators but also their livelihoods. Copyright ensures that artists, authors, and musicians are not only able to express themselves freely but also profit from their works. This encourages the production of culturally significant content and supports the creative industries, which are fundamental to our cultural fibre.

Brand Development and Strategic Advantage:

Trademarks, trade secrets, and industrial designs are invaluable assets for businesses. Trademarks facilitate brand development, instil consumer confidence, and ensure that products and services associated with a particular brand are recognised and trusted. Trade secrets safeguard a company's proprietary processes and know-how, giving them a competitive advantage by preventing rivals from duplicating their methods. Industrial designs safeguard the unique aesthetics of products, enhancing their marketability and setting them apart from competitors.

Innovative Agricultural Practices:

Plant breeders' rights encourage innovation in agriculture by enabling breeders to protect new and distinctive plant varieties. This promotes crop production improvements, contributing to food security and agricultural sustainability. IP incentivises research and development in this critical sector, resulting in more resilient and productive crops.

Cultural and Physical Heritage:

Geographical indications preserve and promote cultural and geographical heritage by safeguarding regionally unique products. This supports local economies and ensures the quality and authenticity of traditional products, benefiting producers and consumers.

Forms of Intellectual Property

COPYRIGHT:

Copyright is a multifaceted and essential kind of intellectual property protection encompassing diverse creative expressions, such as literature, music, art, films, software, and several other forms of creative work. The provision above confers to authors the sole entitlements to duplicate, disseminate, execute, and exhibit their authentic works. The establishment of copyright is an inherent consequence that arises upon the physical manifestation of a creative work, thereby establishing a solid framework for safeguarding the various embodiments of human ingenuity. This type of intellectual property (IP) holds excellent importance within art and culture, as it protects and enables artists, writers, singers, and inventors to secure and derive financial benefits from their intellectual endeavours. Through establishing a harmonious equilibrium between safeguarding intellectual property and facilitating public availability, copyright catalyses the ongoing generation of fresh and inventive material, ultimately enhancing our cultural milieu and fostering the growth of creative sectors.

TRADEMARK:

Trademarks serve as symbolic representations of branding and play a crucial role in establishing consumer confidence. Brands serve as protective mechanisms for symbols, names, phrases, and other distinctive identifiers that differentiate items or services within the commercial sphere. Trademarks play a crucial role in directing consumers towards making well-informed decisions, as they can incorporate various elements such as words, logos, sounds, and even colours. The trademark registration process grants individuals or organisations the exclusive rights to utilise a specific mark about particular goods or services. This develops a distinct and recognisable identity inside the consciousness of consumers. Trademarks play a vital role in enterprises as the fundamental element for establishing brand identification and safeguarding intellectual property. In addition to cultivating consumer loyalty, trademarks guard against brand dilution and counterfeiting, thereby upholding the integrity and reputation of products and services linked to a particular mark.

PATENT:

Patents, fundamental to fostering invention, offer innovators the motivation and safeguard required to advance the frontiers of human understanding. There are two main categories of patents: utility patents, which encompass methods, machinery, articles of production, and compositions of matter, and design patents, which safeguard the aesthetic design of functional objects. Patents bestow upon inventors the privilege of exclusive rights, often 20 years from the filing date, granting them authority over the utilisation and commercial exploitation of their innovations. The safeguard above incentivises inventors for their creative thinking, propelling technological progress and cultivating a competitive environment. Patents, such as technology, medicines, and manufacturing, are crucial in industries that rely on innovation to gain a competitive edge. Patented inventions serve as catalysts for advancement and facilitate the dissemination of information through their public publication.

TRADE SECRETS:

Trade secrets encompass a domain of confidential and proprietary knowledge that serves as the vital essence of several industries. These cover a variety of intellectual assets, including formulas, methods, customer lists, software algorithms, and other confidential knowledge that confer a competitive advantage. In contrast to patents, trade secrets necessitate proactive safeguarding by implementing legal mechanisms such as non-disclosure agreements (NDAs) and rigorous security protocols. Trade secrets play a crucial role in situations where confidentiality is paramount. Technology firms like those in the industry safeguard their software algorithms to sustain a competitive advantage.

Trade secrets provide long-lasting protection if the information stays undisclosed, enabling organisations to maintain their competitive edge and foster innovation.

PROBLEMS ASSOCIATED WITH PROTECTING INTELLECTUAL PROPERTY IN THE DIGITAL DOMAIN.

Safeguarding intellectual property (IP) inside the digital domain poses a complex array of obstacles that require a thorough and flexible approach. The advent of the digital era has significantly altered how intellectual property (IP) is safeguarded, owing to the increased convenience of digital replication and dissemination. The ease with which digital data can be replicated and distributed globally has resulted in widespread piracy and copyright infringement.

The phenomenon of digital piracy has emerged as a widespread concern. The proliferation of file-sharing platforms, torrents, and streaming services has posed significant challenges in regulating the illicit dissemination of protected material. The addition of counterfeit goods within the expansive realm of e-commerce presents a concurrent danger, undermining brand reputation and financial gains.

Digital Reproduction and Distribution:

In the contemporary era of digital technology, the process of replicating and disseminating artistic creations has reached an unparalleled level of convenience and efficiency. Digital files, including many forms such as textual documents, photos, music, and software, can be replicated with exceptional accuracy, and disseminated worldwide in seconds. The seamless duplication of intellectual property poses a significant challenge to conventional approaches regulating its dissemination. Content protected by copyright is especially vulnerable to unlawful replication, resulting in the widespread violation of copyright laws. The enormous quantity of online content presents a challenge for intellectual property owners in efficiently monitoring and enforcing their rights.

Digital Piracy and Counterfeiting:

Digital piracy is a prevalent problem with significant implications for individuals and entities creating and owning intellectual property. The advent of online platforms, including pirate websites and streaming services, has engendered a pervasive dissemination of copyrighted material without requisite authority. The widespread occurrence of piracy infringes on intellectual property rights and presents a significant economic peril. Pirated alternatives frequently result in reduced revenue streams for content creators and owners. Counterfeit goods constitute an additional dimension of this dilemma, particularly in electronic commerce. Counterfeit goods erode brand credibility and lead to substantial economic repercussions for enterprises.

Anonymity And Cybersecurity:

The presence of anonymity within the digital realm presents challenges in identifying and prosecuting individuals involved in intellectual property infringement. The ability for perpetrators to conduct their operations while maintaining anonymity on the internet offers a significant obstacle in tracing their actions. The presence of anonymity, in conjunction with the worldwide scope of the internet, frequently gives rise to jurisdictional complexities when seeking legal recourse against those who engage in infringement. Moreover, the constant and pervasive risk of cyberattacks and data breaches gives rise to significant apprehensions regarding the security of invaluable intellectual property assets. To protect these valuable resources from evil entities and digital risks, it is imperative to implement robust cybersecurity protocols and maintain a state of perpetual alertness.

Evolutionary Progression of Business Models:

The digital era has introduced novel business models challenging conventional intellectual property (IP) protection procedures. The emergence of subscription-based content services, open-source software, and Creative Commons licensing has significantly transformed intellectual property (IP) administration. These models necessitate flexible strategies that can effectively manage the intricate dynamics between intellectual property protection and the ever-changing requirements of the digital marketplace. The perpetual difficulty lies in striking a delicate equilibrium between safeguarding intellectual property (IP) and satisfying customer demands within the dynamic context of the present environment.

International Jurisdiction and Enforcement:

The absence of borders in the realm of the internet presents challenges in enforcing intellectual property (IP) rights across various international authorities. Intellectual property (IP) laws exhibit substantial variation across different countries, posing challenges in attaining uniformity in global IP protection. The enforcement of intellectual property (IP) rights worldwide frequently necessitates intricate legal coordination and can impose significant cost difficulties. The difficulty of bridging jurisdictional barriers and ensuring effective enforcement of intellectual property (IP) on a global scale persists.

User-Generated Content:

The proliferation of user-generated content platforms, including but not limited to social media and content-sharing websites, has significantly increased instances of copyright infringement. The act of unauthorised uploading and sharing of copyrighted information by users is prevalent, leading to a blurred distinction between content production and intellectual property infringement. This occurrence prompts significant inquiries regarding the optimal approach to maintaining a harmonious equilibrium between artistic innovation and intellectual property safeguarding within these digital platforms. Both content creators and media have the complex task of balancing the need to combat copyright infringements with the desire to encourage user-generated content and cooperation.

Technological Advancements:

The rapid pace of technological improvements has a dual nature, as it brings forth both advantageous prospects and complex obstacles in intellectual property (IP) protection. Blockchain technology has the potential to enhance copyright management and offer a means of establishing verifiable evidence of ownership. Nonetheless, it also challenges enforcing intellectual property rights within decentralised digital settings. The capacity of artificial intelligence (AI) to produce remarkably persuasive counterfeit content presents further challenges in the ongoing struggle to address intellectual property (IP) infringement using conventional methods. Adapting to the rapid pace of technology changes and formulating novel techniques for safeguarding intellectual property is imperative.

Data Privacy and Intellectual Property (IP):

The convergence of intellectual property protection with data privacy has various dimensions. The safeguarding of intellectual property frequently encompasses the acquisition and administration of data, giving rise to apprehensions regarding preserving individuals' rights to data privacy. Achieving a harmonious equilibrium between protecting intellectual property (IP) and preserving data privacy rights, particularly in light of dynamic data protection rules such as the General Data Protection Regulation (GDPR), necessitates a nuanced approach. To maintain adherence to data privacy regulations and safeguard intellectual property assets, enterprises must exercise caution in navigating this terrain.

Digital Rights Management (DRM) With Accessibility:

Implementing efficient Digital Rights Management (DRM) systems poses a complex task requiring careful consideration of several factors. The implementation of a robust digital rights management (DRM) system has the potential to discourage piracy and safeguard intellectual property (IP) effectively. However, it is essential to strike a balance, as too stringent measures can lead to consumer dissatisfaction and impede lawful utilisation. The perpetual worry revolves around balancing protecting intellectual property (IP) and delivering a user-friendly experience. Digital rights management (DRM) solutions necessitate a thoughtful approach by content creators and distributors, as they must balance safeguarding their intellectual property (IP) and meeting the demands and expectations of customers.

Education And Awareness:

A considerable segment of the general population and commercial entities needs more awareness of intellectual property rules and their associated consequences. The continuous effort to enhance knowledge and promote understanding among individuals and organisations regarding intellectual property rights and obligations is an ongoing pursuit. This encompasses the promotion of appropriate utilisation of digital content and the discouragement of intellectual property infringement through the implementation of awareness campaigns and educational programs. Enhanced public knowledge has the potential to foster a digital environment characterised by increased respect and adherence to established norms and regulations.

How does the metaverse blur the lines between physical and digital creations?

Immersive Virtual Environments:

The degree of immersion virtual surroundings offer is a crucial determinant in the metaverse. By leveraging cutting-edge technology such as Virtual Reality (VR) and Augmented Reality (AR), individuals can immerse themselves in these simulated settings and interact with digital components in a manner that closely resembles physical presence. Incorporating sensory modalities such as visual, auditory, and haptic feedback in these technologies presents a growing difficulty in discerning between the physical and digital realms. In a virtual environment known as the metaverse, users can engage in a simulated forest setting. Within this digital realm, individuals can visually and audibly hear the sounds of leaves rustling, experience tactile sensations akin to the texture of the virtual ground beneath their feet, and engage in interactive encounters with virtual entities, simulating a realistic encounter with the physical world.

Interconnected Digital and Physical Spaces:

The metaverse frequently expands its reach into the tangible realm using augmented reality. Individuals can retrieve digital information and engage in virtual experiences superimposed onto their physical environment by utilising augmented reality (AR) equipment or smartphone applications. For example, augmented reality (AR) can offer immediate navigation assistance while traversing urban areas or furnish historical context during visits to significant sites. Integrating the physical environment and the digital layer results in a convergence that diminishes the distinctions between the two realms, leading to a cohesive amalgamation.

Ownership And Interaction with Digital Assets:

Individuals inside the metaverse can generate, possess, and engage with digital assets with inherent worth within the virtual and tangible realms. Non-fungible tokens (NFTs) serve as a prominent illustration. Non-fungible tokens (NFTs) establish ownership over distinct digital assets, such as virtual artwork or collectable items. Digital assets can be acquired, exchanged, and traded in a manner akin to tangible assets. A digital painting that can be exhibited within a virtual gallery challenges the traditional distinction between ownership of physical and digital artwork.

Cross-Reality Economic:

The metaverse frequently encompasses economic activity around the trading of digital assets or virtual currency. Individuals can engage in commercial activities, such as conducting business transactions, purchasing, and selling commodities and services, and even creating virtual platforms for commercial purposes. The economy of the metaverse resembles economic systems observed in the actual world, establishing a direct connection between the digital and physical domains. The financial interplay discussed presents an additional complication to delineating these two spheres.

Real-World Applications:

Specific metaverse experiences exhibit innovative methods of integrating with the tangible realm. An example of this phenomenon is the live streaming of virtual concerts and events to real venues, erasing the distinction between attending a physical show and participating in a virtual one. The abovementioned integration augments the perception of a collective reality in which tangible and virtual components interact.

Identity And Social Interaction:

Within the metaverse, individuals frequently establish social connections and construct identities beyond the constraints imposed by physical boundaries. Avatars serve as digital manifestations of one's identity, enabling individuals to express themselves and engage in interactions that transcend the limitations of physical attributes and geographical boundaries. The transformation of one's identity within a digital realm presents a significant departure from conventional understandings of human existence.

What Unique IP difficulties originate from metaverse user-generated content (UGC)?

Ownership And Attribution:

Collaborative content production is a prevalent practice within the metaverse, wherein several people actively participate in advancing virtual settings, artworks, and interactive experiences. The process of ascertaining ownership and ensuring appropriate attribution for these joint products can be complex. In contrast to conventional intellectual property situations, where it is typically feasible to identify individual producers, the collaborative nature of the metaverse presents difficulties in determining the primary ownership and authorship rights.

Remix Culture and Derivative Works:

The metaverse facilitates the development of a remix culture, which promotes the practice of users constructing or altering pre-existing user-generated content (UGC). Frequently, individuals engage in the production of derivative works, causing a fusion of boundaries between the realm of original content and that of adaptations. In the present situation, determining the precise parameters of fair use or transformative production becomes increasingly complex. The phenomenon of remix culture poses a significant challenge to established copyright standards, requiring novel interpretations and legal deliberations.

Virtual Asset Ownership and Copyright:

Within the metaverse, it is a common practice for users to acquire, sell, and exchange virtual assets. These assets encompass many items, such as apparel for avatars, digital companions, and virtual properties. The matter arises when individuals desire to modify or adapt these resources, which may violate the copyright held by the original producers. The intricate issue of reconciling asset providers' rights with users' creative autonomy is a distinctive and multifaceted concern within the metaverse.

Branding And Trademark Issues:

In the metaverse, businesses and people establish virtual storefronts, create branded items, and organise virtual events. This phenomenon raises apprehensions over potential trademark infringement and the dilution of brand identity. The inclusion of established brands in user-generated content (UGC) has the potential to create confusion or injury to existing trademarks. The primary concern revolves around preserving intellectual property rights while nurturing innovation and artistic freedom within the metaverse.

Privacy And Personal Rights:

Using avatars or depictions of actual individuals in user-generated content (UGC) sometimes gives rise to apprehensions over privacy and personal rights. The adverse description, harassment, or defamation experienced within the metaverse can detrimentally impact an individual's reputation. Reconciling the freedom of artistic expression and safeguarding individual rights within the virtual realm is a distinctive obstacle for legal structures and content control.

Licensing And Royalties in Collaborative:

In the metaverse, collaborative user-generated content (UGC) initiatives frequently need more explicit agreements regarding equitable cash distribution and recognition among participants. The inherent collective characteristics of the metaverse give rise to a situation where users' degrees of engagement in a project can differ, posing difficulties in establishing equitable remuneration or revenue distribution frameworks. The establishment of fair partnership agreements assumes critical importance in such circumstances.

Digital Theft and Piracy:

The issue of digital theft and piracy continues to be a significant worry in the metaverse, as users can reproduce or disseminate user-generated content (UGC) without obtaining appropriate authorisation. Copyright infringement can occur as a result of unauthorised copying and dissemination, which can have a direct impact on the original producers. Effectively deterring and addressing digital theft in the decentralised environment of the metaverse necessitates using creative strategies to enforce intellectual property (IP) rights.

Content Moderation and Enforcement:

The enforcement of intellectual property (IP) rights within the metaverse presents distinct issues due to its decentralised and user-centric characteristics. Content moderation and intellectual property (IP) enforcement tools must adapt to the current context to successfully address infringements. This entails removing unauthorised user-generated content (UGC) and the potential initiation of legal proceedings against individuals who violate intellectual property (IP) rights.

Emerging Intellectual Property (IP) Models:

The metaverse is currently positioned as a leading domain in developing intellectual property (IP) paradigms, exemplified by the advent of Non-Fungible Tokens (NFTs). Non-fungible tokens (NFTs) represent ownership of digital assets and offer unique considerations in intellectual property (IP) rights. Potential challenges may occur regarding Non-Fungible Tokens (NFTs) ownership, licensing arrangements, and the interplay between conventional copyright regulations and the rights associated with NFT-based requests. The legal framework concerning intellectual property issues related to non-fungible tokens (NFTs) is now undergoing continuous development.

THE APPLICABILITY OF LEGAL FRAMEWORKS TO THE METAVERSE

1. COPYRIGHT LAW

The legal construct of copyright law confers upon creators and authors the exclusive entitlements to their original works of authorship, guaranteeing their authority over the replication, dissemination, and public exhibition or presentation of their inventions. These works encompass a wide range of creative expressions, including but not limited to literature, visual art, music, and several other forms of artistic expression. The promotion of creativity is facilitated by copyright protection, as it grants creators the opportunity to generate revenue from their creations and safeguard their intellectual property rights for a predetermined period.

Eligible Works:

The domain of copyright law encompasses a wide range of artistic and intellectual creations, encompassing literary works (such as books, articles, and essays), musical compositions and lyrics, dramatic works (including plays and screenplays), choreography, pictorial and graphic works (such as paintings and illustrations), sculptural works, audiovisual works (including films and television shows), and sound recordings. A fundamental criterion to qualify for copyright protection is that the work must possess originality and be recorded in a concrete medium of expression, necessitating its existence in a perceptible or reproducible form.

Exclusive Rights:

Copyright grants creators a bundle of exclusive rights, typically including:

i) *Reproduction:* The right to make copies or recordings of the work.
ii) *Distribution:* The right to control the distribution of documents to the public.
iii) *Public Performance*: The right to publicly display or perform the work (e.g., in concerts or theatres).

iv) Public Display: The right to display the work publicly (e.g., in art exhibitions).

v) Creation of Derivative Works: The right to create new works based on the original (e.g., adaptations, translations, or remixes).

These exclusive rights allow creators to control how their jobs are used, published, and monetised.

Copyright Protection:

The duration of copyright protection is not indefinite. The period of copyright protection exhibits variability across jurisdictions; however, it commonly encompasses the lifespan of the inventor along with an extension of 50 to 70 years after their demise. Once the copyright term has elapsed, the intellectual property transitions into the public domain, granting unrestricted usage rights to any individual.

Copyright Registration:

The provision of copyright protection is frequently inherent in the creation and fixation of a work in a physical medium. Nevertheless, certain nations allow formally registering copyrights through a governmental entity. Recording intellectual property offers a range of advantages, including the capacity to initiate legal proceedings for copyright violation and access to more extensive legal remedies in the event of such breach.

Fair Use and Exceptions:

The field of copyright law has various exceptions and limitations, one of which is commonly referred to as fair use (or fair dealing in certain jurisdictions). Fair use grants individuals the right to utilise copyrighted content in a restricted manner without obtaining explicit permission from the copyright holder. This allowance primarily applies to criticism, commentary, news reporting, education, and research. The nuances of fair use may differ depending on the jurisdiction and are contingent upon legal interpretation.

Moral Rights:

Certain nations acknowledge the existence of moral rights alongside economic rights. Moral rights safeguard the non-economic concerns of artists, encompassing entitlements such as the right to be recognised for their work, the right to object to any disparaging treatment, and the right to avoid misattribution. The purpose of these rights is to safeguard the creator's integrity and reputation.

International Protection:

Copyright protection is granted internationally using agreements such as the Berne Convention for the Protection of Literary and Artistic Works. This provision guarantees that creators originating from a particular nation are afforded copyright protection in other member countries, eliminating the requirement for supplementary registration. International copyright treaties are crucial in promoting global acknowledgement and implementation of copyright protection.

Digital Copyright Issues:

The advent of the digital era has introduced distinctive obstacles to copyright law. The emergence of online piracy, digital distribution, and user-generated material has prompted inquiries regarding the enforcement and adaptation of copyright inside the digital domain. Legislative measures such as the Digital Millennium Copyright Act (DMCA) in the United States are designed to tackle matters about online copyright violation. At the same time, digital platforms and content producers grapple with the intricacies of generating and disseminating digital content.

Licensing and Royalties:

Copyright holders can grant licenses to other parties to utilise their intellectual property in particular manners. Licensing agreements delineate the permissible utilisation of work and frequently entail the remittance of royalties to the copyright proprietor. Collective management organisations (CMOs) are crucial in facilitating copyright licensing and the equitable distribution of rewards to creators.

Limitations Of Existing Law

The metaverse, an interactive and virtual digital environment where users engage in creation, interaction, and collaboration, presents several problems to traditional copyright legislation. One of the main constraints arises from the collective aspect of content generation within the metaverse. In contrast to conventional copyright situations characterised by the creation of a work by a single author or entity, the metaverse frequently involves several users‘ collaborative production of user-generated content (UGC). The intricate nature of these creations might pose challenges in ascertaining ownership and authorship. The current copyright laws, which primarily revolve around individual authorship, need help effectively accommodating the creative process's collaborative and ever-evolving nature. As a result, the metaverse may witness an increase in both the frequency and complexity of conflicts about copyright ownership and the appropriate credit allocation.

Moreover, the metaverse facilitates cultivating a remix culture, wherein users regularly create new content by building upon or modifying current user-generated content (UGC). Although promoting the development of original ideas and inventive thinking, this cultural context presents a complex situation regarding established copyright principles related to derivative works and fair use. Determining what qualifies as proper usage within a metaverse abundant with transformative inventions can be subjective and dynamic. This phenomenon prompts inquiries over the efficacy of current copyright legislation in regulating and safeguarding the wide range of user-generated content (UGC) within the metaverse.

Incorporating digital and physical domains within the metaverse introduces an additional level of intricacy. Augmented reality (AR) applications, such as those mentioned, superimpose digital content over real-world settings. The phenomenon described in the statement blurs the distinction between two separate realities and introduces new and unique copyright problems. The current legal framework may not readily apply to the scenarios involving mixed reality, thus requiring the establishment of new legal frameworks or the interpretation of existing laws to clarify copyright application in these contexts.

Furthermore, the metaverse's expansive scope presents challenges in enforcing copyright. The global nature of users and content creators enables copyright infringement to easily cross geographical boundaries. This phenomenon challenges the conventional understanding of jurisdiction, creating complexities in the consistent application and enforcement of copyright laws. International copyright treaties, such as the Berne Convention, aim to achieve uniformity in copyright protection across different nations. However, given the distinct attributes of the metaverse, it may be necessary to modify existing treaties to effectively manage the complexities associated with this evolving digital realm.

2. TRADEMARK LAW

Trademark law is a specific area within the broader intellectual property (IP) law field. Its primary purpose is to establish legal safeguards and regulations to protect unique symbols, names, phrases, designs, logos, and trade dress. These elements identify and differentiate goods or services within the marketplace. The primary objective of granting exclusive rights to trademark owners is to mitigate customer confusion by enabling them to utilise their trademarks as indicators of the source or origin of their products or services. Trademark law functions to safeguard brands, promote brand identification, and uphold equitable competition within commerce.

Purpose Of Trademark Laws

Trademarks fulfil various significant functions within the realm of commerce. First and foremost, they play a crucial role in establishing and enhancing brand recognition. A meticulously crafted and continuously employed trademark represents a company's distinctiveness, establishing immediate consumer recognition. The awareness of a brand holds significant value as it cultivates trust and loyalty among customers who show a connection between the trademark and a specific standard of excellence and dependability.

Additionally, trademarks play a crucial role in safeguarding consumer interests. Brands protect against ambiguity by guaranteeing that goods or services associated with a specific brand are derived from an officially sanctioned origin. When individuals are presented with a well-established trademark, they can make informed choices regarding their purchases since they know the expected quality and attributes associated with the brand.

Another significant function of trademarks is to build a distinct corporate identity. Utilising a unique brand enables a business to differentiate itself within a highly competitive marketplace. The communication encompasses the corporate identity and the organisation's core principles, standing, and distinctive propositions. The establishment of this identity serves as a potent mechanism for establishing a connection with consumers and distinguishing the enterprise from its rivals.

Trademarks additionally serve as valuable assets for enterprises. Over time, brands that have achieved success have the potential to increase in value and make a substantial contribution to the overall worth of a firm. These intellectual properties have the potential to be licensed to third parties, franchised, or even sold, offering firms supplementary sources of revenue and avenues for expansion.

In addition, trademarks provide firms with a competitive edge by enabling them to differentiate their offerings from their rivals. The differentiation process could foster client loyalty and enhance market share. Trademarks are a strategic instrument for enterprises to establish a competitive advantage and prosper within their sectors.

Furthermore, trademarks assure superior quality. Consumers develop an association between a brand and a particular standard of quality and uniformity. This guarantee aids in the establishment of confidence between organisations and their consumer base, as customers are aware of the anticipated outcomes when encountering a reputable trademark.

Moreover, trademarks serve to streamline marketing and advertising endeavours. These symbols offered by designers help firms establish recognisable brand identities and foster consumer confidence by being concise, memorable, and seamlessly integrated into promotional materials.

Trademarks play a crucial role in enabling worldwide expansion within the global economy. The protection of brands on an international scale enables firms to penetrate new markets while upholding a cohesive corporate identity effectively. Global reach is vital for multinational corporations aiming to develop a global presence.

Finally, trademarks provide legal protection to their proprietors. Exclusive rights are conferred to the individual or entity to utilise the designated mark alone in association with particular goods or services. Trademark owners are granted a legal safeguard that empowers them to initiate legal proceedings against individuals or entities that try to employ marks likely to confuse, thereby safeguarding the brand's credibility and standing. In conclusion, trademarks play a crucial role in facilitating the success of businesses by providing them with essential means to flourish, safeguard their clientele, and establish enduring brand awareness.

TYPES OF TRADEMARKS

A. Word Marks:

Word marks are words or word combinations, usually in conventional typefaces and characters. These entities exhibit remarkable adaptability, making them suitable for diverse sectors and commodities. Prominent instances encompass "Coca-Cola," "Microsoft," and "Amazon."

B. Design Marks:

Design marks encompass various visual aspects, such as graphical components, symbols, or styled fonts, symbolising and representing a particular company. The effects above use visual aesthetics to communicate and establish brand identification. An instance of a well-recognized design mark is the "Apple" logo, which features an iconic apple silhouette.

C. Slogan Marks:

Slogan marks safeguard distinctive catchphrases or slogans closely linked to a brand's promotional initiatives and are frequently employed to fortify brand communication and cultivate a robust brand identity. "Have a Break, have a Kit Kat" is a well-known tagline trademark.

D. Trade Dress:

"Trade dress" refers to a product or service's comprehensive visual presentation and packaging. This may encompass notable colour combinations (e.g., the Tiffany blue hue), distinctive product shapes (e.g., the iconic Coca-Cola bottle), and unusual packaging designs (e.g., the McDonald's Happy Meal box). The primary objective of trade dress is to establish a distinct and uniform visual representation of a product.

E. Service Marks:

Service marks are analogous to trademarks but are mainly linked to services rather than tangible products. Service providers rely on brand identity protection to safeguard their reputations. An instance of this can be observed in the financial sector, where the term "Visa" functions as a service mark denoting the provision of electronic payment services.

F. Certification Marks:

Certification marks indicate that items or services have met specific standards or qualifications established by an autonomous certifying entity. Certified products or services assure buyers they adhere to predetermined criteria, instilling confidence in their quality and reliability. The "Fair Trade Certified" label assures consumers that products have been verified to comply with fair trade standards.

G. Collective Marks:

Collective marks are employed by individuals inside a collective entity or institution to establish a collective identity. These symbols represent a common attribute, association, or inclusion. Professional organisations frequently utilise collective marks to signify affiliation with a particular group. For instance, the National Association of Realtors employs the coordinated pattern "REALTOR®" to denote membership among its constituents.

H. Trade Names:

Trade or company names are the official names under which commercial entities conduct their operations within the legal framework. Although they may not conform to conventional trademark standards, these non-traditional identifiers play a crucial role in business identity. Trademark protection can be obtained for trade names when they are utilised to identify and differentiate particular goods or services. An illustration of this concept may be observed in the case of "General Electric," which functions as both a trade name and a trademark encompassing a diverse range of products and services.

I. Geographical Indications (GIs):

Geographical indications safeguard the names or symbols employed on goods from distinct geographical areas and exhibit attributes or traits closely linked to that location. Illustrative instances encompass "Roquefort," denoting cheese originating from the Roquefort-sur-Soulzon region in France, and "Darjeeling," signifying tea cultivated in the Darjeeling district in India.

J. Three-Dimensional Marks:

Three-dimensional trademarks serve as a means of safeguarding the distinctive shape or arrangement of a product or its packaging. Traditionally, these are employed in instances where the visual attributes of a product are unique and easily identifiable. The distinctive form of a Coca-Cola bottle is safeguarded as a three-dimensional trademark.

K. Sound Marks:

Sound markings are a form of intellectual property that safeguards unique auditory elements closely identified with a particular brand. These acoustic aspects encompass jingles, musical compositions, and other similar components. An illustration of this can be seen in the renowned sound mark of the MGM lion's roar, which has been closely linked with the film company.

L. Motion Marks:

Motion marks safeguard trademarks of moving images, animations, or sequences. Dynamic and memorable brand representations are frequently employed in advertising and branding campaigns.

Different trademarks have distinct benefits and difficulties, prompting firms to combine different types to safeguard their brand identity and intellectual property comprehensively. A comprehensive comprehension of the many categories of trademarks is vital for efficient brand administration and legal safeguarding.

TRADEMARK REGISTRATION

The trademark registration procedure holds significant legal importance, providing many benefits for safeguarding a brand. One key advantage is the provision of a presumption of ownership. When a trademark undergoes registration with a governmental entity such as the United States Patent and Trademark Office (USPTO), it establishes a legal presumption that the individual or entity registered the trademark is the legitimate proprietor of the mark. The assumption facilitates the streamlining of legal proceedings, as the onus of proof is transferred to prospective challengers, who must substantiate their entitlement to utilise the trademark.

One further significant benefit of registration is the provision of exclusive rights on a national scale to utilise the trademark for the designated goods or services. The exclusivity grant gives the brand proprietor the authority to prohibit the utilisation of marks that may confuse consumers about goods or services falling under the same category within the registered jurisdiction. This protection holds significant value in its ability to mitigate brand dilution and minimise customer misunderstanding effectively.

Moreover, the process of trademark registration serves to provide public notification of the existence of the mark. Public databases offer listings of registered trademarks, facilitating the identification and acknowledgement of established defects by competitors and the general populace. The purpose of this public notice is to discourage possible infringers and assist them in preventing the unintentional use of similar effects.

Trademark registration offers a notable benefit in terms of the provision of legal remedies in cases of trademark infringement. The legal entitlement to initiate a lawsuit for trademark infringement in federal courts is granted to owners of registered trademarks. The attainment of a favourable outcome in a legal dispute can lead to the awarding of compensatory monetary compensation, the granting of court orders to prevent specific actions (referred to as injunctive relief), and the provision of various forms of redress aimed at safeguarding the rights of the owner. The legal support considerably enhances the trademark owner's capacity to assert their rights and protect their brand.

Trademark registration can provide firms seeking worldwide expansion with the added benefit of streamlining the process of securing enhanced protection in foreign markets. Brand protection on a global scale can be facilitated by extending registration to other nations, as stipulated in international accords such as the Madrid Protocol. Establishing international security is of utmost importance for organisations that seek to uphold a uniform brand identity and preserve a positive reputation on a global scale.

TRADEMARK DURATION

The time for which trademark protection is granted is contingent upon a range of elements, encompassing the nature of the mark and the specific legal jurisdiction in question. Unregistered or common law trademarks might acquire legal protection using their utilisation in commercial activities. The duration of protection for a mark can be endless as long as the spot remains in use and retains its distinctiveness. Nevertheless, it is essential to note that common law rights are generally constrained to the specific geographical regions where the trademark is actively employed.

In contrast, registered trademarks benefit from a longer duration. The initial registration period spans ten years in numerous nations, such as the United States. Trademark owners can extend the registration for successive ten-year periods without limit, provided they consistently utilise the mark in commercial activities and satisfy the obligatory renewal criteria. The prolonged lifetime of protection offered by this measure allows for preserving exclusive rights for well-established trademarks over an extended period.

The maintenance of registered trademarks frequently necessitates the periodic submission of evidence of usage to the relevant trademark authority. Owners are required to furnish substantiation demonstrating the ongoing utilisation of the brand in commercial activities, thereby strengthening the association between the mark and the goods or services for which it is registered. Non-compliance with these stipulations may lead to the revocation of the registration.

Nevertheless, the assurance of trademark protection is temporary. If a proprietor of a trademark discontinues its utilisation in commercial activities or neglects to uphold the registration appropriately, the brand may forfeit its safeguarding. Maintaining vigilance, actively safeguarding intellectual property, and staying well-informed on renewal and usage criteria are crucial for trademark owners to uphold the ongoing validity and protection of their trademarks. Seeking advice from legal experts specialising in trademark law can offer valuable insights into this matter.

TRADEMARK RIGHTS AND INFRINGEMENT

Trademark rights are legally recognised by registering or using the trademark in commercial activities. Onto registration, a trademark confers onto its proprietor the privilege of exclusive utilisation of the mark in association with designated products or services. The rights above possess a territorial nature, granting their applicability exclusively within the confines of the registered jurisdiction. Trademark infringement arises when a different entity uses a mark that is either similar or identical, which is likely to result in confusion among consumers. It is imperative to acknowledge that trademark owners are responsible for proactively safeguarding their marks. Various remedies are available to address instances of infringement, which may include:

i) Injunctive Relief: A court order that stops the infringing use of the trademark.

ii) Damages: Compensation for financial losses incurred due to the infringement.

iii) Seizure of Counterfeit Goods: Authorities can confiscate counterfeit products bearing the infringing mark.

TRADEMARK DILUTION

Trademark dilution is a legal principle within the realm of trademark law that seeks to safeguard the exceptional attributes of renowned or widely recognised brands; in contrast to the conventional approach of assessing customer misunderstanding, dilution claims centre around the potential harm arising from unauthorised use of a renowned trademark, even without any probable confusion. The primary concept underlying dilution is to safeguard the integrity and worth of a well-known brand by averting its gradual loss of distinctiveness.

The following is a comprehensive elucidation of the concept of trademark dilution.

> Prominent Trademarks:

Trademark dilution is a legal concept specifically applicable to trademarks that have achieved high fame and recognition. These brands have attained notable recognition and distinctiveness within the marketplace. Frequently, renowned trademarks are linked with well-established brands and enjoy substantial recognition among the broader populace.

> Classification of Dilution:

Trademark dilution generally manifests in two distinct forms:

Blurring refers to the illicit utilisation of a well-known trademark, which diminishes its unique characteristics by establishing connections with unrelated goods or services. For instance, if a corporation were to adopt the renowned "Coca-Cola" trademark for marketing bicycles, there is a possibility that this action may attenuate the mark's distinctiveness in the domain of carbonated beverages.

Tarnishment refers to the detrimental impact on the reputation of a renowned trademark resulting from its illicit usage, which associates it with unfavourable or adverse characteristics. As an illustration, utilising the "Disney" trademark by a corporation engaged in adult-oriented entertainment can potentially diminish the pristine reputation commonly associated with the Disney brand.

> **Components of a Dilution Assertion:**

To achieve success in a dilution claim, it is often necessary for the owner of the trademark to establish the following constituent components:

The requisite characteristic of the mark under consideration must possess genuine fame, characterised by a significant degree of recognition and uniqueness.

Unauthorised Use: The defendant must utilise the trademark without obtaining a proper license from the owner of the mark.

The potential harm to distinctiveness arises when the unlawful use of a famous mark is deemed likely to diminish its distinctiveness or degrade its reputation.

> **Strategies for Mitigating the Effects of Dilution:**

Various defences might be raised in response to dilution charges.

Fair Use: Using a well-known trademark may be deemed fair use and not dilution if it serves legitimate purposes such as commentary, criticism, news reporting, education, or parody.

Non-commercial Use: If a trademark is non-commercial and does not provide the impression of being endorsed by the proprietor of the brand, it may not be deemed dilution.

In trademark law, dilution refers to the unauthorised use of a famous mark that weakens its distinctiveness or tarnishes its reputation. To address this issue, various remedies have been established. These

> Potential Remedies

If a dilution claim is successful, remedies can include:

1. *Injunctive Relief:* A court may issue an injunction to stop the defendant from using the mark in a dilutive manner.
2. *Monetary Damages:* The trademark owner may be awarded monetary damages from the dilution.
3. *Corrective Advertising:* Sometimes, a court may order the defendant to run corrective advertising to counteract the dilutive effect.

The legal regulations of trademark dilution exhibit jurisdictional variations, with certain jurisdictions not acknowledging the notion of dilution. Nevertheless, in legal systems where it is applicable, this practice functions as a crucial mechanism for safeguarding the uniqueness and prestige of renowned trademark owners of prominent companies should proactively monitor the market and resort to legal measures when deemed appropriate to protect against dilution and preserve the integrity of their valuable intellectual property.

International Protection

The safeguarding of trademarks on an international scale is an imperative facet of contemporary commerce, particularly for enterprises seeking to extend the reach of their brand beyond national borders. Trademarks possess a geographical characteristic, signifying that their protection is limited to the jurisdiction in which they are registered or actively employed. Firms can utilise several procedures and agreements to safeguard their brands globally.

> Madrid Protocol:

The Madrid Protocol is an influential international agreement streamlining the procedure for safeguarding trademarks across numerous nations. The administration of this entity is under the purview of the World Intellectual Property Organization (WIPO). According to the provisions of the Madrid Protocol, a trademark proprietor can submit a solitary international application within their domestic jurisdiction's trademark office, commonly referred to as the "home office." Subsequently, this application can be utilised to pursue safeguards in numerous member nations participating in the protocol.

Key features of the Madrid Protocol include:

1. *Centralised Filing:* Trademark owners can file one application with their home office, simplifying the administrative process.
2. *Cost Savings:* Filing through the Madrid Protocol can be more cost-effective than filing individual applications in multiple countries.
3. *Single Renewal:* Trademark renewals can also be managed centrally, streamlining maintenance.

> **European Union Trademark (EUTM):**

The European Union provides a centralised system for registering trademarks, referred to as the European Union Trademark (EUTM), formerly recognised as the Community Trademark (CTM). The registration of an EUTM (European Union Trademark) offers comprehensive trademark protection throughout the European Union member states, rendering it a desirable choice for enterprises seeking to conduct operations within the EU.

> **National Filings**

When a corporation wants to safeguard its trademark within certain nations that do not fall under international accords, such as the Madrid Protocol, it must submit separate national trademark registrations for each desired country. Filing domestically might be more labour-intensive and financially burdensome compared to the procedure for foreign filings.

> **Regional Trademark Systems**

Certain regions, such as the African Intellectual Property Organization (OAPI) and the African Regional Intellectual Property Organization (ARIPO), have implemented regional trademark systems that facilitate the submission and safeguarding of trademarks across several member countries within the respective regions.

> WIPO's Global Brand Database

The World Intellectual Property Organization (WIPO) maintains a comprehensive Global Brand Database, which grants users access to a wide range of trademark information from national and international sources. This tool facilitates the search for pre-existing trademarks and evaluates potential trademark disputes for trademark owners seeking to expand their operations globally.

> Enforcement of International Trademarks

After obtaining international protection, trademark owners must diligently exercise their rights by vigorously enforcing their trademarks. Enforcement often entails marketplace surveillance to identify potential instances of infringement, followed by initiating legal measures as deemed required, such as pursuing litigation against those who have infringed on intellectual property rights.

Trademark Licensing And Assignments

Trademark licensing and assignments are crucial in enterprises' strategic management and utilising intellectual property assets, particularly trademarks. Trademark owners can exercise control over the usage of their marks through legal methods, which in turn can give rise to diverse business prospects. The following is a comprehensive elucidation of the concepts of trademark licensing and assignments:

TRADEMARK LICENSING

Trademark licensing is a legal arrangement wherein the trademark owner (the licensor) authorises another party (the licensee) to utilise the trademark, provided that specific predetermined terms and conditions are met. The words above are delineated inside a trademark licensing agreement, constituting a legally enforceable contractual arrangement between the party granting the license (licensor) and the party receiving the request (licensee). The following are essential components of trademark licensing:

1. *Control:* The trademark owner (licensor) retains control over their trademark use, including the quality and standards associated with the products or services bearing the mark.

2. *Scope:* Licensing agreements specify the size of the license, including the territory in which the mark can be used, the duration of the right, and any restrictions on its use.

3. *Fees:* Licenses often involve financial arrangements, such as royalty payments, license fees, or revenue-sharing agreements. These terms are negotiated between the parties.

4. *Quality Control:* To maintain the trademark's integrity, licensors typically have the right to enforce quality control standards and inspect the licensee's products or services.

5. *Exclusivity:* Licensing agreements may grant the licensee exclusive rights to use the trademark in a specific geographic area or for particular products or services. Alternatively, they may be non-exclusive, allowing multiple licensees to use the mark.

6. *Termination:* Licensing agreements outline conditions under which the agreement can be terminated, including breach of contract, failure to meet quality standards or expiration of the deal.

The practice of trademark licensing can offer benefits to both parties involved.

7. *For Licensors:* Trademark owners can generate revenue from licensing their marks, expand their brand's reach into new markets or industries, and increase brand visibility.

8. *For Licensees:* Licensees gain the right to use a recognised and trusted trademark, which can enhance the marketability and credibility of their products or services.

Trademark Assignments:

The trademark assignment process entails transferring ownership of a trademark from the assignor, the present owner, to the assignee, who becomes the new owner. The transfer above is permanent and entails a shift in ownership duly documented and registered with the appropriate trademark authority. The following are essential components of trademark assignments:

1. Transfer of Ownership: In a trademark assignment, all rights and responsibilities associated with the trademark, including its registrations and goodwill, are transferred to the assignee.

2. Legal Documentation: Like licensing agreements, trademark assignments are formalised through a written contract signed by both parties. This contract should clearly state the assignment's terms and conditions.

3. Recordation: Trademark assignments must be recorded with the appropriate trademark office to update the ownership information in the official records.

4. No Control by Assignor: The assignor no longer controls how the mark is used after the assignment. The assignee becomes the new owner and assumes all trademark-related decisions and responsibilities.

Trademark assignments can occur due to various factors, including mergers and acquisitions, divestitures, or transferring ownership of a brand or company division. Terms are commonly employed when the proprietor aims to convey full rights and interests in the trademark.

3. PATENT LAW

The field of patent law pertains to a specific area under intellectual property law, wherein innovators are given exclusive privileges over their inventions for a finite duration, commonly spanning 20 years from the moment of submission. These rights allow inventors to safeguard their discoveries, prohibit unauthorised manufacture, use, or sale of their inventions by others, and potentially generate revenue from their creations through licensing or sales. The following is a comprehensive exposition on the subject of patent law.

TYPES OF PATENTS

1. Utility Patents:

Description: Utility patents are the most common type of patent and cover a wide range of inventions, including processes, machines, manufactured articles, and compositions of matter.

Examples: Utility patents can be granted for technological innovations, pharmaceuticals, manufacturing methods, and other fields. For instance, a new smartphone technology, a novel drug formula, or an improved manufacturing process for a specific material can all be eligible for utility patents.

Duration: Utility patents typically have 20 years from the filing date.

2. Design Patents:

Description: Design patents protect an object's ornamental and non-functional design features. They focus on the visual appearance and aesthetics of the product rather than its functional aspects.

Examples: Design patents can cover the unique design of consumer products, such as the shape of a bottle, the appearance of a piece of jewellery, the pattern on a textile, or the graphical user interface (GUI) of a software application.

Duration: Design patents typically have 15 years from the grant date.

3. Plant Patents:

Description: Plant patents are granted for inventing or discovering a new and distinct variety of plants that can be asexually reproduced. This category is unique to patents and related to agriculture and horticulture advancements.

Examples: Plant patents can be awarded for newly developed plant varieties, such as a new type of rose with distinct characteristics or a hybrid fruit tree with unique qualities.

Duration: Plant patents typically have 20 years from the filing date.

Requirements For Patentability

The requirements for patentability are crucial criteria that an invention must meet to be eligible for a patent. These requirements vary by jurisdiction but generally include the following key elements:

1. Novelty: To be patentable, an invention must be entirely new and not disclosed or publicly available anywhere before the patent application's filing date. This means the design should not have been previously patented, described in a printed publication, publicly used, or sold.

2. Non-Obviousness (Inventive Step): The invention must involve an inventive step or non-obvious advancement beyond what is readily apparent to someone skilled in the relevant field. In other words, it should be something different than an obvious combination of existing knowledge or technologies. This requirement ensures that patents are granted for genuinely innovative and inventive contributions.

3. Usefulness (Utility): The invention must have a practical, real-world application and should not be purely theoretical or non-functional. It should serve a useful purpose and be capable of doing what it claims to do.

4. Enablement and Description: The patent application must provide sufficient detail to enable someone skilled in the field to replicate and use the invention without undue experimentation. This includes clear and complete descriptions, drawings or diagrams, and claims defining the protection scope.

5. Statutory Subject Matter: Patent laws define statutory subject matter in most jurisdictions. Typically, inventions related to technology, processes, machines, articles of manufacture, and compositions of matter are eligible for patent protection. However, abstract ideas, laws of nature, and natural phenomena are usually not patentable subject matter.

6. Written Description and Claims: The patent application should include a written description of the invention that is clear and comprehensive. It should also contain one or more claims defining the specific protection scope sought. Claims are crucial because they delineate what aspects of the invention are protected and can be enforced against potential infringers.

7. Properly Filed Application: The patent application must be filed correctly with the relevant office. This includes submitting the required forms, fees, and documentation per the jurisdiction's requirements.

8. Non-Disclosure Before Filing: In many jurisdictions, inventors are advised to keep their inventions confidential until a patent application is filed. Public disclosure of the story before filing can jeopardise its novelty and patentability.

Meeting these patentability requirements is essential for a successful patent application. Inventors and their legal representatives carefully prepare patent applications to demonstrate how the invention meets these criteria. Patent examiners at the relevant patent office review applications to ensure compliance with these requirements before granting a patent. It's important to note that patent laws and regulations can vary by country, so inventors often seek guidance from patent attorneys or agents familiar with the jurisdiction's specific requirements where they wish to obtain a patent.

The Patent Application Process

A. Invention Disclosure:

The process begins with the inventor(s) documenting their invention clearly and comprehensively. This documentation is critical for preparing a robust patent application. It should include:

i) Detailed descriptions of how the story works.
ii) Diagrams, drawings, or sketches illustrating the invention's design or functionality.
iii) Experimental data, if applicable.
iv) Any prototypes or models of the story.
v) Records of the invention's development, including dates and iterations.

B. Prior Art Search:

A prior art search is conducted to identify existing patents, publications, or public disclosures related to the invention. This search helps determine the novelty of the design and assess the likelihood of obtaining a patent. Patent professionals often use specialised databases and search tools to conduct thorough prior art searches.

C. Consultation with a Patent Attorney:

Inventors typically consult with a patent attorney or agent specialising in intellectual property law. The attorney guides the patenting process during this consultation, including the steps involved, potential challenges, and costs. The attorney helps the inventor make informed decisions about pursuing patent protection.

D. Patent Application Drafting:

The patent attorney works closely with the inventor to draft an application that meets the patent office's requirements. This involves creating various components of the application:

i) *Title:* A concise, descriptive title for the invention.
ii) *Background:* A detailed description of the state of the art in the relevant field, highlighting any problems or challenges that the invention addresses.
iii) *Summary:* An overview of the invention's essential features, advantages, and the problem it solves.
iv) *Detailed Description:* A comprehensive explanation of the invention, including how it works, made or used, and any variations or embodiments.
v) *Claims:* At the heart of the patent application, claims define the specific scope of protection sought for the invention. Well-drafted claims are essential for determining the boundaries of the invention's protection.
vi) *Abstract:* A summary of the invention for publication and search purposes.

Drafting high-quality claims is particularly important, as they are the basis for assessing patent infringement and validity.

E. Filing the Application:

The completed patent application is submitted to the relevant patent office. The application must include the forms and fees required by the jurisdiction where protection is sought. The patent office assigns a filing date, establishing the application's priority.

F. Examination:

The patent office assigns an examiner to review the application. During the examination, the examiner assesses the application for compliance with patentability requirements, including novelty, non-obviousness, usefulness, and proper disclosure. The examiner may conduct their prior art search to evaluate the invention's novelty.

G. Office Actions:

If the examiner identifies issues with the application, they issue office actions. These official communications may request clarifications, amendments, or additional information. Applicants must respond to office actions within a specified timeframe, addressing any concerns the examiner raises.

H. Publication:

In many patent systems, patent applications are published 18 months after the filing or priority date. This publication makes information about the invention available to the public, although the patent has yet to be granted. It allows competitors and the public to become aware of pending patent applications.

I. Grant or Rejection:

The patent office will decide after examination and any necessary amendments or responses to office actions. They will either grant a patent if the invention meets all patentability requirements or reject the application if it does not. If given, the inventor is awarded exclusive rights to the story for a limited period.

J. Maintenance:

After a patent is granted, the owner must pay maintenance fees to keep the patent in force. These fees are typically due periodically throughout the patent's term, and failure to pay them can result in the patent expiring before its full term.

K. Enforcement:

Once granted, patent owners have the legal right to enforce their patents and take legal action against those who infringe on their exclusive rights. Enforcement may involve filing patent infringement lawsuits or pursuing licensing agreements with potential infringers.

Navigating the patent application process can be challenging due to its complexity and legal intricacies. Patent attorneys or agents play a crucial role in helping inventors navigate this process effectively and secure valuable patent protection for their innovations.

OVERVIEW OF TECHNOLOGICAL INNOVATIONS FOR IP PROTECTION IN THE METAVERSE

The preservation of intellectual property (IP) has emerged as a crucial issue within the dynamic and ever-changing realm of the metaverse. The convergence of physical and digital domains has given rise to novel prospects and obstacles in safeguarding intellectual property (IP).

Blockchain is a pioneering technology currently leading the way in safeguarding intellectual property (IP) within the metaverse. Blockchain, an innovative and decentralised ledger system, presents a paradigm-shifting answer. Non-fungible tokens (NFTs), constructed using blockchain technology, have garnered considerable interest. Non-fungible tokens (NFTs) are cryptographic tokens that serve as digital representations of ownership for distinct digital assets, encompassing many forms of creative expression, such as visual art, music, or virtual properties. The investments are securely held on blockchain platforms such as Ethereum, facilitating transparent and auditable documentation of ownership and origin. Non-fungible tokens (NFTs) verify and safeguard digital creations inside the metaverse, empowering creators to establish their ownership rights and receive royalties upon subsequent resale of their products.

Digital watermarking is a technology that is utilised to safeguard intellectual property. The methodology above encompasses concealing covert data within digital media formats, such as photographs or videos. Watermarks can incorporate pertinent details regarding the originator, copyright status, or utilisation rights. Digital watermarks in the metaverse have the potential to discourage illicit utilisation and facilitate the process of attribution. Artists can incorporate watermarks into their digital artworks or merchandise, establishing unequivocally their continued ownership and authority over their creations.

Significant advancements have been achieved in intellectual property (IP) safeguarding within the metaverse using artificial intelligence (AI) and machine learning. These systems can monitor extensive virtual environments and identify copyright infringement or unlawful utilisation occurrences. Content recognition systems driven by artificial intelligence (AI) can analyse virtual environments, detect copyrighted content, and notify authors or rights holders about potential infringements. Implementing this proactive method enables creators to maintain their intellectual property rights effectively.

Furthermore, metaverse systems currently include intellectual property (IP) protection methods. Virtual worlds such as Decentral and The Sandbox have established intellectual property (IP) policies that delineate explicit requirements for authors and users to safeguard copyright and trademark rights. These rules frequently provide provisions for reporting and resolving intellectual property conflicts within the platform.

DIGITAL RIGHTS MANAGEMENT (DRM), BLOCKCHAIN, AND OTHER EMERGING SOLUTIONS

In the dynamic landscape of the metaverse, protecting digital rights and intellectual property (IP) has become increasingly critical. Various emerging solutions, including Digital Rights Management (DRM) and blockchain technology, are being employed to address these challenges and ensure the rights and ownership of creators are upheld.

1. Digital Rights Management (DRM):

DRM is a technology and set of strategies to control access to and use of digital content. In the metaverse, DRM is crucial in protecting digital assets, ensuring that only authorised users can access, modify, or distribute them. Critical aspects of DRM in the metaverse include:

i) Access Control: DRM systems can enforce access controls, limiting who can enter virtual spaces and interact with digital content. This is particularly important in protecting exclusive experiences and proprietary assets.

ii) Content Encryption: DRM can encrypt digital assets, making it difficult for unauthorised users to intercept or copy them. This safeguards sensitive content, such as virtual goods and unique creations.

2. Blockchain Technology:

Blockchain technology has gained prominence in the metaverse for securing digital ownership and provenance through Non-Fungible Tokens (NFTs). NFTs, built on blockchain networks like Ethereum, provide transparent and immutable records of requests for digital assets. This technology offers:

i) Provenance Tracking: Blockchain enables tracking an asset's ownership history, proving its authenticity and origin. In the metaverse, this is vital for establishing the legitimacy of virtual items and art.

ii) Ownership Transparency: NFTs make ownership transparent, allowing creators to assert their rights over digital creations and potentially earn royalties from resales within virtual worlds.

iii) Smart Contracts: Blockchain-based smart contracts automate transactions and agreements, ensuring creators receive compensation when their digital assets are used or sold within the metaverse.

Emerging solutions in the metaverse also include AI-powered content recognition systems, which monitor virtual environments for instances of copyright infringement. These systems use machine learning algorithms to identify and report unauthorised use of copyrighted material, aiding in enforcing IP rights.

REFORMS TO EXISTING IP LAWS AND REGULATIONS FOR THE METAVERSE

Proposed reforms to existing intellectual property (IP) laws and regulations for the metaverse are essential to address this digital frontier's unique challenges and opportunities. Elaborating further on these proposed reforms

1. Recognition of Virtual Property Rights:

In the metaverse, users invest significant time and resources in acquiring virtual assets, including virtual real estate, digital fashion items, and in-game collectables. Recognising virtual property rights would mean acknowledging the inherent value of these digital assets and granting users legal ownership. Such reforms would provide users with explicit rights to buy, sell, trade, and protect virtual property, similar to real-world property rights. This recognition is essential to create a sense of ownership and trust within virtual economies.

2. Enhanced Copyright Protection for Virtual Creations:

User-generated content (UGC) is central to the metaverse's dynamic environment. To better protect creators and their creations, proposed reforms may focus on streamlining the copyright registration process for virtual content. More precise guidelines and definitions regarding copyright infringement within virtual environments are also necessary. These reforms would empower creators to assert their intellectual property rights over digital works and seek appropriate infringement remedies.

3. NFT and Blockchain Integration:

Non-fungible tokens (NFTs) and blockchain technology have emerged as powerful tools for establishing ownership and provenance of digital assets in the metaverse. Proposed reforms could involve integrating NFTs and blockchain into existing IP frameworks. This would enable creators to easily prove the authenticity and ownership of their digital creations using immutable blockchain records. Additionally, it could facilitate the collection of royalties for secondary sales of virtual assets, ensuring creators benefit from the resale of their works.

4. Cross-Border IP Enforcement:

The metaverse operates globally, and IP disputes can often cross jurisdictional boundaries. Proposed reforms should focus on international cooperation and harmonisation of IP enforcement. This might entail creating standardised procedures for addressing cross-border IP disputes, streamlining legal processes, and promoting collaboration between jurisdictions to ensure fair and consistent enforcement of IP rights.

5. Privacy and Data Ownership:

The metaverse generates vast amounts of user data, raising concerns about privacy and data ownership. Reforms should address these issues by establishing clear data ownership and protection guidelines within virtual environments. Users should have control over their data and provide informed consent for its use. Privacy-enhancing technologies and regulations are necessary to safeguard users' digital identities and data.

6. Fair Use and Transformative Works:

As users in the metaverse engage in creative activities, reforms may consider revising fair use and transformative works doctrines. These revisions would acknowledge the unique nature of virtual environments, where users often remix and transform existing content to create new and innovative experiences. Striking a balance between protecting original creators' rights and fosteringcreative expression within the metaverse is crucial.

CROSS-JURISDICTIONAL CHALLENGES AND THE NEED FOR INTERNATIONAL COOPERATION

Cross-jurisdictional challenges in the metaverse reflect this digital space's global and interconnected nature. The need for international cooperation arises from the following elaborated aspects:

1. Complex Legal Frameworks:

The metaverse transcends geographical boundaries, making applying traditional national legal frameworks challenging. Virtual environments are often hosted on servers located in one country but accessed by users worldwide. This complexity raises questions about which jurisdiction's laws and regulations should govern interactions and disputes. International cooperation is essential to establish clear guidelines for resolving such jurisdictional conflicts.

2. Divergent IP Laws:

Intellectual property laws, including copyright, trademarks, and patents, vary significantly from one country to another. In the metaverse, where users create and share content across borders, divergent IP laws can lead to clarity and certainty. Creators may inadvertently infringe on IP rights, not realising that what is permissible in one jurisdiction may constitute infringement in another. International cooperation can help align IP protections and enforcement mechanisms to provide clarity and consistency for creators and rights holders.

3. Data Privacy Concerns:

Data privacy is paramount in the metaverse, where extensive user data is collected and processed. Regulations like the GDPR have a global reach, affecting any organisation that handles data from EU residents, regardless of location. Cross-border data flows and international data transfer regulations require cooperation to ensure compliance and protect user privacy. International standards and agreements can facilitate this cooperation.

4. Jurisdictional Conflicts:

Disputes arising in the metaverse can involve multiple parties from different countries, leading to jurisdictional conflicts. Determining which legal system has authority over a particular case can be complex and time-consuming. International cooperation is essential to establish protocols for resolving conflicts efficiently, ensuring access to justice, and preventing legal disputes from becoming overly burdensome.

5. Cybersecurity and Cybercrime:

The metaverse is not immune to cybersecurity threats and cybercrime, which can originate from anywhere worldwide. Effective responses to cyber threats require international collaboration, sharing of threat intelligence, and coordinated efforts to track down and prosecute cybercriminals. Cybersecurity standards and practices can be developed through global consensus, enhancing the overall security of the metaverse.

6. Taxation and Economic Implications:

Virtual economies within the metaverse generate substantial economic activity, including revenue from virtual asset sales and virtual businesses. Taxation in virtual environments is a complex issue, with the potential for double taxation and inconsistent tax treatment across borders. International cooperation can help establish fair and transparent tax frameworks, ensuring that economic activity in the metaverse is appropriately taxed and regulated.

7. Standardisation and Interoperability:

The metaverse encompasses a multitude of platforms and virtual worlds, each with its technical specifications and rules. Achieving interoperability and standardisation across these platforms ensures a seamless and user-friendly experience. International cooperation can facilitate the development of common technical standards and protocols, making it easier for users to navigate and interact within the metaverse.

8. Cultural and Societal Differences:

Cultural norms and societal expectations regarding virtual behaviours vary widely across countries and regions. What is considered acceptable in one culture might be offensive or unacceptable in another. International cooperation can help establish guidelines for respectful and inclusive virtual interactions, taking into account cultural sensitivities and diversity.

CHAPTER III

Virtual Goods Marketplaces: Consumer Protection and Economic Considerations

INTRODUCTION

In the contemporary period, characterised by the constant progression of technology and the pervasive integration of digital elements into various facets of human existence, virtual goods markets have become a prominent and distinctive element within the contemporary digital economy. These online platforms exhibit dynamic characteristics and function as virtual marketplaces, facilitating the exchange of intangible assets such as in-game items, virtual real estate, digital art, and collectables.

The Progression of Virtual Goods Marketplaces

The emergence of virtual goods marketplaces can be attributed to the early stages of online gaming communities. During the late 1990s and early 2000s, a new phenomenon emerged in the form of Massively Multiplayer Online Games (MMOs) such as "EverQuest" and "Ultima Online." These games presented a unique concept wherein players could acquire or earn virtual objects within the digital realm of the game. The emergence of this innovative manifestation of virtual assets, be it a scarce weapon, an enchanted elixir, or a highly sought-after virtual steed, captivated the imagination of gamers. Players quickly realised that these virtual assets possessed tangible value, both within the confines of the game and in external contexts.

In these simulated environments, participants commenced informal exchanges, trading their diligently acquired virtual assets between themselves. The outcome manifested as a grassroots phenomenon, characterised by a basic virtual economy that functioned within the game's environment. The initial occurrences of in-game trade served as the foundation upon which virtual goods marketplaces would eventually emerge.

The increasing popularity of virtual asset trading has led to a corresponding rise in the need for specialised platforms to support these transactions effectively. During the mid-2000s, the initial virtual goods marketplaces formed in response to the growing market need. The emergence of media such as Player Auctions and G2G has garnered significant attention since they have facilitated the buying, selling, and trading of in-game items, accounts, and currency among players. These marketplaces expanded beyond the confines of individual gaming worlds, establishing a centralised platform for a growing worldwide community of fans interested in virtual assets.

The proliferation of virtual goods marketplaces has extended beyond the realm of games. During the 2010s, the emergence of virtual worlds such as "Second Life" and "Decentraland" led to a growing interest in virtual real estate as a highly desirable asset. Emerging marketplaces like The Sandbox and Somnium Space have allowed users to acquire, develop, and monetise virtual land. This event represented a significant turning point in developing these marketplaces, demonstrating their ability to adapt and expand beyond particular specialised markets.

Nevertheless, the most essential stage of this evolutionary process occurred when blockchain technology was incorporated in the latter part of the 2010s and continues to be relevant in the contemporary era. The notion of Non-Fungible Tokens (NFTs) was created by blockchain technology, allowing for the tokenisation and verification of ownership for digital assets. Abruptly, those involved in art, music, digital creation, and collecting discovered a ground-breaking and innovative platform to exchange digital artwork, music compositions, collectable items, and other related commodities. Marketplaces like OpenSea, Rarible, and Foundation have arisen as the focal points of a digital renaissance, fundamentally reshaping societal perceptions and valuations of digital creation.

In addition to the realm of art, virtual goods marketplaces are undergoing a process of increasing diversification. The virtual economy has expanded to include various elements such as digital fashion, avatars, virtual concerts, and immersive experiences. These additions have introduced novel aspects to the virtual economy. Fashion businesses use these platforms to connect with technologically adept audiences, while musicians produce virtual concerts and release unique NFT songs.

Overview Of Existing Literature on Virtual Goods Marketplaces, Consumer Protection, And Economic Aspects.

Virtual Goods Exchanges:

Early Development and Evolution: This research vividly depicts the earliest days of virtual goods markets. It demonstrates how these platforms emerged naturally from online gaming communities. Players initiated the trading of digital assets due to the scarcity and desirability of virtual items. This grassroots growth exemplifies the symbiotic relationship between participants and virtual economies.

Multiple Applications: Researchers investigated their adaptability as virtual product marketplaces expanded beyond the gaming industry. For instance, studies illuminate how virtual land ownership became a sought-after commodity in the virtual real estate industry. This expansion exemplified how virtual product marketplaces can transcend specific niches and serve multiple industries.

Blockchain technology and non-fungible tokens. Scholars investigate the tokenisation of digital assets and its repercussions. They explore how blockchain enables the creation of one-of-a-kind digital collectables and works of art, thereby transforming the relationship between artists and collectors and digital creativity.

Consumer Security:

Fraud and Scams: The research delves deep into users' multifaceted challenges within consumer protection. This includes a comprehensive analysis of various fraudulent activities, such as fake listings, phishing, and account theft. Researchers investigate the complexities of these strategies and suggest countermeasures to improve user security.

Regulatory Strategies: Besides comprehending the obstacles, some academics investigate regulatory frameworks designed to protect users in virtual goods marketplaces. They investigate government interventions, legal mechanisms, and the role of market policies in guaranteeing fair and secure transactions. This study investigates the delicate equilibrium between innovation and regulation.

Economic Factors:

Impact on the Economy: Economics studies analyse the transformative effects of virtual goods marketplaces. For instance, analysts examine the transition from traditional revenue models to microtransactions and in-game purchases in the gaming industry. They evaluate how this shift impacts user engagement, the profitability of game developers, and the gaming landscape.

Regulatory Approaches:

Recent research investigates the environmental impact of virtual product marketplaces, particularly in the context of blockchain technology and non-fungible tokens. Scholars investigate the energy consumption of blockchain networks, posing crucial issues regarding the technology's viability. They propose strategies for addressing environmental concerns while preserving the advantages of blockchain technology.

Copyright and Intellectual Property:

The intricate relationship between virtual commodities marketplaces and intellectual property is an essential area of research. Examining instances of copyright infringement sheds light on the difficulties of safeguarding creators' rights in a decentralised digital ecosystem. This field of study seeks innovative solutions that balance innovation and intellectual property protection.

Governance of Platforms:

Scholarly research on platform governance examines the rules and policies that influence virtual goods marketplaces. This includes content moderation practices, dispute resolution mechanisms, and platforms' role in ensuring compliance and impartiality. Researchers investigate the impact of platform governance on user experiences and trust.

Social and Cultural Impact:

Beyond economic and regulatory aspects, research demonstrates the profound social and cultural effects of virtual goods marketplaces. This includes the emergence of online communities and fandoms and the complex social interactions encircling virtual items. Scholars investigate the impact of these markets on digital culture, identity, and social dynamics.

IDENTIFICATION OF GAPS

One of the critical issues in the field of regulation and governance is the presence of gaps. These gaps refer to the areas where regulation and governance mechanisms could be improved or improved. This can lead to challenges and problems in ensuring effective regulation and governance practices.

Lack of Global Regulatory Frameworks:

The need for comprehensive worldwide regulatory frameworks within virtual commodities marketplaces is an intricate and diverse problem that engenders numerous noteworthy challenges and controversies. In the following discussion, we will examine these facets more comprehensively.

Jurisdictional Complexity:

The absence of comprehensive international regulations gives rise to a scenario wherein virtual commodities marketplaces are compelled to navigate through a complex network of laws at the national, regional, and local levels. The complexity emerges due to the operation of these marketplaces in a digital environment that extends beyond conventional geographical limits. Consequently, marketplaces frequently encounter uncertainty regarding the applicable set of regulations in each scenario, thereby giving rise to potential challenges of a legal and operational nature.

The presence of controversy is a direct result of the intricate nature of this jurisdictional framework. Various stakeholders, such as platform operators, users, and regulators, may possess divergent perspectives regarding the appropriate approach to tackle the complexities presented by this situation. Some proponents push for harmonising rules and regulations to streamline compliance processes, whereas others support localised alternatives that prioritise national sovereignty.

Inadequate Consumer Protection:

The need for standardised international legislation implies that customers in different geographical areas may experience disparate degrees of protection when participating in transactions inside virtual goods markets. Certain countries or regions may possess substantial consumer rights and well-established processes for resolving disputes, while others may exhibit deficiencies in such safeguards.

Controversies frequently centre on matters about fairness and equity. Individuals residing in areas with less robust consumer protection measures may encounter a situation where they are placed in an unfavourable position when confronted with conflicts or instances of deceitful practices. The disparity above underscores the necessity for implementing consistent and all-encompassing rules for safeguarding consumers, irrespective of their geographical location.

One of the primary issues that arise in the enforcement realm is the presence of various challenges.

Challenges in Enforcement:

The enforcement of legislation across international borders presents a multifaceted and arduous undertaking. Virtual commodities markets have the potential to establish their main offices in a particular country, while their servers and equipment may be situated in distinct legal countries. Moreover, the users of these platforms are geographically dispersed, posing challenges for regulatory bodies in efficiently monitoring and enforcing regulations.

The issue of accountability for misconduct in marketplaces gives rise to controversy. Regulatory bodies in a particular area may possess restricted authority over a marketplace based in a different country. The presence of jurisdictional fragmentation might give rise to potential avenues for marketplaces to circumvent regulatory scrutiny, raising questions regarding the efficacy of regulatory measures.

Debate Over Platform Accountability:

The absence of comprehensive international regulatory frameworks has given rise to a highly disputed discourse surrounding the responsibility and liability of virtual goods marketplace platforms. There is a contention that media should be more proactive in overseeing user conduct, moderating content, and preventing fraudulent activities to safeguard consumers. This method is perceived to guarantee a marketplace with enhanced safety and security.

Conversely, a compelling contention exists that an overabundance of platform control and moderation may impede innovation and curtail freedom of expression. The issue of finding an appropriate equilibrium between the platforms' responsibilities and users' autonomy is a crucial area of disagreement. Diverse stakeholders possess differing viewpoints regarding the optimal balance in this regard.

Emergence of Self-Regulation:

Without comprehensive worldwide legislation, several virtual commodities markets have assumed the responsibility of implementing self-regulatory mechanisms and codes of behaviour. The primary objective of these programs is to effectively tackle pressing issues about safeguarding consumer interests, preventing fraudulent activities, and ensuring the appropriate moderation of information.

Nevertheless, there are ongoing debates regarding the efficacy of self-regulation. There is a debate about the effectiveness of self-regulation in ensuring consumer protection and market integrity comparable to that of formal legislation. Furthermore, there are apprehensions regarding the possibility of self-regulation being susceptible to the impact of marketplace operators' interests.

THE IMPORTANCE OF INTERNATIONAL COOPERATION

Resolving the deficiency in global regulatory frameworks necessitates establishing international collaboration and coordination among governments and regulatory entities. Developing uniform regulations that effectively address the needs of consumers, maintain market integrity, and promote innovation is a multifaceted and time-consuming endeavour.

There is potential for controversy regarding the viability of attaining significant levels of international collaboration. Disparate interests and priorities among many nations can impede the establishment of a unified global regulatory framework.

Global Copyright Enforcement:

The issue of global copyright enforcement is a complex and contentious topic within the context of virtual goods marketplaces. It revolves around the challenges of enforcing copyright and intellectual property rights in a digital ecosystem that operates across national and international borders. Here, we'll explore the nuances and controversies associated with global copyright enforcement:

1. Cross-Border Nature of Virtual Goods Marketplaces:

Virtual goods marketplaces are inherently international. Creators, buyers, and sellers can be located in different countries or regions, making it challenging to apply copyright laws consistently. This cross-border nature of virtual goods transactions creates a jurisdictional quagmire for copyright enforcement.

2. Disparate Copyright Laws:

Different countries have their copyright laws and regulations, often with variations in duration, exceptions, and enforcement mechanisms. This diversity of legal frameworks complicates efforts to enforce copyright globally.

3. Digital Piracy and Infringement:

Virtual goods marketplaces are susceptible to digital piracy and copyright infringement. Users may create and distribute copyrighted content without authorisation, leading to disputes and legal challenges.

4. Legal Challenges:

Enforcing copyright across borders involves navigating complex legal processes, including international treaties and agreements. The legal challenges of pursuing copyright infringement cases in multiple jurisdictions can be prohibitively expensive and time-consuming.

5. Lack of International Harmonization:

Controversy arises from the need for international harmonisation of copyright laws. While efforts such as the Berne Convention and TRIPS Agreement aim to establish common standards, there are gaps and variations in implementation across countries. This need for harmonisation makes creating a seamless global enforcement framework challenging.

6. Digital Challenges:

The digital nature of virtual goods complicates copyright enforcement further. Digital assets are easily replicable and transferable, challenging tracking and preventing unauthorised distribution. This raises questions about the adequacy of traditional copyright enforcement mechanisms in the digital age.

7. Role of Platform Operators:

Controversy exists regarding the role of platform operators in copyright enforcement. Some argue that platforms should implement robust content recognition and takedown mechanisms to prevent the listing and sale of copyrighted material without permission. However, others express concerns about the potential for overzealous content removal and the impact on legitimate user-generated content.

8. Emerging Technologies:

Emerging technologies like blockchain and decentralised marketplaces introduce new challenges and opportunities for copyright enforcement. Blockchain's transparency can aid in tracking ownership and provenance, but it also poses questions about the role of blockchain in enforcing copyright.

MARKET DOMINANCE

In virtual goods marketplaces, market dominance refers to the situation in which a single platform or marketplace obtains a significant and frequently overwhelming share of a particular market segment. This dominance can manifest in various ways, such as having the most users, conducting the highest volume of transactions, or offering the widest selection of goods and services within a particular niche or industry. Here is a comprehensive explanation of market dominance, its associated controversies, and its implications:

DEFINITION OF MARKET LEADERSHIP

Market dominance occurs when a virtual goods marketplace or platform becomes the dominant actor in a particular sector, holding a disproportionately large market share compared to competitors. This dominance may result from user numbers, transaction volume, brand recognition, and various products and services.

Market Dominance and Controversy:

1. Limited Competition: The potential for little competition is one of the most contentious aspects of market dominance. When a single platform reaches a near-monopoly position, it may discourage new entrants and impede innovation. The absence of competition can reduce the dominant platform's incentives to improve its services or decrease its fees, potentially harming consumers and stifling market growth.

2. Pricing and Fee Structures: Dominant platforms can dictate pricing and fee structures. Controversy may arise when these platforms increase fees or modify pricing models, affecting sellers and consumers. The perception of high costs or abrupt changes as exploitative raises concerns about fairness, affordability, and openness.

3. Data Privacy and Management: Market-dominant platforms frequently amass immense amounts of user data. This raises questions regarding data control and privacy. Users may be concerned about how their data is collected, utilised, and potentially monetised by these platforms, leading to discussions regarding privacy policies and data ownership.

User Experience and Confidence:

User Experience: Dominant platforms attract users due to their convenience and large user bases. However, sometimes this convenience comes at the expense of user experience. Controversies may emerge if users experience sluggish customer support response times, lack of innovation, or inadequate dispute resolution mechanisms.

Trust is a crucial component of market dominance. Users frequently place their confidence in dominant platforms due to their familiarity and perceived stability. Controversies may emerge if security breaches, unscrupulous practices, or user disputes erode trust between users and the platform.

Regulatory and Antitrust Issues:

As market dominance develops, it frequently attracts the attention of regulatory bodies and competition authorities. Controversies may revolve around whether dominant platforms engage in anticompetitive practices, such as stifling competition with their market dominance, engaging in predatory pricing, or unfairly favouring their products and services.

Regulatory Debates: Regulatory debates can be contentious due to divergent perspectives on the required scope of regulatory intervention. Others advocate for a hands-off approach that emphasises market forces and consumer choice.

ALTERNATIVES AND INNOVATIONS

Innovations: Dominance in a particular epoch does not guarantee future dominance. Controversies may arise when disruptive innovations or alternative platforms challenge the established dominant entity. These innovations can either strengthen the supremacy of extant platforms or undermine their market hold.

User Retention and Switching Costs:

User Lock-In: User lock-in and switching costs associated with dominant platforms can generate controversy. Even if dissatisfied, users who have invested significant time, effort, or money in a particular platform may need help to move to an alternative. This raises ethical concerns regarding the platform's obligation to facilitate switching.

Decentralised Alternatives:

In virtual goods marketplaces, decentralised alternatives refer to emerging platforms and systems that seek to reduce the traditional centralisation and control held by a single entity or platform operator. These decentralised alternatives are intended to give users greater control over their digital assets and transactions, empowering them. Here, we will examine the concept of decentralised alternatives, the debates they engender, and their implications.

Definition of Decentralized Alternatives:

Definition: Decentralized alternatives in virtual goods marketplaces are platforms and systems that operate on decentralised technologies, primarily blockchain. Unlike traditional centralised marketplaces, where control and decision-making authority rest with a single entity, decentralised alternatives distribute control among users or nodes.

CONTROVERSY SURROUNDING DECENTRALIZED ALTERNATIVES

Centralisation vs. Decentralization: Centralization, seen in traditional virtual goods marketplaces, offers convenience and user-friendly experiences. However, it also concentrates power and decision-making in the hands of platform operators, leading to concerns about potential abuses and lack of user control. Decentralisation, on the other hand, empowers users by giving them complete control over their assets but can be seen as less user-friendly and more complex.

Scalability and Efficiency: Decentralized systems, particularly those built on blockchain technology, often face challenges related to scalability and efficiency. These systems' consensus mechanisms and decentralised nature can make them slower and less cost-effective than their centralised counterparts. These limitations can be controversial, as they impact the practicality of decentralised alternatives for mass adoption.

User Experience: User experience on decentralised platforms can be controversial. Some users may find the interfaces less intuitive and the processes more complex than centralised platforms. Balancing user-friendliness with decentralisation remains an ongoing challenge.

Regulatory Compliance: Decentralized alternatives may face regulatory challenges due to their decentralised nature. Regulators may need help identifying responsible parties and enforcing compliance with existing laws and regulations. This raises questions about the legal and regulatory clarity needed to navigate decentralised ecosystems.

EMPOWERING USERS AND OWNERSHIP

Ownership of Digital Assets: Decentralized alternatives aim to empower users by granting them full rights and control over their digital assets. Users hold their private keys, which are essential for accessing and managing their assets. While this ownership is empowering, it can also be controversial if users lose access to their private keys, as there may be no central authority to assist with recovery.

Reduced Intermediaries: Decentralized platforms eliminate or reduce the need for intermediaries, such as centralised market operators or banks. This can lead to cost savings and increased user control. However, controversies may emerge regarding the potential loss of consumer protection mechanisms and dispute resolution services typically provided by intermediaries.

OPENNESS AND TRANSPARENCY

Transparency: Decentralized platforms often emphasise openness due to the public nature of blockchain technology. All transactions and ownership records are publicly accessible and verifiable on the blockchain, reducing the potential for fraud and mismanagement. However, this transparency can also lead to controversies concerning the exposure of user data and financial information.

Open Source: Many decentralised platforms are built on open-source principles, allowing anyone to review and contribute to their code. While this openness fosters innovation, it can also lead to controversies related to code vulnerabilities and potential security risks if not properly managed.

CHALLENGES IN ADOPTION

User Adoption: Decentralized alternatives may face challenges in user adoption due to the learning curve associated with blockchain technology and the potential complexity of decentralised systems. Controversies may arise regarding the readiness of the general population to transition from centralised to decentralised platforms.

Network Effects: Centralized platforms often benefit from network effects, where the platform's value increases as more users join. Decentralised alternatives may need help to overcome this network effect, making attracting a critical mass of users and content creators difficult.

REGULATORY ADAPTATION

Regulatory Challenges: Regulatory authorities are in the process of adapting to the emergence of decentralised alternatives. Controversies may arise as regulators seek to balance fostering innovation and ensuring compliance with existing regulations. The challenge lies in creating a regulatory framework accommodating decentralised ecosystems' unique features and challenges.

Digital Labour and Commodification: Digital labour and commodification are crucial in virtual product marketplaces, reflecting how digital assets are produced, purchased, and valued. Here, we will examine these concepts, the controversies they engender, and their implications in greater depth:

Digital Labour and Commodification Definition: Digital labour refers to the endeavours, skills, and creative work individuals contribute to creating, modifying, or improving digital assets within virtual goods marketplaces. This includes generating digital art, designing in-game items, and extending software.

Digital assets, such as virtual goods or creative content, become commodified when regarded as tradable commodities. Like traditional markets, these assets are ascribed a value, bought, sold, and frequently exchanged within virtual goods marketplaces.

DISPUTE CONCERNING DIGITAL LABOUR AND COMMODIFICATION:

Equitable Compensation: The equitable compensation of individuals engaged in digital labour is a central point of contention. Creators may put significant time and effort into producing valuable digital assets. Still, disputes can arise over whether they receive adequate compensation, particularly in cases where purchases are resold or traded multiple times.

Concerns exist regarding the possible exploitation and precariousness of digital workers. In virtual goods marketplaces, freelance creators and vendors may experience unstable income, lack of job security, and unequal bargaining power in transactions with larger platforms or buyers.

Regarding the ownership and control of digital assets, disputes may arise. Creators may question who retains the ultimate rights to their work and how those rights are transferred or maintained during asset transactions. Intellectual property and copyright concerns can be contentious.

Work-Life Boundaries: The nature of digital labour in online marketplaces for virtual products blurs the lines between work and leisure. Creators frequently engage in these activities as a form of self-expression or as a pastime, but the potential for monetary gain complicates the definition of work-life boundaries.

SOCIOECONOMIC CONSEQUENCES

Income Inequality: In virtual product marketplaces, the commodification of digital assets can contribute to income inequality. Some creators may experience significant financial success, while others struggle to make a living. Controversy may arise concerning the equitable distribution of wealth in these ecosystems.

Digital Divide: Factors such as access to technology, education, and economic resources can influence the ability to engage in digital labour and benefit from commodification. The digital divide may be a source of contention, as only some have equal access to virtual product marketplaces.

Considerations of an Ethical Nature: Ethical Treatment of Workers There may be ethical debates regarding the treatment of digital labourers. Fair compensation, working conditions, and the ethical responsibilities of platform operators and consumers toward those providing digital labour may be questioned.

The commodification of digital assets raises philosophical concerns regarding transforming creative work into tradable goods. Some argue that the commodification of digital content can devalue its inherent artistic or creative qualities.

Platform Policies and Administration: Platform Rules: Platform rules and policies that regulate digital labour and commodification can generate controversy. Creators and sellers may be concerned about platform fees, content restrictions, and dispute resolution procedures, which can impact their earnings and legal rights.

Governance Models: Some virtual product marketplaces use decentralised governance models, allowing users to participate in platform decision-making. This can contribute to controversies regarding balancing user autonomy and platform governance in decentralised systems.

ANALYSIS OF CONSUMER PROTECTION ISSUES IN ONLINE MARKETPLACES FOR VIRTUAL PRODUCTS

In the digital economy, consumer protection in marketplaces for virtual goods is paramount, as these platforms present unique challenges and opportunities for assuring the safety and well-being of users. Let's thoroughly analyse consumer protection issues in online marketplaces for virtual products.

Fraudulent Activities:

Fraudulent activities in virtual goods marketplaces encompass a wide range of deceptive practices aimed at obtaining financial gain or valuable assets at the expense of users. These activities pose a significant consumer protection issue and require comprehensive measures to prevent and address them. Let's elaborate in more detail on fraudulent activities in virtual goods marketplaces:

Types of Fraudulent Activities:

Identity Theft: Fraudsters may steal personal information, such as usernames, passwords, or credit card details, to impersonate legitimate users and engage in fraudulent transactions.

Phishing: Phishing attempts involve creating fake websites or emails that mimic legitimate virtual goods marketplaces to trick users into disclosing sensitive information.

Deceptive Listings: Sellers may misrepresent products or services in their listings, leading buyers to make purchases based on false information.

Advance-Fee Fraud: Scammers may ask users to pay an upfront fee for a promised product or service, only to disappear after receiving payment without delivering the promised item.

Account Takeovers: Fraudsters may gain unauthorised access to user accounts, steal valuable assets (such as virtual items or currency), and manipulate account settings.

Impact of Fraudulent Activities:

Financial Loss: Users who fall victim to fraud can suffer financial losses. They may pay for non-existent goods, services, or virtual items or experience unauthorised transactions on their accounts.

Identity Theft: Identity theft can result in severe consequences, including unauthorised access to personal information, compromised financial accounts, and even legal issues.

Loss of Trust: Incidents of fraud can erode trust in the virtual goods marketplace platform, making users hesitant to engage in transactions or participate in the marketplace.

Consumer Protection Measures:

User Verification: Implementing robust user verification processes, such as two-factor authentication and identity verification, can help prevent unauthorised access and identity theft.

Transaction Monitoring: Real-time monitoring of transactions can identify suspicious behaviour, such as unusual login locations or high-value transactions, prompting further investigation.

Education: It is essential to educate users about everyday fraudulent activities and how to recognise and report them. Platforms should provide clear guidelines and resources to help users protect themselves.

Customer Support: Having responsive customer support available to assist users who suspect fraudulent activities is crucial. Promptly addressing reported incidents can minimise the impact on affected users.

Reporting Mechanisms: Establishing easy-to-use reporting mechanisms for users to report fraudulent activities, suspicious listings, or unauthorised account access is essential.

Security Measures: Continuous improvement of security measures, including encryption, secure payment processing, and regular security audits, can help protect user data and financial transactions.

Community Moderation: Implementing community moderation and content monitoring can help identify and remove deceptive listings and suspicious user behaviour.

Legal Consequences:

Regulatory Compliance: Virtual goods marketplaces must comply with relevant laws and regulations related to consumer protection and online transactions. This includes data protection laws, privacy regulations, and fraud prevention measures.

Cooperation with Authorities: Platforms should cooperate with law enforcement and regulatory authorities when investigating and prosecuting fraud cases. This includes sharing necessary information and evidence.

COUNTERFEIT GOODS

Counterfeit goods are imitations or fake products designed to look genuine but produced without the proper authorisation or adherence to quality standards. In virtual goods marketplaces, selling counterfeit digital items or misrepresenting virtual assets is a significant consumer protection concern. Here's a more detailed exploration of the issue of counterfeit goods in virtual goods marketplaces:

Definition of Counterfeit Goods:

> **Counterfeit Digital Items:** In virtual goods marketplaces, counterfeit digital items refer to fake or unauthorised copies of virtual assets, such as in-game items, software, or digital art. These counterfeit items are often presented as genuine, deceiving buyers.

Impact of Counterfeit Goods:

> **Consumer Deception:** Users may unknowingly purchase counterfeit digital items, believing they are genuine. This can lead to disappointment, financial loss, or dissatisfaction.
> **Brand Reputation:** Counterfeit goods on a platform can harm the reputation of the venue and the creators or brands whose items are being counterfeited.

Consumer Protection Measures:

> **Stringent Verification:** Virtual goods marketplaces should implement rigorous verification processes for sellers and digital items. This includes verifying the authenticity and ownership of digital assets before they are listed for sale.
> **User Reporting:** Encourage users to report suspicious listings or digital items they suspect to be counterfeit. Establish precise reporting mechanisms and a responsive system for addressing such reports.
> **Swift Removal:** Platforms should swiftly remove counterfeit listings once they are identified or reported. This prevents further user exposure to fraudulent items.
> **Quality Control:** Implement measures to ensure digital items meet specific standards. This may involve reviewing item descriptions, images, and other relevant information for authenticity.
> **Educational Resources:** Provide educational materials to users on identifying counterfeit digital items. Educating users about the risks and signs of counterfeit goods can empower them to make informed choices.
> **Legal and Regulatory Compliance:** Comply with intellectual property

laws and regulations related to digital assets. Collaborate with creators, brands, and rights holders to enforce copyright and trademark protections.

Intellectual Property Considerations:

> **Copyright Protection:** Digital creators and artists should know their rights regarding their creations. Platforms can play a role in enforcing copyright protections and taking down infringing content.
> **Trademark Protection:** Brands should protect their trademarks within virtual goods marketplaces to prevent counterfeit items with logos or names.

Dispute Resolution:

> **Efficient Dispute Resolution:** Implement efficient dispute resolution mechanisms for users who purchase counterfeit goods. These mechanisms should provide a fair process for resolving disputes and ensuring that affected users are compensated appropriately.

Legal Consequences:

> **Legal Actions:** Virtual goods marketplaces should be prepared to cooperate with legal authorities and rights holders in case of copyright or trademark infringement claims related to counterfeit goods.

DATA PRIVACY AND SECURITY

Data privacy and security are critical concerns in virtual goods marketplaces, as these platforms handle many user data and financial transactions. Protecting user information and ensuring data security are essential for building trust and maintaining a safe environment. Here's a detailed exploration of data privacy and security issues in virtual goods marketplaces:

Data Privacy Concerns:

i) Data Collection: Virtual goods marketplaces collect user data, including personal information, payment details, and transaction histories. Users may need to be more concerned about the extent and purpose of data collection.

ii) User Consent: Users want to know how their data is used and shared. They expect transparency and the ability to provide informed consent for data processing activities.

ii) Data Retention: Users may worry about how long their data is stored and whether it's securely deleted when no longer needed.

Data Security Concerns:

i) Data Breaches: Data breaches can lead to the exposure of sensitive user information, including usernames, passwords, and payment data. This can result in identity theft and financial fraud.

ii) Unauthorised Access: Unauthorized access to user accounts or databases can lead to the misuse of data or the manipulation of transactions.

Impact of Data Privacy and Security Issues:

i) Loss of Trust: Data breaches or privacy violations can lead to a loss of trust among users, damaging the reputation of the virtual goods marketplace.

ii) Financial Loss: Data breaches can result in financial losses for users who become victims of fraud or unauthorised transactions.

Consumer Protection Measures:

i) Encryption: Implement robust encryption protocols to protect user data during transmission and storage.

ii) Secure Payment Processing: Ensure that payment is processed through specific, trusted channels to protect users' financial information.

iii) Data Minimization: Collect only the data necessary for platform functionality and communicate the purpose of data collection to users.

iv) Consent Mechanisms: Provide users with clear options to provide or withhold consent for data processing activities. Allow them to review and modify their data preferences.

v) Privacy Policies: Maintain transparent and easily accessible privacy policies that outline how user data is collected, used, and protected.

vi) User Access Controls: Enable users to control their data, including the ability to delete their accounts and associated data.

vii) Data Retention Policies: Establish apparent data retention and deletion policies. Delete user data that is no longer necessary for platform operations.

viii) Security Audits: Regularly conduct security audits and assessments to identify vulnerabilities and address potential threats.

ix) Incident Response Plan: Develop and implement an incident response plan to address data breaches and security incidents effectively.

x) Compliance with Regulations: When applicable, ensure compliance with data privacy regulations such as GDPR (General Data Protection Regulation) and CCPA (California Consumer Privacy Act).

User Education:

i) Data Literacy: Educate users about data privacy and security best practices, such as creating strong passwords, enabling two-factor authentication, and recognising phishing attempts.

ii) Reporting Mechanisms: Provide clear instructions on reporting suspicious activity or potential data breaches.

Legal and Regulatory Compliance:

i) Data Protection Regulations: Adhere to data protection regulations and consumer privacy laws applicable to the platform's jurisdiction.

ii) Notification Requirements: Comply with legal requirements related to data breach notifications, including notifying affected users and relevant authorities in case of a breach.

DISPUTE RESOLUTION

Dispute resolution is critical to consumer protection in virtual goods marketplaces, as conflicts and disagreements between buyers and sellers are common. A well-designed dispute resolution system can help ensure fairness and trust within the platform. Here's a more detailed exploration of dispute resolution in virtual goods marketplaces:

Types of Disputes:

i) Non-Delivery: Users may dispute transactions where they paid for goods or services but have yet to receive them.

ii) Misrepresentation: Disputes can arise when buyers receive items that do not match their descriptions, such as digital goods that were advertised falsely.

iii) Quality Disputes: Users may disagree about the quality or condition of virtual goods, particularly in cases where subjective judgments come into play.

Impact of Inadequate Dispute Resolution:

i) User Dissatisfaction: Poorly resolved disputes can lead to dissatisfaction among users involved in the transaction. Unsatisfied users may have a negative perception of the platform.

ii) Loss of Trust: Repeated unresolved disputes can erode trust in the virtual goods marketplace, discouraging users from future transactions.

Consumer Protection Measures:

i) Transparent Guidelines: Virtual goods marketplaces should have clear and accessible guidelines for dispute resolution. Users should understand the process and their rights.

ii) Efficiency: Dispute resolution processes should be efficient and timely, minimising the disruption to users' experiences.

iii) Impartiality: The dispute resolution system must be impartial, ensuring fair outcomes for all parties involved.

iv) User-Friendly: The process should be user-friendly, with intuitive interfaces and clear instructions for users to follow.

v) Documentation: Encourage users to keep records of transactions and communication in case a dispute arises. This documentation can help resolve disagreements.

vi) Customer Support: Provide responsive customer support that can assist users in initiating and navigating the dispute resolution process.

vii) Third-Party Mediation: In complex or contentious cases, platforms may consider involving third-party mediators or arbitrators to reach a fair resolution.

Transparency:

i) Communication: Maintain open and transparent communication with users involved in disputes. Keep them informed about the status of their case and expected timelines for resolution.

ii) Decision Rationale: In cases where platform administrators or moderators make decisions, explain the findings to ensure transparency.

Legal and Regulatory Compliance:

i) Consumer Protection Laws: Comply with consumer protection laws and regulations related to dispute resolution. These may include requirements for offering refunds or exchanges.

ii) Dispute Resolution Regulations: Be aware of specific regulations or industry standards related to dispute resolution in digital marketplaces.

Continuous Improvement:

i) Feedback Mechanisms: Encourage users to provide feedback on their dispute resolution experiences. Use this feedback to make improvements to the process.

ii) Monitoring and Evaluation: Continuously monitor the effectiveness of the dispute resolution system and evaluate its impact on user satisfaction and trust.

User Education:

i) Dispute Prevention: Educate users on how to avoid common disputes, such as by thoroughly reviewing product descriptions, communicating with sellers, and documenting transactions.

ii) Dispute Resolution Process: Provide information on how the dispute resolution process works and how users can initiate a dispute if necessary.

MISLEADING PRACTICES

Misleading practices in virtual goods marketplaces involve deceptive tactics, false advertising, or hidden fees that can harm consumers' trust and overall experience. These practices undermine consumer protection and require vigilant measures to prevent and address them. Here's an in-depth exploration of misleading practices in virtual goods marketplaces:

Types of Misleading Practices:

i) False Advertising: Sellers may exaggerate the features or qualities of their virtual goods in listings, leading buyers to expect something different from what they receive.

ii) Hidden Fees: Some virtual goods marketplaces may charge hidden fees, such as transaction fees, that are not disclosed to users during purchase.

iii) Bait-and-Switch: This tactic involves advertising one virtual item or service to attract buyers, only to provide something different or of lower quality after the purchase.

Impact of Misleading Practices:

i) User Disappointment: Misleading practices can lead to user satisfaction when they receive items that match their expectations.

ii) Financial Loss: Hidden fees or deceptive pricing can result in unexpected financial burdens for users.

iii) Loss of Trust: Repeated incidents of misleading practices can erode trust in the virtual goods marketplacc and deter users from participating.

Consumer Protection Measures:

i) Transparency in Listings: Ensure sellers provide accurate and detailed descriptions of their virtual goods or services. Any limitations, conditions, or potential fees should be disclosed in listings.

ii) Transparent Pricing: Display pricing information prominently, including any additional fees or charges. Users should clearly understand the total cost before making a purchase.

iii) Review Mechanisms: Implement user review and rating systems that allow buyers to share their experiences and provide feedback on sellers. This can help identify sellers with a history of misleading practices.

iv) Quality Control: Establish quality control measures to verify the accuracy of product or service descriptions and to identify listings that may involve misleading practices.

v) User Reporting: Encourage users to report misleading practices or deceptive listings. Provide transparent reporting mechanisms and a responsive system for addressing such reports.

vi) Educational Resources: Educate users about common misleading tactics and how to recognise them. Users who are informed are less likely to fall victim to deceptive practices.

Legal and Regulatory Compliance:

i) Advertising Standards: Adhere to advertising standards and regulations that require truth. Avoid false or exaggerated claims in listings.

ii) Price Transparency Laws: Comply with laws and regulations that mandate price transparency, including clear and accurate pricing information.

Responsive Actions:

i) Immediate Action: Take swift action to investigate and address reported misleading practices. This may involve removing deceptive listings or suspending sellers who engage in such practices.

ii) Refunds or Compensation: In cases where users have been harmed due to misleading practices, consider offering refunds or compensation to affected users.

Continuous Monitoring:

i) Regular Audits: Conduct periodic audits of listings and transactions to identify potential cases of misleading practices.

ii) Feedback Mechanisms: Encourage users to provide feedback on their experiences, including instances of misleading practices. Use this feedback to improve the platform's policies and enforcement.

ACCESSIBILITY AND USER EDUCATION

Accessibility and user education are crucial aspects of consumer protection in virtual goods marketplaces. Ensuring that all users, regardless of their digital literacy or experience, can access and use the platform safely is essential. Here's a detailed exploration of accessibility and user education in virtual goods marketplaces:

Accessibility Concerns:

i) Digital Literacy: Some users may need more digital literacy or experience, making them more vulnerable to online risks, scams, and deceptive practices.

ii) Language Barriers: Users who need to improve in the primary language of the platform may need help understanding terms of service, product descriptions, or user reviews.

iii) User with Disabilities: Ensuring the platform is accessible to users with disabilities, such as visual or hearing impairments, is crucial for inclusivity.

Impact of Inadequate Accessibility and User Education:

i) Vulnerability: Users with limited digital literacy may be more vulnerable to scams, deceptive practices, or poor purchasing decisions.

ii) User Frustration: Users who encounter language barriers or inaccessible features may become frustrated and discouraged from using the platform.

Accessibility and User Education Measures:

i) User-Friendly Interface: Design the platform with a user-friendly interface that is intuitive and easy to navigate, minimising the learning curve for users.

ii) Language Options: Offer multiple language options for the platform's interface, product descriptions, and user support to accommodate users from diverse linguistic backgrounds.

iii) Accessibility Features: Ensure the platform adheres to accessibility standards, providing features like alt text for images, keyboard navigation, and compatibility with screen readers for disabled users.

iv) Educational Resources: Develop and provide educational resources for users with varying levels of digital literacy. These resources can include guides on safe online practices, recognising scams, and understanding their rights and responsibilities as consumers.

v) Interactive Tutorials: Create interactive tutorials or onboarding processes that guide new users through the platform's features and safety measures.

vi) In-Platform Support: Offer in-platform support channels, such as chatbots or help centres, to assist users in real-time. Make these support options easily accessible from the platform's interface.

vii) Clear Policies: Maintain clear and concise terms of service, privacy policies, and community guidelines that are easily understandable by users of all backgrounds.

viii) Multimedia Content: Use multimedia content, such as videos or infographics, to convey critical information and safety tips more engagingly.

ix) Feedback Mechanisms: Encourage users to provide feedback on their experiences, including any difficulties they encounter regarding accessibility or understanding platform policies.

User Empowerment:

i) Privacy Controls: Allow users to control their privacy settings, data sharing preferences, and notification preferences to empower them to customise their experience.

ii) Digital Literacy Programs: Consider offering digital literacy programs or partnerships with organisations that promote digital literacy to educate users on safe online practices.

Legal and Regulatory Compliance:

i) Accessibility Laws: Comply with accessibility laws and regulations that mandate digital platforms to be accessible to disabled users.

ii) Consumer Protection Laws: Ensure the platform adheres to consumer protection laws, including transparency and user education regulations.

REGULATION AND COMPLIANCE

Regulation and compliance are essential aspects of consumer protection in virtual goods marketplaces. These platforms often operate in a complex legal landscape, and adhering to relevant laws and regulations is crucial to ensure the safety and rights of users. Here's a more detailed exploration of regulation and compliance in virtual goods marketplaces:

Regulatory Challenges:

i) Global Operations: Virtual goods marketplaces often operate globally, meaning they must navigate many regional and national regulatory frameworks. This can be challenging due to the varying legal requirements in different jurisdictions.

ii) Consumer Protection Laws: Virtual goods marketplaces must comply with consumer protection laws that govern online transactions, product descriptions, and the resolution of disputes. These laws protect consumers from fraud, misrepresentation, and unfair practices.

iii) Data Protection Regulations: Platforms must also adhere to data protection regulations, such as GDPR in the European Union or CCPA in California, when handling user data. These laws impose strict requirements on data privacy and security.

Impact of Non-Compliance:

i) Legal Consequences: Non-compliance with consumer protection and data privacy regulations can result in legal actions, fines, and penalties. This can harm the platform's reputation and financial stability.

ii) User Trust: Users may lose trust in the platform if they perceive it as disregarding their rights and safety due to non compliance.

Compliance Measures:

i) Legal Expertise: Virtual goods marketplaces should have legal experts or teams closely monitoring and interpreting relevant laws and regulations, especially in the platform's operating regions.

ii) Regional Compliance: Customize platform policies, terms of service, and practices to align with the specific regulations in each jurisdiction. For example, they provide clear refund policies in compliance with local laws.

iii) Transparent Communication: Communicate to users how the platform complies with various laws and regulations. This includes explaining how their data is used, their consumer rights, and how disputes are resolved.

iv) Cooperation with Authorities: Cooperate with regulatory and law enforcement agencies when necessary. This includes sharing information and evidence for investigations or regulatory compliance.

v) User Data Protection: Prioritize robust data protection measures, including encryption, secure storage, and user data control settings to comply with data privacy regulations.

Cross-Border Transactions:

i) Currency Conversion and Fees: Disclose how currency conversion is handled and any associated fees for cross-border transactions to ensure transparency for international users.

ii) Tax Compliance: Comply with international tax regulations, including VAT (Value Added Tax) or GST (Goods and Services Tax), as applicable to digital transactions.

Continuous Compliance:

i) Monitoring and Audits: Continuously monitor and audit platform practices to ensure ongoing compliance with changing regulations and identify areas needing adjustment.

ii) Regular Legal Updates: Stay informed about changes in consumer protection, data privacy, and tax laws in various regions to adapt platform policies accordingly.

User Rights and Protections:

i) Refund and Cancellation Policies: Clearly outline refund and cancellation policies that adhere to consumer protection laws, allowing users to exercise their rights.

ii) Data Access and Deletion: Enable users to access and delete their data in compliance with data privacy regulations.

iii) Dispute Resolution: Provide transparent and compliant dispute resolution mechanisms to protect user rights.

EXAMINATION OF REGULATORY FRAMEWORKS AND LEGAL CHALLENGES IN PROTECTING CONSUMERS IN VIRTUAL ENVIRONMENTS.

Examining regulatory frameworks and legal challenges in protecting consumers in virtual environments is essential for understanding how virtual goods marketplaces navigate the complex legal landscape and ensure consumer safety. Here's a detailed exploration of this topic:

Regulatory Frameworks in Virtual Environments:

> **Global vs. Regional Regulations:** Virtual goods marketplaces often operate globally, challenging complying with various regional and national regulations. Some regions, like the European Union, have enacted comprehensive data protection regulations (e.g., GDPR), while others may have specific laws governing online transactions and consumer rights.

> **Digital and Crypto Assets:** The rise of cryptocurrencies and blockchain technology has introduced unique regulatory challenges in virtual environments. Regulations surrounding the sale and exchange of digital and crypto assets vary significantly by jurisdiction.

> **Virtual Property and Ownership:** Virtual environments often involve virtual property or assets (e.g., in-game items or digital art). Determining these assets' legal ownership, transferability, and protection can be complex.

Legal Challenges in Protecting Consumers:

> **Jurisdictional Complexity:** The global nature of virtual goods marketplaces means that legal disputes can span multiple jurisdictions. Determining which jurisdiction's laws apply can take time and effort, leading to conflicts and delays in dispute resolution.

> **Data Privacy and Cross-Border Data Flows:** Virtual goods marketplaces handle user data, often across borders. Compliance with data privacy regulations like GDPR and ensuring secure cross-border data flows can be legally complex and resource-intensive.

> **Consumer Rights and Refunds:** Ensuring that users have access to their rights, such as the right to refunds, can be complicated due to global variations in consumer protection laws.

> **Intellectual Property Rights:** The sale of virtual goods may involve intellectual property rights, which can be challenging to enforce in virtual environments. Copyright and trademark infringements are common issues.

> **Emerging Technologies:** As virtual environments evolve, augmented reality (AR) and virtual reality (VR) introduce novel legal challenges related to user safety, content moderation, and liability.

Legal Measures to Protect Consumers:

> **Customised Policies:** Platforms should customise their policies, terms of service, and practices to comply with the specific regulations in each jurisdiction.

> **Legal Expertise:** Maintaining a legal team or consulting legal experts is crucial to effectively interpreting and navigating complex regulations.

> **Transparency:** Platforms should communicate to users how they comply with various laws and regulations, including data privacy, consumer protection, and intellectual property rights.

> **User Empowerment:** Provide users with tools and information to exercise their rights, such as data access, deletion, and dispute resolution mechanisms.

> **Data Protection:** Prioritize robust data protection measures, including encryption and secure data storage, to comply with data privacy regulations.

Collaboration with Regulatory Authorities:

> **Cooperation:** Platforms should cooperate with regulatory authorities and law enforcement agencies, especially in fraud, copyright infringement, or other legal violations.

> **Sharing Information:** Be prepared to share information and evidence as required by regulatory investigations or compliance checks.

Ongoing Monitoring and Adaptation:

> **Regular Audits:** Continuously monitor and audit platform practices to ensure ongoing compliance with changing regulations and identify areas needing adjustment.

> **Legal Updates:** Stay informed about changes in laws and regulations in various regions and adapt platform policies accordingly.

DISCUSSION OF CONSUMER RIGHTS AND RESPONSIBILITIES IN VIRTUAL GOODS TRANSACTIONS.

Discussing consumer rights and responsibilities in virtual goods transactions is crucial for ensuring a fair and safe marketplace environment. Users should know their consumer rights and duties when engaging in virtual goods transactions. Here's a comprehensive exploration of this topic:

Consumer Rights in Virtual Goods Transactions:

1. Right to Accurate Information:

> Consumers have the right to expect the information provided about virtual goods, such as in-game items, digital art, or software, to be accurate and truthful.
> This includes accurate descriptions, specifications, and claims about the virtual goods in listings.

2. Right to Privacy:

> Consumers have the right to privacy and data protection. Virtual goods marketplaces should adhere to data privacy laws and protect users' personal information.
> Users should be informed about how their data is collected, used, and stored within the platform.

3. Right to Transparency:

> Consumers have the right to transparency regarding platform policies and procedures.
> This includes clear and easily accessible information about terms of service, refund and return policies, and dispute resolution mechanisms.

4. Right to Fair Pricing:

> Consumers should not be subject to deceptive pricing practices or hidden fees when purchasing virtual goods.
> Pricing information should be presented transparently, and any additional charges should be disclosed.

5. Right to Data Control:

> Users have the right to control their data within the platform.
> This includes accessing, modifying, or deleting their data as privacy regulations allow.

6. Right to Refunds and Returns:

> Depending on the platform's policies and relevant laws, consumers may have the right to request refunds or returns for virtual goods that do not meet their expectations or are defective.
> These policies should be clear and accessible to users.

7. Right to Dispute Resolution:

> Consumers have the right to dispute transactions and seek resolution for issues related to virtual goods purchases.
> The dispute resolution process should be fair, impartial, and accessible to users.

Consumer Responsibilities in Virtual Goods Transactions:

1. Informed Decision-Making:

> Consumers are responsible for making informed decisions. This involves thoroughly reviewing product descriptions, seller ratings, and user reviews before purchasing.
> Consumers need to understand what they are buying to avoid dissatisfaction.

2. Security Practices:

> Users are responsible for taking measures to protect their accounts and personal information. This includes using strong and unique passwords, enabling two-factor authentication, and being cautious about sharing personal data.

3. Respect for Platform Policies:

> Consumers should adhere to the platform's terms of service, community guidelines, and policies. Engaging in activities that violate these rules can result in account suspension or other consequences.

4. Honest Communication:

> Consumers should communicate honestly and provide accurate information to the platform and other users when engaging in transactions or disputes.
> Deceptive or fraudulent behaviour is not acceptable and can have consequences.

5. Dispute Reporting:

> If consumers encounter issues with a transaction, they are responsible for reporting the problem promptly to the platform and following the provided dispute resolution process.
> Reporting problems helps maintain the integrity of the marketplace.

6. Compliance with Laws:

> Consumers should comply with applicable laws and regulations when buying and selling virtual goods. This includes respecting copyright and trademark rights and adhering to tax laws for digital transactions.

7. Data Security Awareness:

> Users should be cautious about sharing personal or financial information with sellers or other users. Awareness of phishing attempts

and online scams is essential for their protection.

8. Respect for Others:

> Consumers should treat other users, including sellers and buyers, with respect. Harassment, discrimination, or abusive behaviour is unacceptable and can lead to consequences.

9. Responsibility for Account:

> Users are responsible for the security of their accounts. This includes ensuring the confidentiality of login credentials and promptly reporting unauthorised access.

10. Adherence to Refund and Return Policies:

> Consumers should adhere to the platform's specific refund and return policies when seeking refunds or returns for virtual goods.
> Following these policies helps streamline the resolution process.

VALUATION OF THE ECONOMIC IMPACT AND SIGNIFICANCE OF VIRTUAL GOODS MARKETPLACES.

The economic impact and significance of virtual goods marketplaces are substantial and continue to grow as digital economies expand. These marketplaces have evolved from niche platforms into thriving ecosystems with profound financial implications. Here's a comprehensive valuation of their economic impact and significance:

Market Size and Revenue Generation:

1. **Gaming Industry:** The gaming industry primarily contributes to the virtual goods market. It includes in-game items, character skins, virtual currency, and loot boxes. In 2020, the global video game industry was estimated at approximately $159.3 billion, with significant revenue coming from virtual goods and microtransactions.
2. **Digital Collectibles:** Non-fungible tokens (NFTs) have surged in popularity, enabling the sale of digital collectables like digital art, virtual

trading cards, and virtual pets. High-profile NFT sales, such as Beeple's artwork selling for $69 million, have showcased the economic significance of digital collectables.

3. Virtual Real Estate: Virtual real estate markets are emerging in virtual worlds and metaverse platforms. Users buy, sell, and develop virtual land, with some transactions reaching substantial values akin to the real estate market in the physical world.

4. Digital Art Market: Digital art has grown significantly, particularly with artists selling their creations as NFTs. Renowned artists have achieved multimillion-dollar sales for digital art pieces, demonstrating the market's economic impact.

Job Creation and Employment:

i) The growth of virtual goods marketplaces has led to job creation across various sectors, including game development, digital artistry, customer support, and platform management.

ii) This job creation extends to skilled professionals and gig workers who provide services related to virtual goods and their ecosystems.

Impact on the Gaming Industry:

i) Virtual goods have become a significant revenue stream for the gaming industry. Games monetise through in-game purchases, loot boxes, and virtual item sales.

ii) They also impact player engagement, as players often seek virtual items to enhance their gaming experiences.

Cultural and Social Significance:

i) Virtual goods have cultural and social significance as they shape virtual economies within games and online communities. These digital ecosystems have unique currencies, trade dynamics, and value systems.

ii) They contribute to user experiences, allowing individuals to express themselves, signal their status, and form identities within virtual communities.

Investment and Speculation:

i) Investors and speculators participate in virtual goods markets, trading virtual items and investing in virtual assets. The emergence of virtual asset investment markets and the use of cryptocurrencies add to the market's significance.
ii) The rise of blockchain-based virtual goods provides secure ownership and investment opportunities for digital assets.

Real-World Impact:

i) The economic impact of virtual goods extends to the real world, with individuals earning substantial income from virtual goods sales, virtual property investments, and digital art creations.
ii) Some virtual real estate transactions have reached values comparable to physical real estate, and artists have achieved fame and fortune through virtual art sales.

Technological Advancements:

i) The development and sale of virtual goods drive technological advancements, particularly in blockchain and NFT technologies.
ii) Blockchain provides secure ownership and provenance tracking for digital assets with applications beyond virtual goods.

Digital Art Market:

i) Digital art has experienced significant growth thanks to NFTs. High-profile artists have achieved multimillion-dollar sales for their digital artworks.
ii) The digital art market has expanded its reach and economic significance through NFT platforms.

Economic Challenges:

i) Virtual goods marketplaces face fraud, scams, counterfeiting, and regulatory concerns. Addressing these issues is crucial for maintaining trust and stability.

ii) Regulatory compliance and consumer protection are critical areas of concern.

User-Generated Content:

i) Virtual goods enable users to monetise their creativity and skills by creating and selling items and experiences within virtual ecosystems.
ii) This fosters a culture of entrepreneurship and innovation.

Global Reach and Cross-Platform Integration:

i) Virtual goods marketplaces operate globally, providing opportunities for users and businesses worldwide to participate in the digital economy.
ii) Cross-platform integration allows virtual items to be used across different games or worlds, expanding their economic impact.

Social and Psychological Impact:

i) Virtual goods have social and psychological significance, allowing users to express themselves, signal status, and form identities within virtual communities.
ii) They contribute to user experiences and engagement.

Emerging Trends:

i) Emerging trends include the rise of metaverse concepts, virtual fashion, and integration with augmented and virtual reality (AR/VR) technologies.
ii) These trends add to the market's economic significance and open new opportunities.

ANALYSIS OF THE FACTORS INFLUENCING VIRTUAL GOODS PRICES AND MARKET DYNAMICS.

Analysing the factors affecting virtual goods prices and market dynamics is essential to comprehend how these digital assets are purchased, sold, and valued within virtual goods marketplaces. Here is a comprehensive analysis of these variables:

Scarcity and Rarity:

> **Limited Supply:**Virtual goods with a limited supply or intentionally made scarce tend to be more valuable. Game developers or virtual goods marketplaces can create this scarcity by controlling the release of items or making them available for a limited time. Players often desire things that are difficult to obtain.

Popularity and Demand:

> **User Demand:**User demand is the most influential factor in virtual goods pricing. If users highly desire a virtual item due to its aesthetics, functionality, or rarity, its price can skyrocket. Demand drives competition among buyers.

> **Fandom and Collectability:** Items associated with popular franchises, characters, or fandoms often command higher prices. Collectors are willing to pay a premium for items related to their favourite intellectual properties.

Utility and Functionality:

> **In-Game Advantages:** Within gaming, virtual goods that provide players with in-game advantages, such as enhanced abilities or increased performance, are typically priced higher. Players are willing to invest in items that improve their gameplay experience.

> **Functional Items:** Some virtual goods have practical applications beyond gaming. For example, virtual real estate in metaverse platforms like Decentraland can be used for various purposes, including hosting events or setting up businesses. The utility these items offer can significantly influence their prices.

Branding and Reputation:

> **Branded Content:** Virtual goods associated with well-known brands or franchises can carry higher price tags due to brand recognition and the perceived value associated with those brands.

> **Creator Reputation:** In digital art and collectables, the creator's or artist's reputation can significantly impact the pricing of their works.

Established artists often fetch higher prices for their creations.

Supply Control and Artificial Scarcity:

> **Controlled Releases:** Virtual goods marketplaces or game developers may strategically control the release of items to create artificial scarcity. This tactic encourages users to act quickly to acquire items before they become unavailable, driving up prices.
> **Limited-Time Events:** Time-limited events or promotions can increase demand for virtual goods by creating a sense of urgency among users to obtain them before they disappear. This heightened demand can lead to price spikes.

Secondary Market Factors:

> **Resale Market:** The existence of secondary markets, where users can buy and sell virtual goods to other users, adds complexity to pricing dynamics. Users may speculate on items, buying them with the expectation of reselling them at a profit.
> **Marketplaces and Auctions:** The design and mechanics of virtual goods marketplaces and auction systems can influence pricing. Bidding mechanisms, listing fees, and marketplace policies play a role in determining prices.

Technological Advancements:

> **Blockchain and NFTs:** Using blockchain technology and non-fungible tokens (NFTs) has introduced transparency, provenance tracking, and verifiable ownership of virtual goods. These technological advancements can affect pricing, especially in the digital art and collectables markets.

Platform Policies and Fees:

> **Transaction Fees:** Virtual goods marketplaces often charge fees for listing, selling, and transferring items. Higher fees can increase item prices, as sellers may pass these costs on to buyers.
> **Licensing and Royalties:** Some platforms pay creators or brand owners royalties for virtual goods sales. These royalties can impact item pricing

and profitability for both creators and sellers.

Community and Social Influences:

> **Community Values:** Virtual goods prices can be influenced by the values and preferences of the user community. What users collectively consider valuable can have a significant impact on pricing.
> **Social Status:** Users may purchase virtual goods to signal their social status or affiliation within online communities. This can impact the perceived value of those items.

Economic Factors:

> **Currency Exchange Rates:** Virtual goods often involve virtual currencies, and exchange rates between virtual and real-world currencies can influence pricing. Additionally, the fluctuation of cryptocurrencies can affect the value of virtual goods.
> **Inflation:** Some virtual economies may experience inflation over time, causing gradual price increases for virtual goods.

Regulatory Environment:

> **Regulatory Changes:** Regulation changes like taxation on virtual goods transactions can influence pricing dynamics and user behaviour. Compliance with evolving laws is essential for market stability.

User Behaviour:

> **Market Speculation:** Some users engage in speculative behaviour, buying virtual goods with the expectation that their prices will rise over time. This can influence pricing and market volatility.
> **Consumer Confidence:** User trust in the virtual goods marketplace, including protection against fraud and scams, can significantly impact pricing and overall market health.

EXAMINATION OF VIRTUAL CURRENCY SYSTEMS AND THEIR ROLE IN VIRTUAL GOODS TRANSACTIONS.

Examining virtual currency systems and their role in virtual goods transactions reveals the fundamental financial infrastructure that underpins these digital economies. Virtual currencies are the lifeblood of virtual goods marketplaces, serving as the medium of exchange for buying and selling digital assets. Here, we explore their significance and impact on virtual goods transactions.

Virtual Currency Systems in Virtual Goods Transactions:

Virtual currencies are digital or virtual representations of value that enable users to transact within virtual goods marketplaces and online ecosystems. These currencies have distinct roles in facilitating virtual goods transactions:

i) Primary Medium of Exchange: Virtual currencies are users' primary means to buy, sell, and trade virtual goods. Whether in gaming environments, virtual worlds, or digital art platforms, users typically use virtual currencies to acquire virtual items, assets, or experiences.

ii) Diverse Virtual Economies: Different virtual goods marketplaces may have unique virtual currencies. For example, popular games like "Fortnite" have their in-game currencies, while virtual worlds like "Second Life" have their own money (Linden Dollars). This diversity reflects the specialised economies within these digital ecosystems.

iii) Cross-Platform Compatibility: Some virtual currencies are designed to be interoperable across multiple platforms and games. This cross-platform compatibility allows users to use the same money in different virtual environments, enhancing flexibility and utility.

iv) Incentive Mechanisms: Game developers and virtual goods marketplaces often use virtual currencies as incentives. They reward users with virtual currency for specific actions or achievements, encouraging user engagement and spending within the ecosystem.

v) Monetisation Strategy: Virtual currencies are integral to the monetisation strategies of game developers and platform operators. Users may purchase virtual currency with real money, and these transactions form a significant source of revenue for the creators of virtual goods.

vi) Microtransactions: Virtual currencies enable microtransactions, allowing users to make small purchases, such as virtual items or cosmetic enhancements. This model has become prevalent in the gaming industry and contributes to the economic viability of free-to-play games.

Role in Economic Dynamics:

The presence of virtual currencies fundamentally shapes the economic dynamics of virtual goods transactions:

i) Price Flexibility: Virtual currencies provide flexibility in pricing virtual goods. Creators and sellers can set item prices in terms of virtual currency, and these prices are not directly tied to real-world currency values. This flexibility allows for experimentation with pricing strategies.

ii) Market Speculation: Virtual currencies may be subject to market speculation, with users buying and holding them in anticipation of potential price increases. This speculation can affect currency exchange rates and, consequently, the prices of virtual goods.

iii) Economic Growth: Successful virtual currencies can drive economic growth within virtual ecosystems. A thriving virtual currency system encourages user engagement, content creation, and financial activities, fostering a vibrant digital economy.

iv) User Behaviour: Users' behaviour, including spending patterns and investment decisions related to virtual currencies, plays a crucial role in shaping market dynamics. A confident user base is likelier to participate actively in virtual goods transactions.

v) Currency Exchange Services: Virtual currency systems often include exchange services that allow users to convert virtual currency into real-world currency and vice versa. These services provide liquidity to the virtual economy and enable users to realise the value of their virtual assets.

Challenges and Regulation:

Virtual currency systems also face challenges and regulatory considerations. Fraud, money laundering, and tax compliance have prompted governments and regulatory bodies to scrutinise virtual currencies in virtual goods transactions.

i) Money Laundering and Illicit Activities: Virtual currencies can be used for money laundering and financing illicit activities due to their relative anonymity. This has led to concerns among regulators regarding the potential misuse of virtual currencies for criminal purposes.

ii) Taxation and Reporting: Taxation of virtual currency transactions can be complex, and reporting requirements vary by jurisdiction. Users and businesses involved in virtual goods transactions may need help understanding and complying with tax regulations.

iii) Market Volatility: The value of virtual currencies can be highly volatile, subject to rapid fluctuations. Users and businesses may face significant financial risks when holding or trading virtual currencies.

iv) Regulatory Uncertainty: The regulatory landscape of virtual currencies is evolving in many countries. Clear and consistent regulations can create certainty for users and businesses operating in virtual currency systems.

v) Cybersecurity Risks: Virtual currency systems are attractive targets for cyberattacks. Security breaches can result in losing users' virtual currency holdings and personal information.

vi) Cross-Border Transactions: Virtual currencies operate globally, making cross-border transactions familiar. However, different jurisdictions' varying regulations and compliance requirements can complicate international transactions.

vii) AML and KYC Requirements: Some jurisdictions impose anti-money laundering (AML) and know-your-customer (KYC) requirements on virtual currency service providers. These requirements can be burdensome and expensive to implement.

viii) Regulatory Responses: Regulators in various countries are taking steps to address these challenges. They may introduce licensing and registration requirements for virtual currency service providers, implement AML regulations, and enhance consumer protection measures.

ix) Digital Asset Classification: The classification of virtual currencies and digital assets varies by jurisdiction. Some are considered commodities, while others are seen as securities. The type can affect the regulatory framework applied to them.

DISCUSSION OF THE RELATIONSHIP BETWEEN VIRTUAL GOODS MARKETS AND TRADITIONAL ECONOMIES.

The intricate and developing dynamics characterise the interaction between virtual goods markets and traditional economies. The impact of virtual goods, referring to digital or intangible assets, has extended beyond the virtual realm and now significantly affects economic activity in the physical world. The interaction between the digital and conventional domains engenders several discernible characteristics.

The significance of virtual goods markets in terms of their economic influence should be considered. The needs mentioned above, encompassing gaming, digital art, virtual real estate, and other sectors, have experienced substantial growth and emerged as noteworthy contributors to the world economy. Within the gaming industry, a notable proportion of the overall earnings is derived from the sale of virtual goods, amounting to billions of dollars annually. The significant economic impact extends beyond mere revenue statistics, as it also stimulates the generation of employment opportunities. The virtual goods business has emerged as an essential contributor to employment opportunities, encompassing a wide range of workers with varying skill sets, including highly skilled professionals and individuals engaged in gig work. This industry has had a distinctive impact on the overall employment environment.

Including real-world investments in virtual commodities introduces this association to an additional level of intricacy. The act of users often converting actual currency into virtual assets imbues these digital commodities with discernible value. Prominent transactions, as demonstrated by selling non-fungible token (NFT) based digital artworks for significant amounts, highlight the considerable economic value of these intangible assets. Moreover, the speculative characteristic of investments in virtual goods resembles conventional asset categories, as investors speculate over the prospective value of these digital assets. This phenomenon leads to fluctuations in prices and creates chances for investment.

Cross-platform integration is an additional aspect of this association, as the convergence of virtual commodities continues to blur the barriers between digital and conventional economies. The assets are being developed to achieve interoperability, enabling users to utilise their digital holdings across various virtual contexts. It is worth noting that certain virtual commodities can be exchanged or transformed into tangible currency, thereby establishing a connection between virtual and conventional forms of monetary exchange and subsequently influencing the structure of the financial domain.

Virtual commodities exert a substantial impact on cultural and social domains. Users can customise their digital identities, exhibit individuality, and indicate their social standing within virtual networks. These assets play a significant role in shaping digital identities and interactions within these groups. In addition, virtual goods markets have fostered a robust ecosystem of creators of digital content, offering artists, designers, and innovators opportunities for acknowledgement and financial gain.

Nevertheless, this complex interconnection has its challenges. Consumer protection issues, such as fraud, scams, and counterfeiting, give rise to concerns that necessitate a proactive approach to safeguard customer confidence and maintain stability within the market. In addition, the increasing economic significance of virtual commodities has attracted regulatory scrutiny, leading governments to consider strategies for imposing taxes, implementing regulations, and overseeing transactions inside this rapidly expanding digital marketplace.

Moreover, traditional sectors are also adapting to the emergence of virtual product markets. Fashion brands, such as those in the industry, have expanded their operations to include virtual fashion, while real estate corporations are allocating resources towards virtual land and property investments. The metaverse, a notion encompassing the cohabitation of users within communal virtual environments, has garnered considerable attention from prominent technological corporations such as Meta (formerly known as Facebook). This trend signifies a merging of conventional enterprises with virtual realms.

ANALYSIS OF CURRENT POLICIES AND REGULATIONS RELATED TO VIRTUAL GOODS MARKETPLACES.

Consumer Protection and Terms of Service: Current policies and regulations in virtual goods marketplaces often focus on consumer protection by establishing terms of service and refund policies. However, the extent of protection can vary widely between platforms. Some marketplaces provide clear and comprehensive terms of service that outline user rights and responsibilities, including refund procedures. In contrast, others may need more transparent policies, potentially leaving consumers with limited recourse in case of disputes or dissatisfaction with virtual goods. Some platforms also employ age verification measures to safeguard minors from engaging in potentially harmful transactions, reflecting an effort to protect vulnerable users.

Digital Property Rights and Licensing Agreements: The treatment of digital property rights in virtual goods is a subject of ongoing regulatory scrutiny. While some virtual goods are regarded as items with transferable ownership, others may have more limited rights. Creators and platform operators often enter into licensing agreements, particularly for virtual goods based on intellectual property rights. These agreements define the terms under which virtual goods can be bought, sold, and used within the virtual ecosystem, aiming to balance the interests of creators, operators, and users.

Taxation, Reporting, and AML/KYC: Taxation on virtual goods sales is an area where regulations can significantly impact virtual economies. Different jurisdictions apply varying tax rates or exemptions to these transactions. Reporting requirements for income generated from virtual goods sales can also differ, posing challenges for users and businesses to comply with tax regulations. Anti-money laundering (AML) regulations, particularly in regions with stricter financial oversight, may require virtual goods platforms to implement know-your-customer (KYC) measures to verify users' identities in high-value transactions, adding a layer of regulatory complexity.

Intellectual Property Protection and Counterfeit Goods: Regulations concerning intellectual property protection are vital in combatting counterfeit virtual goods. Marketplaces typically have policies to remove or prohibit the sale of counterfeit items, but enforcement can vary. The Digital Millennium Copyright Act (DMCA) in the United States allows copyright owners to send notices to virtual goods platforms requesting the removal of infringing content. Compliance with these notices is essential to avoid legal repercussions and underscores the intersection of intellectual property and virtual goods regulation.

Secondary Markets and Platform Liability: Secondary markets for virtual goods, where users can resell items, present regulatory challenges. Some platforms regulate and facilitate secondary market transactions, while others may restrict or prohibit them. Additionally, platform liability protections vary by jurisdiction. In certain regions, marketplaces are considered intermediaries rather than liable parties in transactions, which can impact their legal responsibilities regarding user-generated content and commerce.

Decentralised Marketplaces and Cross-Border Transactions: The rise of decentralised virtual goods marketplaces, often facilitated by blockchain technology, introduces novel regulatory considerations. These platforms may operate outside traditional regulatory frameworks, challenging conventional notions of jurisdiction and oversight. Moreover, the prevalence of cross-border transactions in virtual goods markets complicates regulatory enforcement, prompting international efforts to harmonise regulations through organisations like the Financial Action Task Force (FATF).

POLICYMAKERS SHOULD ENHANCE CONSUMER PROTECTION AND FOSTER A HEALTHY VIRTUAL GOODS MARKETPLACE.

i) Standardise Consumer Protection Measures: Policymakers should collaborate with virtual goods marketplaces to establish standardised consumer protection measures. These measures should encompass clear and transparent terms of service that outline user rights and responsibilities. Standardisation ensures that consumers enjoy consistent protection, regardless of their platform. It can also simplify regulatory compliance for businesses.

ii) Age Verification and Content Ratings: Mandating age verification mechanisms, such as age-gating, can help prevent minors from accessing virtual goods that may be inappropriate for their age. Additionally, policymakers can promote the implementation of content rating systems similar to those used in the entertainment industry. These systems enable users to make informed choices about the virtual goods they consume, enhancing child safety and responsible use.

iii) Educational Initiatives: Policymakers should allocate resources to educational initiatives to raise user awareness about the virtual goods marketplace. These initiatives can include online campaigns, guides, and workshops to teach users to recognise and avoid scams, counterfeit goods, and other fraudulent activities. Informed users are better equipped to protect themselves and make wise purchasing decisions.

iv) Enhance Intellectual Property Protections: Strengthening intellectual property (IP) protection regulations is crucial to combat counterfeit goods in virtual marketplaces. Policymakers can encourage marketplaces to implement robust anti-counterfeit measures, such as automated content recognition systems. Additionally, it provides copyright holders with straightforward and efficient channels for reporting infringement, ensuring the timely removal of infringing content.

v) Taxation and Reporting Guidelines: Policymakers should collaborate with tax authorities to develop comprehensive taxation guidelines for virtual goods transactions. Given the international nature of these markets, clear guidelines on cross-border transactions are essential. These guidelines should also address reporting requirements, ensuring businesses and users understand their tax obligations when engaging in virtual goods sales.

vi) Anti-Money Laundering (AML) and Know Your Customer (KYC) Regulations: Craft AML and KYC regulations that consider the unique characteristics of virtual goods transactions. These regulations should balance preventing illicit financial activities, such as money laundering and terrorist financing while respecting user privacy. Platforms should be required to implement risk-based AML and KYC measures for high-value transactions, helping deter criminal activities.

vii) Regulate Secondary Markets: Policymakers can introduce regulations governing secondary markets for virtual goods. These regulations should clarify the rights and responsibilities of users and marketplaces in secondary transactions. By doing so, policymakers can prevent fraud and ensure that users have fair and transparent opportunities to resell virtual goods they no longer need.

viii) Blockchain and Decentralized Marketplaces: Acknowledging the growth of decentralised virtual goods marketplaces powered by blockchain technology, policymakers should proactively develop a regulatory framework. This framework should address jurisdictional challenges and provide taxation, consumer protection, and dispute resolution guidelines in these decentralised ecosystems. Policymakers should seek input from experts and stakeholders in blockchain technology to create effective and adaptable regulations.

ix) International Cooperation: Recognizing the global nature of virtual goods transactions, policymakers should engage in international cooperation efforts. Collaborate with other countries and international organisations, such as the Financial Action Task Force (FATF), to harmonise regulations for cross-border transactions. This cooperation can prevent regulatory arbitrage and enhance the effectiveness of consumer protection measures.

x) Consumer Feedback Mechanisms: Encourage virtual goods marketplaces to establish transparent and user-friendly feedback mechanisms. These mechanisms allow users to report issues, provide seller feedback, and share their experiences. Publicly available feedback can serve as a valuable resource for users in assessing the trustworthiness of sellers, contributing to a safer marketplace.

xi) Transparency in Virtual Currency Use: Promote transparency in the use of virtual currencies within virtual goods marketplaces. Ensure that users can access clear and understandable terms and conditions regarding the conversion rates, fees, and limitations of virtual currency usage. Transparent practices enhance trust and prevent unexpected financial surprises for users.

xii) Regular Audits and Compliance Checks: Policymakers should institute a system of regular audits and compliance checks for virtual goods marketplaces. Independent auditors can verify that platforms adhere to established regulations, ensuring that consumer protection measures are implemented effectively. Non-compliance should result in penalties or sanctions to incentivise adherence to rules.

xiii) Consumer Rights Awareness: Launch initiatives to raise awareness of consumer rights in virtual goods transactions. Ensure that users are well-informed about their rights, including the right to refunds, data privacy protections, and accessible dispute resolution processes. Knowledgeable consumers are more likely to assert their rights and make informed decisions.

xiv) Adaptive Regulations: Acknowledge virtual goods markets' dynamic and rapidly evolving nature. Develop regulatory frameworks that are adaptive and responsive to technological advancements and changing market dynamics. Regularly review and update regulations to ensure their continued relevance and effectiveness.

xv) Engage Stakeholders: Policymakers should engage with industry stakeholders, including virtual goods marketplaces, creators, users, and advocacy groups. Collaboration and consultation with these stakeholders can lead to more practical, effective, and balanced regulations that consider the perspectives and needs of all parties involved.

Virtual Employment and Labour Law: Rights and Protections for Metaverse Workers

INTRODUCTION

Virtual Employment

Virtual employment, also known as remote work or telecommuting, refers to a work arrangement where individuals perform their duties and responsibilities primarily from a location other than a physical office or workplace. Instead of being present at a traditional brick-and-mortar office, virtual employees use digital technologies and communication tools to carry out their work-related tasks. Here's a more detailed breakdown:

1. Location Independence:

Virtual employment allows workers to carry out their job responsibilities from a location of their choice, such as their home, a co-working space, a coffee shop, or any place with internet connectivity. This flexibility in work location is one of the defining features of virtual employment.

2. Technology-Centric:

Virtual employment relies heavily on technology and digital tools. Employees use computers, laptops, smartphones, internet connections, and various software applications to access company systems, communicate with colleagues and clients, collaborate on projects, and perform tasks.

3. Varied Roles and Industries:

Virtual employment encompasses various job roles and industries. While some positions are naturally suited for remote work (e.g., software development, content writing, digital marketing), technological advances have made it possible for many traditional office roles to transition to virtual employment arrangements.

4. Flexibility:

Virtual employment often offers flexibility regarding work hours and schedules. Employees may have more control over their daily routines, allowing them to balance work with personal commitments and preferences.

5. Communication Tools:

Effective communication is crucial in virtual employment. Workers use video conferencing, messaging apps, email, and project management software to communicate with colleagues and supervisors, exchange information, and coordinate tasks.

6. Remote Team Collaboration:

Virtual employment often involves collaborating with colleagues who may be located in different time zones or regions. Team members must work together seamlessly despite physical distance.

Metaverse Workers

Metaverse workers actively engage in economic activities, social interactions, and creative endeavours within the virtual and interconnected digital universe. The metaverse combines augmented reality (AR), virtual reality (VR), and the internet to create an immersive and expansive digital environment. Here's a more detailed explanation:

The Metaverse: The metaverse represents a collective virtual space where users, often characterised by avatars or digital personas, interact with each other, digital entities, and computer-generated environments. It is a multi-dimensional, digital universe that goes beyond traditional internet browsing.

Roles and Activities: Metaverse workers participate in various positions and activities within the metaverse, which may include:

i) Content Creators: Design, build, and create virtual objects, assets, environments, or experiences.

ii) Developers: Design and program software, applications, and systems within the metaverse.

iii) Entrepreneurs: Establish businesses and services that operate exclusively within the metaverse, such as virtual real estate, entertainment venues, and virtual goods shops.

iv) Moderators: Oversee and manage virtual communities and spaces, ensuring adherence to rules and guidelines.

v) Service Providers: Offer services within the metaverse, such as event planning, customer support, or entertainment.

Economic Transactions: Economic activities within the metaverse often involve virtual currencies or digital assets unique to the metaverse. Users may engage in transactions, such as buying, selling, trading, or creating virtual items, experiences, or services.

i) Virtual Identity: Metaverse workers typically create and customise avatars or digital representations of themselves to navigate and interact within the metaverse. These avatars can be highly personalised and may differ from users' real-world identities.

ii) Virtual Societies: The metaverse includes social spaces, communities, and virtual worlds where metaverse workers can socialise, collaborate, and establish relationships with other users. It serves as both a workspace and a venue for leisure and entertainment.

iii) Emerging Legal and Economic Structures: The metaverse is a relatively new concept, and its economic and legal structures are still evolving. This includes addressing intellectual property, taxation, virtual property rights, and labour laws specific to the metaverse.

THE SIGNIFICANCE OF EMPLOYMENT AND LABOUR LAW IN THE METAVERSE

Employment and labour law must be addressed in the metaverse for multiple reasons, as it presents unique challenges and opportunities that must be carefully considered:

1. Worker Protections:

Workers may be vulnerable to exploitation, unfair treatment, and unregulated working conditions in the metaverse. Labour laws provide a safety net to protect workers from abuse, ensuring they receive fair compensation, reasonable working hours, and a safe working environment.

2. Worker Classification:

Precise worker classification is crucial in the metaverse. If workers are misclassified as independent contractors, they may miss out on essential benefits like minimum wage, overtime pay, and access to healthcare or retirement plans.

3. Intellectual Property:

The metaverse involves the creation and exchange of virtual assets and content. Well-defined intellectual property laws are essential to prevent unauthorised copying or use of virtual products and to protect creators' rights.

4. Taxation and Revenue:

Taxation laws need to adapt to economic activity in the metaverse generating income. Proper taxation ensures governments collect revenue from this digital economy, contributing to public services and infrastructure.

5. Virtual Property Rights:

Many metaverse users invest significant time and resources in acquiring virtual property, such as virtual real estate or in-game items. Establishing legal frameworks for virtual property rights is critical to protect these investments.

6. Privacy and Data Security:

The metaverse collects and processes user data. Privacy laws should ensure that user information is protected and data breaches are minimised. Regulations must define how data is collected, stored, and used within virtual environments.

7. Workplace Safety:

In the metaverse, even virtual workplaces where workers engage in tasks may exist. Workplace safety regulations should extend to these digital environments to prevent worker harm.

8. Dispute Resolution:

Disputes can arise in the metaverse, necessitating mechanisms for resolution. Virtual courts or alternative dispute resolution processes designed for digital spaces are vital for ensuring fair outcomes.

9. Accessibility:

Legal provisions should require that metaverse content and spaces are accessible to individuals with disabilities. This ensures equal opportunities for participation and prevents discrimination.

10. Anti-Discrimination Laws:

Discrimination based on race, gender, religion, disability, or other factors should be prohibited in the metaverse, just as in traditional workplaces.

11. Worker Mobility:

Metaverse work arrangements often transcend geographical boundaries. Labour laws must accommodate remote work and address issues related to visas and immigration for international metaverse workers.

12. Emerging Challenges:

The metaverse is a rapidly evolving environment with new technologies and behaviours. Legal frameworks must remain flexible and adaptive to address emerging challenges and unanticipated issues.

13. Economic Growth:

A well-regulated metaverse can stimulate economic growth by providing legal certainty. This encourages businesses and entrepreneurs to invest in metaverse-related ventures, leading to innovation and job creation.

14. Consumer Protection:

Many metaverse activities involve economic transactions. Consumer protection laws must apply to safeguard individuals against fraud, scams, and unfair practices within virtual economies.

15. Global Harmonization:

Given the global nature of the metaverse, international cooperation is vital. Harmonising labour and employment laws across borders helps create a consistent and fair legal environment, preventing jurisdictional conflicts and ensuring equal protection for workers worldwide.

CURRENT AND PROSPECTIVE METAVERSE APPLICATIONS IN VARIOUS INDUSTRIES

As a conceptual framework, the metaverse can profoundly transform various sectors by establishing immersive and interconnected digital worlds. Although the metaverse is now in its nascent phase, numerous businesses are actively investigating its possible uses, with several already making notable progress. Moreover, several other industries hold substantial promise for future integration within the metaverse. The present discourse will delineate the existing and prospective implementations of the metaverse across diverse sectors.

GAMING AND ENTERTAINMENT

The metaverse is already making significant strides in the gaming and entertainment industry and has tremendous potential for further innovation. Here's an overview of current and potential applications within this sector:

Current Applications:

i) **Virtual Worlds and Games**: Several virtual worlds and online games operate as metaverse-like environments. These platforms allow players to create avatars, interact with others, and participate in various activities.

ii) **Social Experiences**: Social gaming platforms within the metaverse enable users to meet friends, attend virtual events, and engage in various leisure activities like dancing, parties, or simply hanging out.

iii) **Virtual Concerts and Performances**: Artists and musicians have embraced the metaverse to host virtual concerts and performances, reaching global audiences in immersive digital venues.

iv) **Live Streaming and Esports**: Live streaming platforms within the metaverse enable gamers and content creators to broadcast their gameplay, providing entertainment to viewers and monetising their content.

Potential Applications:

i) **Immersive VR and AR Gaming**: Virtual reality (VR) and augmented reality (AR) technologies will offer more immersive and realistic gaming experiences. Gamers can explore highly detailed virtual environments and interact with objects as if they were in the physical world.

ii) **Cross-Platform Gaming**: The metaverse can facilitate cross-platform gaming, enabling players on different devices to interact and compete in the same virtual space seamlessly.

iii) **Persistent Universes**: Games and virtual worlds within the metaverse could offer endless universes where changes made by players have lasting impacts, creating dynamic and evolving game worlds.

iv) **User-Created Content**: Metaverse gaming platforms might empower users to create and sell in-game assets, levels, and experiences, fostering a user-generated content ecosystem.

v) Digital Collectibles and NFTs: The metaverse could popularise digital collectables and non-fungible tokens (NFTs) tied to in-game items, characters, and experiences. Gamers can buy, sell, and trade unique digital assets.

vi) Virtual Reality Esports: Esports within the metaverse could become highly immersive, with VR headsets allowing players to move and interact physically in virtual arenas.

vii) Interactive Storytelling: Metaverse gaming can push the boundaries of interactive storytelling, enabling players to shape the narrative and influence the game world's outcome.

viii) Cinematic Experiences: Virtual cinema within the metaverse can offer cinematic experiences where users watch movies and TV shows in shared virtual theatres, enhancing the sense of community.

ix) Themed Entertainment: Theme parks and entertainment venues in the metaverse can recreate immersive experiences inspired by popular franchises, allowing fans to explore and interact in their favourite fictional worlds.

x) Education and Learning Games: Educational institutions can use the metaverse to create engaging learning games, simulations, and virtual field trips that make learning fun and interactive.

xi) Augmented Reality Adventures: Augmented reality games in the metaverse can merge the digital and physical worlds, encouraging users to explore their real-world surroundings while interacting with virtual elements.

xii) Live Interactive Streaming: Enhanced interactive streaming in the metaverse could enable viewers to actively participate in gameplay, making content consumption a more engaging experience.

xiii) Narrative and Role-Playing Experiences: Role-playing games within the metaverse can provide deeply immersive narratives and character-driven experiences, blurring the lines between gaming and storytelling.

The gaming and entertainment industry is at the forefront of metaverse development, continuously pushing the boundaries of what's possible in digital entertainment. As technology advances and user adoption grows, the metaverse is poised to become a central hub for gaming, social interaction, and entertainment experiences, creating new opportunities for creators and consumers.

EDUCATION

The metaverse holds immense potential to transform the field of education by providing innovative, immersive, and collaborative learning experiences. Here are current and potential applications of the metaverse in education:

Current Applications:

i) **Virtual Classrooms and Conferencing**: Some educational institutions and organisations use the metaverse to host virtual classrooms and conferences. Students can attend classes, lectures, and meetings using avatars and interact in real-time.

ii) **Virtual Field Trips**: Metaverse platforms offer virtual field trip experiences where students can explore historical sites, museums, and natural wonders without leaving their homes or classrooms.

iii) **Collaborative Learning**: The metaverse fosters collaborative learning through shared virtual spaces, enabling students and educators to collaborate on projects, experiments, and presentations.

iv) **Professional Development**: Educators can use the metaverse for professional development, attending workshops, conferences, and training sessions in virtual environments.

Potential Applications:

i) **Immersive Learning Environments**: The metaverse can provide highly immersive learning environments where students can interact with 3D models, simulations, and historical recreations for subjects like science, history, and art.

ii) **Virtual Laboratories**: In subjects requiring experimentation, virtual laboratories can offer students a risk-free and accessible way to conduct experiments and practice scientific methods.

iii) **Language Learning**: Language learners can engage in immersive language environments within the metaverse, practising conversations with native speakers or exploring virtual cultural experiences.

iv) **Virtual Campus Tours**: Educational institutions can create virtual campuses within the metaverse, allowing prospective students to explore facilities and get a feel for the campus before making enrolment decisions.

v) Online Tutoring and Support: Metaverse platforms can facilitate online tutoring and support services, with students receiving personalised assistance from educators or peers in virtual spaces.

vi) Adaptive Learning: AI-driven adaptive learning systems can be integrated into the metaverse, tailoring educational content and challenges to individual students' abilities and progress.

vii) Cultural and Historical Education: Students can travel back in time or to distant locations within the metaverse, gaining deep insights into historical events, cultures, and archaeological sites.

viii) Art and Creativity: The metaverse can be a hub for art and creativity education, offering virtual studios, galleries, and workshops for aspiring artists and designers.

ix) Personalised Learning Paths: Metaverse-based education platforms can track students' progress and adapt content to their learning styles and needs, providing a customised learning path.

x) Accessible Education: The metaverse can enhance accessibility for students with disabilities, offering tools and features that cater to diverse learning needs.

xi) Global Collaboration: Students worldwide can collaborate on projects, cultural exchanges, and research, fostering international perspectives and cross-cultural understanding.

xii) Virtual Career Fairs: Educational institutions can host virtual career fairs within the metaverse, connecting students with employers and industry professionals

xiii) Educational Content Marketplaces: Users can buy, sell, or share educational content and resources within the metaverse, creating a marketplace for teachers and educators.

xiv) Continuing Education: Professionals seeking further education or certifications can access courses and training programs in the metaverse, enhancing lifelong learning opportunities.

xv) Interactive Assessments: Assessments and quizzes can become more interactive and engaging within the metaverse, offering immediate feedback and adaptive challenges.

The metaverse has the potential to revolutionise education by making learning more engaging, accessible, and collaborative. As technology continues to advance and educational institutions embrace virtual learning, the metaverse will likely play a pivotal role in shaping the future of education.

REAL ESTATE AND ARCHITECTURE

The metaverse is poised to bring transformative changes to the real estate and architecture industries, offering innovative solutions for design, visualisation, and property exploration. Here are current and potential applications of the metaverse in these fields:

Current Applications:

i) Virtual Property Tours: Real estate agents and developers use the metaverse to offer virtual property tours. Prospective buyers can explore homes and commercial spaces using virtual reality (VR) or augmented reality (AR) technologies.

ii) Architectural Visualization: Architects and designers use the metaverse for 3D modelling and visualisation of building designs. This allows stakeholders to experience and review architectural plans in immersive virtual environments.

iii) Virtual Showrooms: Furniture and interior design companies are creating virtual showrooms in the metaverse where customers can browse and interact with virtual furniture and decor items.

iv) Collaborative Design: Architects, engineers, and clients can collaborate on building projects within the metaverse, making real-time adjustments to designs and layouts.

Potential Applications:

i) Virtual Property Transactions: Real estate transactions could occur entirely in a digital environment in the metaverse. This includes virtual property auctions, contract signings, and property deeds stored on the blockchain for added security.

ii) Virtual Property Development: Real estate developers could create and visualise entire neighbourhoods and urban landscapes in the metaverse, allowing stakeholders to explore and provide input on development projects before construction begins.

iii) Architectural Design Iteration: Architects and designers can use the metaverse for rapid design iterations, testing various concepts and gathering feedback from clients and collaborators in virtual spaces.

iv) Interactive Neighbourhood Planning: City planners and government agencies can use the metaverse to engage with communities in the urban planning process, visualising proposed developments and gathering public input.

v) Sustainable Design Simulations: The metaverse can facilitate simulations of sustainable building designs, allowing architects and engineers to assess energy efficiency, environmental impact, and resource management in real-time.

vi) Virtual Property Management: Property managers can use the metaverse to monitor and manage real estate assets remotely, from tracking maintenance needs to addressing tenant concerns through virtual service desks.

vii) Property Investment: Investors can explore virtual representations of properties and assess potential investments in the metaverse, accessing detailed data on market trends and property performance.

viii) Historical Preservation: Preservationists can use the metaverse to digitally recreate historical buildings and landmarks, ensuring their legacy and educating future generations about architectural heritage.

ix) Virtual Reality Walkthroughs: Prospective buyers and tenants can take virtual reality tours of properties, customising interior designs, layouts, and decor choices to visualise their potential future spaces.

x) Building Training Simulations: Construction workers and maintenance personnel can undergo training and simulations in the metaverse to learn about building systems, safety procedures, and equipment operation.

xi) Virtual Events: Real estate companies can host virtual property showcases, expos, and industry events in the metaverse, connecting buyers, sellers, and industry professionals.

xii) Property Data Visualization: Data analysts and real estate professionals can use the metaverse to visualise complex property data, helping to identify trends and investment opportunities.

xiii) Global Property Marketplace: A metaverse-based marketplace could facilitate the buying, selling, and trading virtual properties and land, forming a new form of digital real estate investment.

The metaverse offers real estate and architecture professionals an immersive and collaborative platform to rethink traditional property development, design, and transaction approaches. As these industries continue to explore metaverse applications, they may witness enhanced efficiency, greater accessibility, and improved stakeholder engagement in property-related activities.

RETAIL AND E-COMMERCE

The metaverse has the potential to revolutionise the retail and e-commerce industries, offering new ways for consumers to shop, interact with brands, and make purchasing decisions. Here are current and potential applications of the metaverse in retail and e-commerce:

Current Applications:

i) **Virtual Showrooms**: Some retail brands have established virtual showrooms within the metaverse where users can explore and interact with digital representations of products and merchandise.

ii) **Virtual Try-Ons**: Virtual try-on experiences allow consumers to use augmented reality (AR) to try on clothing, accessories, and makeup before purchasing.

iii) **Brand Engagement**: Brands use the metaverse to engage consumers through virtual events, product launches, and marketing campaigns, creating interactive and memorable experiences.

iv) **Digital Art and Collectibles**: The metaverse has become a marketplace for digital art and collectables, with artists and creators selling unique digital assets as non-fungible tokens (NFTs).

Potential Applications:

i) **Immersive Shopping Environments**: The metaverse can offer fully immersive virtual shopping environments where consumers navigate digital malls and stores, interacting with products and virtual staff.

ii) **Personalised Shopping Experiences**: AI and data analytics can personalise metaverse shopping experiences, recommending products, styles, and brands tailored to individual preferences and browsing history.

iii) **Virtual Pop-Up Stores**: Retailers can host virtual pop-up stores within the metaverse, offering limited-time products, collaborations, and exclusive discounts to attract and engage customers.

iv) Virtual Fashion Shows: Fashion brands can host virtual fashion shows, enabling users to watch runway presentations and purchase items directly from the virtual showrooms.

v) Customisation and Personalization: Metaverse-based retailers can offer deep customisation options, allowing customers to personalise products, from clothing designs to home furnishings.

vi) Social Shopping: Users can shop with friends and social connections in the metaverse, enhancing the social aspect of e-commerce through shared virtual experiences.

vii) Blockchain-Based Supply Chains: Blockchain technology can be used to transparently track the origins and authenticity of products, fostering trust and reducing counterfeiting in the metaverse.

viii) Virtual Payment Methods: The metaverse can introduce virtual currencies and payment methods specific to virtual environments, streamlining transactions and reducing friction.

ix) Extended Reality (XR) Shopping: Extended reality technologies like VR and AR can create mixed-reality shopping experiences where digital and physical worlds merge for enhanced product exploration.

x) Interactive Product Reviews: Users can access detailed and immersive product reviews within the metaverse, gaining insights through 3D models, demonstrations, and user-generated content.

xi) Digital Fitting Rooms: Virtual fitting rooms can offer more accurate and detailed try-on experiences, allowing users to assess how clothing and accessories fit and move in 3D.

xii) Metaverse-Exclusive Products: Brands may release metaverse-exclusive items or digital fashion collections, creating a unique virtual clothing and accessories market.

xiii) Social Commerce Integration: Social media and e-commerce can merge within the metaverse, enabling users to discover, share, and purchase products seamlessly.

xiv) Virtual Home Shopping: Consumers can explore and furnish virtual homes within the metaverse, visualising how furniture and decor items fit into their living spaces.

xv) Global Market Access: The metaverse transcends geographic boundaries, giving retailers access to a worldwide customer base and eliminating traditional limitations of physical stores.

The metaverse's potential to offer immersive, interactive, and personalised shopping experiences has garnered significant interest from retailers and e-commerce businesses. As technology and user adoption evolve, the metaverse will likely become a prominent channel for retail and e-commerce activities, redefining how consumers shop and engage with brands.

HEALTHCARE

The metaverse can transform the healthcare industry by offering innovative solutions for patient care, medical training, and healthcare management. Here are current and potential applications of the metaverse in healthcare:

Current Applications:

i) **Telemedicine and Virtual Consultations**: Some healthcare providers have adopted metaverse-like technologies for telemedicine, allowing patients to consult with healthcare professionals remotely through video conferencing and virtual appointments.

ii) **Medical Training and Simulation**: Medical students and professionals use metaverse platforms to train simulations, practice surgical procedures, and improve diagnostic skills in virtual environments.

iii) **Mental Health and Therapy**: Therapists and counsellors use the metaverse for virtual therapy sessions, creating safe and immersive spaces for mental health support.

iv) **Patient Education**: Virtual reality (VR) and augmented reality (AR) applications provide patients with interactive educational experiences that help them better understand medical conditions, treatments, and procedures.

Potential Applications:

i) **Immersive Medical Training**: The metaverse can offer highly realistic and immersive medical training scenarios, enabling healthcare professionals to practice complex procedures, surgeries, and emergency responses in a virtual environment.

ii) **Remote Surgery and Telehealth**: Surgeons could perform remote surgery with robotic systems and advanced haptic feedback technologies, offering life-saving interventions across geographical distances.

iii) Medical Records and Data Visualization: Healthcare providers can use the metaverse to visualise patient data, medical records, and diagnostic images in 3D, making it easier to analyse and understand complex medical information.

iv) Healthcare Team Collaboration: Multi-disciplinary healthcare teams can collaborate in virtual spaces within the metaverse to discuss patient cases, share insights, and coordinate care plans.

v) Rehabilitation and Physical Therapy: Patients can undergo virtual rehabilitation and physical therapy sessions within the metaverse, making exercises and recovery more engaging and monitored by healthcare professionals.

vi) Patient Support Groups: Patients with chronic conditions or rare diseases can connect with support groups and peers in the metaverse, fostering community and shared experiences.

vii) Medical Research and Drug Discovery: Researchers can use metaverse environments to visualise and simulate complex biological processes, accelerating drug discovery and medical research.

viii) Emergency Response Training: First responders and healthcare workers can train for disaster response and emergencies in realistic virtual environments.

ix) Healthcare Resource Allocation: Hospital administrators can use the metaverse to optimise resource allocation, such as beds, equipment, and staff, during healthcare crises and pandemics.

x) Accessible Healthcare: The metaverse can enhance accessibility for disabled patients, providing virtual healthcare services tailored to various needs and abilities.

xi) Health and Wellness Apps: In immersive environments, metaverse-based apps can encourage users to adopt healthier lifestyles through gamified wellness challenges, virtual fitness classes, and health tracking

xii) Clinical Trials and Drug Testing: Clinical trials can be conducted in the metaverse, enabling researchers to recruit and monitor participants more efficiently and securely.

xiii) Patient Monitoring: Wearable devices and sensors integrated with the metaverse can continuously monitor patients' vital signs, providing real-time health data and early warning alerts.

xiv) Crisis Intervention: Mental health professionals can provide crisis intervention and support within the metaverse during emergencies and natural disasters.

xv) Global Medical Collaboration: Healthcare professionals worldwide can collaborate on research, share best practices, and provide real-time medical expertise within a virtual global healthcare network.

The metaverse's potential to improve healthcare accessibility, enhance medical training, and provide innovative solutions for patient care has significant implications for the future of healthcare. As the technology matures and regulatory frameworks adapt, the metaverse will likely play a pivotal role in advancing healthcare delivery and medical innovation.

WORK AND BUSINESS

The metaverse has the potential to revolutionise the way work and business are conducted, offering new opportunities for remote collaboration, innovation, and entrepreneurship. Here are current and potential applications of the metaverse in work and business:

Current Applications:

i) Virtual Offices: Some companies have established virtual office spaces within the metaverse, where employees can gather for meetings, discussions, and collaborative work using avatars.

ii) Remote Meetings and Conferences: Metaverse platforms host remote meetings, conferences, and events, allowing participants to engage in virtual environments.

iii) Product Demonstrations: Businesses use the metaverse to showcase products and conduct demonstrations in virtual showrooms or exhibits.

iv) Networking and Professional Development: The metaverse facilitates networking events and professional development opportunities where participants can connect with industry peers and experts.

Potential Applications:

i) Immersive Remote Work: The metaverse can offer fully immersive remote work environments, allowing teams to collaborate seamlessly across geographic boundaries in virtual offices that mimic physical workplaces.

ii) Virtual Trade Shows and Exhibitions: Businesses can host virtual trade shows, expos, and exhibitions within the metaverse, attracting global audiences and offering interactive product showcases.

iii) Entrepreneurial Ecosystems: The metaverse can foster entrepreneurial ecosystems where start-ups and innovators collaborate, access funding, and engage with mentors and experts in virtual incubators and accelerators.

iv) Marketplace for Digital Products: Businesses can create and sell digital products, services, and assets within the metaverse, including virtual real estate, digital art, virtual fashion, and virtual event tickets.

v) Cross-Platform Collaboration: The metaverse can facilitate cross-platform collaboration, enabling users on various devices and platforms to work together in shared virtual spaces.

vi) Global Talent Pools: Businesses can tap into global talent pools by hiring and collaborating with individuals worldwide in metaverse-based projects.

vii) Innovation Hubs: Innovation hubs and research centres within the metaverse can support interdisciplinary collaboration, driving innovation in various fields.

viii) Blockchain-Based Contracts and Transactions: Smart contracts and blockchain technology can be integrated into the metaverse for secure and automated business transactions and agreements.

ix) Corporate Training and Onboarding: Businesses can use the metaverse for employee training, onboarding, and skill development in immersive virtual environments.

x) Virtual Business Incubation: The metaverse can provide a platform for business incubation programs, offering resources, mentorship, and funding opportunities to start-ups and entrepreneurs.

xi) Simulated Business Environments: Business schools and organisations can create simulated business environments within the metaverse for realistic business simulations and case studies.

xii) Virtual Corporate Headquarters: Companies can establish virtual corporate headquarters, complete with offices, boardrooms, and collaborative spaces for remote work and decision-making.

xiii) Business Analytics and Data Visualization: Metaverse platforms can offer advanced visualisation tools, allowing businesses to analyse complex data in three-dimensional virtual environments.

xiv) Augmented Reality Commerce: Augmented reality commerce within the metaverse can enable customers to try on products virtually, visualise items in their physical space, and make informed purchase decisions.

xv) Secure Virtual Transactions: Enhanced security features can ensure secure financial transactions, intellectual property protection, and confidential business meetings within the metaverse.

The metaverse's potential to transform work and business environments is significant, offering opportunities for global collaboration, innovation, and the creation of new business models. As technology advances, the metaverse will likely play a central role in shaping the future of work and entrepreneurship.

SOCIAL NETWORKING

Social networking within the metaverse has the potential to revolutionise how people connect, communicate, and interact in digital spaces. Here are current and potential applications of the metaverse in social networking:

Current Applications:

i) Virtual Social Spaces: Some metaverse platforms, such as Facebook Horizon, offer virtual social spaces where users can create avatars, interact with friends, and engage in various activities.

ii) Virtual Events: Social events, gatherings, and parties take place in the metaverse, allowing users to attend concerts, exhibitions, and parties with friends and strangers.

iii) Avatar-Based Interactions: Users create and customise avatars representing them in the virtual world, enabling them to express themselves and socialise uniquely.

iv) User-Generated Content: Users can create and share user-generated content, including virtual art, experiences, and environments, for others to explore and enjoy.

Potential Applications:

i) Immersive Social Interaction: The metaverse can offer more immersive and realistic social interactions, with users engaging in activities like dancing, sports, and shared hobbies in virtual spaces.

ii) Cross-Platform Socialization: Users on various devices and platforms can interact seamlessly in shared metaverse environments, fostering inclusivity and broadening social connections.

iii) Virtual Communities: The metaverse can host virtual communities centred around shared interests, hobbies, and passions, allowing users to find and connect with like-minded individuals.

iv) Global Language Learning: Language learners can immerse themselves in language communities within the metaverse, practising conversations with native speakers and learning through interactive experiences.

v) Metaverse Dating and Relationships: Virtual dating and relationship-building platforms can provide unique and creative ways for individuals to meet and connect with potential partners.

vi) Virtual Real Estate and Social Hangouts: Users can purchase and personalise virtual real estate within the metaverse, creating social hubs, nightclubs, and social gathering spaces for friends and communities.

vii) Social Commerce Integration: Users can discover and purchase products from friends' virtual stores and showrooms, combining social interactions with e-commerce activities.

viii) Virtual Museums and Galleries: Artists and curators can create virtual museums and galleries within the metaverse, offering visitors immersive art and cultural experiences.

ix) Educational Social Spaces: Students can gather in virtual study groups and academic communities, creating a collaborative learning and knowledge-sharing environment.

x) Virtual Family Reunions: Families separated by distance can gather in the metaverse for virtual reunions, celebrations, and shared experiences.

xi) Mental Health and Support: Virtual support groups and counselling services within the metaverse can provide individuals with spaces to seek help, share experiences, and connect with peers facing similar challenges.

xii) Privacy and Control: Users can have more control over their personal data and privacy settings within the metaverse, enhancing their comfort and safety while socialising online.

xiii) Virtual Travel and Exploration: Users can explore virtual replicas of famous landmarks and travel destinations, allowing for virtual tourism and cultural experiences.

xiv) Emotional and Immersive Communication: Users can convey emotions and gestures more realistically through their avatars, enhancing the emotional depth of their virtual interactions.

xv) Social Impact Initiatives: Social organisations and non-profits can leverage the metaverse to raise awareness, host virtual fundraisers, and engage communities in social causes.

The metaverse has the potential to redefine social networking by offering immersive, inclusive, and creative ways for individuals to connect and engage in digital environments. As the metaverse ecosystem grows and evolves, it will likely become a central hub for social interactions, relationships, and cultural exchange in the digital age.

ART AND CREATIVITY

The metaverse presents exciting opportunities for artists and creators to explore, share, and collaborate on various artistic and creative endeavours. Here are current and potential applications of the metaverse in the realm of art and creativity:

Current Applications:

i) Virtual Galleries and Studios: Artists can showcase their work in virtual galleries and studios within the metaverse, reaching global audiences and engaging with art enthusiasts.

ii) Digital Art Sales: Artists can sell digital art as non-fungible tokens (NFTs) within the metaverse, offering buyers unique and collectable digital assets.

iii) Collaborative Art Projects: Artists and creators can collaborate on projects within the metaverse, working together to produce digital art, music, literature, and more.

iv) Virtual Art Exhibitions: Art exhibitions and cultural events are hosted within the metaverse, bringing together artists, curators, and audiences in immersive virtual spaces.

Potential Applications:

i) Immersive Art Creation Tools: The metaverse can offer advanced and intuitive 3D modelling, sculpting, and painting tools for artists to create immersive and interactive digital art.

ii) Augmented Reality Art: Artists can create augmented reality (AR) art installations that users can experience in their physical surroundings using AR devices.

iii) Virtual Art Studios: Collaborative virtual art studios within the metaverse can provide a shared space for artists to work together on large-scale projects.

iv) Digital Fashion and Wearable Art: Designers can create virtual and wearable art pieces that users can customise and wear within the metaverse, showcasing unique styles and expressions.

v) Art Education and Workshops: Virtual art schools and workshops can offer immersive learning experiences, allowing students to attend art classes and receive critiques from instructors and peers.

vi) Interactive Art Installations: Artists can design installations that respond to user interactions within the metaverse, creating dynamic and engaging experiences.

vii) Artistic Cultural Preservation: Cultural institutions and organisations can use the metaverse to preserve and share cultural heritage through virtual museums and historical recreations.

viii) Virtual Art Auctions: Auction houses can host virtual art auctions within the metaverse, enabling collectors to bid on and purchase artwork in a digital environment.

ix) Digital Art Curation: Curators can organise and curate virtual exhibitions and collections, offering unique experiences for art enthusiasts and researchers.

x) Community Art Projects: Communities can collaborate on community art projects, murals, and public art installations in the metaverse.

xi) Artistic Performance Spaces: The metaverse can offer virtual spaces for artists to perform live art shows, music concerts, and multimedia performances.

xii) Art-Based Social Networks: Social networks within the metaverse can focus on artistic connections, allowing artists and enthusiasts to share their work, collaborate, and provide feedback.

xiii) Artistic NFT Marketplaces: NFT marketplaces within the metaverse can become hubs for buying, selling, and trading digital art assets, including paintings, music, animations, and more.

xiv) Digital Art Residencies: Artists can participate in virtual art residencies, gaining access to resources, mentorship, and collaborative opportunities within the metaverse.

xv) Virtual Art Therapy: Art therapists can use the metaverse to provide virtual art therapy sessions, offering creative and therapeutic experiences to individuals seeking support.

The metaverse offers a dynamic and innovative platform for artists and creatives to explore new artistic expression, collaboration, and distribution forms. As technology advances, it will continue to shape the future of the art and creativity landscape, offering exciting opportunities for artists and art enthusiasts alike.

FINANCE AND BANKING

The metaverse can introduce significant innovations and disruptions in the finance and banking industry. Here are current and potential applications of the metaverse in finance and banking:

Current Applications:

i) Virtual Banking: Some financial institutions have begun experimenting with virtual banking services within the metaverse, allowing users to perform basic financial transactions and inquiries.

ii) Blockchain and Cryptocurrencies: Cryptocurrencies and blockchain technology are already integral to the metaverse, with many virtual worlds and assets built on blockchain platforms.

iii) Virtual Real Estate Investment: Investors can purchase virtual real estate within the metaverse, often using cryptocurrencies or virtual currencies, with the potential for profit through appreciation or development.

Potential Applications:

i) Metaverse Banking Services: Full-fledged virtual banks can provide a wide range of financial services within the metaverse, including savings accounts, loans, and investments.

ii) Virtual Payment Systems: The metaverse can introduce virtual payment systems and digital currencies specific to virtual environments, facilitating seamless transactions and commerce.

iii) Blockchain-Based Financial Instruments: Financial instruments such as smart contracts, tokenised assets, and decentralised finance (DeFi) protocols can be integrated into the metaverse, offering new investment opportunities.

iv) Virtual Stock Markets: Virtual stock markets and trading platforms can allow users to invest in virtual and real-world assets, facilitating global trading and investment opportunities.

v) Virtual Banking for Digital Assets: Metaverse banks can provide secure custody, lending, and trading services for digital assets such as NFTs and virtual real estate.

vi) Financial Education and Simulation: Virtual financial education programs and simulations within the metaverse can help users learn about investing, budgeting, and financial planning.

vii) Virtual Financial Advisors: AI-driven virtual financial advisors can provide users with personalised financial advice and investment recommendations within the metaverse.

viii) Decentralised Autonomous Organizations (DAOs): DAOs can be formed within the metaverse for decentralised governance and decision-making in financial and investment matters.

ix) Virtual Crowdfunding and Investment: Start-ups and businesses can raise capital through virtual crowdfunding campaigns and investment rounds within the metaverse.

x) Virtual Credit and Lending: Metaverse users can access virtual credit and lending services to fund virtual projects, businesses, and investments.

xi) Virtual Asset Management: Asset managers and investment firms can offer virtual asset management services, providing users with diversified portfolios of virtual and real-world assets.

xii) Virtual Insurance Services: Insurance companies can offer virtual insurance products to protect virtual assets and investments within the metaverse.

xiii) Cross-Platform Asset Portability: Users can seamlessly transfer and utilise digital assets and virtual currencies across different metaverse platforms and virtual worlds.

xiv) Secure Identity and Verification: Advanced identity and verification systems within the metaverse can enhance security and prevent fraud in financial transactions.

xv) Virtual Financial Conferences: Finance and investment conferences, seminars, and networking events can be hosted within the metaverse, connecting professionals and enthusiasts worldwide.

The metaverse's potential impact on finance and banking extends beyond traditional financial services, introducing novel concepts, technologies, and opportunities for individuals and businesses. As the metaverse ecosystem evolves, the financial industry will likely adapt and innovate in response to these transformative developments.

TRAVEL AND TOURISM

The travel and tourism industry is poised to undergo significant changes and enhancements by incorporating the metaverse. Here are current and potential applications of the metaverse in travel and tourism:

Current Applications:

i) Virtual Travel Experiences: Some travel companies offer virtual travel experiences that allow users to explore destinations and attractions within the metaverse.

ii) Virtual Tourism Promotion: Through immersive virtual campaigns, tourism boards and organisations use the metaverse to promote destinations, cultural experiences, and attractions.

iii) VR Destination Marketing: Virtual reality (VR) technology is used for destination marketing, offering potential travellers the chance to visit and experience a location virtually before planning a trip.

iv) Virtual Tours and Guides: Virtual tour guides and experiences within the metaverse provide users with narrated tours of historical sites, landmarks, and museums.

Potential Applications:

i) Immersive Virtual Travel: The metaverse can offer highly immersive virtual travel experiences where users can explore realistic 3D replicas of destinations worldwide, including famous landmarks, natural wonders, and cultural sites.

ii) Travel Booking and Reservations: Metaverse-based travel agencies can facilitate travel bookings, reservations, and itineraries, providing users with a one-stop platform for planning trips.

iii) Virtual Travel Agents: AI-driven virtual travel agents can assist users in planning personalised travel experiences, offering recommendations, booking accommodations, and providing travel assistance within the metaverse.

iv) Interactive Travel Planning: Users can collaborate within the metaverse with friends and travel companions to plan trips, explore destinations, and make group travel decisions.

v) Virtual Travel Events: Tourism boards and travel companies can host virtual travel events, expos, and showcases within the metaverse, allowing travellers to learn about destinations and connect with travel experts.

vi) Cultural and Historical Immersion: Travelers can engage in deep cultural and historical immersion within the metaverse, participating in virtual festivals, ceremonies, and re-enactments.

vii) Virtual Adventure Tourism: Adventure seekers can embark on virtual adventure tours within the metaverse, experiencing extreme sports, wildlife encounters, and exploration in a safe digital environment.

viii) Virtual Destination Weddings: Couples can host virtual destination weddings, allowing friends and family worldwide to attend and celebrate within the metaverse.

ix) Language and Cultural Learning: Language learners can immerse themselves in virtual language and cultural experiences, practising languages and gaining insights into local customs and traditions.

x) Virtual Travel Communities: Users can join virtual travel communities and forums within the metaverse, sharing travel stories, tips, and recommendations with fellow travellers.

xi) Virtual Travel Souvenirs: Travelers can collect virtual souvenirs and memorabilia from their metaverse travel experiences, creating a digital travel journal.

xii) Sustainable Travel Initiatives: The metaverse can promote sustainable and eco-friendly travel practices, encouraging users to explore destinations with minimal environmental impact,

xiii) Virtual Reality in Airlines: Airlines can incorporate VR technology into in-flight entertainment, offering passengers virtual travel experiences during long-haul flights.

xiv) Virtual Travel Education: Educational institutions can use the metaverse for virtual travel education, offering students experiential learning opportunities and field trips to global destinations.

xv) Travel Accessibility: The metaverse can enhance travel accessibility for individuals with mobility challenges, allowing them to virtually experience destinations and cultural events.

The metaverse's potential to offer immersive and accessible travel experiences has the potential to transform how people plan, experience, and share their travel adventures. As technology advances, the metaverse will likely become integral to the travel and tourism industry, providing innovative solutions for travellers and businesses.

MANUFACTURING AND DESIGN

The metaverse can potentially revolutionise the manufacturing and design industries by offering new tools, collaborative environments, and innovative solutions. Here are current and potential applications of the metaverse in manufacturing and design:

Current Applications:

i) Virtual Prototyping: Some manufacturers and design firms use the metaverse for virtual prototyping, allowing designers and engineers to create and test product prototypes in digital environments.

ii) Collaborative Design: Teams of designers and engineers collaborate within the metaverse to work on product designs, making real-time adjustments and improvements.

iii) Training Simulations: Manufacturers use the metaverse for employee training and simulations, helping workers learn about machinery, safety procedures, and manufacturing processes.

iv) Supply Chain Visualization: The metaverse is used to visualise and optimise supply chain processes, helping manufacturers track and manage inventory, logistics, and production.

Potential Applications:

i) Immersive Product Design: Designers can create highly detailed and immersive product prototypes within the metaverse, allowing for 3D exploration and user feedback.

ii) Virtual Factories: Manufacturers can build and operate virtual factories within the metaverse, simulating production processes, machinery, and quality control.

iii) Digital Twins: The metaverse can be used for digital twin simulations, where virtual representations of physical products and systems are created, allowing for real-time monitoring and analysis.

iv) Augmented Reality Manufacturing: Augmented reality (AR) can be integrated into the metaverse to assist workers in assembly tasks and quality control within physical manufacturing facilities.

v) Supply Chain Transparency: Blockchain technology integrated into the metaverse can enhance supply chain transparency, traceability, and authenticity for manufactured goods.

vi) Customisation and Personalization: Manufacturers can offer highly customised and personalised products through metaverse-based configurators, allowing customers to design their products.

vii) Collaborative 3D Printing: 3D printing enthusiasts and professionals can collaborate on projects within the metaverse, sharing 3D models and designs for additive manufacturing.

viii) Virtual Material Testing: Materials scientists and engineers can conduct virtual material testing and simulations within the metaverse, exploring the properties of various materials and their performance in different conditions.

ix) Virtual Showrooms for Manufacturing Equipment: Industrial machinery manufacturers can create virtual showrooms within the metaverse, allowing potential customers to explore and understand complex machinery before purchasing.

x) Remote Machine Operation: Manufacturers can operate and monitor machinery remotely through metaverse interfaces, reducing the need for on-site presence and improving efficiency.

xi) Sustainable Manufacturing Simulations: Manufacturers can use the metaverse for simulations focusing on sustainability, energy efficiency, and waste reduction in manufacturing processes.

xii) Digital Design Collaboration: Industrial designers and engineers can collaborate on product design and development projects within the metaverse, fostering global collaboration and innovation.

xiii) Safety Training and Compliance: The metaverse can offer realistic training simulations and compliance programs for manufacturing workers, reducing workplace accidents.

xiv) Virtual Quality Control: Manufacturers can use the metaverse to conduct virtual quality control inspections, ensuring product quality and consistency.

xv) Global Manufacturing Networks: The metaverse can connect manufacturers from different regions, enabling global manufacturing networks for outsourcing, production, and distribution.

The metaverse offers manufacturing and design professionals a dynamic and collaborative platform to reimagine traditional product development, production, and quality control approaches. As technology advances and industries embrace virtual environments, the metaverse will likely play a central role in shaping the future of manufacturing and design.

SPORTS AND FITNESS

The metaverse has the potential to transform the sports and fitness industries by offering new ways for athletes, fans, and fitness enthusiasts to engage in sports, training, and physical activities. Here are current and potential applications of the metaverse in sports and fitness:

Current Applications:

i) Virtual Sporting Events: Some sports organisations and teams have started hosting virtual sporting events, allowing fans to watch and participate in e-sports and virtual sports competitions.

ii) Virtual Fitness Classes: Fitness instructors offer virtual fitness classes within the metaverse, providing users with live or recorded workouts they can follow from home.

iii) Sports Simulation Games: Sports simulation games within the metaverse offer users the chance to participate in virtual versions of their favourite sports, such as soccer, basketball, and racing.

iv) Training and Coaching Apps: Athletes and fitness enthusiasts use metaverse-based training and coaching apps to improve their skills and receive expert guidance.

Potential Applications:

i) Immersive Sports Experiences: The metaverse can offer highly immersive sports experiences, allowing users to participate in virtual versions of real-world sports or engage in fantasy sports leagues.

ii) Virtual Sports Arenas: Sports teams can build virtual sports arenas and stadiums within the metaverse, hosting virtual matches, concerts, and events with global audiences.

iii) Virtual Athlete Training: Athletes can undergo virtual training and practice sessions to improve their skills and strategies and analyse gameplay in a realistic digital environment.

iv) Augmented Reality Sports: Augmented reality (AR) technology can be integrated into the metaverse to enhance real-world sports experiences, such as providing live statistics and player data during matches.

v) Fan Engagement and Interactivity: Fans can engage with their favourite sports teams and athletes through metaverse-based fan clubs, interactive experiences, and virtual meet-and-greet events.

vi) Virtual Sports Equipment Testing: Sports equipment manufacturers can use the metaverse for virtual testing and prototyping of sporting goods, ensuring performance and safety.

vii) Athlete Recovery and Rehabilitation: Injured athletes can undergo virtual rehabilitation and recovery programs, working with physical therapists and trainers within the metaverse.

viii) Sports Analytics and Simulation: Coaches and analysts can use the metaverse for in-depth sports analytics, game simulations, and strategy development.

ix) Virtual Sports Academies: Young athletes can enrol in virtual sports academies, receiving coaching, training, and mentorship within the metaverse.

x) E-Sports Integration: E-sports tournaments and leagues can be fully integrated into the metaverse, allowing players and fans to engage in competitive gaming experiences.

xi) Global Fitness Communities: Fitness enthusiasts can join global fitness communities and challenges within the metaverse, connecting with trainers and like-minded individuals.

xii) Virtual Obstacle Courses and Challenges: Fitness enthusiasts can engage in virtual obstacle courses and fitness challenges, combining physical and digital elements for exciting workouts.

xiii) Health and Wellness Monitoring: Wearable devices and sensors integrated with the metaverse can monitor users' health and performance during physical activities, offering real-time feedback.

xiv) Virtual Marathon Races: Running enthusiasts can participate in virtual marathon races, exploring virtual racecourses and competing with participants worldwide.

xv) Fitness Gamification: Fitness apps within the metaverse can incorporate gamification elements, motivating users to achieve fitness goals through interactive challenges and rewards.

The metaverse's potential to offer immersive sports and fitness experiences, training opportunities, and fan engagement is vast. As technology advances, the metaverse will likely become integral to how sports are experienced as spectators and participants and how fitness and physical activities are conducted and monitored.

ENVIRONMENTAL CONSERVATION

The metaverse has the potential to play a significant role in environmental conservation efforts by raising awareness, facilitating education, and enabling innovative solutions. Here are current and potential applications of the metaverse in environmental conservation:

Current Applications:

i) Virtual Conservation Campaigns: Environmental organisations and conservationists use the metaverse to launch virtual campaigns to raise awareness about critical environmental issues.

ii) Virtual Nature Reserves: Some metaverse platforms offer virtual nature reserves where users can explore and learn about ecosystems, wildlife, and conservation efforts.

iii) Environmental Education: Virtual educational programs within the metaverse teach users about biodiversity, climate change, sustainable practices, and wildlife conservation.

iv) Virtual Wildlife Tours: Wildlife enthusiasts and conservationists offer virtual wildlife tours, allowing users to observe and learn about animals in their natural habitats.

Potential Applications:

i) Immersive Environmental Education: The metaverse can provide highly immersive educational experiences, allowing users to explore virtual ecosystems, witness the effects of climate change, and understand conservation challenges.

ii) Virtual Conservation Workshops: Conservation organisations can conduct virtual workshops, enabling participants to learn about and engage in hands-on conservation activities like habitat restoration and tree planting.

iii) Citizen Science Projects: Metaverse-based citizen science projects can encourage users to collect and contribute environmental data, aiding researchers in monitoring biodiversity, pollution, and climate patterns.

iv) Virtual Reality Wildlife Conservation: Wildlife conservationists can use virtual reality (VR) technology within the metaverse to simulate wildlife habitats and behaviour for research and education.

v) Eco-Tourism Initiatives: Eco-tourism operators can offer virtual eco-tours, allowing users to experience and appreciate natural wonders, remote landscapes, and endangered species without physical impact.

vi) Sustainable Lifestyle Simulations: Users can engage in simulations within the metaverse to practice sustainable living, make eco-friendly choices, and understand the environmental consequences of their actions.

vii) Virtual Reforestation Projects: Environmental organisations can host virtual reforestation projects, enabling users to participate in tree-planting initiatives and track the impact of their contributions.

Environmental Impact Assessment: Architects and urban planners can use the metaverse for virtual ecological impact assessments, helping design sustainable and eco-friendly cities and infrastructure.

1. Virtual Marine Conservation: Marine biologists and conservationists can study and protect marine ecosystems through VR simulations and educational programs within the metaverse.

2. Virtual Clean-Up Initiatives: Users can participate in virtual clean-up events, removing digital representations of pollution and waste from virtual environments while learning about real-world clean-up efforts.

3. Green Technology Showcases: Companies developing sustainable technologies can showcase their innovations within the metaverse, raising awareness about eco-friendly solutions.

4. Environmental Policy and Advocacy: Environmental advocacy groups can host virtual conferences and meetings within the metaverse to discuss and advocate for environmental policies and conservation strategies.

5. Virtual Wildlife Conservation Centers: Users can explore virtual wildlife conservation centres, interact with endangered animals in digital habitats, and learn about conservation efforts to protect these species.

6. Carbon Footprint Calculators: Users can access the Metaverse's carbon footprint calculators and tools to measure their environmental impact and receive recommendations for reducing emissions.

7. Virtual Conservation Fundraising: Environmental organisations can host virtual fundraising events and campaigns within the metaverse to support conservation initiatives and projects.

The metaverse's immersive and educational capabilities make it a powerful tool for promoting environmental awareness, engaging people in conservation efforts, and fostering a deeper understanding of the natural world. The metaverse will likely become a vital platform for addressing global environmental challenges as technology evolves.

LEGAL AND GOVERNANCE

The metaverse presents opportunities and challenges in legal and governance systems. Here are current and potential applications of the metaverse in legal and governance:

Current Applications:

i) Digital Laws and Regulations: Some metaverse platforms have implemented rules and regulations governing user behaviour, transactions, and virtual property rights.

ii) Intellectual Property Protection: Intellectual property (IP) laws are applied within the metaverse to protect digital assets, including virtual art, designs, and content.

iii) Virtual Courts: In some metaverse environments, virtual courts or dispute resolution mechanisms exist to address conflicts and enforce community rules.

iv) Virtual Property Rights: Users in the metaverse have property rights over their virtual assets, protected by the platform's terms of service and legal agreements.

Potential Applications:

i) Metaverse Legal Frameworks: Legal experts can develop comprehensive legal frameworks tailored explicitly to the metaverse, addressing issues like virtual property rights, digital contracts, and disputes.

ii) Virtual Citizenship: Users could be offered virtual citizenship within specific metaverse communities, each governed by its rules and regulations.

iii) Digital Identity and Privacy: The metaverse can implement advanced digital identity and privacy protections, allowing users to control their data and identity within virtual spaces.

iv) Smart Contracts and Legal Automation: Smart contracts within the metaverse can automate legal processes, such as transactions, agreements, and contract enforcement.

v) Virtual Law Firms: Law firms specialising in metaverse-related legal matters can provide legal advice and representation to individuals and businesses operating within virtual environments.

vi) Blockchain-Based Legal Records: Legal records, contracts, and agreements can be stored on blockchain platforms within the metaverse, ensuring transparency and immutability.

vii) Metaverse Arbitration Services: Arbitration services within the metaverse can offer efficient and cost-effective dispute resolution for virtual conflicts and transactions.

viii) Virtual Government and Governance Models: Metaverse platforms can experiment with virtual governments and governance models, allowing users to participate in decision-making processes for platform rules and regulations.

ix) Cross-Platform Legal Standards: The metaverse may require cross-platform legal standards and interoperability agreements to ensure consistent governance and legal protections.

x) Legal Education and Training: Virtual law schools and training programs can prepare professionals to navigate metaverse-related legal challenges.

xi) Environmental and Property Rights: As virtual real estate becomes more valuable, legal frameworks will be needed to address issues like environmental conservation, zoning regulations, and property disputes within the metaverse.

xii) Virtual Law Enforcement: Metaverse platforms may establish virtual law enforcement agencies to enforce rules and regulations, investigate virtual crimes, and maintain order.

xiii) Consumer Protections: Legal frameworks within the metaverse can include consumer protection laws to safeguard users from fraud, scams, and unfair business practices.

xiv) Metaverse Taxation: Governments may implement virtual taxation policies to collect revenue from economic activities within the metaverse, requiring new tax regulations and enforcement mechanisms.

xv) Legal Research and Knowledge Sharing: Virtual law libraries and knowledge-sharing platforms can help legal professionals access resources and collaborate on metaverse-related legal cases and issues.

The metaverse's rapid growth and complexity present unique legal challenges and opportunities. Legal experts, governments, and metaverse platforms must work together to develop robust legal and governance systems that protect user rights, ensure fairness, and promote trust within virtual environments. As the metaverse evolves, it will require ongoing legal innovation and adaptation.

TRANSPORTATION

The metaverse has the potential to revolutionise transportation in various ways, offering new opportunities for travel, mobility, and logistical solutions. Here are current and potential applications of the metaverse in vehicles:

Current Applications:

i) Virtual Travel Experiences: Some metaverse platforms offer virtual travel experiences, allowing users to explore digital replicas of real-world destinations and transportation modes.

ii) Virtual Transport Simulation: Transportation professionals use the metaverse for simulation and training purposes, such as pilot training, route planning, and traffic management.

Potential Applications:

i) Immersive Virtual Travel: The metaverse can provide highly immersive virtual travel experiences, allowing users to explore destinations, historical eras, and fantasy worlds virtually.

ii) Virtual Public Transportation: Cities can create virtual public transportation systems within the metaverse, offering users a virtual subway or bus experience to navigate virtual cityscapes.

iii) Autonomous Vehicle Testing: Autonomous vehicle manufacturers can use the metaverse for safe and realistic testing of self-driving cars, trucks, and drones in diverse virtual environments.

iv) Digital Twin Cities: Urban planners and architects can create digital twin cities within the metaverse, allowing them to model and simulate transportation infrastructure, traffic patterns, and urban development.

v) Virtual Mobility Services: Virtual mobility-as-a-service (MaaS) platforms within the metaverse can provide users access to various virtual transportation options, from horse-drawn carriages to futuristic spacecraft.

vi) Virtual Travel Agencies: Travel agencies can offer virtual travel services, enabling users to plan and book virtual vacations, complete with virtual transportation and accommodations.

vii) Transportation Information Portals: Metaverse platforms can serve as information portals for real-world transportation, offering users real-time updates on public transit schedules, traffic conditions, and flight information.

viii) Virtual Airport Experiences: Users can navigate virtual airports, complete with security checks, boarding procedures, and virtual flights to global destinations.

ix) Ridesharing and Carpooling: Users can participate in virtual ridesharing and carpooling services within the metaverse, reducing the environmental impact of transportation.

x) Transportation for Individuals with Disabilities: Virtual transportation options can be designed to cater specifically to individuals with disabilities, offering accessible and inclusive mobility solutions.

xi) Virtual Cargo Transport: Companies can use the metaverse for virtual cargo transport and logistics, optimising supply chains and delivery routes.

xii) Sustainable Transportation Campaigns: Environmental organisations can launch virtual campaigns within the metaverse to promote sustainable transportation choices, such as cycling, electric vehicles, and public transit.

xiii) Virtual Travel Communities: Users can join virtual communities within the metaverse, sharing travel stories, recommendations, and transportation tips.

xiv) Transportation Safety Training: Transportation professionals can undergo virtual training and simulations within the metaverse, enhancing their skills and preparedness for real-world scenarios.

xv) Transportation Data Analytics: Researchers and policymakers can use metaverse-based data analytics tools to analyse transportation data, improve traffic management, and plan future infrastructure needs.

The metaverse offers the transportation industry a platform for innovation, education, and user engagement. By leveraging virtual environments and technologies, transportation professionals can explore new possibilities for sustainable, efficient, and inclusive mobility solutions.

VIRTUAL EMPLOYMENT OPPORTUNITIES IN THE METAVERSE

TYPES OF VIRTUAL EMPLOYMENT

Virtual employment opportunities encompass a wide range of job types and industries. As technology advances and remote work becomes more prevalent, the variety of virtual job options continues to grow. Here are some common types of virtual employment opportunities:

Remote Office Jobs:

> **Customer Support Representatives**: Providing customer service and support remotely via phone, email, or chat.

> **Administrative Assistants**: Managing tasks such as scheduling, data entry, and document management from a home office.

> **Data Entry Clerks**: Input and managed data remotely in various databases and systems.

> **Virtual Assistants**: Remotely providing administrative, scheduling, and personal support to clients and businesses.

Digital Marketing and Communications:

> **Digital Marketers**: Managing online advertising campaigns, social media marketing, SEO, and content creation.
> **Content Writers and Bloggers**: Creating written content for websites, blogs, and marketing materials.
> **Social Media Managers**: Managing and curating social media profiles and content for businesses and organisations.
> **Email Marketers**: Creating and managing email marketing campaigns for businesses.

Information Technology and Development:

> **Software Developers**: Coding, testing, and developing software applications and websites.
> **IT Support Specialists**: Providing technical support and troubleshooting for hardware and software issues remotely.
> **Web Designers and Developers**: Creating and maintaining websites, web applications, and user interfaces.
> **Cybersecurity Specialists**: Protecting digital assets and networks from cyber threats and attacks.

Creative and Design:

> **Graphic Designers**: Creating visual content, including logos, graphics, and branding materials.
> **Illustrators**: Producing digital illustrations and artwork for various media.
> **Video Editors**: Edit and produce video content for online platforms and marketing.
> **3D Artists and Animators**: Creating 3D models and animations for gaming, film, and advertising.

Education and Online Teaching:

> **Online Teachers and Tutors**: Educating students remotely in various subjects and skills.

> **eLearning Course Developers**: Creating and managing online courses and educational materials.
> **Virtual Language Instructors**: Teaching languages to students worldwide through virtual platforms.
> **Online Educational Consultants**: Providing guidance and support to educational institutions transitioning to online learning.

Healthcare and Telemedicine:

> **Telehealth Professionals**: Remotely offering medical consultations, therapy sessions, and healthcare services.
> **Medical Transcriptionists**: Transcribing medical records and notes from audio recordings.
> **Healthcare IT Specialists**: Managing healthcare information systems and technology remotely.
> **Online Nutritionists and Health Coaches**: Providing dietary and wellness guidance via virtual sessions.

Consulting and Professional Services:

> **Management Consultants**: Offering business strategy and management advice to clients remotely.
> **Financial Consultants**: Providing financial planning, analysis, and advisory services online.
> **Legal Consultants**: Remotely offering legal advice, contract reviews, and legal research.
> **HR and Talent Consultants**: Assisting businesses with HR processes, talent acquisition, and employee management virtually.

Freelancing and Gig Work:

> **Freelance Writers**: Writing articles, blog posts, copywriting, and other content on a project basis.
> **Freelance Designers**: Providing graphic design, web design, and other creative services as independent contractors.
> **Freelance Developers**: Coding, programming, and web development on a project-by-project basis.
> **Rideshare and Food Delivery Drivers**: Gig workers using platforms

like Uber, Lyft, and DoorDash to offer transportation and food delivery services.

Virtual Sales and E-commerce:

> **Sales Representatives**: Selling products or services remotely through online platforms and virtual meetings.
> **E-commerce Managers**: Managing online stores, product listings, and e-commerce operations.
> **Affiliate Marketers**: Promoting products and earning commissions through online affiliate marketing programs.

Research and Data Analysis:

> **Market Researchers**: Conducting market research and analysis for businesses remotely.
> **Data Analysts**: Analyzing data, generating reports, and providing data-driven insights.
> **Academic Researchers**: Engaging in research projects and literary studies from home.

These are just a few examples of the diverse virtual employment opportunities in today's digital economy. The key to finding the right virtual job is identifying your skills, interests, and career goals and exploring options that align with your strengths and preferences.

JOB ROLES AND RESPONSIBILITIES IN THE METAVERSE

The metaverse is an evolving concept, and job responsibilities within it are still developing and evolving. As technology advances and the metaverse grows, new career opportunities and responsibilities emerge. Here are some potential job responsibilities and roles in the metaverse:

1. Metaverse Architect:

Responsibilities: Metaverse architects are responsible for designing and constructing the virtual landscapes, structures, and environments that comprise the metaverse. They must consider user experience, spatial design, and interactivity. Architects collaborate with developers and artists to bring virtual spaces to life.

2. Virtual Reality Developer:

Responsibilities: Virtual reality (VR) developers create immersive experiences within the metaverse. They write code, develop 3D models, and design interactive elements. VR developers may work on gaming, education, training, or entertainment applications.

3. Metaverse UI/UX Designer:

Responsibilities: UI/UX designers in the metaverse focus on user interfaces and experiences. They design virtual interfaces that allow users to navigate, interact, and communicate within the metaverse. This role requires a deep understanding of 3D design principles and user behaviour in virtual environments.

4. Metaverse Community Manager:

Responsibilities: Community managers are responsible for building, growing, and maintaining virtual communities within the metaverse. They facilitate discussions, manage online forums, resolve conflicts, and ensure a positive and engaging user experience.

5. Metaverse Event Coordinator:

Responsibilities: Event coordinators plan and organise virtual events, conferences, and gatherings within the metaverse. They handle logistics, coordinate speakers or performers, manage schedules, and oversee the technical aspects of virtual events.

6. Metaverse Marketer:

Responsibilities: Metaverse marketers promote metaverse platforms, experiences, and content to a broad audience. They use digital marketing strategies, social media, and advertising campaigns to attract users and generate interest in metaverse offerings.

7. Virtual Goods Designer:

Responsibilities: Virtual goods designers create digital assets and items users can buy, trade, or use within the metaverse. This may include clothing, accessories, virtual real estate, and unique digital collectables, often sold as NFTs (Non-Fungible Tokens).

8. Metaverse Data Analyst:

Responsibilities: Data analysts in the metaverse collect and analyse user data to gain insights into user behaviours and trends. They use this data to inform decision-making, improve user experiences, and optimise metaverse platforms.

9. Metaverse Security Specialist:

Responsibilities: Security specialists protect metaverse platforms from cyber threats, unauthorised access, and fraud. They implement security measures, conduct audits, and respond to security incidents to safeguard virtual environments and user data.

10. Metaverse Lawyer or Legal Consultant:

Responsibilities: Legal professionals specialising in the metaverse offer legal advice on various issues, such as intellectual property rights, virtual property disputes, and compliance with metaverse regulations. They draft contracts and provide legal representation as needed.

11. Metaverse Educator or Trainer:

Responsibilities: Educators and trainers in the metaverse develop and deliver educational content, tutorials, and training programs. They use virtual platforms to teach skills, disseminate knowledge, and enhance users' understanding of metaverse technologies.

12. Metaverse Healthcare Provider:

Responsibilities: Healthcare providers offer virtual healthcare services, consultations, and therapy sessions within the metaverse. They may diagnose, treat, and provide medical advice to users in virtual environments, leveraging telemedicine technology.

These roles represent just a fraction of the potential career paths in the metaverse, and many other specialised positions are emerging as the metaverse evolves. It's important to note that the metaverse job landscape is highly interdisciplinary, drawing from fields such as technology, design, social sciences, law, and healthcare. As the metaverse becomes more integrated into our lives, the demand for skilled professionals in these roles is expected to increase significantly.

ADVANTAGES AND CHALLENGES OF VIRTUAL EMPLOYMENT

Virtual employment, alternatively referred to as remote work, telecommuting, or teleworking, has many benefits, although it has its accompanying difficulties. Let us delve into both facets with greater depth:

Advantages of Virtual Employment:

1. Flexibility:

> **Work Hours:** Virtual employment offers the flexibility to set one's work hours, making it easier to accommodate personal commitments or preferred schedules.
> **Location Independence:** Employees can work from anywhere with an internet connection, allowing them to choose a workspace that suits their needs.

2. Cost Savings:

> **Reduced Commuting Costs:** Virtual employees save money on commuting expenses, including fuel, public transportation fares, and vehicle maintenance.

> **Lower Work-Related Expenses:** Employees can save on work attire, lunches, and daily expenses associated with office-based work.

3. Access to a Global Talent Pool:

Employers can tap into a vast talent pool, not limited by geographic boundaries, to hire individuals with specialised skills and experiences worldwide.
This diversity can lead to increased creativity, innovation, and problem-solving within the organisation.

4. Increased Productivity:

Many virtual employees report higher productivity levels when working remotely due to reduced office distractions, quieter work environments, and the ability to customise their workspaces.
The time saved from commuting can also be redirected towards work-related tasks.

5. Environmental Benefits:

Virtual employment contributes to reduced carbon emissions and environmental impact by decreasing the number of daily commutes.
Reduced office energy consumption and waste production further contribute to environmental sustainability.

6. Improved Work-Life Balance:

Virtual employment allows for better work-life balance, enabling employees to spend more time with family and pursue personal interests and hobbies.
This balance can lead to reduced stress and increased overall job satisfaction.

7. Customised Workspaces:

Employees can create personalised workspaces at home, optimising comfort and productivity.

Customisation extends to factors like lighting, temperature, and ergonomic furniture.

8. Leveraging Technology:

Virtual employment relies on advanced technology and communication tools like video conferencing, project management software, and collaboration platforms.
These tools enhance remote collaboration, information sharing, and efficiency.

9. Business Continuity:

Virtual employment provides business continuity, allowing organisations to maintain operations during unforeseen disruptions like natural disasters or public health emergencies.

Challenges of Virtual Employment:

1. Isolation and Loneliness:

> Remote employees may experience feelings of isolation and loneliness due to reduced face-to-face interactions with colleagues.
> The absence of in-person social interactions can affect team cohesion and morale.

2. Communication Challenges:

> Virtual employment introduces communication challenges, including misunderstandings arising from text-based communication, delayed responses, and the lack of non-verbal cues.
> Effective communication becomes crucial, often requiring more precise written communication and proactive engagement.

3. Work-Life Boundaries:

> Remote employees may need help establishing clear boundaries between work and personal life. Without the physical separation of an

office, it can be challenging to "log off" from work.
> This can lead to potential burnout, as employees may feel pressure to be available around the clock.

4. Distractions at Home:

> Home environments can be distracting, with family members, pets, or household chores competing for attention during work hours.
> Maintaining focus and concentration can be challenging.

5. Technical Issues:

> Virtual employment relies on technology, making employees vulnerable to technical glitches, internet outages, and software problems.
> These issues can disrupt work and cause frustration.

6. Security Concerns:

> Protecting sensitive company data and information can be more challenging in virtual employment. Cybersecurity risks, including data breaches, phishing attacks, and malware, must be addressed.
> Employees need to follow stringent security protocols and practices.

7. Difficulty in Monitoring and Managing Teams:

> Managers may find it challenging to supervise and monitor remote teams. Ensuring accountability, tracking progress, and fostering teamwork requires innovative approaches and communication.

8. Lack of Access to Resources:

> Remote employees may have access to different resources and equipment than in-office workers, potentially affecting their effectiveness and collaboration ability.

9. Career Development:

> Virtual employees may perceive limited opportunities for career

advancement, networking, and mentorship compared to their in-office counterparts.

> It may require additional effort to build professional relationships and seek career growth.

10. Time Zone Differences:

> Collaborating across different time zones can lead to scheduling conflicts, delayed responses, and difficulties in arranging real-time meetings and discussions.

11. Dependence on Self-Motivation:

> Virtual employment relies on self-motivation and discipline. Employees must manage their time effectively, meet deadlines, and remain productive without direct supervision.

While virtual employment offers significant advantages, addressing the associated challenges is essential for employees and employers to maximise the benefits of remote work. Many organisations are adopting strategies, policies, and technologies to overcome these challenges and create successful virtual work environments.

LABOUR LAW FRAMEWORK FOR THE METAVERSE

Establishing a legal structure about labour within the metaverse is a multifaceted and dynamic endeavour that necessitates a meticulous examination of current legislation, the distinctive characteristics of virtual employment, and the difficulties posed by this nascent technology. The following is an analysis of the fundamental components of establishing a labour law framework for the metaverse.

Review of Existing Labour Laws:

i) **Comprehensive Legal Assessment:** Conduct a thorough assessment of labour laws in jurisdictions with prevalent metaverse work. Analyse how existing labour laws apply to virtual employment, remote work, and virtual environments.

ii) Identification of Relevant Laws: Identify the specific labour laws and regulations applicable to metaverse workers. This includes laws related to employment contracts, minimum wage, working hours, employee benefits, and occupational health and safety.

iii) Adaptation to Digital Environments: Recognize that traditional labour laws were primarily designed for in-person employment. Assess how these laws can be adapted to address the unique characteristics and challenges of the metaverse, such as remote work arrangements, virtual property rights, and digital identity.

Applicability to the Metaverse:

i) Determining Relevance: Examine which aspects of existing labour laws are still relevant and essential in virtual work within the metaverse. For example, fundamental rights such as non-discrimination and equal pay remain applicable.

ii) New Challenges: Acknowledge that the metaverse introduces new challenges that traditional labour laws may not fully cover. These challenges include defining virtual property rights, establishing digital identity protection, and addressing remote work issues.

iii) Balancing Traditional and Virtual: Strive to balance applying traditional labour laws and creating new regulations tailored to the metaverse. In some cases, existing laws may provide a foundation upon which specialised metaverse labour laws can be built.

Identification of Gaps and Challenges:

i) Virtual Property Rights: Recognize the challenges related to virtual property rights within the metaverse. Develop mechanisms for determining ownership, transfer, and protection of virtual assets and property.

ii) Digital Identity Protection: Address the protection of digital identities in virtual environments, ensuring that metaverse workers' personal information is secure and their privacy is respected.

iii) Cross-Border Work: Consider the complexities of employing workers in different countries within the metaverse. This includes navigating tax laws, immigration requirements, and legal frameworks that vary across borders.

iv) Worker Classification: Define clear criteria for classifying metaverse workers as either independent contractors or employees, as this classification has significant implications for benefits and legal protections.

v) Virtual Harassment and Discrimination: Develop policies and regulations to combat harassment, discrimination, and other harmful behaviours in virtual environments, aiming to provide a safe and inclusive metaverse work environment.

vi) Workplace Safety: Establish guidelines and regulations to ensure the safety and well-being of metaverse workers, including measures to prevent virtual harm or abuse and promote mental health support.

Need for Specialized Labour Regulations:

i) Tailored to Metaverse: Recognize that specialised labour regulations may be necessary to address the unique characteristics of the metaverse. These regulations should specifically be designed to protect the rights and interests of metaverse workers.

ii) Virtual Property Rights: Develop regulations that define and protect virtual property rights, ensuring that metaverse workers have legal ownership and control over their virtual assets.

iii) Digital Identity Protection: Enact regulations safeguarding digital identities and personal information within the metaverse, including data privacy and cybersecurity provisions.

iv) Dispute Resolution: Create mechanisms for dispute resolution within the metaverse, including virtual courts or arbitration services, to address conflicts that may arise in digital workspaces.

v) Employment Contracts: Establish guidelines for virtual employment contracts, including terms and conditions, compensation, and dispute resolution clauses, taking into account the unique nature of virtual work.

International Collaboration:

i) Multilateral Agreements: Encourage collaboration among countries and regions to establish multilateral agreements or standards for metaverse labour regulations. This can help harmonise legal frameworks and facilitate cross-border virtual employment.

ii) International Organizations: Engage with international organisations, such as the United Nations or the International Labour Organization (ILO), to coordinate efforts in addressing global challenges related to metaverse work.

iii) Global Best Practices: Explore and adopt international best practices in metaverse labour regulation, drawing from successful approaches worldwide.

Ongoing Adaptation:

i) Regular Reviews: Commit to regular reviews and updates of metaverse labour regulations to ensure they remain relevant and effective in a rapidly evolving technological landscape.

ii) Flexibility: Design regulations with built-in flexibility to adapt to emerging technologies, changing work practices, and new challenges that may arise in the metaverse.

iii) Feedback Mechanisms: Establish mechanisms for feedback from metaverse workers, employers, and other stakeholders to improve and refine labour regulations continuously.

Creating a comprehensive labour law framework for the metaverse requires a multi-pronged approach that combines elements of existing labour laws with specialised regulations tailored to virtual work environments. International cooperation and adaptability are crucial to addressing the unique challenges and opportunities presented by the metaverse in labour law.

FUNDAMENTAL RIGHTS APPLICABLE TO METAVERSE WORKERS

Metaverse workers are entitled to certain fundamental rights and protections like any other workers. While the specific application of these rights within the metaverse may require some adaptation, the core principles remain relevant. Here are fundamental rights applicable to metaverse workers:

1. Right to Fair Compensation:

> Metaverse workers have the right to receive fair and equitable compensation for their work, including wages, salaries, bonuses, and

other forms of remuneration.
> In the metaverse, this right extends to virtual economies and digital transactions, ensuring workers are compensated appropriately for their contributions, whether in virtual or real-world currency.

2. Right to Equal Treatment and Non-Discrimination:

> Metaverse workers should not be subjected to discrimination based on factors such as race, gender, age, religion, sexual orientation, or disability.
> This right also applies to virtual spaces, ensuring all individuals are treated equally and respectfully within digital work environments.

3. Right to a Safe and Healthy Workplace:

> Metaverse workers have the right to a safe and healthy work environment. This extends to both physical workplaces and virtual spaces.
> Employers should ensure the well-being of metaverse workers, addressing digital safety concerns, preventing harassment, and promoting mental health support.

4. Right to Privacy and Data Protection:

> Metaverse workers maintain the right to privacy, even in digital environments. Personal data should be handled carefully and in compliance with data protection regulations.
> Employers and platforms operating within the metaverse should safeguard the personal information of workers and users.

5. Right to Freedom of Association and Collective Bargaining:

> Metaverse workers can form associations, unions, or other organised groups to collectively represent their interests and negotiate with employers.
> This right extends to virtual spaces, allowing workers to organise and advocate for fair working conditions and compensation.

6. Right to Intellectual Property:

> Workers in the metaverse often create intellectual property, including digital assets, designs, and content. They have the right to own and control these creations, subject to contractual agreements.
> Employers should respect the intellectual property rights of metaverse workers and specify ownership rights in employment contracts.

7. Right to Fair Working Hours and Rest:

> Metaverse workers should not be subjected to excessively long working hours that could lead to burnout or health issues.
> The right to rest and leisure also applies to virtual work, ensuring workers have time to disconnect from their digital tasks and maintain a healthy work-life balance.

8. Right to Freedom of Expression and Opinion:

> Metaverse workers retain the right to freedom of expression and opinion, provided they do not engage in harmful or abusive behaviours.
> This right allows workers to express their thoughts, ideas, and concerns within digital workspaces, contributing to open and constructive communication.

9. Right to Fair Termination and Dispute Resolution:

> Metaverse workers have the right to fair and just termination procedures, including clear reasons for termination and the opportunity to dispute unfair dismissals.
> Employers should establish mechanisms for dispute resolution within the metaverse, ensuring that conflicts are addressed impartially and effectively.

10. Right to Training and Professional Development:

> Metaverse workers have the right to access training, education, and opportunities for professional development to enhance their skills and career prospects.

> Employers should support metaverse workers' continuous growth and skill-building, adapting training programs to meet virtual work demands.

These fundamental rights protect metaverse workers' well-being, dignity, and ownership. Employers, governments, and regulatory bodies should work together to ensure that these rights are respected and upheld within the dynamic and evolving landscape of the metaverse. Additionally, ongoing discussions and adaptations may be necessary to address emerging challenges and opportunities in the virtual work environment.

HEALTH AND SAFETY CONSIDERATIONS IN VIRTUAL WORK ENVIRONMENTS

Health and safety considerations in virtual work environments are crucial for ensuring workers' well-being within the metaverse or other digital spaces. While the risks in virtual environments may differ from those in traditional workplaces, they are nonetheless significant. Here are essential health and safety considerations for virtual work environments:

1. Digital Ergonomics:

i) **Workspace Setup**: Encourage metaverse workers to set up their virtual workspaces ergonomically, considering factors like screen placement, chair comfort, and keyboard and mouse positioning.
ii) **Preventing Digital Strain**: Prolonged virtual reality (VR) or augmented reality (AR) headsets can cause discomfort. Workers should take regular breaks to avoid digital eye strain and motion sickness.

2. Mental Health and Well-being:

i) **Isolation and Loneliness**: Acknowledge the potential for isolation and loneliness in virtual work environments. Encourage social interaction and provide opportunities for team bonding.
ii) **Work-Life Balance**: Emphasize the importance of maintaining a healthy work-life balance. Encourage regular breaks, set boundaries, and discourage overworking.

3. Virtual Harassment and Bullying:

i) Anti-Harassment Policies: Implement and enforce anti-harassment and anti-bullying policies within virtual environments. Ensure that workers know how to report and address such issues.

ii) Moderation and Reporting Tools: Provide tools and mechanisms for users to report harassment or inappropriate behaviour. Implement moderation features to maintain a safe environment.

4. Cybersecurity and Data Privacy:

i) Data Protection: Safeguard personal and sensitive data within virtual workspaces. Implement encryption, access controls, and robust cybersecurity measures to protect against data breaches.

ii) Training and Awareness: Train metaverse workers on cybersecurity best practices, including identifying phishing attempts and maintaining secure online behaviours.

5. Virtual Property Rights:

i) Ownership and Control: Ensure workers understand their rights and responsibilities concerning virtual property and assets within the metaverse. Establish clear guidelines for the license and transfer of virtual assets.

6. Workplace Safety in Virtual Reality:

i) Physical Safety: For VR headset workers, ensure a safe physical environment free from obstacles or hazards that could lead to accidents.

ii) Limiting Physical Strain: Be mindful of the potential for physical strain and discomfort when using VR equipment for extended periods. Encourage users to take regular breaks and perform stretches.

7. Technical Support and Training:

i) Technical Assistance: Provide technical support for metaverse workers to address hardware or software issues promptly. This can reduce frustration and improve productivity.

ii) Training: Offer comprehensive training on how to use virtual environments and tools effectively and safely.

8. Emergency Preparedness:

i) Virtual Emergency Procedures: Establish emergency procedures within virtual work environments, such as evacuation plans or protocols for handling virtual emergencies (e.g., in-game incidents).
ii) Communication Channels: Ensure workers can quickly communicate with colleagues and supervisors in emergencies or urgent situations.

9. Legal and Ethical Considerations:

i) Compliance with Regulations: Comply with regulations and laws about virtual work, data protection, and cybersecurity.
ii) Ethical Behaviour: Promote ethical behaviour and decision-making within virtual environments, reinforcing respect for others' rights and property.

10. Regular Assessments and Feedback:

i) Health and Safety Audits: Conduct regular assessments and audits of virtual work environments to identify and mitigate potential health and safety risks.
ii) Feedback Mechanisms: Establish mechanisms for workers to provide feedback on health and safety concerns and improvements.

It's essential for organisations and employers to actively prioritise health and safety in virtual work environments, just as they do in traditional workplaces. This includes providing resources, training, and support to metaverse workers to ensure their physical and mental well-being while operating within digital spaces. Regularly reviewing and updating health and safety protocols is crucial in an ever-evolving technological landscape.

COLLECTIVE BARGAINING AND UNIONIZATION IN THE METAVERSE

Collective bargaining and unionisation in the metaverse are emerging issues that raise unique challenges and opportunities for workers and employers. These traditional labour concepts are gradually extending into virtual work environments. Here's an exploration of collective bargaining and unionisation in the metaverse:

Collective Bargaining in the Metaverse:

i) Definition: Collective bargaining involves negotiations between workers (often represented by labour unions) and employers to determine the terms and conditions of employment, such as wages, benefits, working hours, and workplace rules.

ii) Virtual Workplaces: In the metaverse, collective bargaining can occur within virtual workplaces, where avatars or digital representations of workers, union representatives, and employers engage in negotiations

iii) Digital Contracts: Collective bargaining agreements in the metaverse may involve the creation of digital contracts that specify terms of employment and virtual property rights within the digital workspace.

Unionisation in the Metaverse:

i) Formation of Virtual Unions: Workers in the metaverse can form virtual unions or labour organisations to represent their interests and advocate for improved working conditions collectively.

ii) Membership: Workers can become members of virtual unions, just as they would in traditional labour unions. These unions may be specific to particular metaverse platforms or industries.

iii) Collective Voice: Virtual unions give workers a voice to negotiate with employers, address concerns, and seek improvements in virtual workspaces.

Unique Challenges and Considerations:

i) Digital Identity: Protecting metaverse workers' digital identities and privacy is paramount, especially when they engage in collective bargaining or unionisation activities.

ii) Virtual Property Rights: Defining and protecting virtual property rights within collective bargaining agreements is essential, as these agreements may involve the ownership of digital assets and resources.

iii) Cross-Border Issues: The metaverse is open to more than geographical boundaries, which can complicate collective bargaining and unionisation efforts when workers are spread across different countries.

iv) Virtual Harassment: Addressing virtual harassment and bullying within virtual unions is crucial to ensure a safe and respectful environment for all participants.

Benefits of Collective Bargaining and Unionization in the Metaverse:

i) Improved Worker Rights: Collective bargaining and unionisation can establish clear employment terms, protection against unfair treatment, and access to collective benefits.

ii) Advocacy and Representation: Virtual unions can advocate for the interests of metaverse workers and represent their concerns to employers and metaverse platform operators.

iii) Fair Compensation: Negotiations can lead to modest compensation structures, including wages, bonuses, and benefits, that reflect the contributions of metaverse workers.

iv) Safety and Well-being: Unions can play a role in ensuring the safety and well-being of workers within virtual environments, addressing issues of harassment or discrimination.

Legal and Regulatory Considerations:

i) Recognition: Determining whether virtual unions are legally recognised entities within the metaverse or if they need to operate under real-world legal frameworks.

ii) Cross-Border Regulations: Addressing legal and regulatory complexities when workers from different countries engage in collective bargaining and unionisation efforts within the metaverse.

iii) Data Privacy: Complying with data privacy and cybersecurity regulations to protect union members' personal information and data.

Ethical and Cultural Aspects:

i) Ethical Behaviour: Encouraging ethical behaviour and respectful communication within virtual unions to maintain a positive and constructive working environment.

ii) Cultural Sensitivity: Recognizing the diversity of metaverse workers and the potential for cultural differences in understanding and participating in collective bargaining and unionisation activities.

Collective bargaining and unionisation in the metaverse will likely evolve as virtual work becomes more prevalent. Both workers and employers will need to adapt to these new digital landscapes, considering the unique challenges and opportunities they present while upholding the rights and well-being of all participants. Legal and regulatory frameworks will also play a crucial role in shaping the future of labour relations in the metaverse.

ROLE OF LABOUR UNIONS IN REPRESENTING METAVERSE WORKERS' INTERESTS

Labour unions play a critical role in representing the interests of metaverse workers, just as they do for traditional workers in physical workplaces. Their role in the metaverse encompasses various functions and responsibilities to ensure that metaverse workers are protected, empowered, and fairly treated. Here's an overview of the role of labour unions in representing metaverse workers' interests:

Negotiating Employment Terms:

i) Collective Bargaining: Labour unions negotiate with employers and metaverse platform operators to establish fair employment terms and conditions. This includes agreements on wages, benefits, working hours, and workplace rules specific to the metaverse.
ii) Digital Contracts: Unions may work to develop digital contracts that outline the terms of employment and virtual property rights within virtual workspaces.

Advocacy and Representation:

i) Voice for Workers: Unions serve as a collective voice for metaverse workers, ensuring their concerns, needs, and grievances are effectively communicated to employers and platform operators.
ii) Conflict Resolution: Unions advocate for workers in disputes with

employers, helping to resolve conflicts and reach fair solutions, whether related to compensation, virtual property, or workplace safety.

Safety and Well-being:

i) **Virtual Workspace Safety**: Unions work to ensure the safety and well-being of metaverse workers within virtual environments. This includes addressing issues of harassment and discrimination and providing a respectful digital work environment.

ii) **Mental Health Support**: Unions may advocate for mental health support and resources for metaverse workers who may face unique stressors and challenges associated with virtual work.

Legal and Regulatory Compliance:

i) **Data Privacy**: Unions may advocate for and monitor compliance with privacy regulations to protect metaverse workers' personal information and data.

ii) **Cybersecurity**: Addressing cybersecurity concerns and advocating for measures to safeguard workers against cyber threats, including data breaches or virtual property theft.

Education and Training:

i) **Skills Development**: Unions can facilitate training and skills development programs specific to metaverse work, helping workers enhance their abilities and adapt to evolving technologies.

ii) **Awareness**: Unions raise awareness among metaverse workers about their rights, responsibilities, and the potential risks and benefits associated with virtual work.

Cross-Border Representation:

i) **Global Workforce**: As the metaverse transcends geographical boundaries, unions may represent the interests of metaverse workers from different countries and advocate for cross-border labour rights and protections.

Advocacy for Fair Compensation:

i) Wage Equality: Unions ensure that metaverse workers receive fair compensation commensurate with their contributions, skills, and the value they bring to the virtual workspace.

Promoting Ethical Behaviour:

i) Ethical Conduct: Unions promote ethical behaviour and respectful communication within virtual environments, fostering a positive and inclusive working culture.

Influence on Platform Policies:

i) Policy Advocacy: Unions can influence platform policies and practices by discussing with metaverse platform operators and advocating for worker-friendly policies and protections.

Labour unions play a crucial role in ensuring that metaverse workers are protected and have a voice in shaping the future of work within virtual environments. They help maintain a balance of power between workers and employers or platform operators, advocating for fair treatment, rights, and equitable compensation within the rapidly evolving landscape of the metaverse.

POTENTIAL MODELS FOR COLLECTIVE REPRESENTATION AND NEGOTIATION

Collective representation and negotiation models for metaverse workers are still evolving due to virtual work environments‘ unique challenges and opportunities. Here are some potential models that can be adapted and explored:

1. Virtual Trade Unions:

Definition: Similar to traditional trade unions, virtual trade unions are organisations formed by metaverse workers to collectively represent their interests and negotiate with employers or platform operators.

Platform Agnostic: These unions are not tied to a specific metaverse platform, allowing them to represent workers across various virtual environments.

Membership-Based: Workers voluntarily become members of these unions to access collective bargaining, advocacy, and support services.

2. Virtual Collective Bargaining Platforms:

Definition: Digital platforms or spaces designed explicitly for collective bargaining and negotiations between metaverse workers and employers or platform operators.

Virtual Meeting Spaces: These platforms can provide virtual meeting rooms where avatars of union representatives and management can convene for negotiations.

Digital Contracts: Agreements reached through these platforms can be recorded as digital contracts, ensuring transparency and accountability.

3. Industry-Specific Guilds:

Definition: Guilds are organisations that bring together metaverse workers from a specific industry or profession. They focus on industry-specific issues and negotiations.

Skill and Industry Focus: Guilds can cater to professionals in game development, virtual architecture, digital art, and more.

Advocacy and Networking: Besides bargaining, they can offer networking opportunities, skill development, and advocacy for industry-specific rights.

4. Decentralised Autonomous Organizations (DAOs):

Definition: DAOs are blockchain-based organisations governed by smart contracts and decentralised decision-making. Metaverse workers can participate in DAOs to collectively represent their interests.

Transparent Decision-Making: DAOs use blockchain technology to ensure decision-making and resource allocation transparency.

Digital Tokens and Assets: DAOs can issue digital tokens or assets as rewards for members' contributions, creating a system of incentives.

5. Cross-Platform Labour Federations:

Definition: Labour federations that unite multiple virtual trade unions or guilds, working together to advocate for the rights of metaverse workers across different platforms.

Coordination and Advocacy: These federations facilitate coordination among member unions, allowing them to share best practices resources and collaborate on advocacy efforts.

Cross-Platform Agreements: They can negotiate cross-platform agreements that establish common standards for virtual work.

6. Government-Supported Initiatives:

Definition: Government agencies or bodies can establish initiatives or councils dedicated explicitly to addressing labour issues in the metaverse.

Regulatory Oversight: These initiatives may have the regulatory authority or serve as advisory bodies, ensuring that labour rights are protected within virtual environments.

Public-Private Partnerships: Collaboration between governments, unions, and industry stakeholders can create effective frameworks for metaverse labour regulation.

7. Collaborative Virtual Spaces:

Definition: Collaborative virtual environments, such as virtual town halls or forums, where metaverse workers, employers, and representatives can engage in open discussions and negotiations.

Transparent Dialogue: These spaces promote transparent and inclusive dialogue, allowing all parties to express their views and concerns.

Mediation and Conflict Resolution: Virtual spaces can include mediation and conflict resolution mechanisms to facilitate agreements.

8. Blockchain-Based Reputation Systems:

Definition: Reputation systems built on blockchain technology can help establish trust and reputation within the metaverse. Workers with solid reputations may have enhanced negotiation power.

Verified Credentials: Blockchain can verify workers' credentials, skills, and experience, providing them with a strong bargaining position.

Negotiation Mediation: Smart contracts on blockchain platforms can facilitate negotiations by automating certain aspects of agreements.

Hybrid Models: Combine elements of the above models to create hybrid approaches that suit the unique needs of metaverse workers and the specific industry or platform in which they operate.

It's important to note that the effectiveness of these models may vary based on factors such as the metaverse platform, the nature of virtual work, and the legal and regulatory environment. Additionally, the evolution of technology and the metaverse may lead to the emergence of new models and approaches for collective representation and negotiation in the future.

COMPLIANCE AND ENFORCEMENT MECHANISMS

Compliance and enforcement mechanisms in the context of metaverse labour regulations are essential to ensure employers and workers adhere to established rules and agreements. These mechanisms help maintain a fair and just working environment within virtual spaces. Here are some compliance and enforcement mechanisms for metaverse labour regulations:

1. Virtual Labour Inspectors:

Monitoring: These inspectors or automated bots continuously monitor virtual workplaces, observing worker activities, employer practices, and adherence to labour laws within the metaverse.

Alerts: If violations or irregularities are detected, virtual labour inspectors can send alerts or notifications to relevant parties, including regulatory bodies.

Real-time Data: Collect and analyse real-time data on working conditions, hours, wages, and any incidents of harassment or discrimination occurring within virtual environments.

2. Digital Compliance Certifications:

Verification Process: Organizations responsible for issuing digital compliance certifications conduct thorough audits and assessments of virtual workplaces to verify compliance with metaverse labour regulations.

Certification Criteria: Establish clear criteria and benchmarks that virtual workplaces must meet to obtain certification, including minimum wage standards, workplace safety measures, and virtual property rights protections.

Validity Period: Certifications may have a limited validity period, requiring virtual workplaces to undergo periodic reviews to maintain their compliant status.

3. Blockchain-Based Smart Contracts:

Automation: Smart contracts on blockchain platforms automatically execute predefined actions based on specific conditions. For instance, they can ensure that workers receive their virtual currency payments immediately upon completing tasks.

Immutable Records: Blockchain records transactions and agreements transparently and tamper-resistantly, providing an immutable record of employment terms and compensation.

Dispute Resolution: Smart contracts can include dispute resolution mechanisms, automatically triggering mediation or arbitration processes when disputes arise.

4. Virtual Dispute Resolution Platforms:

User-Friendly Interfaces: These platforms offer user-friendly interfaces that allow workers and employers to initiate dispute resolution processes within the metaverse quickly.

Mediation and Arbitration: Trained mediators and arbitrators, or AI-driven systems, can facilitate negotiations, helping parties reach mutually acceptable resolutions.

Enforceable Outcomes: Once agreements are reached, intelligent contracts can enforce the agreed-upon outcomes, ensuring compliance with the resolution.

5. In-Game Reporting and Moderation Systems:

Reporting Tools: Metaverse platforms and games can integrate reporting tools that enable users to report violations, harassment, or unethical behaviour directly within the virtual environment.

Responsive Moderation: A team of human moderators or AI algorithms can swiftly review and address reported issues, applying appropriate penalties, warnings, or sanctions.

Transparency: Transparency in the moderation process ensures that actions taken against violators are visible to the community, enhancing trust

6. Cross-Platform Agreements:

Standardisation: Cross-platform agreements aim to standardise labour regulations, virtual property rights, and ethical conduct guidelines across various metaverse platforms.

Enforcement Mechanisms: These agreements may include enforcement mechanisms, such as penalties for platforms that fail to comply with agreed-upon standards.

Regulatory Oversight: Independent bodies or coalitions can oversee the implementation of cross-platform agreements and ensure compliance.

7. International Cooperation and Treaties:

International Frameworks: Countries and regions can collaborate to create international frameworks and treaties addressing cross-border employment within the metaverse.

Consistency: These agreements promote consistent enforcement of labour regulations, making it challenging for entities to evade compliance by operating in different jurisdictions.

Dispute Resolution: International cooperation can establish mechanisms for cross-border dispute resolution and the harmonisation of legal standards.

8. Whistleblower Protection Programs:

Anonymity: Whistleblower protection programs offer a secure platform for workers to report violations anonymously, safeguarding them against potential retaliation.

Legal Safeguards: Legal protections may include provisions for job reinstatement, compensation for damages, or penalties for employers found guilty of retaliation against whistleblowers.

Public Awareness: Programs promote public awareness about the importance of reporting labour violations and encourage a culture of accountability.

9. Government Oversight and Regulation:

Regulatory Authority: Governments can designate regulatory bodies or agencies responsible for overseeing and enforcing metaverse labour regulations.

Auditing and Inspection: Regular audits and inspections can be conducted to ensure compliance with labour laws, with regulatory bodies having the authority to impose fines or sanctions for violations.

Legal Actions: Regulatory bodies can initiate legal actions against entities or individuals that violate metaverse labour regulations.

10. Public Transparency and Reporting:

Published Reports: Virtual workplaces may be required to publish annual or periodic reports detailing their compliance with metaverse labour regulations, including data on wages, virtual property rights, and workplace safety.

Consumer Awareness: Publicizing compliance reports raises consumer awareness, allowing users to make informed choices when engaging with virtual workplaces.

Accountability Pressure: Transparency pressures virtual workplaces to maintain high standards, as violations can result in public scrutiny and reputational damage.

These detailed compliance and enforcement mechanisms are crucial for creating a safe, ethical, and fair metaverse work environment, ensuring that the rights and well-being of metaverse workers are protected and upheld. Implementing these mechanisms can help maintain integrity and trust within the virtual workforce.

ETHICAL CONSIDERATIONS AND FUTURE OUTLOOK

Ethical considerations in the metaverse are vital as this digital space continues to evolve and influence various aspects of society, including work, entertainment, and social interactions. Examining these ethical dimensions is essential for ensuring that the metaverse develops in a way that benefits individuals and communities. Here's a look at some of the key ethical considerations and the future outlook of the metaverse:

Digital Inclusion and Accessibility:

> *Ethical Concern*: Many individuals, particularly those with disabilities and from disadvantaged backgrounds, may face barriers to accessing the metaverse, resulting in digital exclusion.
> *Future Outlook*: Efforts to enhance digital inclusion will likely involve initiatives like affordable internet access, accessible user interfaces, and adaptive technologies to cater to a broader range of users.

Digital Identity and Privacy:

> *Ethical Concern*: Protecting users' digital identities and personal data is crucial to prevent unauthorised surveillance, data breaches, and privacy violations.
> *Future Outlook*: Advancements in decentralised identity solutions and privacy-preserving technologies like zero-knowledge proofs will empower users to control their data more.

Digital Divide:

> *Ethical Concern*: Bridging the digital divide is imperative to ensure equitable access to the metaverse across demographics and regions.
> *Future Outlook*: Initiatives involving government subsidies, community centres with internet access, and low-cost devices aim to reduce the digital divide and provide equal opportunities for all.

Virtual Harassment and Safety:

> *Ethical Concern*: Addressing virtual harassment and ensuring the safety of metaverse users from abusive behaviour is essential.
> *Future Outlook*: Enhanced reporting mechanisms, proactive moderation, and stricter enforcement of policies against harassment will contribute to safer virtual environments.

Data Ownership and Control:

> *Ethical Concern*: Determining who owns and controls virtual assets and property within the metaverse is a complex moral issue.
> *Future Outlook*: Developing transparent and standardised frameworks for virtual property rights and innovative contract technology will facilitate fair ownership and control.

Ethical AI and Automation:

> *Ethical Concern*: Ethical considerations include addressing job displacement due to automation, mitigating algorithmic bias, and ensuring responsible AI use.
> *Future Outlook*: Ethical guidelines, regulatory frameworks, and industry standards will evolve to promote responsible AI development and unbiased automation practices.

Intellectual Property and Creativity:

> *Ethical Concern*: Balancing protecting intellectual property rights with fostering innovation and creativity in the metaverse is a perpetual moral challenge.
> *Future Outlook*: Ongoing discussions will shape legal and ethical frameworks that balance protecting creators' rights and encouraging collaborative innovation.

Digital Addiction and Mental Health:

> *Ethical Concern*: Addressing potential digital addiction and its impact on mental health is a pressing moral issue.

> *Future Outlook*: Increasing awareness of digital addiction and responsible metaverse use will likely lead to developing guidelines for healthy engagement and digital detox programs.

Labour Rights and Fair Compensation:

> *Ethical Concern*: Ensuring that metaverse workers are compensated, protected from exploitation, and have the right to unionise is a central moral challenge.
> *Future Outlook*: Ongoing discussions on labour laws and regulations will focus on adapting them to cover virtual work while emphasising fair compensation and workers' rights.

Environmental Impact:

> *Ethical Concern*: Minimizing the ecological impact of the metaverse, including energy consumption and electronic waste, is a growing ethical consideration.
> *Future Outlook*: Eco-friendly technologies, energy-efficient practices, and sustainability initiatives will be prioritised to reduce the metaverse's carbon footprint.

Accountability and Governance:

> *Ethical Concern*: Establishing clear accountability and governance structures to prevent abuses of power and ensure ethical behaviour within the metaverse is crucial.
> *Future Outlook*: Ethical standards, self-regulation, and third-party audits will contribute to more responsible governance and ethical conduct within the metaverse.

Cybersecurity and Digital Security:

> *Ethical Concern*: Protecting users from cyber threats and ensuring data security are critical ethical considerations.
> *Future Outlook*: Continuous advancements in cybersecurity technologies, user education, and robust encryption will safeguard users and digital assets.

Cross-Cultural Sensitivity:

> *Ethical Concern*: Promoting cross-cultural sensitivity to prevent cultural misunderstandings and conflicts within the metaverse is essential.
> *Future Outlook*: Education and awareness campaigns will foster cultural understanding and respectful interactions in virtual spaces, reducing potential cultural clashes.

Ethical AI Assistants and Chatbots:

> *Ethical Concern*: Ensuring that AI assistants and chatbots provide unbiased, fair, and honest responses and recommendations is critical.
> *Future Outlook*: Continuous AI ethics research, audits, and user feedback will drive the development of AI systems that adhere to ethical standards.

Public Participation and Decision-Making:

> *Ethical Concern*: Involving the public and diverse stakeholders in shaping the metaverse's future to prevent the concentration of power is a critical ethical consideration.
> *Future Outlook*: Efforts to engage the public in governance and policymaking will result in more inclusive and transparent metaverse development.

The future of the metaverse relies on addressing these ethical considerations thoughtfully and collaboratively. As technology and society evolve, ongoing dialogues, responsible innovation, and regulatory frameworks will be essential in shaping a metaverse that aligns with ethical principles, respects individual rights, and contributes positively to society.

CHAPTER V

Virtual Economy Taxation: Exploring Challenges and Opportunities in the Metaverse

INTRODUCTION

The emergence and rapid growth of the metaverse have ushered in a new era of digital interaction, creativity, and commerce. Within these immersive virtual worlds, individuals and businesses engage in various economic activities, from buying virtual real estate to trading non-fungible tokens (NFTs) and providing virtual services. As the metaverse expands, so do the challenges and opportunities surrounding taxation within this digital realm.

Virtual economy taxation is a multifaceted topic that demands attention from policymakers, tax authorities, and economists. It raises essential questions about how to adapt traditional tax frameworks to the unique characteristics of virtual economies. This exploration explores the intricacies of taxing the metaverse, identifying the challenges tax authorities face and the opportunities that arise in this ever-evolving landscape.

The metaverse presents various challenges, from classifying and valuing digital assets to navigating cross-border transactions in a global virtual space. Furthermore, the pseudonymous nature of virtual worlds raises concerns about tax evasion and financial anonymity. Innovative business models, such as virtual asset trading platforms and metaverse real estate development, add further complexity to taxation.

Despite these challenges, virtual economy taxation offers governments, businesses, and users many opportunities. Blockchain technology and smart contracts can streamline tax calculations and payments, increasing transparency and compliance. In-world taxation mechanisms within virtual environments can generate revenue for these digital economies. Collaboration between tax authorities and virtual world developers can yield effective and tailored tax policies.

This exploration will delve deeper into the challenges and opportunities surrounding taxation in the metaverse, offering insights into the evolving landscape of virtual economy taxation and the measures needed to ensure a fair and effective tax framework in this digital frontier.

FISCAL DIFFICULTIES IN THE METAVERSE

The metaverse, an expansive digital domain of interconnected virtual worlds, is swiftly emerging as a significant catalyst in digital advancements. In the vast expanse of the digital realm, individuals and corporations partake in many economic endeavours, encompassing the exchange of digital assets and virtual currencies and the production and sale of virtual goods and services. Nevertheless, the expeditious development of the metaverse has given rise to many financial obstacles that necessitate meticulous examination.

The fiscal challenges encountered inside the metaverse entail a multifaceted array of concerns involving taxation, revenue generation, economic governance, and regulatory supervision. The ongoing evolution of the digital ecosystem has brought to light the growing issues related to fiscal matters. This study examines the complex fiscal challenges that arise in the metaverse, focusing on the problems faced by policymakers, tax authorities, and users as they navigate this unfamiliar domain.

One of the primary obstacles encountered in the metaverse pertains to the issue of taxation. Establishing a taxation framework for virtual transactions, digital assets, and the build-up of wealth poses a significant and complex obstacle. The presence of cross-border economic operations within the metaverse introduces additional complexities to the tax environment, giving rise to inquiries over jurisdictional matters and tax responsibilities.

The assessment of digital assets, frequently influenced by speculation and characterised by swift value swings, introduces an additional level of intricacy. The presence of privacy and pseudonymity within the metaverse poses a significant obstacle for tax authorities in their efforts to ascertain and oversee users' financial transactions. This situation can raise concerns about tax evasion and the preservation of financial anonymity.

Additionally, regulatory gaps and uncertainties within the nascent metaverse ecosystem pose significant challenges to enforcing tax regulations and establishing effective economic governance mechanisms. Establishing effective governance mechanisms is crucial for maintaining stability and managing financial crises in virtual economies.

Practical challenges necessitating resolution include transaction monitoring, enforcement of tax compliance, and adjustment to evolving business models, such as those based on blockchain economies.

As the metaverse progresses and reaches a more advanced stage, tackling these financial challenges effectively becomes increasingly crucial. Collaboration among governments, virtual world developers, and users is necessary to balance promoting innovation and economic growth and maintaining equitable taxation and financial stability within the digital frontier. This study aims to investigate further the complexities of the aforementioned budgetary difficulties and the strategies necessary to traverse them within the metaverse effectively.

REGULATORY AND DISCIPLINARY COMPLEXITIES

Legal and jurisdictional complexities in the metaverse are multifaceted and pose significant challenges as virtual environments transcend physical boundaries and traditional legal frameworks. These complexities arise from the metaverse's global nature and virtual worlds' unique characteristics. Here are some critical aspects of these complexities:

Cross-Border Transactions:

In the context of the metaverse, cross-border transactions refer to economic activities that occur across international borders within virtual worlds and digital environments. These transactions present a variety of unique obstacles and factors:

Jurisdictional Complexity:

In the physical world, transactions are typically subject to the laws and regulations of the country where they occur. However, because the metaverse transcends physical borders, determining which jurisdiction's laws apply takes time and effort. This complexity may result in jurisdictional disputes and legal ambiguity.

Taxation:

Taxing transnational transactions within the metaverse can be especially difficult. Different nations may have other tax regulations, making determining where economic value is generated difficult. Tax authorities must consider several issues to determine how to tax virtual assets, digital currencies, and economic activities in virtual environments.

Regulatory Oversight:

In some jurisdictions, virtual transactions may involve financial assets or activities subject to regulatory oversight. Compliance with regulations can be complex, as various nations may have different rules and requirements for virtual transactions.

International transactions raise concerns regarding consumer protection. Users engaging in virtual commerce may have a different level of protection than in traditional trades, and resolving disputes across international borders can take time and effort.

Valuation of Digital Assets:

Determining the value of digital assets in cross-border transactions can be complex. Values of virtual assets such as non-fungible tokens, virtual real estate, and in-game items can fluctuate and be speculative. This complicates customs duties, import/export regulations, and taxation matters.

In cross-border transactions, digital contracts and agreements are frequently utilised. Nonetheless, the enforceability of these contracts can vary from jurisdiction to jurisdiction, creating uncertainty when disputes arise.

Virtual currencies in the metaverse may have different countries' values and exchange rates. This can affect the cost and viability of international transactions, particularly when converting virtual currencies into conventional fiat currencies.

Virtual World Administration: Frequently, virtual realms have their governance structures and regulations. The terms of service and community guidelines established by the platform provider may apply to users. It can be challenging to balance these platform-specific rules and international legal standards.

Several Strategies And Considerations Are Necessary To Address The Difficulties Associated With Cross-Border Transactions In The Metaverse:

International Cooperation: Governments and regulatory entities should collaborate on harmonising virtual economies and international transaction regulations as part of international cooperation. International agreements and standards may aid in reducing legal ambiguities.

Innovation in Taxation: Tax authorities should investigate innovative tax policies tailored to the metaverse, considering the distinctive characteristics of virtual assets and transactions.

Education of Users: Users engaging in international transactions within virtual environments should be educated on the legal and regulatory aspects of their activities. This can aid users in making informed decisions and reduce legal risks.

Digital Identity Verification: Implementing robust digital identity verification systems within virtual worlds can improve security and regulatory compliance, simplifying identifying and tracing users engaged in cross-border transactions.

Dispute Resolution Mechanisms: Virtual worlds should establish efficient and accessible dispute resolution mechanisms to address cross-border disputes, possibly in collaboration with international organisations.

Addressing these cross-border transaction issues as the metaverse evolves is essential for assuring legal clarity, user protection, and the responsible growth of global virtual economies.

i) Digital Property Rights: Digital property rights in the metaverse include virtual assets' ownership, management, and transmission, such as virtual real estate, in-game items, non-fungible tokens (NFTs), and digital currencies. These rights present unique difficulties and complexities because they frequently exist in a domain where the line between physical and digital property is blurred. Here are essential considerations regarding digital property rights:

ii) Ownership Ambiguity: Determining and enforcing possession of virtual assets within the metaverse can be difficult. Users may have virtual property rights within a specific platform or game, but these rights are frequently governed by platform-specific terms of service rather than traditional property laws.

iii) Platform Control: Control Exercised by Platforms Virtual worlds and platforms exert considerable control over digital property rights. They can modify the rules regulating ownership, access, and use of virtual assets, influencing the perception of ownership's security.

iv) Interoperability: The metaverse consists of a multitude of virtual environments and platforms. Users may possess virtual assets on one platform, but interoperability issues may impede their transfer to or use in other virtual environments.

v) Intellectual Property Concerns: Users can create and own virtual content, including artwork, music, and objects. Especially when user-generated content is involved, intellectual property rights, copyright infringement, and licensing issues in the metaverse are complex.

vi) Legal Status: The legal standing of virtual property rights varies by jurisdiction. Some nations have partially recognised virtual property rights, while others have not. This inconsistency contributes to legal uncertainty.

vii) Valuation and Appraisal: The values of virtual assets in the metaverse can fluctuate and be speculative. Determining the fair market value of these assets, particularly for taxation or legal purposes, can be challenging.

viii) Ownership Transfers: In-game or platform-specific mechanisms are frequently utilised when transferring ownership of virtual assets, whether through transactions or gifts. It is essential to ensure the security and enforceability of these transfers.

ix) Platform Shutdowns: Users may lose access to digital assets when a virtual world or platform ceases operations. This raises concerns regarding the longevity of digital property rights' security.

Several measures can be taken to address these challenges and establish a framework for digital property rights in the metaverse:

i) Standardisation: Developing industry standards and best practices that provide consistent rules and guidelines for digital property rights across virtual worlds and platforms is possible.

ii) Legal Recognition: Governments and legal authorities can work to elucidate the legal status of virtual property rights and establish recognition and enforcement mechanisms.

iii) Blockchain and NFTs: Using blockchain technology and non-fungible tokens can increase the transparency and security of digital property rights. These technologies can provide immutable ownership and provenance documents for digital assets.

iv) Interoperability Standards: Developers can work together to establish interoperability standards that enable the transfer and use of virtual assets between distinct virtual worlds.

v) User Education: Users should be educated on the terms of service agreements and ownership rights of the virtual platforms they participate in. Comprehending the restrictions and liberties associated with digital property rights is crucial.

vi) Dispute Resolution: Establishing efficient and accessible dispute resolution mechanisms for virtual property disputes can aid in protecting user rights and ensuring fair outcomes.

Digital property rights are fundamental to the economic and social fabric of the metaverse. Addressing these rights' complexities will be crucial for fostering user trust and assuring the responsible development of virtual economies as the metaverse evolves.

CONTRACTUAL AGREEMENTS

Contractual agreements within the metaverse refer to digital contracts and agreements that govern various interactions, transactions, and activities between users and entities in virtual environments. These agreements are essential for defining the terms and conditions under which users engage with virtual platforms, trade virtual assets, and interact with one another. However, the unique characteristics of the metaverse introduce several complexities and considerations regarding contractual agreements:

i) Digital and Smart Contracts: Contracts in the metaverse are often executed digitally using smart contracts, self-executing agreements with the contract terms directly written into code. These contracts automate transactions and interactions but may not always align with traditional contract law.

ii) Enforceability: The enforceability of digital and intelligent contracts can vary by jurisdiction. Some countries may recognise and enforce these contracts, while others may have different legal frameworks. This can lead to uncertainties in legal protection.

iii) Terms of Service Agreements: Virtual platforms typically require users to agree to their terms of service, which often contain clauses related to property rights, content usage, and dispute resolution. Users may need help understanding or reading these agreements, which can raise questions about informed consent.

iv) User-Generated Content: Users often create and share content within virtual worlds, including virtual art, music, or virtual real estate. Contracts related to creating and sharing user-generated content can be complex, especially when intellectual property rights and licensing are involved.

v) Privacy and Data Usage: Contracts within the metaverse can involve collecting and using user data. Privacy considerations and data protection regulations add a layer of complexity to these agreements.

vi) Interoperability: Users often engage with multiple virtual platforms, and their interactions may involve contractual agreements with different terms and conditions. Ensuring that these agreements are compatible and do not conflict can be challenging.

vii) Platform Control: Virtual platform providers exercise significant control over the terms and enforcement of contracts. Users may need more ability to negotiate or contest these terms.

To address these complexities and ensure the effectiveness of contractual agreements within the metaverse, several steps can be taken:

i) **Standardisation:** Industry standards and best practices for digital and smart contracts can be developed to provide consistency and clarity in contractual agreements within the metaverse.

ii) **Legal Frameworks:** Governments and legal authorities can work to establish legal frameworks that recognise and provide guidance on the enforcement of digital and smart contracts in the metaverse.

iii) **User Education:** Users should be educated about the terms and conditions of virtual platforms and the agreements they enter into. Clear and accessible explanations of contractual terms can promote informed consent.

iv) **Data Privacy and Security:** Data usage and privacy contracts should adhere to data protection regulations and best practices to safeguard user information.

v) **Dispute Resolution:** Efficient and accessible mechanisms for dispute resolution should be in place to address conflicts arising from contractual agreements within virtual environments.

Contractual agreements are the foundation of economic and social interactions in the metaverse. As the metaverse continues to evolve, it is essential to navigate the complexities surrounding these agreements to protect the rights and interests of users and ensure a fair and transparent virtual environment.

JURISDICTIONAL CONFLICTS

Jurisdictional conflicts in the metaverse refer to the legal disputes and challenges when determining which country's laws and regulations should apply to activities, transactions, and arguments within virtual environments. These conflicts result from the borderless nature of the metaverse and the complexity of using traditional legal frameworks in virtual worlds. Here are some critical aspects of jurisdictional disputes in the metaverse:

i) Cross-Border Transactions: Users in the metaverse can engage in economic activities, such as virtual property transactions or digital currency trading, with participants worldwide. Determining which jurisdiction's laws govern these transactions can be challenging, especially when the physical location of the parties involved is only sometimes apparent.

ii) Legal Ambiguity: The legal status of virtual property and virtual assets varies from one country to another. Some countries have recognised virtual property rights, while others have not. This inconsistency adds ambiguity to the legal landscape and complicates jurisdictional matters

iii) Regulatory Variances: Different countries have varying regulatory frameworks for virtual economies, digital currencies, and online gaming. These regulatory variances can lead to conflicts between users and businesses in multiple jurisdictions.

iv) Content and Speech Laws: Jurisdictional conflicts can also extend to issues related to content moderation and freedom of speech within virtual worlds. Some countries have strict content regulations, while others emphasise freedom of expression. Balancing these differences can be challenging.

v) Taxation: Tax authorities may have jurisdictional conflicts when taxing virtual transactions and assets spanning multiple countries. Determining which country has the right to tax these activities can be a contentious issue.

vi) Legal Enforcement: Enforcing judgments and legal decisions across borders in the metaverse can be complicated. A court order in one country may not have direct authority or enforceability in another, creating challenges for users seeking legal recourse.

To address jurisdictional conflicts in the metaverse, several strategies and considerations are essential:

i) International Cooperation: Governments and international organisations can collaborate to create common standards and agreements for governing activities within the metaverse. Such cooperation can help reduce conflicts and provide clarity in cross-border legal matters.

ii) Legal Harmonization: Efforts should be made to harmonise legal frameworks related to virtual property rights, taxation, content regulation, and other aspects of the metaverse. This can help create a more predictable and consistent legal environment.

iii) User Education: Users should know the potential jurisdictional conflicts and legal implications of their actions within virtual environments. Clear information about applicable laws and regulations can promote responsible behaviour.

iv) Dispute Resolution Mechanisms: Establishing efficient and accessible mechanisms for resolving cross-border disputes, possibly through virtual courts or international arbitration, can help users seek legal remedies when needed.

v) Blockchain and Smart Contracts: Using blockchain technology and smart contracts can help automate and enforce legal agreements transparently and borderless, potentially reducing jurisdictional conflicts.

vi) Legal Innovation: Governments and legal experts should explore innovative legal solutions specific to the metaverse, considering its unique characteristics and challenges.

Navigating jurisdictional conflicts in the metaverse is a complex and evolving issue requiring international collaboration and legal framework adaptability. Addressing these conflicts will ensure legal clarity and user protection within this virtual frontier as the metaverse grows and matures.

USER IDENTITIES AND ANONYMITY

User identities and anonymity are fundamental aspects of the metaverse, presenting opportunities and challenges. In the metaverse, users often operate under pseudonyms or digital personas, which can provide a sense of privacy and freedom. However, this anonymity also raises concerns about accountability, security, and legal compliance. Here are some key considerations regarding user identities and anonymity in the metaverse:

Opportunities:

i) Privacy and Freedom of Expression: Anonymity in the metaverse allows users to explore and express themselves without fearing real-world consequences. It fosters a space for creativity, experimentation, and free expression.

ii) Personal Security: Anonymity can protect users from harassment, doxxing, or cyberbullying if their real identities are exposed. It can also provide a layer of protection against identity theft.

iii) Inclusivity: Anonymity can promote inclusivity by allowing individuals from diverse backgrounds to participate in the metaverse without revealing potentially stigmatised or discriminated-against aspects of their identities.

iv) Digital Activism: Anonymity can empower individuals to engage in digital activism and advocacy without fearing retribution. It has played a crucial role in facilitating social and political change in the digital realm.

Challenges:

i) Accountability: Anonymity can hinder accountability, making it difficult to identify individuals responsible for illegal or harmful activities within the metaverse, such as fraud, harassment, or cybercrimes.

ii) Legal Compliance: Legal authorities may face difficulties enforcing laws and regulations within the metaverse when user identities are concealed. This can lead to challenges in investigating and prosecuting virtual crimes.

iii) Content Moderation: Anonymity can be misused to disseminate harmful or illegal content, making content moderation and removing offensive material more challenging.

iv) Economic Transactions: In virtual economies, anonymity can raise concerns about the traceability of financial transactions, potentially facilitating money laundering and tax evasion.

v) Identity Verification: Establishing trust and verifying users' identities for certain activities, such as virtual property transactions or age-restricted content, can be problematic in an anonymous environment.

To address these challenges and opportunities related to user identities and anonymity in the metaverse, the following strategies and considerations may be helpful:

i) User Education: Users should be educated about the benefits and risks of anonymity and the importance of responsible behaviour within virtual environments.

ii) Digital Identity Verification: Implementing digital identity verification systems within the metaverse can enhance security and accountability while allowing users to maintain pseudonymity.

iii) Moderation and Reporting Mechanisms: Virtual platforms should establish effective content moderation and reporting mechanisms to address harmful behaviour or illegal content, even in an anonymous environment.

iv) Legal Frameworks: Governments and international organisations may need to adapt and develop legal frameworks to address crimes and disputes involving anonymous users within the metaverse.

v) Innovative Technologies: Leveraging emerging technologies like blockchain for identity verification or artificial intelligence for content moderation can help balance anonymity and accountability.

Balancing the benefits of user anonymity with the need for accountability and security is an ongoing challenge in the metaverse. Striking the right balance will require technological solutions, legal frameworks, and user education to ensure the metaverse remains safe and inclusive for all participants.

CONSUMER PROTECTIONS

Consumer protections in the metaverse are essential to safeguard users from fraud, scams, and unfair practices within virtual environments. These protections ensure users have a safe and transparent experience when engaging in economic activities, transactions, and interactions within the metaverse. Here are vital considerations regarding consumer protections in the metaverse:

Challenges:

i) Virtual Scams and Fraud: In the metaverse, users may encounter scams, fraudulent schemes, and deceptive practices, such as Ponzi schemes, fake virtual goods, or phishing attempts, which can result in financial losses.

ii) Security Risks: Virtual environments can be susceptible to security breaches, hacking, and data breaches that put users' personal information and assets at risk.

iii) Privacy Concerns: Users may have concerns about the collection and use of their data within virtual platforms, raising questions about data privacy and consent.

iv) Content Regulation: Balancing freedom of expression with the need to protect users from harmful or offensive content can be challenging. Content moderation policies need to be robust and transparent.

v) Payment Disputes: Disputes related to virtual transactions, such as disputes over virtual property purchases or virtual currency transactions, may require mechanisms for resolution and compensation.

Opportunities:

i) Transparency: Establishing clear and transparent rules and policies within virtual platforms can empower users to make informed decisions and protect themselves from fraudulent activities.

ii) Education: Educating users about potential risks and best practices in the metaverse can help them recognise and avoid scams and fraudulent schemes.

iii) Content Moderation: Effective content moderation mechanisms can help protect users from harmful or offensive content while preserving freedom of expression within virtual worlds.

iv) Dispute Resolution: Implementing efficient and accessible dispute resolution mechanisms can allow users to resolve conflicts and seek remedies when they encounter issues within the metaverse.

v) Regulatory Frameworks: Governments and regulatory bodies can adapt existing consumer protection laws and develop new regulations specific to the metaverse to address emerging challenges and protect users' rights.

To enhance consumer protections in the metaverse, the following strategies and considerations may be helpful:

i) Platform Policies: Virtual platforms should establish and enforce clear policies regarding user behaviour, content moderation, data privacy, and financial transactions.

ii) User Education: Providing users with information and resources to recognise and report scams and fraud is crucial. Education campaigns and user guides can be valuable tools.

iii) Data Protection: Platforms should implement robust data protection measures, including encryption and secure storage, to safeguard users' personal information.

iv) Trust and Safety Teams: Platforms can create trust and safety teams dedicated to monitoring and addressing user concerns, including scams, harassment, and other security issues.

v) Regulatory Engagement: Platforms should engage with relevant regulatory authorities to ensure compliance with consumer protection laws and regulations in different jurisdictions.

vi) Technological Solutions: Leveraging technologies like blockchain for secure transactions or AI for content moderation can enhance consumer protection.

Consumer protections are vital to building trust and confidence in the metaverse. By addressing the challenges and opportunities related to user safety and fairness, the metaverse can provide a more secure and enjoyable experience for users engaging in virtual activities and transactions.

CONTENT REGULATION

Content regulation in the metaverse involves defining and enforcing rules and policies for creating, distributing, and consuming digital content within virtual environments. It is a complex and evolving aspect of virtual worlds, aiming to strike a balance between promoting freedom of expression, ensuring user safety, and complying with legal and ethical standards. Here are vital considerations regarding content regulation in the metaverse:

Challenges:

i) Freedom of Expression: Virtual environments often celebrate creativity and diverse forms of expression. Striking a balance between allowing users to express themselves freely and protecting against harmful or offensive content can be challenging.

ii) Hate Speech and Harassment: The metaverse is not immune to hate speech, harassment, or offensive content. Implementing effective moderation mechanisms to address these issues is crucial for creating a safe and inclusive environment.

iii) Age-Appropriate Content: Virtual worlds may have users of varying ages, and ensuring that content is age-appropriate can be difficult. Platforms must consider how to restrict certain content based on users' ages.

iv) Cultural Sensitivity: Content acceptable in one culture may be offensive in another. Virtual platforms may need to navigate cultural differences when regulating content.

v) Moderation Scale: The sheer volume of user-generated content in the metaverse makes content moderation challenging. Platforms must find efficient ways to review and address content violations.

Opportunities:

i) User Safety: Effective content regulation can protect users from harassment, hate speech, and harmful content, ensuring a more enjoyable and secure experience.

ii) Community Standards: Establishing clear and transparent community standards and content policies can empower users to understand the rules and expectations within virtual environments.

iii) Age Verification: Implementing age verification mechanisms can help ensure that age-appropriate content is accessible to the right users.

iv) Cultural Inclusivity: Platforms can promote cultural inclusivity by providing users with tools to filter or customise their content experiences based on their artistic preferences.

v) Legal Compliance: Content regulation can help platforms and users comply with relevant laws and regulations, reducing legal risks and liabilities.

To enhance content regulation in the metaverse, the following strategies and considerations may be helpful:

i) Clearly Defined Policies: Virtual platforms should establish clear and comprehensive content policies that outline prohibited content, community standards, and enforcement procedures.

ii) Reporting Mechanisms: Platforms should provide users with easy and efficient ways to report content violations, ensuring a responsive approach to addressing issues.

iii) Moderation Tools: Implementing AI-powered content moderation tools and employing human moderators can help platforms review and manage content effectively.

iv) Age Restrictions: Platforms should develop mechanisms for age verification and content age ratings to protect younger users from age-inappropriate content.

v) Cultural Sensitivity: Platforms can offer content customisation options that allow users to filter content based on their artistic preferences.

vi) Legal Compliance: Platforms should stay informed about relevant laws and regulations in different jurisdictions and adjust their content policies accordingly.

Content regulation is an ongoing challenge in the metaverse, requiring a delicate balance between promoting freedom of expression and ensuring a safe and inclusive environment. By implementing clear policies, efficient moderation mechanisms, and user-friendly reporting tools, virtual platforms can help foster a positive and responsible digital community within the metaverse.

TAXATION

Taxation in the metaverse is a complex and evolving area, encompassing the collection of taxes on various economic activities and transactions that occur within virtual worlds and digital environments. It presents unique challenges and opportunities due to the borderless and decentralised nature of the metaverse. Here are vital considerations regarding taxation in the metaverse:

Challenges:

i) Cross-Border Transactions: Economic activities within the metaverse often involve participants from different countries engaging in virtual property transactions, digital asset trading, and virtual currency exchanges. Determining which jurisdiction has the right to tax these transactions can take time and effort.

ii) Digital Assets Valuation: Virtual assets, including NFTs, virtual real estate, and in-game items, can have fluctuating and speculative values. Tax authorities need help in valuing these assets for tax purposes.

iii) Pseudonymity and Privacy: The pseudonymous nature of the metaverse can make it challenging for tax authorities to identify and track users involved in economic activities. Ensuring tax compliance and preventing tax evasion can be difficult.

iv) Regulatory Gaps: The regulatory landscape for virtual economies is still evolving, with many jurisdictions needing clear guidelines on taxation in the metaverse. This can create uncertainty and compliance challenges.

v) Blockchain and Cryptocurrency: Virtual transactions often involve blockchain technology and digital currencies. Taxation of cryptocurrencies and blockchain-based assets is a complex and rapidly changing field.

Opportunities:

i) Revenue Generation: Taxation in the metaverse can generate revenue for governments, potentially contributing to economic growth and funding public services.

ii) Innovation: Tax authorities can explore innovative policies and mechanisms tailored to the metaverse, leveraging blockchain technology and smart contracts to automate tax collection.

iii) International Cooperation: Collaborative efforts among countries can lead to international agreements and standards for taxing cross-border virtual transactions, reducing tax evasion risks.

iv) Transparency: Blockchain technology can provide transparent and auditable records of virtual transactions, enhancing tax enforcement and reducing tax fraud.

v) User Education: Educating users about their tax obligations in the metaverse can promote compliance and reduce legal risks.

To address taxation challenges in the metaverse, the following strategies and considerations may be helpful:

i) International Collaboration: Governments should collaborate internationally to develop common standards and agreements for taxing virtual transactions and assets, ensuring consistency and fairness.

ii) Regulatory Clarity: Regulatory bodies should work to provide clear and updated guidelines on taxation in the metaverse, offering legal certainty to users and businesses.

iii) Blockchain Integration: Leveraging blockchain technology for tax collection and reporting can enhance transparency and streamline tax processes.

iv) User Reporting: Virtual platforms can implement mechanisms for users to report their virtual income and transactions for tax purposes, similar to traditional tax reporting.

v) Smart Contracts: Tax authorities can explore using smart contracts to automate tax collection and reporting within virtual economies.

Taxation in the metaverse is a dynamic field that requires adaptation to the evolving nature of digital economies. As the metaverse continues to grow and develop, governments and regulatory bodies will play a vital role in ensuring fair and effective taxation practices within this virtual frontier.

LEGAL RECOGNITION

Legal recognition in the context of the metaverse refers to acknowledging and validating various virtual entities, such as virtual property, virtual corporations, digital contracts, and virtual identities, within the legal frameworks of different jurisdictions. Achieving legal recognition for these virtual entities is essential for establishing clear rights and responsibilities in the metaverse. Here are vital considerations regarding legal recognition in the metaverse:

Challenges:

i) Virtual Property Rights: Determining the legal status of virtual property rights, including virtual real estate and in-game items, can be challenging. While virtual assets may have significant value, they often exist in a legal grey area.

ii) Virtual Corporations: Virtual entities like virtual corporations or organisations operating within virtual worlds lack clear legal recognition. This raises questions about their legal rights, obligations, and liabilities.

iii) Digital Contracts: Digital contracts and agreements within the metaverse may not always align with traditional contract laws. Legal recognition and enforceability can vary by jurisdiction.

iv) Intellectual Property: Issues related to intellectual property rights within the metaverse, including copyright and trademark, are complex, especially when user-generated content is involved.

v) Digital Identities: The legal recognition of digital identities and pseudonyms used in the metaverse is evolving. Users often operate under pseudonyms, making identity verification and legal accountability challenging.

Opportunities:

i) Property Rights: Establishing legal recognition for virtual property rights can provide users with clear ownership and protection against unauthorised transfers or disputes.

ii) Business Entities: Recognizing virtual corporations and organisations can facilitate legitimate economic activities and promote innovation within virtual economies.

iii) Enforceable Contracts: Ensuring that digital contracts are legally enforceable can give users confidence to engage in virtual transactions and agreements.

iv) Intellectual Property Protection: Defining the legal status of intellectual property within the metaverse can protect creators and encourage the development of original content.

v) Consumer Rights: Legal recognition can help protect the rights and interests of consumers participating in virtual economies and transactions.

To enhance legal recognition in the metaverse, the following strategies and considerations may be helpful:

i) Legal Frameworks: Governments and legal authorities should work to adapt existing legal frameworks or create new ones that address the unique challenges posed by virtual entities and activities within the metaverse.

ii) International Cooperation: Collaboration among countries can lead to international agreements and standards for recognising virtual entities and property rights, promoting consistency and clarity.

iii) Blockchain and Smart Contracts: Leveraging blockchain technology and smart contracts can enhance the metaverse's transparency and enforceability of legal agreements and property rights.

iv) User Education: Users should be educated about their legal rights and responsibilities within virtual environments, ensuring informed participation.

v) Dispute Resolution: Establishing accessible and efficient dispute resolution mechanisms, possibly through virtual courts or online arbitration, can provide users with a means to seek legal remedies.

Legal recognition establishes trust, accountability, and protection within the metaverse. As virtual economies and digital environments evolve, addressing the complexities of legal recognition will be crucial for users and businesses operating in this digital frontier.

DISPUTE RESOLUTION

Dispute resolution in the metaverse involves the mechanisms and processes to address conflicts, disputes, and legal issues among users, entities, or participants within virtual environments. Effective dispute resolution is essential for maintaining a fair and secure metaverse where users can resolve conflicts and seek necessary remedies. Here are vital considerations regarding dispute resolution in the metaverse:

Challenges:

i) **Cross-Border Conflicts**: Disputes in the metaverse can involve users and entities from different countries, leading to jurisdictional complexities and conflicts of laws.

ii) **Virtual Property Disputes**: Disputes related to virtual property, including ownership disputes and virtual real estate conflicts, can be complex due to the unique nature of virtual assets.

iii) **Contractual Disagreements**: Digital contracts and agreements within virtual environments may sometimes align with traditional contract laws, leading to disputes over the interpretation and enforcement of contract terms.

iv) **Content and Harassment Disputes**: Conflicts related to offensive or harmful content, harassment, or intellectual property infringement require effective mechanisms for resolution.

v) **Fraud and Scams**: Users may encounter fraudulent schemes or scams within virtual worlds, necessitating mechanisms to investigate and address such issues.

Opportunities:

i) Fairness and Trust: Effective dispute resolution mechanisms build trust within the metaverse by ensuring users can seek justice and resolution.

ii) Protection of Rights: Dispute resolution processes protect the rights and interests of users, providing them with recourse when they encounter harmful or unfair activities.

iii) Legal Clarity: Clear and accessible dispute resolution mechanisms contribute to legal clarity, enhancing user confidence in virtual environments.

iv) Innovation: The metaverse can leverage innovative technologies like blockchain-based dispute resolution or virtual courts to streamline and automate dispute resolution processes.

v) User Empowerment: Empowering users with the ability to address disputes and conflicts fosters a sense of agency and responsibility within virtual communities.

To enhance dispute resolution in the metaverse, the following strategies and considerations may be helpful:

i) Mechanisms for Reporting: Virtual platforms should provide clear and accessible tools for users to report disputes and conflicts, ensuring that issues are promptly addressed.

ii) Mediation and Arbitration: Virtual platforms can offer mediation or arbitration services to help users resolve disputes more informally and quickly.

iii) Virtual Courts: Establishing virtual courts or online dispute resolution platforms tailored explicitly to the metaverse can give users formal legal recourse.

iv) Blockchain and Smart Contracts: Leveraging blockchain technology and smart contracts can automate and enhance the transparency of dispute resolution processes.

v) Legal Assistance: Virtual platforms may provide users with legal assistance or resources to navigate complex disputes.

vi) User Education: Educating users about the dispute resolution mechanisms and their rights within the metaverse is essential for informed participation.

vii) Legal Frameworks: Governments and regulatory bodies can work to adapt and develop legal frameworks that address the unique challenges of dispute resolution in virtual environments.

Dispute resolution is critical to building a fair, secure, trustworthy metaverse. By implementing effective mechanisms and providing users with access to transparent and accessible resolution processes, virtual platforms can ensure that users have the means to address conflicts and seek remedies when they encounter issues within the metaverse.

VALUATION AND CLASSIFICATION OF VIRTUAL ASSETS

The valuation and classification of virtual assets in the metaverse are crucial for determining the worth, ownership, and legal status of digital goods and property within virtual environments. These assets include virtual real estate, in-game items, non-fungible tokens (NFTs), digital currencies, and more. Here are critical considerations regarding the valuation and classification of virtual assets:

A. Valuation Challenges

Lack of Tangibility: Virtual assets exist solely in digital form and need a physical presence, making their valuation less intuitive than physical assets.

Fluctuating Value: The value of virtual assets can be highly volatile and subject to rapid changes, influenced by factors like demand, rarity, and popularity.

Subjective Value: The perceived value of virtual assets can vary widely among users, making it challenging to establish objective valuation standards.

Speculative Nature: Some virtual assets are traded as speculative investments, further complicating valuation due to market speculation.

Non-Uniformity: Different virtual worlds and platforms may have distinct economic systems and asset valuation methods.

B. Valuation Approaches

Market-Based Valuation: This approach relies on the prices at which virtual assets are bought and sold in secondary markets. It considers supply and demand dynamics.

Income-Based Valuation: Income-generating virtual assets, such as virtual real estate, can be valued based on the revenue generated through rent or user activity.

Cost-Based Valuation: Some virtual assets may have a straightforward cost of creation or acquisition, which serves as their value.

Scarcity and Rarity: The rarity and lack of virtual assets, often reflected in their attributes or metadata, can influence their valuation.

C. Classification Challenges

Legal Recognition: Determining the legal status of virtual assets varies by jurisdiction, and some countries may not recognise virtual property rights.

Ownership Rights: Classifying virtual assets as property can raise questions about ownership rights and the ability to transfer or trade them.

Intellectual Property: Virtual assets may contain elements subject to intellectual property rights, complicating their classification and use.

D. Classification Approaches

Virtual Property: Some virtual assets are classified as virtual property, entitling users to ownership and property rights.

Virtual Goods: Virtual goods are assets that can be consumed or used within virtual environments, such as in-game items.

Non-Fungible Tokens (NFTs): NFTs are specific virtual assets representing ownership of a unique item or content. They are often used for digital art, collectables, and virtual real estate.

Virtual Currency: Digital currencies within virtual environments may be classified as a means of exchange rather than property.

To address valuation and classification challenges in the metaverse, various strategies and considerations may be helpful:

Legal Frameworks: Governments and legal authorities should work to adapt existing legal frameworks or develop new ones that recognise and guide the valuation and classification of virtual assets.

Industry Standards: Virtual platforms and developers can establish industry standards and best practices for valuing and classifying virtual assets.

Blockchain Technology: Leveraging blockchain technology for virtual asset ownership records and metadata can enhance transparency and traceability, making classifying and valuing assets easier.

User Education: Educating users about valuing and classifying virtual assets within specific virtual environments can promote responsible participation and investment.

Market Data: Giving users access to real-time market data for virtual assets can help inform their valuation decisions.

Valuation and classification are foundational aspects of the virtual economy in the metaverse. As the metaverse evolves, establishing clear and transparent standards for these processes will be essential for creating a trustworthy and stable virtual environment.

TAX EVASION AND ADMINISTRATION

In the context of the metaverse, tax evasion and enforcement pose significant challenges for governments and regulatory agencies. Tax evasion is the deliberate evasion or underreporting of tax obligations in virtual economies. In contrast, enforcement refers to the actions to ensure compliance with tax laws and regulations in virtual environments. The following are essential factors to consider regarding tax evasion and enforcement in the metaverse:

Challenges:

i) Pseudonymity and Privacy: Users in the metaverse often operate under pseudonyms or digital personas, making it challenging for tax authorities to identify and track individuals or entities involved in virtual transactions.

ii) Cross-Border Transactions: Economic activities within virtual worlds often span multiple countries, leading to jurisdictional complexities and difficulty tracking taxable events.

iii) Valuation and Reporting: Determining the accurate value of virtual assets and transactions can be challenging, as virtual assets often need more apparent market values, and users may only sometimes report their virtual income accurately.

iv) Blockchain and Cryptocurrency: Using blockchain technology and cryptocurrencies in virtual environments can further complicate tax enforcement, as these technologies enable increased privacy and can facilitate tax evasion.

v) Regulatory Gaps: The regulatory landscape for taxing virtual economies is still evolving, with many jurisdictions needing clear guidelines and frameworks for tax enforcement in the metaverse.

Enforcement Approaches:

i) Digital Footprints: Tax authorities may leverage digital footprints and transaction records within virtual platforms to identify users or entities engaged in significant economic activities.

ii) User Reporting: Virtual platforms can implement mechanisms for users to report their virtual income and transactions for tax purposes, similar to traditional tax reporting.

iii) Blockchain Analysis: Analysing blockchain transactions associated with virtual currencies and NFTs can provide insights into taxable events and help identify tax evaders.

iv) International Collaboration: Governments can collaborate internationally to develop common standards and agreements for taxing cross-border virtual transactions, reducing tax evasion risks.

v) Legal Frameworks: Governments and regulatory authorities can work to adapt and develop legal frameworks that address the unique challenges of tax enforcement in virtual environments.

vi) User Education: Educating users about their tax obligations within the metaverse can promote tax compliance and reduce legal risks.

Technological Solutions:

i) Blockchain Transparency: Leveraging blockchain technology can enhance the transparency and traceability of virtual transactions, making it more challenging for users to engage in tax evasion.

ii) Smart Contracts: Tax authorities can explore using smart contracts to automate tax collection and reporting within virtual economies, ensuring accurate tax compliance.

iii) Data Analytics: Advanced data analytics tools can help tax authorities analyse large datasets from virtual platforms to detect patterns and anomalies related to tax evasion.

iv) Cross-Platform Integration: Collaborative efforts between virtual platforms and tax authorities can facilitate the exchange of information and data to enhance tax enforcement.

Addressing tax evasion and enforcement challenges in the metaverse requires a combination of regulatory adaptation, international cooperation, and technological innovation. As virtual economies evolve, governments and regulatory bodies must develop effective strategies to uphold tax laws and regulations, promoting fairness and revenue generation within virtual environments.

Cross-border transactions and international cooperation

Cross-border transactions within the metaverse encompass economic activity, exchanges of digital assets, and transfers of virtual property between users and entities situated in distinct countries or jurisdictions within virtual settings. International collaboration is paramount in effectively tackling the intricacies and difficulties resulting from such transactions. This discourse aims to comprehensively analyse cross-border transactions and the significance of international cooperation inside the metaverse.

> **Global Nature**: The metaverse is a digital realm where users from all corners of the world participate. Virtual environments and online games are accessed by individuals regardless of their geographical location. As a result, economic activities and transactions within these virtual worlds inherently involve cross-border interactions.

> **Virtual Property**: Virtual real estate, in-game items, and digital assets can be owned and traded by users from different countries. For example, a user in the United States might purchase virtual real estate in a virtual world operated by a company based in South Korea.

> **Virtual Currency Exchange**: Users often engage in cross-border transactions when converting virtual currencies from one game or virtual platform to another or exchanging virtual currency for cryptocurrencies like Bitcoin or Ethereum.

> **NFT Sales**: Non-fungible tokens (NFTs) representing digital collectables,

art, or virtual property are frequently bought and sold internationally through online marketplaces. These transactions involve users and collectors from various countries.

Challenges and Considerations:

i) Jurisdictional Complexity: The decentralised and borderless nature of the metaverse creates jurisdictional complexities. Determining which country has the authority to regulate and tax cross-border virtual transactions can take time and effort.

ii) Regulatory Differences: Different countries have distinct regulations related to virtual assets, cryptocurrencies, and digital property rights. Compliance with these varying regulations can be cumbersome for users and global virtual platforms.

iii) Legal Recognition: The recognition of virtual property rights and transactions can vary significantly. Some jurisdictions may fully recognise virtual property rights, while others may have limited or no credit, impacting users' legal protections.

iv) Consumer Protection: Cross-border transactions can raise consumer protection concerns. Users engaging in international virtual transactions may have access to different consumer rights and protections than they do in their home countries.

International Cooperation:

i) Regulatory Harmonization: Governments and regulatory bodies can engage in international cooperation efforts to harmonise regulations related to virtual transactions, digital property rights, and virtual currencies. Such harmonisation can reduce regulatory fragmentation and inconsistencies.

ii) Taxation Agreements: Countries can establish taxation agreements or treaties to address the taxation of cross-border virtual transactions. These agreements help ensure that tax liabilities are appropriately assigned among jurisdictions.

iii) Information Sharing: Collaboration among countries can involve sharing information about virtual asset transactions. This information exchange can assist in tracking and enforcing tax and regulatory compliance.

iv) Global Standards: Developing international standards and best practices for virtual asset transactions and digital property rights can promote consistency and fairness in cross-border activities. These standards can provide a common framework for users and platforms to follow.

v) User Education: Educating users about the potential legal and tax implications of cross-border transactions is essential. Users should be aware of the regulatory landscape and the impact of engaging in international virtual activities.

vi) Blockchain and Transparency: Leveraging blockchain technology's transparency and traceability can enhance international cooperation. Blockchain provides a verifiable and auditable record of virtual transactions, which can assist in regulatory and tax enforcement.

International cooperation is crucial for addressing the complexities of cross-border transactions in the metaverse. As virtual economies continue to grow and evolve, governments, regulatory authorities, and virtual platforms must work together to create a stable and inclusive global digital ecosystem that fosters responsible and secure cross-border interactions. This cooperation can lead to a more harmonised and consistent regulatory environment for virtual activities, benefiting users and the metaverse.

TAX MODELS AND APPROACHES

Traditional taxation models and their limitations

Traditional taxation models typically applied to physical assets and income, may encounter limitations due to their unique characteristics when used in the metaverse and virtual economies. Here are some traditional taxation models and their rules in this context:

INCOME TAX

Income taxation, a traditional taxation model applied to individuals' earnings, can encounter several limitations when used in the metaverse and virtual economies due to their unique characteristics:

1. Valuation Challenges: Determining the accurate value of virtual income in the metaverse can be complex. Virtual assets, currencies, and digital items may not have clear market values, which fluctuate significantly.

2. Multisource Income: In the metaverse, individuals can earn virtual income from various sources, such as selling virtual assets, providing virtual services, or participating in virtual events. Tracking and aggregating income from these diverse sources can be challenging.

3. Cross-Border Transactions: Virtual income in the metaverse often involves cross-border transactions, making it difficult to determine the source and location of income for tax purposes. International cooperation and agreements may be necessary to address cross-border taxation.

4. Pseudonymity: Users in the metaverse often operate under pseudonyms or digital personas, concealing their real-world identities. This pseudonymity can make it challenging for tax authorities to identify and track individuals earning virtual income.

5. Tax Evasion: The pseudonymous nature of the metaverse can create opportunities for tax evasion, as users may underreport their virtual income or engage in untraceable transactions.

6. Lack of Traditional Employment: In the metaverse, traditional employment models may not apply, as users can earn income through diverse virtual activities that may not resemble traditional jobs.

7. Volatility: The value of virtual assets and virtual currencies can be highly volatile, leading to fluctuations in virtual income. Taxation based on the fair market value at receipt may not accurately reflect the income's actual economic value.

8. Ownership and Property Rights: Determining the ownership and property rights associated with virtual assets and income can be challenging. Some virtual assets may need more ownership structures.

Property taxation, a traditional tax model applied to physical real estate and assets, encounters several limitations when extended to the metaverse and virtual property due to the unique characteristics of these digital assets:

1. Intangibility and Digital Nature: Virtual property, such as virtual real estate and digital assets in the metaverse, lacks physical presence. Taxing intangible digital assets can be challenging, as traditional property tax models are designed for physical objects and land.

2. Ownership Challenges: Determining ownership of virtual property can be complex. In some virtual environments, users may have property rights, but these rights may not align with traditional property laws. Ownership of virtual property is often recorded on the platform's database, which may need legal recognition

3. Valuation: Valuing virtual property for tax purposes is challenging because virtual assets do not have inherent physical or market values. Their value can be highly subjective and volatile, making it difficult to assess their worth accurately.

4. Cross-Border Ownership: Virtual property ownership often transcends national boundaries, with users from different countries owning and trading virtual assets within the same virtual environment. This complicates the determination of the appropriate tax jurisdiction.

5. Transfer and Sale: Taxation of virtual property transactions, such as the sale or transfer of virtual real estate, may be challenging to implement, as these transactions do not involve physical deeds or titles.

6. Ownership Rights: The nature of ownership rights in the metaverse can be uncertain. Users may have rights to use and modify virtual property but not actual ownership rights in the traditional sense. Taxing these rights can be legally complex.

7. Pseudonymity and Privacy: Many users in the metaverse operate under pseudonyms or digital personas, concealing their real-world identities. This pseudonymity can make it challenging for tax authorities to identify and track virtual property owners.

8. Regulatory Variability: Different jurisdictions may have varying approaches to taxing virtual property, leading to regulatory disparities and potential tax avoidance or confusion.

SALES TAXATION

Sales taxation, a traditional tax model applied to the sale of goods and services, faces several limitations when extended to the metaverse and virtual economies due to their unique characteristics:

1. Intangibility of Digital Goods: In the metaverse, many transactions involve digital goods and services, such as virtual items, virtual real estate, and digital content. These items need a physical form, making it challenging to determine the point of sale and apply traditional sales tax models designed for tangible goods.

2. Virtual Currency Transactions: Virtual currencies, like in-game currencies or cryptocurrencies, are commonly used for transactions within virtual environments. Taxing these currencies can be complex, as they do not fit the traditional definition of goods or services.

3. Cross-Border Transactions: Virtual economies are often global, with users from different countries participating in transactions. Determining the appropriate tax jurisdiction and rate for cross-border transactions can take time and effort.

4. Pseudonymity and Privacy: Users in the metaverse often operate under pseudonyms or digital personas, concealing their real-world identities. This pseudonymity can make it difficult for tax authorities to identify and track individuals involved in virtual transactions.

5. Lack of Physical Presence: Traditional sales tax models often rely on physical presence within a specific jurisdiction to trigger tax obligations. In the metaverse, users can conduct transactions without a physical presence, creating uncertainty in tax liability.

6. Valuation Challenges: Determining the value of virtual goods and services for taxation purposes can be complex, as these values may need to be more consistent and readily apparent, and they can fluctuate over time.

7. Regulatory Variability: Different jurisdictions may have varying approaches to taxing virtual transactions, leading to regulatory disparities and potential tax avoidance or confusion.

VALUE-ADDED TAX (VAT)

Value-added tax (VAT), a traditional consumption tax applied at each stage of the production and distribution of goods and services, faces several limitations when extended to the metaverse and virtual economies due to their unique characteristics:

1. Intangibility of Digital Goods and Services: Many transactions in the metaverse involve digital goods, services, or virtual assets, which lack a physical presence. VAT systems were primarily designed for tangible goods and services, making applying VAT to intangible digital products challenging.

2. Virtual Currencies: Virtual currencies, such as in-game or cryptocurrencies, are often used in virtual economies. Taxing these currencies under VAT can be complex, as they do not fit the traditional definition of goods or services, and their values may fluctuate significantly.

3. Cross-Border Transactions: Virtual economies in the metaverse are inherently global, with users from different countries participating in transactions. Determining the appropriate VAT jurisdiction and rate for cross-border virtual transactions can be challenging.

4. Pseudonymity and Privacy: Users in the metaverse frequently operate under pseudonyms or digital personas, concealing their real-world identities. This pseudonymity can make it difficult for tax authorities to identify and track individuals involved in virtual transactions.

5. Lack of Physical Presence: Traditional VAT models often rely on physical presence within a specific jurisdiction to trigger tax obligations. In the metaverse, users can conduct transactions without a physical presence, creating uncertainty in tax liability.

6. Valuation Challenges: Determining the value of virtual goods and services for VAT purposes can be complex, as these values may need to be more consistent and readily apparent and can fluctuate over time.

7. Regulatory Variability: Different jurisdictions may have varying approaches to taxing virtual transactions, leading to regulatory disparities and potential tax avoidance or confusion.

Capital gains taxation, a traditional tax model applied to the profits earned from the sale or exchange of capital assets, encounters several limitations when extended to the metaverse and virtual holdings due to their unique characteristics:

1. Valuation Challenges: Determining the accurate value of virtual assets for capital gains taxation can be complex. Virtual assets, such as virtual real estate, digital items, or cryptocurrencies, may lack clear market values, and their values can be highly speculative and volatile.

2. Multisource Gains: In the metaverse, individuals can generate capital gains from various sources, including selling virtual assets, trading virtual currencies, or participating in virtual asset speculation. Tracking and aggregating gains from these diverse sources can be challenging.

3. Cross-Border Transactions: Virtual economies in the metaverse are often global, with users from different countries engaging in virtual asset transactions. Determining the appropriate tax jurisdiction and addressing cross-border capital gains taxation can be complex.

4. Pseudonymity and Privacy: Users in the metaverse often operate under pseudonyms or digital personas, concealing their real-world identities. This pseudonymity can make it challenging for tax authorities to identify and track individuals earning capital gains from virtual assets.

5. Lack of Traditional Ownership Rights: Virtual assets may not grant traditional ownership rights like physical assets. Users often have rights to use, trade, or modify virtual assets but may not have ownership rights. Defining and taxing these rights can be legally complex.

6. Regulatory Variability: Different jurisdictions may have varying approaches to taxing capital gains, and these approaches may not align with the unique characteristics of virtual assets. Regulatory disparities can lead to tax avoidance or confusion.

CORPORATE TAXATION

Corporate taxation, a traditional tax model applied to businesses and corporations, faces several limitations when extended to the metaverse and virtual companies due to their unique characteristics:

1. Virtual Entity Recognition: Determining the legal and tax status of virtual entities and businesses operating in the metaverse can be challenging. These entities may need a physical presence or traditional corporate structures, making applying standard corporate tax rules difficult.

2. Ownership and Control: Virtual entities may not have traditional ownership structures or hierarchical management. Ownership and control can be decentralised, with multiple users contributing to decision-making and revenue generation, complicating the attribution of tax liabilities.

3. Cross-Border Operations: Virtual businesses in the metaverse can operate across national borders, making it difficult to determine the appropriate tax jurisdiction and address cross-border corporate taxation challenges.

4. Pseudonymity and Privacy: Users and entities in the metaverse often operate under pseudonyms or digital personas, concealing their real-world identities. This pseudonymity can make it challenging for tax authorities to identify and track the beneficial owners of virtual businesses.

5. Diverse Revenue Sources: Virtual businesses can generate revenue from various sources, such as selling virtual assets, virtual services, advertising, and virtual real estate. Tracking and aggregating revenue from these diverse sources can be complex.

6. Intangible Assets: Virtual businesses may hold valuable intangible assets, such as virtual or intellectual property, which can be challenging to value and tax effectively.

7. Regulatory Variability: Different jurisdictions may have varying approaches to taxing virtual businesses, and these approaches may not align with the unique characteristics of virtual economies. Regulatory disparities can lead to tax avoidance or confusion.

Cross-border taxation, which involves taxing economic activities and transactions that cross national boundaries, faces several limitations when applied to the metaverse and virtual economies due to their unique characteristics:

1. Jurisdictional Complexity: The decentralised and borderless nature of the metaverse can create challenges in determining which country or jurisdiction has the right to tax cross-border virtual transactions. Traditional tax laws may need help to adapt to these complexities.

2. Pseudonymity and Privacy: Users and entities in the metaverse often operate under pseudonyms or digital personas, concealing their real-world identities. This pseudonymity can make it difficult for tax authorities to identify and track individuals or entities engaged in cross-border transactions.

3. Virtual Economies: The metaverse features virtual economies that are not bound by physical geography. Virtual assets and virtual currencies can be easily transferred and traded across borders, challenging applying traditional tax models designed for physical economies.

4. Digital Asset Valuation: Determining virtual assets' value and income for cross-border taxation can be complex. These assets may not have clear market values, which can fluctuate significantly.

5. Regulatory Variability: Countries may have varying approaches to taxing virtual transactions, assets, and businesses. This regulatory variability can lead to disparities and potential tax avoidance.

6. Multisource Income: Users and entities in the metaverse often generate income from various sources, including selling virtual assets, providing virtual services, and participating in virtual events. Tracking and aggregating income from these diverse sources for cross-border taxation can be challenging.

7. Cross-Border Virtual Corporations: Virtual entities and corporations in the metaverse can operate globally, making determining their tax liability in multiple jurisdictions challenging.

8. Lack of Physical Presence: Traditional tax models often rely on physical presence within a specific jurisdiction to trigger tax obligations. In the metaverse, users and entities can engage in transactions without a physical presence, creating uncertainty in tax liability.

USER REPORTING

User reporting, a method of taxation that relies on individuals and entities to self-report their income and transactions for tax purposes, faces several limitations when applied to the metaverse and virtual economies due to their unique characteristics:

1. Pseudonymity and Privacy: Users and entities in the metaverse often operate under pseudonyms or digital personas, concealing their real-world identities. This pseudonymity can make it challenging for tax authorities to identify and verify the accuracy of user-reported data.

2. Complex Income Sources: In the metaverse, individuals and entities can generate income from various sources, including virtual asset sales, virtual services, virtual real estate transactions, and virtual events. Reporting and tracking income from these diverse sources can be complex and subject to underreporting.

3. Cross-Border Transactions: Virtual economies in the metaverse are global, with users from different countries engaging in cross-border transactions. Users may need to know their tax obligations in other jurisdictions or accurately report cross-border income.

4. Valuation Challenges: Determining the value of virtual assets and virtual income for tax reporting purposes can be complex, as these assets may need clear market values, and their values can fluctuate significantly.

5. Regulatory Variability: Different countries may have varying approaches to taxing virtual transactions and income, leading to regulatory disparities and potential tax avoidance.

6. Compliance and Enforcement: Relying solely on user reporting for tax compliance can be challenging to enforce, as some users may be tempted to underreport or evade taxes in the pseudonymous environment of the metaverse

7. Record Keeping: Users and entities may need more adequate record-keeping practices in virtual environments, making providing accurate and verifiable tax reports difficult.

INNOVATIVE TAX MODELS FOR THE METAVERSE

Innovative tax models tailored to the metaverse and virtual economies are essential to address these digital realms' unique challenges and opportunities. Here are some innovative tax models that governments and regulatory bodies may consider:

A Virtual Asset Transaction Tax is a model designed to generate revenue from transactions involving virtual assets within the metaverse and virtual economies. This innovative tax model addresses the unique challenges and opportunities presented by the digital realm of virtual assets, including virtual real estate, digital items, non-fungible tokens (NFTs), and other intangible digital properties. Here's an overview of the Virtual Asset Transaction Tax:

Model:

i) Taxable Transactions: This tax is levied on specific transactions within virtual environments. These transactions may include purchasing, selling, exchanging, or transferring virtual assets.

ii) Tax Rate: A predetermined tax rate or percentage is applied to the transaction value. This rate may vary depending on factors such as the type of virtual asset, the transaction size, or the virtual platform's policies.

iii) Point of Collection: The tax can be collected at the end of the sale or transfer within the virtual environment. Virtual platforms or blockchain networks can facilitate this collection process.

iv) Automated Collection: Blockchain technology and smart contracts can be leveraged to automate tax collection, ensuring that taxes are deducted and remitted in real time during transactions.

Advantages:

i) Revenue Generation: Virtual asset transactions have become a significant part of the digital economy, and taxing these transactions can generate revenue for governments or regulatory bodies.

ii) Transparency: Using blockchain technology can clarify and trace transactions, reducing the potential for tax evasion or fraud.

iii) Fairness: It ensures that individuals and entities engaging in virtual asset transactions contribute to the tax base, promoting justice in taxation.

iv) Automation: Blockchain-based tax collection can be highly automated, reducing administrative burdens on taxpayers and tax authorities.

Challenges:

i) Valuation: Determining the accurate value of virtual assets for tax purposes can be challenging, as their values can be subjective, volatile, or based on user demand.

ii) Regulatory Coordination: Ensuring consistent taxation rules and regulations across virtual platforms and jurisdictions may require international cooperation and coordination.

iii) Privacy: Balancing the need for tax collection with user privacy and pseudonymity within the metaverse can be a delicate challenge.

iv) User Education: Users may need to be educated about their tax obligations within virtual environments to promote compliance.

v) Compliance: Ensuring that all virtual asset transactions are reported and taxed can be complex, especially in decentralised virtual environments.

Implementing a Virtual Asset Transaction Tax requires careful consideration of these challenges and the development of clear rules and regulations. Collaboration among governments, regulatory bodies, virtual platforms, and users is crucial in shaping an effective and equitable taxation framework for virtual assets in the metaverse.

VIRTUAL CURRENCY TRANSACTION

A Virtual Currency Transaction Tax is a model designed to generate revenue from transactions involving virtual currencies within the metaverse and virtual economies. This innovative tax model addresses the unique challenges and opportunities presented by the digital realm of virtual currencies, including in-game coins, cryptocurrencies, and other digital tokens. Here's an overview of the Virtual Currency Transaction Tax:

Model:

i) **Taxable Transactions**: This tax is levied on specific transactions involving virtual currencies. These transactions may include purchases, sales, exchanges, or transfers of virtual currencies.

ii) **Tax Rate**: A predetermined tax rate or percentage is applied to the transaction value denominated in virtual currency. The tax rate may vary depending on factors such as the type of virtual currency, the transaction size, or the virtual platform's policies.

iii) **Point of Collection**: The tax can be collected at the end of a transaction within the virtual environment. Virtual platforms or blockchain networks can facilitate this collection process.

iv) **Automated Collection**: Blockchain technology and smart contracts can be leveraged to automate tax collection, ensuring that taxes are deducted and remitted in real time during transactions.

Advantages:

i) **Revenue Generation**: Virtual currency transactions have become a significant part of the digital economy, and taxing these transactions can generate revenue for governments or regulatory bodies.

ii) **Transparency**: Using blockchain technology can clarify and trace transactions, reducing the potential for tax evasion or fraud in virtual currency transactions.

iii) **Fairness**: It ensures that individuals and entities engaging in virtual currency transactions contribute to the tax base, promoting justice in taxation.

iv) **Automation**: Blockchain-based tax collection can be highly automated, reducing administrative burdens on taxpayers and tax authorities.

Challenges:

i) Valuation: Determining the accurate value of virtual currency transactions for tax purposes can be challenging, as virtual currency values can be highly volatile and vary across different virtual platforms.

ii) Regulatory Coordination: Ensuring consistent taxation rules and regulations for virtual currencies across different platforms and jurisdictions may require international cooperation and coordination.

iii) Privacy: Balancing the need for tax collection with user privacy and pseudonymity within the metaverse can be a delicate challenge, especially with cryptocurrencies known for their privacy features.

iv) User Education: Users may need to be educated about their tax obligations within virtual environments to promote compliance, especially when using digital currencies.

v) Compliance: Ensuring that all virtual currency transactions are reported and taxed can be complex, especially in decentralised virtual environments.

Implementing a Virtual Currency Transaction Tax requires careful consideration of these challenges and the development of clear rules and regulations. Collaboration among governments, regulatory bodies, virtual platforms, and users is crucial in shaping an effective and equitable taxation framework for virtual currencies in the metaverse.

DIGITAL REAL ESTATE PROPERTY TAX

A Digital Real Estate Property Tax is a model designed to generate revenue from virtual real estate holdings within the metaverse and virtual economies. This innovative tax model addresses digital real estate's unique challenges and opportunities, including virtual land, properties, and locations. Here's an overview of the Digital Real Estate Property Tax:

Model:

i) Taxable Assets: This tax is levied on virtual real estate holdings within virtual environments. These assets may include virtual land, buildings, venues, and other digital properties.

ii) Tax Assessment: The value of digital real estate is assessed based on factors such as the size of the property, its location within the virtual world, use, and perceived value within the virtual community.

iii) Tax Rate: A predetermined tax rate or percentage is applied to the assessed value of digital real estate holdings. The tax rate may vary depending on the virtual property type, location, or the virtual platform's policies.

iv) Point of Collection: The tax can be collected periodically (e.g., annually or semi-annually) from virtual property owners within the virtual environment. Virtual platforms or blockchain networks can facilitate this collection process.

v) Blockchain and Transparent Records: To enhance transparency and traceability, blockchain technology can record and verify virtual property ownership and tax payments.

Advantages:

i) Revenue Generation: Taxing digital real estate holdings can generate revenue for governments or regulatory bodies and contribute to virtual infrastructure or services funding.

ii) Encourages Development: Property owners may be incentivised to develop and improve their virtual properties, leading to a more vibrant and diverse virtual landscape.

iii) Adaptability: The model can be adapted from traditional property tax models used in the physical world, making it familiar to taxpayers.

iv) Transparency: Blockchain technology can clarify the suitability of virtual property ownership and tax payments.

Challenges:

i) Valuation: Determining the accurate value of virtual real estate holdings for tax purposes can be challenging, as virtual property values can be subjective, volatile, and may not have clear market comparisons.

ii) Regulatory Coordination: Ensuring consistent taxation rules and regulations for virtual real estate across different virtual platforms and jurisdictions may require international cooperation and coordination.

iii) Privacy: Balancing the need for tax collection with user privacy and pseudonymity within the metaverse can be a delicate challenge, as virtual property owners may prefer to remain anonymous.

iv) User Education: Users may need to be educated about their tax obligations regarding virtual real estate holdings within virtual environments to promote compliance.

v) Enforcement: Ensuring that all virtual property owners report and pay property taxes may require robust enforcement mechanisms.

Implementing a Digital Real Estate Property Tax requires careful consideration of these challenges and the development of clear rules and regulations. Collaboration among governments, regulatory bodies, virtual platforms, and virtual property owners is crucial in shaping an effective and equitable taxation framework for virtual real estate in the metaverse.

BLOCKCHAIN-BASED TRANSACTION FEES

Blockchain-Based Transaction Fees are a taxation model designed to generate revenue by imposing small fees on transactions conducted on blockchain networks within the metaverse and virtual economies. This innovative tax model leverages blockchain technology's transparency and automation to collect transaction fees. Here's an overview of Blockchain-Based Transaction Fees:

Model:

i) Taxable Transactions: This model imposes a small fee on various blockchain transactions within virtual environments. These transactions can include asset transfers, innovative contract executions, and other blockchain-based activities.

ii) Tax Rate: The tax rate is typically a small percentage of the transaction value. It can vary depending on the type of transaction, blockchain network, or virtual platform's policies.

iii) Point of Collection: The tax is automatically deducted at the end of the blockchain transaction. Intelligent contracts or blockchain protocols facilitate this automated collection process.

iv) Transparency: All transactions and tax collections are recorded on the blockchain, providing transparency and auditability.

v) Real-Time Collection: Blockchain technology allows real-time tax collection as transactions occur, ensuring immediate revenue generation.

Advantages:

i) Revenue Generation: Blockchain-based transaction fees can provide a steady source of revenue for governments or regulatory bodies in the metaverse.

ii) Automation: The tax collection process is highly automated, reducing administrative burdens on taxpayers and tax authorities.

iii) Transparency: The blockchain's transparency and immutability ensure that tax collections are accurately recorded and verifiable.

iv) Real-Time Compliance: Tax compliance is ensured in real-time, minimising the risk of tax evasion or non-compliance.

Challenges:

i) Valuation: Determining the appropriate tax rate for different types of blockchain transactions may be challenging, as values can vary significantly.

ii) Privacy: Balancing the need for tax collection with user privacy and pseudonymity within blockchain transactions can be complex.

iii) Cross-Blockchain Transactions: Addressing taxation for transactions that involve multiple blockchain networks or interoperable virtual environments may require coordination and standardised tax rules.

iv) User Education: Users may need to be educated about blockchain-based transaction fees and their tax obligations within virtual environments.

v) Regulatory Coordination: Consolidating taxation rules across blockchain networks and virtual platforms may require international cooperation and coordination.

Implementing Blockchain-Based Transaction Fees in the metaverse requires careful consideration of these challenges and the development of clear rules and regulations. Collaboration among governments, regulatory bodies, virtual platforms, and users is essential in shaping an effective and equitable taxation framework for blockchain transactions within virtual environments.

VIRTUAL BUSINESS REVENUE TAX

A Virtual Business Revenue Tax is a taxation model designed to generate revenue from virtual businesses operating within the metaverse and virtual economies. This innovative tax model addresses digital companies' unique challenges and opportunities, including in-world shops, entertainment venues, service providers, and other virtual enterprises. Here's an overview of the Virtual Business Revenue Tax:

Model:

i) Taxable Entities: This tax levies on revenue earned by virtual businesses operating within virtual environments. Virtual companies can include shops, entertainment venues, service providers, content creators, and other digital enterprises.

ii) Revenue Assessment: Virtual businesses must report revenue generated within the virtual environment. Payment is assessed based on the income earned from virtual transactions, virtual services, or other income sources within the metaverse.

iii) Tax Rate: A predetermined tax rate or percentage is applied to the reported revenue. The tax rate may vary depending on factors such as the type of virtual business, its size, or the virtual platform's policies.

iv) Point of Collection: The tax is collected periodically (e.g., monthly or quarterly) from virtual business owners within the virtual environment. Virtual platforms or blockchain networks can facilitate this collection process.

v) Blockchain and Transparent Records: To enhance transparency and traceability, blockchain technology can record and verify virtual business revenue and tax payments.

Advantages:

i) Revenue Generation: Taxing virtual businesses can provide a steady source of revenue for governments or regulatory bodies in the metaverse.

ii) Promotes Entrepreneurship: The model encourages entrepreneurship and innovation within the metaverse by allowing virtual businesses to operate legally and contribute to the virtual economy.

iii) Transparency: Blockchain-based recording ensures transparency and auditability of virtual business revenue and tax payments.

iv) Fairness: It ensures that virtual businesses contribute to the tax base, promoting justice in taxation.

Challenges:

i) Revenue Reporting: Ensuring accurate reporting of virtual business revenue may require mechanisms to prevent underreporting or evasion.

ii) Valuation: Determining the appropriate tax rate for different types of virtual businesses and their revenue sources can be challenging.

iii) Privacy: Balancing the need for tax collection with user privacy and pseudonymity within the metaverse can be complex.

iv) User Education: Virtual business operators may need to know their tax obligations within virtual environments.

v) Regulatory Coordination: Ensuring that taxation rules are consistent across different virtual platforms and jurisdictions may require international cooperation and coordination.

Implementing a Virtual Business Revenue Tax in the metaverse requires careful consideration of these challenges and the development of clear rules and regulations. Collaboration among governments, regulatory bodies, virtual platforms, and virtual business operators is essential in shaping an effective and equitable taxation framework for virtual businesses within virtual environments.

METAVERSE USER INCOME TAX

A Metaverse User Income Tax is a taxation model designed to generate revenue from individuals and entities operating within the metaverse and virtual economies. This innovative tax model addresses the unique challenges and opportunities of digital activities and income sources within virtual environments. Here's an overview of the Metaverse User Income Tax:

Model:

i) Taxable Entities: This tax levies on the income earned by individuals and entities within the metaverse. It applies to various virtual activities, including virtual jobs, virtual property sales, virtual services, content creation, and other income sources within the virtual environment.

ii) Income Reporting: Users and entities within the metaverse must report their virtual income. This includes revenue from virtual transactions, services, events, and other virtual economic activities.

iii) Tax Rate: A predetermined tax rate or percentage is applied to the reported income. The tax rate may vary depending on factors such as the type of income, the income amount, or the virtual platform's policies.

iv) Point of Collection: The tax is collected periodically (e.g., annually or semi-annually) from metaverse users and entities within the virtual environment. Virtual platforms or blockchain networks can facilitate this collection process.

v) Blockchain and Transparent Records: To enhance transparency and traceability, blockchain technology can record and verify user and entity income and tax payments.

Advantages:

i) Revenue Generation: Taxing metaverse users and entities can provide a steady source of revenue for governments or regulatory bodies in the metaverse.

ii) Fairness: It ensures that individuals and entities engaged in income-generating activities within the metaverse contribute to the tax base, promoting justice in taxation.

iii) Transparency: Blockchain-based recording ensures transparency and auditability of income and tax payments.

iv) Automation: Blockchain and smart contracts can facilitate real-time tax collection, reducing administrative burdens on both taxpayers and tax authorities.

Challenges:

i) Income Reporting: Ensuring accurate reporting of virtual income may require mechanisms to prevent underreporting or evasion.

ii) Valuation: Determining the appropriate tax rate for different virtual income sources can be challenging.

iii) Privacy: Balancing the need for tax collection with user privacy and pseudonymity within the metaverse can be complex.

iv) User Education: Metaverse users and entities may need to know their tax obligations within virtual environments.

v) Regulatory Coordination: Ensuring that taxation rules are consistent across different virtual platforms and jurisdictions may require international cooperation and coordination.

Implementing a Metaverse User Income Tax requires careful consideration of these challenges and the development of clear rules and regulations. Collaboration among governments, regulatory bodies, virtual platforms, and metaverse users and entities is essential in shaping an effective and equitable taxation framework for virtual income within virtual environments.

CLEVER CONTRACT-BASED TAXES

Clever Contract-Based Taxes are a taxation model that leverages blockchain technology and smart contracts to automate the tax collection process within the metaverse and virtual economies. This innovative tax model aims to ensure real-time tax compliance and reduce the administrative burden on taxpayers and tax authorities. Here's an overview of Smart Contract-Based Taxes:

Model:

i) Taxable Transactions: Smart contracts are deployed on blockchain networks within the metaverse to calculate and deduct taxes from specific types of transactions automatically. These transactions can include asset transfers, virtual services, content sales, virtual property transactions, and other taxable activities within the virtual environment.

ii) Tax Rate: Each smart contract is programmed with a predefined tax rate or percentage applicable to the specific type of transaction it governs. The tax rate may vary based on transaction value, style, or virtual platform policies.

iii) Real-Time Deduction: When a taxable transaction occurs, the smart contract automatically calculates the tax amount based on the transaction parameters and deducts the tax from the transaction value in real-time.

iv) Transparency and Traceability: All tax transactions and deductions are recorded on the blockchain, providing transparency and auditability of tax payments and ensuring that tax authorities can verify compliance.

Advantages:

i) Real-Time Compliance: Smart contract-based taxes ensure immediate tax compliance as transactions occur, minimising the risk of tax evasion or non-compliance.

ii) Automation: The tax collection process is highly automated, reducing administrative burdens on taxpayers and tax authorities.

iii) Transparency: Blockchain technology provides clarity and immutability, ensuring that tax collections are accurately recorded and verifiable.

iv) Accuracy: Smart contracts can precisely calculate tax amounts based on predefined rules, reducing potential tax reporting and collection errors.

Challenges:

i) Development and Deployment: Creating and deploying smart contracts for various taxable transactions within the metaverse may require technical expertise and resources.

ii) Privacy: Balancing the need for tax collection with user privacy and pseudonymity within the metaverse can be complex.

iii) User Education: Users may need to be educated about using intelligent contract-based taxes and their tax obligations within virtual environments.

iv) Regulatory Coordination: Ensuring that taxation rules encoded in smart contracts are consistent across different virtual platforms and jurisdictions may require international cooperation and coordination.

v) Adaptability: Smart contracts must be adaptable to evolving virtual environments and taxation requirements.

Implementing Smart Contract-Based Taxes in the metaverse requires careful consideration of these challenges and the development of clear rules and regulations. Collaboration among governments, regulatory bodies, virtual platforms, and blockchain developers is essential in shaping an effective and equitable taxation framework based on intelligent contracts within virtual environments.

OPPORTUNITIES FOR REVENUE GENERATION

Taxation of virtual income and transactions within the metaverse and virtual economies is an evolving and complex area, and the specific rules and regulations may vary by jurisdiction. However, there are some general principles and considerations to keep in mind:

Taxation of Virtual Income:

> **Virtual Jobs and Earnings**: In some jurisdictions, income earned through virtual employment, such as in-game jobs or virtual services, may be subject to taxation. This includes revenue from virtual world platforms, online gaming, content creation, and more.
> **Virtual Asset Sales**: Profit from buying and selling virtual assets, including virtual real estate, digital items, and NFTs, may be considered taxable income. The tax treatment may depend on factors like the frequency of transactions and the intent to make a profit.
> **Mining and Staking**: Earnings from cryptocurrency mining or staking, which can be integral to some virtual economies, may be subject to income tax, capital gains tax, or other relevant taxes.
> **Gifts and Donations**: Some virtual economies involve gifting or donating virtual assets or currencies. The tax implications of these transactions may vary, but they could have gift tax consequences.

Taxation of Virtual Transactions:

> **Transaction Taxes**: Some jurisdictions may impose taxes on virtual transactions, such as sales tax, value-added tax (VAT), or goods and services tax (GST). Applying these taxes depends on the specific nature of the transaction and the jurisdiction's tax laws.
> **Crypto-to-Fiat Conversion**: When converting virtual currencies (cryptocurrencies) to fiat currencies, users may be required to report capital gains for tax purposes. The tax rate and reporting requirements can vary widely.
> **In-Game Purchases**: Many virtual worlds and online games involve microtransactions and in-game purchases. Whether these purchases are subject to tax can depend on regional laws and the classification of virtual

items as digital goods or services.

Reporting and Compliance:

> **Record-Keeping**: Users engaging in virtual income and transactions should maintain accurate records of their activities, including transaction histories, earnings, and expenses related to virtual assets.
> **Tax Reporting**: In many jurisdictions, individuals and entities must report their virtual income and transactions when filing annual tax returns. This includes reporting any capital gains or losses from virtual asset transactions.
> **Tax Payment**: Taxes on virtual income and transactions are typically paid in the relevant fiat currency, and taxpayers may need to convert their virtual earnings into fiat for this purpose.

Legal and Jurisdictional Considerations:

> **Jurisdictional Differences**: Taxation rules can vary significantly between countries and regions. Users should be aware of the specific tax regulations in their jurisdiction and seek guidance from tax professionals.
> **Virtual Platforms**: Some virtual platforms may have tax reporting mechanisms or partnerships with tax authorities to facilitate tax compliance.
> **Cryptocurrency Reporting**: If virtual transactions involve cryptocurrencies, users may need to report these transactions to tax authorities, especially if there are capital gains or losses.
> **Tax Treaties**: In cross-border virtual transactions, tax treaties between countries can impact the taxation of virtual income and transactions. Double taxation agreements may also apply.

Given the complexity and evolving nature of virtual economy taxation, it's crucial for individuals and entities engaged in virtual activities to consult with tax professionals who are knowledgeable about virtual economies and the tax laws in their jurisdiction. Additionally, staying informed about updates in tax regulations related to virtual economies is essential to ensure compliance and avoid potential tax liabilities.

LICENSING AND REGULATION OF VIRTUAL BUSINESSES

The licensing and regulation of virtual businesses within the metaverse and virtual economies are complex and evolving areas that require careful consideration by governments and regulatory bodies. These virtual businesses can encompass various activities, including gaming, content creation, virtual real estate development, virtual goods sales, and more. Here are key aspects and considerations regarding the licensing and regulation of virtual businesses.

Regulatory Frameworks:

i) Emerging Field: Virtual business regulation is still emerging, and regulatory frameworks often need to catch up to the rapid growth of virtual economies. Governments and regulators are working to catch up with these developments.

ii) Jurisdictional Differences: Regulations can vary significantly between countries and regions, leading to jurisdictional challenges in the metaverse.

Types of Virtual Businesses:

i) Gaming: Game developers and publishers operating within virtual worlds may need to comply with gaming industry and virtual economy regulations.

ii) Content Creation: Content creators, including YouTubers, streamers, and virtual artists, may need to navigate copyright, intellectual property, and online content regulations.

iii) Virtual Real Estate: Developers and investors in virtual real estate may face property-related regulations, land-use laws, and tax obligations.

iv) Virtual Goods and NFTs: Sales of virtual goods, including NFTs (Non-Fungible Tokens), may involve consumer protection laws, securities regulations, and taxation.

Licensing and Registration:

i) Business Licensing: Virtual businesses may need licenses or permits to operate legally. The requirements can vary by jurisdiction and the type of business.

ii) Virtual Land Ownership: Some virtual platforms may require users to register and pay fees for virtual land ownership, which can be subject to platform-specific rules.

Consumer Protection:

i) Virtual Goods Sales: Regulations related to virtual goods sales often focus on consumer protection, ensuring that users are informed about purchases and have recourse in case of issues.

ii) Payment Processing: Virtual businesses that handle real-world financial transactions may need to comply with payment processing regulations to protect users' financial information.

Intellectual Property and Copyright:

Copyright Infringement:

Virtual businesses must respect intellectual property rights and avoid infringing on copyrights, trademarks, or patents. Regulations may govern how user-generated content is used and shared.

Taxation:

> **Income and Transaction Taxes**: Virtual businesses may be subject to income taxes, sales taxes, or other forms of taxation depending on their revenue streams and the jurisdiction in which they operate.

Privacy and Data Protection:

> **User Data**: Regulations such as GDPR in the European Union and similar laws in other regions may apply to virtual businesses that collect and process user data.

Blockchain and Cryptocurrency:

> **Regulatory Clarity**: Virtual businesses dealing with blockchain technology, cryptocurrencies, or virtual currencies may need to navigate

evolving regulatory landscapes related to these technologies.

User Agreements and Terms of Service:

> **Platform Rules**: Many virtual businesses operate within virtual platforms with their terms of service and community guidelines. Compliance with these rules is essential.

International Considerations:

> **Cross-Border Operations**: Virtual businesses with global operations must consider how international regulations and agreements impact their activities.
> **Legal Recognition**: Some countries may need to recognise virtual assets, which can complicate international regulation legally.

Regulatory Compliance and Reporting:

> **Transparency**: Virtual businesses may need to maintain transparency regarding their operations, revenue, and user interactions to demonstrate compliance with regulations.

Enforcement:

> **Enforcement Challenges**: Enforcing regulations in virtual environments can be challenging due to pseudonymity, privacy concerns, and the decentralised nature of some platforms.
> **User Identities**: In virtual environments, users often interact under pseudonyms or remain completely anonymous. This makes it difficult for authorities to identify and track individuals engaged in illegal or non-compliant activities.
> **Verification**: Establishing the real-world identity of users can be challenging, as virtual platforms may require little identity verification during registration.
> **Evolving Technologies**: The metaverse and virtual economies are characterised by rapid technological advancements. Regulations and enforcement efforts may need help to keep up with these changes.
> **Emerging Challenges**: New technologies, such as decentralised finance

(DeFi) and blockchain-based games, introduce novel enforcement challenges that may need clear precedents.

> **Regulatory Complexity**: The complex and evolving nature of virtual economies and their intersection with traditional legal frameworks can make enforcement challenging for authorities.

As the metaverse develops, the virtual business regulatory landscape will likely evolve. It's crucial for virtual business operators to stay informed about local and international regulations, seek legal counsel when necessary, and proactively address compliance issues to operate within the bounds of the law and protect users. Collaboration between governments, virtual platforms, and the virtual business community can help establish transparent and fair regulatory frameworks.

POLICY IMPLICATIONS AND CONSIDERATIONS

Balancing Taxation and Innovation In The Metaverse

Balancing taxation and innovation in the metaverse is a complex and delicate task. Tax is necessary to fund public services infrastructure and ensure a fair distribution of resources. At the same time, fostering innovation is crucial for the growth and development of the metaverse and virtual economies. Here are some strategies and considerations for striking a balance between taxation and innovation:

Clear Regulatory Frameworks:

> **Clarity**: Governments and regulatory bodies should provide clear and comprehensive regulations for virtual economies. Uncertainty can stifle innovation.

> **Adaptability**: Regulations should be adaptable to technological advancements and changing business models within the metaverse.

Taxation Models:

> **Innovation-Friendly Taxation**: Taxation models should be designed to encourage innovation rather than hinder it. For example, tax incentives for research and development (R&D) in virtual technologies can stimulate

innovation.

> Progressive Taxation: Taxation should be developed, meaning those with higher incomes or more extensive virtual holdings pay a proportionally larger share. This can promote fairness while allowing innovation to thrive.

Education and Awareness:

> User Education: Educating metaverse users and virtual businesses about their tax obligations and benefits can lead to better compliance and a more innovation-friendly environment.

Sandbox Approaches:

> Regulatory Sandboxes: Some governments have introduced regulatory sandboxes that allow innovative businesses to operate within defined boundaries for a limited time, allowing regulators to better understand new technologies and business models.

Collaboration:

> Public-Private Collaboration: Collaboration between governments, regulatory bodies, and the private sector can lead to the development of innovative solutions for taxation and regulation that consider the unique nature of the metaverse.
> Cross-Border Collaboration: International cooperation and collaboration on taxation and regulation are essential due to the global nature of virtual economies.

Blockchain and Transparency:

> Blockchain Technology: Utilizing blockchain for transparent record-keeping and taxation can help ensure compliance while fostering trust in the metaverse.

Encouraging Investment:

> **Incentives for Investment**: Governments can offer tax incentives for individuals and businesses that invest in metaverse-related technologies, startups, or infrastructure.

Risk Mitigation:

> **Risk Assessment**: Governments can work to identify and mitigate potential risks associated with new virtual technologies and business models rather than stifling them with overly cautious regulations.

Innovation Hubs:

> **Designated Innovation Zones**: Some regions may consider establishing certain areas or zones within the metaverse as innovation hubs with favourable tax and regulatory environments.

Public Input:

> **Stakeholder Engagement**: Involve stakeholders, including virtual platform operators, developers, and users, in the policymaking process to ensure that regulations strike the right balance.

Balancing taxation and innovation in the metaverse requires a nuanced and collaborative approach. Recognising that the metaverse is a rapidly evolving space is essential, and overburdensome taxation and regulation can stifle its potential. At the same time, responsible taxation and regulation are necessary to address issues such as consumer protection, financial stability, and taxation of virtual assets.

Ultimately, achieving the right balance between taxation and innovation in the metaverse will require ongoing dialogue, adaptability, and a willingness to experiment with new approaches that promote economic growth and participants' welfare within the virtual economy.

CHAPTER VI

Cryptocurrency Regulation in Virtual Economies: Legal and Economic Implications

INTRODUCTION

The advent of cryptocurrencies, exemplified by prominent examples such as Bitcoin and Ethereum, has constituted a significant upheaval in finance. Digital currencies have caused significant disruptions to conventional financial institutions by providing an alternative method of conducting transactions and preserving value that surpasses the limitations imposed by geographical boundaries and traditional financial intermediaries. By doing so, they have sparked a surge of interest and creativity inside virtual economies on a global scale. Nevertheless, the potential for disruption is accompanied by many issues, hence requiring the establishment of regulatory frameworks to tackle them effectively.

The regulation of cryptocurrency within virtual economies is a significant and intricate matter within the contemporary global financial environment. Cryptocurrencies provide the potential for enhanced financial inclusivity, improved efficiency in cross-border transactions, and broadened availability of financial services. Conversely, these entities have been linked to various potential hazards, including fraudulent activities, illicit financial transactions, and fluctuations in market stability.

The objective of this study is to thoroughly explore the complex realm of cryptocurrency regulation, with a particular emphasis on its legal and economic ramifications. In an era characterised by the growing convergence of the virtual and physical domains, it becomes crucial to examine the responses of governments, regulatory entities, and financial institutions to the complexities presented by digital assets.

The regulatory framework for cryptocurrencies is complex and covers various matters. This study aims to examine the issue of consumer protection, which assumes great significance due to the vulnerability of persons targeted by fraudulent activities and thefts in the realm of Bitcoin. Implementing anti-money laundering (AML) and know-your-customer (KYC) legislation is of utmost importance in safeguarding against the illicit utilisation of cryptocurrencies.

Furthermore, the topic of discussion will encompass the taxation of cryptocurrencies, which presents a multifaceted matter subject to divergence across different jurisdictions. Consequently, users and enterprises face the intricate task of navigating a complex tax legislation and regulations network. Certain types of cryptocurrencies, particularly initial coin offerings (ICOs) and tokens, have prompted inquiries regarding their classification as securities, subjecting them to the regulatory framework of securities legislation.

In addition, the increasing use of cryptocurrencies is raising concerns about the stability of conventional financial systems. It is imperative for regulators to diligently oversee and mitigate potential systemic risks that may emerge from the convergence of the cryptocurrency and traditional economic domains.

Moreover, the inherent transnational characteristic of cryptocurrency transactions poses a distinctive obstacle. Cryptocurrencies, characterised by their decentralised nature and worldwide reach, frequently transcend certain jurisdictions' boundaries, raising inquiries over the applicable legislative framework.

The careful equilibrium between regulation and innovation significantly affects economic growth and technical progress. The potential for revolutionary impact on other industries extends beyond banking, as exemplified by the creation of cryptocurrency, mainly through blockchain technology. Nevertheless, excessively stringent restrictions have the potential to impede this innovation and drive it into clandestine practices.

Overseeing cryptocurrencies in virtual economies is a complex and swiftly developing domain. The domain pertains to the intricate legal and economic considerations that governments and regulatory entities confront to safeguard consumers, uphold financial stability, and promote innovation within an ever-expanding digital realm. This endeavour aims to elucidate the complex dynamics shaping virtual economies' future and the broader economic landscape.

OVERVIEW OF RELEVANT LITERATURE ON CRYPTOCURRENCY REGULATION

An overview of relevant literature on cryptocurrency regulation reveals a rich and diverse body of research that spans legal, economic, and technological perspectives. Scholars, policymakers, and practitioners have extensively explored the challenges and opportunities of regulating cryptocurrencies. Here are some key themes and notable contributions from the literature:

Regulating Cryptocurrencies in the United States: Current Issues and Future Directions" by Golumbia (2019)

The scholarly study "Regulating Cryptocurrencies in the United States: Current Issues and Future Directions" by Golumbia (2019) examines the regulatory landscape of cryptocurrencies in the United States. The paper provides insights into the challenges, complexities, and potential future orientations for cryptocurrency regulation within the U.S. Here is an overview of the paper's main points and contributions:

The paper begins with a discussion of the status of cryptocurrency regulation in the United States. It emphasises cryptocurrencies' decentralised and borderless character, making it difficult to implement traditional regulatory frameworks effectively.

Golumbia investigates the duties and responsibilities of numerous regulatory agencies, including the U.S. Securities and Exchange Commission (SEC), the Commodity Futures Trading Commission (CFTC), the Financial Crimes Enforcement Network (FinCEN), and state-level regulators. Each agency views cryptocurrencies differently, resulting in a fragmented regulatory landscape.

The paper investigates whether specific cryptocurrencies and initial coin offerings (ICOs) should be considered securities. This classification has substantial implications for regulatory oversight and investor protection.

It identifies the challenges and complexities of regulating cryptocurrencies, including jurisdictional issues, technological advancements, and the character of the crypto space as it evolves. The author emphasises the difficulty of keeping up with the industry's swift advances.

Future Regulatory Directions: Golumbia investigates possible future regulatory directions for cryptocurrencies in the United States. This includes discussions regarding regulatory clarity, the possibility of amending existing laws, and international cooperation to address cross-border issues.

The paper highlights the delicate balance regulators must achieve between fostering innovation in the blockchain and cryptocurrency and protecting consumers and investors from potential risks and fraud.

"Regulating Cryptocurrencies in the United States: Current Issues and Future Directions" provides an insightful analysis of the challenges and opportunities surrounding cryptocurrency regulation in the United States. It underscores the need for regulatory frameworks to address cryptocurrencies' unique characteristics while fostering innovation and assuring investor protection. This paper is handy for policymakers, legal experts, and academics who wish to comprehend the evolving regulatory landscape for cryptocurrencies in the United States.

"Crypto Tokens and Initial Coin Offerings as a New Way of Crowdfunding - the Regulatory Aspects" by Górka and Kairys (2019):

The research paper "Crypto tokens and Initial Coin Offerings as a New Form of Crowdfunding - the Regulatory Aspects" by Górka and Kairys (2019) examines the regulatory aspects surrounding crypto tokens and Initial Coin Offerings (ICOs), with a focus on their role as a new form of crowdfunding. Here is a summary of this paper's main points and contributions:

The paper introduces the concepts of crypto tokens and initial coin offerings (ICOs). Crypto tokens are blockchain-based digital assets, whereas ICOs are fundraising events where tokens are sold to investors. The authors highlight the inventiveness of these fundraising mechanisms.

The paper discusses how initial coin offerings (ICOs) have emerged as a revolutionary form of crowdfunding. It demonstrates their potential to democratise fundraising by enabling entrepreneurs and projects to access a global pool of investors without conventional intermediaries.

Górka and Kairys investigate the regulatory challenges presented by ICOs. They emphasise that the rapid evolution of ICOs has made it challenging for regulators to keep up with innovation. This includes concerns regarding investor protection, fraud, and the possibility of using ICOs for unlawful activities.

The authors investigate whether initial coin offerings (ICOs) should be categorised as securities offerings subject to applicable securities regulations. This classification has significant implications for conducting and regulating initial coin offerings.

This paper provides a comparative analysis of ICO regulations in various jurisdictions, highlighting the need for a global consensus on regulating these fundraising mechanisms. The United States, the European Union, and Switzerland are among the nations whose approaches are examined.

Górka and Kairys provide regulatory and policymaker recommendations to address the regulatory challenges ICOs pose. They emphasise the need for clarity, regulatory sandboxes for experimentation, and international cooperation.

In its conclusion, the paper summarises the key takeaways and reiterates the need for a balanced regulatory approach that encourages innovation while safeguarding investors and preserving market integrity.

The article "Crypto Tokens and Initial Coin Offerings as a New Way of Crowdfunding - the Regulatory Aspects" adds to the increasing literature on ICOs and crowdfunding in cryptocurrency. It provides valuable insights into the complexities and challenges of regulating these innovative fundraising methods. It emphasises the need for regulatory solutions that encourage responsible innovation in the blockchain and cryptocurrency industries. This study interests legal scholars, policymakers, and industry participants who wish to comprehend the evolving regulatory landscape of initial coin offerings (ICOs) and crypto tokens.

"Taxation of Cryptocurrencies: A Worldwide Review" by Deloitte (2020)

"Taxation of Cryptocurrencies: A Worldwide Review" by Deloitte (2020) is a comprehensive report that provides insights into the taxation of cryptocurrencies globally. The report provides an in-depth analysis of how various nations approach the taxation of cryptocurrency transactions and holdings. Here is a summary of the report's main points and findings:

Introduction to Cryptocurrency Taxation The report begins by explaining the significance of comprehending cryptocurrency taxation. Due to their digital and decentralised character, cryptocurrencies such as Bitcoin and Ethereum have unique tax considerations.

Classification for Tax Purposes The report by Deloitte discusses how various nations classify cryptocurrencies for tax purposes. Typical categories include property, currency, and commodity. These classifications have substantial implications for the taxation of cryptocurrencies.

Capital Gains Tax: This report examines the application of capital gains tax to cryptocurrency transactions. It discusses the taxation of profits derived from purchasing and selling cryptocurrencies and emphasises differences in tax rates and thresholds across nations.

Deloitte investigates the taxation of cryptocurrency-related revenue, including mining rewards, airdrops, and staking rewards. It discusses the tax treatment of income generated through these activities.

The report provides insight into the reporting requirements for cryptocurrency transactions. It discusses the need for individuals and businesses to keep accurate documents of their cryptocurrency transactions and to report them to the appropriate tax authorities.

Anti-Avoidance Measures: Deloitte investigates the anti-avoidance measures implemented by some countries to prevent tax evasion and assure compliance with cryptocurrency taxation laws.

International Taxation: The report discusses the difficulties and opportunities associated with international cryptocurrency taxation. It discusses double taxation and the significance of international cooperation in this regard.

Case Studies: The report by Deloitte includes case studies of selected countries, which provide comprehensive insights into how particular nations approach cryptocurrency taxation. These case studies provide a more profound comprehension of regional tax policy variations.

Implications for the Economy: The report briefly comments on the economic importance of cryptocurrency taxation. It discusses how tax policies influence cryptocurrencies' adoption, investment, and economic activity.

Future Patterns: Deloitte concludes by discussing possible future taxation trends for cryptocurrencies. It emphasises the need for continuous regulatory innovations to keep up with the rapidly changing cryptocurrency landscape.

This Deloitte report is a valuable resource for individuals, businesses, tax professionals, and policymakers navigating the complex world of cryptocurrency taxation. It emphasises the need for international coordination in addressing the tax-related challenges posed by cryptocurrencies, as well as the significance of remaining up to date on local tax laws and regulations. Compliance and informed decision-making are aided by the report's global perspective, which provides a comprehensive overview of cryptocurrency taxation in various countries.

DISCUSSION OF LEGAL FRAMEWORKS AND REGULATIONS IN DIFFERENT JURISDICTIONS

Legal frameworks and regulations for cryptocurrencies and blockchain technology vary significantly across jurisdictions. The approach to regulating these technologies depends on the country's legal, economic, and political landscape. Here is a discussion of some notable legal frameworks and regulations in various jurisdictions:

1. United States:

The United States has a complicated regulatory environment for cryptocurrencies. The SEC classifies specific tokens as securities and enforces securities laws, whereas the CFTC classifies others as commodities. The IRS taxes cryptocurrencies as property and transactions are subject to capital gains tax.

State-level regulations vary, with New York's BitLicense being one of the strictest state-specific regulations, mandating cryptocurrency businesses to obtain a license.

2. The European Union:

The European Union seeks to establish a uniform regulatory framework for cryptocurrencies across its member states. The proposal for Markets in Crypto Assets (MiCA) seeks to establish clear regulations for issuing and trading digital assets.

Fifth Anti-Money Laundering Directive (5AMLD) mandates AML and Know Your Customer (KYC) requirements for cryptocurrency enterprises, including exchanges and wallet providers.

3. China:

China takes a strict stance on virtual currencies. In 2017, it prohibited cryptocurrency exchanges and ICOs—the government's continued crackdown on cryptocurrency-related activities, including mining operations.

4. Japan:

Since 2017, Japan has recognised cryptocurrencies as legitimate forms of payment. The Payment Services Act regulates and mandates licensing for cryptocurrency exchanges. Additionally, Japan enforces stringent AML and KYC measures.

5. Singapore:

Singapore is renowned for its progressive cryptocurrency regulatory framework. The Payment Services Act, which will go into effect in 2020, mandates that cryptocurrency businesses register and comply with AML and KYC regulations.
Singapore promotes fintech and blockchain innovation actively.

6. Switzerland:

Switzerland is renowned for its cryptocurrency-friendly regulatory framework. The Swiss Financial Market Supervisory Authority (FINMA) is provided with explicit guidelines for ICOs. The Crypto Valley in Zug is a central location for blockchain and cryptocurrency enterprises.

7. South Korea:

South Korea has enacted regulations to resolve cryptocurrency risks, requiring exchanges to verify users' identities.
AML regulations apply to cryptocurrency transactions, and the government intends to tax cryptocurrency gains.

8. India:

The Supreme Court lifted the cryptocurrency banking prohibition imposed by the Reserve Bank of India (RBI) in India, which the RBI had set. The government is contemplating a cryptocurrency regulation and taxation bill.

9. Australia:

Australia's regulatory framework for cryptocurrency exchanges focuses predominantly on AML and KYC regulations. AUSTRAC (Australian Transaction Reports and Analysis Centre) registration is required. Australia has also enacted regulations to secure the safety of exchanges' cryptocurrency holdings.

10. Canada:

Canada has a permissive attitude toward cryptocurrencies. AML and KYC measures are the primary regulatory focus for cryptocurrency enterprises. The nation has experimented with CBDC initiatives and promotes the development of blockchain technology.

These jurisdictional variations reflect the global diversity of cryptocurrency and blockchain regulatory approaches. Participants in the cryptocurrency space must be aware of and compliant with the specific regulations in their respective regions as these frameworks continue to evolve in tandem with the rapidly changing cryptocurrency landscape. Clarity in legal and regulatory matters is essential for fostering innovation, protecting consumers, and preserving the integrity of financial markets.

EXAMINATION OF EXISTING STUDIES ON THE ECONOMIC IMPACT OF CRYPTOCURRENCY REGULATION

Market Behaviour and Volatility

Market behaviour and volatility in the context of cryptocurrency regulation are areas of significant interest and study. Cryptocurrency markets are known for their inherent volatility, which regulatory developments can exacerbate. Here, we'll explore the relationship between regulatory actions and market behaviour:

i) Impact of Regulatory Announcements: Cryptocurrency markets are susceptible to news and regulatory announcements. Market participants react swiftly when governments or regulatory bodies state their stance on cryptocurrencies. Joyous news, such as regulatory clarity or acceptance, often leads to price surges, while negative information, such as impending bans or restrictive regulations, can trigger sharp declines in cryptocurrency prices. This rapid market response to regulatory news underscores the importance of regulatory certainty for market stability.

ii) Increased Volatility: Research has shown that regulatory events increase market volatility. Sudden regulatory changes or crackdowns can create uncertainty, prompting traders and investors to adjust their positions rapidly. This heightened volatility can present both opportunities and risks. Traders may seek to profit from price swings, while long-term investors may face increased uncertainty about the market's stability.

iii) Market Sentiment and Investor Behaviour: Regulatory actions can significantly influence market sentiment. Positive regulatory developments often boost investor confidence and attract new participants, leading to bullish sentiment. Conversely, negative regulatory news can trigger fear and uncertainty, causing panic selling and bearish sentiment. The interplay between market sentiment and regulatory events can amplify price movements.

iv) Long-Term Impact on Market Stability: While short-term volatility is expected in response to regulatory news, the long-term impact of regulation on market stability is less clear-cut. Some researchers argue that well-defined and investor-friendly rules can attract institutional investors and promote long-term market stability. Others contend that excessive regulation can stifle innovation and deter market participants, potentially limiting long-term growth.

v) Global Variation in Regulatory Impact: It's important to note that the impact of regulation can vary by jurisdiction. Different countries have adopted diverse approaches to cryptocurrency regulation, ranging from welcoming and supportive to highly restrictive. As a result, cryptocurrency market behaviour and volatility may differ significantly from region to region, depending on the local regulatory environment.

vi) Ongoing Regulatory Evolution: Cryptocurrency markets are dynamic, and regulations continue to evolve. This means the relationship between law and market behaviour is subject to change. Regulatory clarity and consistency are crucial in mitigating excessive volatility, as uncertainty can lead to irrational market reactions.

The interplay between cryptocurrency regulation and market behaviour is complex and evolving. Regulatory actions and announcements have the potential to influence market sentiment, trigger rapid price movements, and impact the overall stability of cryptocurrency markets. As the cryptocurrency industry matures and regulatory frameworks develop, understanding and managing the effects of regulation on market behaviour remain critical for participants and observers of these dynamic markets.

Market Liquidity

Market liquidity in the context of cryptocurrency refers to the ease with which digital assets can be bought or sold in the market without causing significant price fluctuations. It is a crucial aspect of any financial market, including cryptocurrencies, and directly impacts trading efficiency, price stability, and overall market health. Here's a more detailed explanation of market liquidity in the cryptocurrency space:

i) Market Orders and Liquidity: Liquidity is typically assessed by examining the depth of the order book on cryptocurrency exchanges. The order book displays the number of buy and sell orders at various price levels. Many buy and sell orders close to the current market price indicate high liquidity. Traders can execute large market orders without significantly impacting the price.

ii) Bid-Ask Spread: The bid-ask spread represents the difference between the highest price a buyer is willing to pay (the bid) and the lowest price a seller accepts (the ask). A narrow spread suggests high liquidity, as there is minimal difference between buying and selling prices. A broader reach may indicate lower liquidity.

iii) Volume: Trading volume is a crucial indicator of liquidity. High trading volume means a large number of transactions are occurring, indicating active participation in the market. Higher trading volumes often correspond to greater liquidity.

iv) Impact of Liquidity on Price: Large trades can be executed in liquid markets without causing significant price fluctuations. In illiquid markets, attempting to buy or sell a substantial cryptocurrency can lead to price slippage, where the execution price deviates from the expected price.

v) Market Orders vs. Limit Orders: Traders can use market orders or limit orders when executing trades. Market orders are executed immediately at the prevailing market price, while limit orders specify a particular price a trader is willing to buy or sell. In liquid markets, market orders are more likely to be filled at the desired price.

vi) Liquidity Providers: Market makers and liquidity providers are crucial in maintaining liquidity. These entities continuously place buy and sell orders in the market, narrowing the bid-ask spread and increasing market depth.

vii) Impact of Regulatory Measures: Regulatory actions and measures can influence market liquidity. Stricter regulations may deter market participants, leading to reduced liquidity. Conversely, laws that enhance transparency and investor protection can attract more participants, potentially increasing liquidity.

viii) Cryptocurrency Liquidity vs. Traditional Markets: Cryptocurrency markets are generally less liquid than traditional financial markets like stocks or foreign exchange. This lower liquidity can lead to greater price volatility and potential risks and offers opportunities for traders and investors.

ix) Regional Variations: Liquidity levels can vary by cryptocurrency exchange and region. Some businesses may have higher liquidity for specific cryptocurrencies, while others may have lower liquidity. Additionally, liquidity can differ between cryptocurrency trading pairs.

Overall, liquidity is a critical factor in cryptocurrency markets. High liquidity promotes price stability, efficient trading, and a more attractive environment for market participants. Traders and investors often consider liquidity when choosing exchanges and assets to trade, as it can impact the ease of executing orders and the potential for price slippage. Regulators and market participants continue to work towards improving liquidity and market integrity in the cryptocurrency space.

Innovation and Investment

Innovation and investment in cryptocurrency are closely intertwined and play pivotal roles in shaping the development and evolution of blockchain technology and digital assets. Here's a detailed exploration of the relationship between innovation and investment in the cryptocurrency sector:

1. Innovation as a Driver of Investment:

> Cryptocurrency innovation often catalyses investment. New and ground-breaking technologies, protocols, and applications attract the attention of investors seeking to participate in the next wave of innovation.
> Projects that introduce novel solutions to real-world problems or offer improvements over existing financial systems tend to garner significant investment interest.

2. Venture Capital (VC) Investment:

> VC firms have been instrumental in funding cryptocurrency and blockchain projects. They identify promising start-ups and provide capital to fuel their development and growth.
> VC investment is crucial in the early stages of a project's lifecycle, helping it reach milestones and achieve viability.

3. Initial Coin Offerings (ICOs):

> ICOs have been a popular method for cryptocurrency projects to raise capital directly from the public. Investors purchase project tokens during ICOs to anticipate future utility or value appreciation.
> ICOs democratised access to investment opportunities, enabling more individuals to participate in cryptocurrency projects.

4. Tokenisation and Asset Digitization:

> Innovation in tokenisation has enabled the representation of real-world assets (such as real estate, art, and stocks) as digital tokens on blockchain networks.
> This innovation has the potential to unlock previously illiquid assets and create new investment opportunities for a global audience.

5. Defi (Decentralized Finance) Innovation:

> DeFi projects have introduced novel financial products and services built on blockchain technology. These include lending, borrowing, yield

farming, and decentralised exchanges.

> DeFi innovation has attracted substantial investment as it disrupts traditional financial intermediaries and offers decentralised alternatives.

6. Blockchain Interoperability and Scalability:

> Innovations aimed at enhancing blockchain interoperability and scalability have attracted investment. Solutions that enable different blockchains to communicate and process transactions more efficiently are of particular interest.

> Scalability innovations aim to address blockchain network congestion and high transaction fees.

7. Regulatory Considerations:

> Regulatory clarity and compliance also play a role in investment decisions. Projects that align with existing regulations or demonstrate a commitment to regulatory compliance may be perceived as lower-risk investments.

> Innovations that address regulatory concerns, such as anti-money laundering (AML) and know-your-customer (KYC) requirements, can enhance a project's appeal to institutional investors.

8. Risks and Due Diligence:

> While innovation drives investment, investors also conduct thorough due diligence to assess the legitimacy and viability of projects.

> Investment in cryptocurrencies and blockchain projects carries inherent risks, including technological, regulatory, and market risks. Investors carefully evaluate these risks before allocating capital.

9. Long-Term Impact:

> The relationship between innovation and investment in the cryptocurrency sector is dynamic and ongoing. Successful innovations can attract additional investment, fostering further development.

> The long-term impact of innovation and investment is still unfolding, with the potential to reshape various industries beyond finance.

Innovation and investment are mutually reinforcing in the cryptocurrency space. Innovative projects attract investment capital, and investment enables further innovation and development. This symbiotic relationship has driven the rapid evolution of blockchain technology and digital assets, making the cryptocurrency sector one of the global economy's most dynamic and transformative areas.

ICO Activity

Initial Coin Offerings (ICOs) have been a prominent fundraising method in the cryptocurrency space. ICO activity refers to how blockchain and cryptocurrency projects raise capital by selling newly created tokens to investors. Here's an in-depth look at ICO activity and its key aspects:

1. Fundraising Mechanism:

> ICOs are a crowdfunding method where cryptocurrency projects create and issue their tokens, often on a blockchain platform like Ethereum.
> Investors participate in ICOs by purchasing these tokens, typically using widely accepted cryptocurrencies such as Bitcoin (BTC) or Ethereum (ETH).

2. Token Creation and Distribution:

> Projects create a specific quantity of tokens, which may represent various forms of utility or ownership within the project's ecosystem.
> These tokens are typically distributed to investors during the ICO in exchange for their contributions, which can be in cryptocurrencies or fiat currencies.

3. Investor Participation:

> ICOs have attracted many participants, including retail investors, institutional investors, and cryptocurrency enthusiasts.
> The level of investor participation can significantly impact the success of an ICO.

4. Use of Funds:

> ICOs are intended to raise capital for various purposes, including project development, platform expansion, marketing, and operational expenses.
> Project teams outline their funding goals and how they plan to use the proceeds in whitepapers or other documents.

5. Whitepapers:

> ICOs are typically accompanied by whitepapers detailing the project's objectives, technical aspects, team background, and the problem the project aims to solve.
> Investors use whitepapers to assess the project's viability and potential return on investment.

6. Regulatory Considerations:

> ICOs have faced regulatory scrutiny in many jurisdictions. The legal status of ICOs varies by country, and some have implemented regulations to protect investors and prevent fraud.
> Compliance with relevant securities and financial regulations is crucial to conducting an ICO.

7. Risks and Rewards:

> ICOs present opportunities for high returns, but they also carry significant risks. The value of tokens purchased during ICOs can be volatile, and there is a risk of losing the entire investment.
> Due diligence and careful evaluation of ICO projects are essential to manage risks.

8. Evolution of ICOs:

> The ICO landscape has evolved. In the early days, ICOs were often launched with minimal oversight and regulation. However, increased regulatory scrutiny and concerns about fraudulent ICOs have led to changes in the industry.
> Security Token Offerings (STOs) and Initial Exchange Offerings (IEOs)

have emerged as alternative fundraising methods with different regulatory considerations.

9. Investor Protection:

> Investor protection has become a focus in the ICO space. Regulatory efforts aim to ensure that investors receive adequate information and safeguards.
> Some jurisdictions have introduced requirements for projects to conduct KYC checks on participants and provide detailed disclosures.

10. Global Impact:

> ICOs have raised billions of dollars for blockchain and cryptocurrency projects worldwide. They have funded many initiatives, from decentralised applications (dApps) and innovative contract platforms to blockchain infrastructure and tokenised assets.

ICO activity has played a significant role in the growth and development of the cryptocurrency ecosystem. While ICOs have presented opportunities for fundraising and innovation, they have also faced challenges related to regulatory compliance and investor protection. The evolving regulatory landscape and the emergence of alternative fundraising methods continue to shape the landscape of blockchain capital formation.

Market Participants and Behaviour

Market participants and their behaviour are central to the dynamics of cryptocurrency markets. Understanding the roles and behaviours of different actors in these markets is crucial for comprehending price movements, liquidity, and overall market trends. Here's an exploration of the various market participants and their behaviours:

1. Retail Traders:

> Retail traders are individual investors who participate in cryptocurrency markets. They can range from beginners to experienced traders.

> Retail traders often use online exchanges to buy, sell, and hold cryptocurrencies. Their behaviour can be influenced by factors such as news, sentiment, and technical analysis.

2. Institutional Investors:

> Institutional investors include hedge funds, asset management firms, family offices, and other large financial institutions that allocate capital to cryptocurrencies.
> Institutional participation has grown significantly in recent years, contributing to increased market liquidity and the development of institutional-grade infrastructure.

3. Miners:

> Miners are individuals or organisations validating and adding blockchain transactions through mining.
> Economic incentives drive their behaviour as they seek rewards through cryptocurrency, transaction, or mining fees. Mining operations require significant computational power and energy resources.

4. Whales:

> Whales are individuals or entities that hold a substantial amount of a specific cryptocurrency. They can influence markets by making large trades.
> Whales' behaviour can include buying or selling large amounts of cryptocurrency to manipulate prices, create liquidity, or realise profits.

5. Market Makers:

> Market makers provide liquidity to cryptocurrency markets by continuously placing buy and sell orders.
> They aim to profit from the bid-ask spread—the difference between buying and selling prices. Market makers help reduce price volatility and ensure smoother trading.

6. Arbitrageurs:

> Arbitrageurs seek to profit from price differences of the same cryptocurrency on different exchanges. They buy low on one sale and sell high on another.
> Their actions help equalise prices across exchanges and maintain market efficiency.

7. HODLers:

> HODLers (a misspelling of "hold") are long-term investors who buy cryptocurrencies to hold them for an extended period, often regardless of short-term price fluctuations.
> HODLers believe in the long-term potential of cryptocurrencies and are less concerned with daily price movements.

8. Day Traders:

> Day traders are active traders who seek to profit from short-term price fluctuations within a single day. They may enter and exit positions multiple times in a day.
> Day trading requires technical analysis, chart patterns, and a deep understanding of market psychology.

9. Algorithmic Traders:

> Algorithmic traders use automated trading bots or algorithms to execute trades based on predefined criteria and strategies.
> These traders can react to market conditions quickly and may engage in high-frequency trading (HFT) to capitalise on fleeting opportunities.

10. Regulatory Authorities:

> Regulatory bodies and authorities oversee cryptocurrency markets in many jurisdictions. They enforce anti-money laundering (AML) rules, investor protection, and market integrity.
> Regulatory behaviour can influence market behaviour by imposing trading restrictions, enforcing KYC/AML requirements, and investigating

fraud.

11. Developers and Innovators:

> Developers and innovators within cryptocurrency are responsible for creating new blockchain projects, protocols, and decentralised applications (dApps).
> Their behaviour is driven by the desire to solve real-world problems, enhance blockchain technology, and introduce novel use cases.

12. Media and Influencers:

> Media outlets, social media influencers, and crypto-specific news sources shape market sentiment through news coverage, analysis, and commentary.
> Their statements and reports can influence the behaviour of retail investors and traders.

Understanding the behaviour of these diverse market participants is essential for predicting and interpreting cryptocurrency market movements. The cryptocurrency market's unique characteristics, including high volatility and 24/7 trading, can lead to rapid and sometimes irrational price changes, making it crucial for participants to stay informed and exercise caution. Additionally, regulatory developments and market sentiment often impact participant behaviour and market outcomes.

Taxation and Revenue

Taxation and revenue generation related to cryptocurrencies are essential aspects of the regulatory framework in many jurisdictions. Taxation involves imposing taxes on cryptocurrency transactions, holdings, and activities. Here's an in-depth look at taxation and revenue aspects in the cryptocurrency space:

1. Taxation of Cryptocurrency Transactions:

> Cryptocurrency transactions may be subject to various taxes, including

capital gains, income, and transaction-specific taxes.

> Capital Gains Tax: Profits from the sale or exchange of cryptocurrencies are typically subject to capital gains tax. The tax rate may vary based on factors such as holding duration and local tax laws.

> Income Tax: Cryptocurrency received as income, such as mining rewards or salary payments in crypto, is subject to income tax. The value of the accepted cryptocurrency at the time of receipt is often used for tax calculations.

2. Tax Reporting and Compliance:

> Tax authorities in many countries require individuals and businesses to accurately report cryptocurrency transactions and holdings. Non-compliance may result in penalties and legal consequences.

> Reporting requirements may include providing transaction details, disclosing wallet addresses, and maintaining records of cryptocurrency-related activities.

3. Cryptocurrency Mining Taxation:

> Cryptocurrency mining is subject to taxation in some jurisdictions. Depending on the tax laws, miners may need to report and pay taxes on the rewards they receive, either as income or as self-employment income.

4. Taxation of Cryptocurrency Gifts and Donations:

> Some countries levy taxes on gifts and donations of cryptocurrency. The tax treatment varies, with exemptions or deductions available for charitable contributions in some cases.

5. Taxation of Cryptocurrency as Property:

> In many jurisdictions, cryptocurrencies are treated as property rather than currency. This means that every cryptocurrency transaction is a taxable event, potentially leading to complex tax calculations for traders.

6. Taxation of Cryptocurrency Exchanges:

> Cryptocurrency exchanges are often required to report certain user information to tax authorities to ensure that users comply with tax laws.
> Some countries also impose taxes on cryptocurrency exchange profits, similar to traditional stock exchanges.

7. Cross-Border Transactions and International Taxation:

> Cross-border cryptocurrency transactions can pose challenges for tax authorities. Tax treaties and international cooperation efforts are evolving to address tax evasion and ensure proper taxation of global cryptocurrency activities.

8. Revenue Generation for Governments:

> Taxation of cryptocurrencies can generate revenue for governments, contributing to national budgets and public services.
> Tax revenue from cryptocurrency activities may be used to fund infrastructure, education, healthcare, and other government programs.

9. Challenges in Taxation:

> Taxation of cryptocurrencies presents unique challenges due to their digital and decentralised nature. Tracking transactions, determining fair market values, and enforcing compliance can be complex.
> Cryptocurrency tax regulations often must catch up to the rapidly evolving technology, creating ambiguity and compliance challenges.

10. Regulatory Clarity:

> Many governments are working to provide more explicit guidance on cryptocurrency taxation to reduce uncertainty for taxpayers and facilitate compliance.
> Regulatory clarity can encourage responsible cryptocurrency use and investment while discouraging tax evasion.

Taxation and revenue aspects of cryptocurrencies are critical for governments and taxpayers alike. As the cryptocurrency market grows, governments adapt their tax policies to address this emerging asset class, enhance tax compliance, and ensure that cryptocurrency activities contribute to national revenue streams. However, cryptocurrencies' complex and evolving nature poses ongoing challenges in developing and enforcing tax regulations. Individuals and businesses involved in cryptocurrency need to stay informed about tax requirements in their respective jurisdictions and seek professional advice when necessary to ensure compliance.

Exchange Operations

Exchange operations are a fundamental component of the cryptocurrency ecosystem. Cryptocurrency exchanges are the primary platforms for buying, selling, and trading digital assets. Understanding how these exchanges function and their impact on the cryptocurrency market is crucial for anyone involved in the crypto space. Here's an overview of exchange operations:

1. Trading Pairs:

> Cryptocurrency exchanges offer various trading pairs, allowing users to exchange one cryptocurrency for another or fiat currency (e.g., BTC/USD, ETH/BTC).
> Major exchanges typically provide various trading pairs to cater to different user preferences.

2. Order Types:

> Exchanges offer different order types, including market orders, limit orders, stop-limit orders, and more.
> Market orders are executed immediately at the current market price, while limit orders specify a desired price at which the trade should occur.

3. Liquidity:

> Liquidity on an exchange refers to the ease with which assets can be bought or sold without affecting the price significantly.

> High liquidity is essential for efficient trading, as it minimises price slippage and allows users to enter and exit positions quickly.

4. Order Book:

> The order book displays a list of buy (bids) and sells (asks) orders at various price levels.
> Traders use the order book to assess market depth and make informed trading decisions.

5. Trading Fees:

> Exchanges charge trading fees on transactions. These fees may vary based on trading volume, user type (maker or taker), and the exchange's fee structure.
> Some exchanges offer fee discounts or benefits to users who hold their native tokens.

6. Security Measures:

> Exchange security is a critical aspect of operations. Robust security measures include cold storage of user funds, two-factor authentication (2FA), and regular security audits.
> Security breaches and hacks have historically significantly impacted exchanges and their users.

7. User Verification:

> Many exchanges require user verification, called Know Your Customer (KYC) procedures to comply with legal and regulatory requirements.
> KYC verification typically involves providing identification documents and personal information.

8. Regulatory Compliance:

> Exchanges must adhere to regulatory requirements in their operating jurisdictions. This may include AML (Anti-Money Laundering) and CFT (Counter-Terrorist Financing) measures.

> Some exchanges seek licenses and regulatory approvals to operate legally in specific regions.

9. Stablecoins and Fiat Integration:

> To facilitate trading and withdrawals, exchanges often integrate stablecoins (e.g., USDT, USDC) and offer fiat currency trading pairs.
> These assets provide a stable value reference amid the volatility of cryptocurrencies.

10. Trading Interface:

> User-friendly trading interfaces are essential for attracting traders. Exchanges typically offer a range of tools, including price charts, technical analysis indicators, and trading bots.

11. Market Data and Analysis:

> Exchanges often provide market data, including historical price charts, trading volume, and order book data.
> Traders and analysts use this information to analyse market trends and make informed decisions.

12. Support and Customer Service:

> Exchange customer service is crucial for addressing user inquiries, resolving issues, and providing assistance.
> Responsiveness and reliability of customer support are factors that users consider when choosing an exchange.

13. Listing and Delisting:

> Exchanges decide which cryptocurrencies to list for trading. They may add or remove coins and tokens based on market demand, security, and regulatory considerations.

Exchange operations are central in cryptocurrency markets, providing users access to digital assets and trading opportunities. However, users should exercise caution when selecting an exchange and consider security, regulatory compliance, fees, and user experience to ensure a safe and efficient trading experience. Additionally, staying informed about the latest developments in the cryptocurrency exchange space is essential, as it can impact the overall cryptocurrency market and user portfolios.

Blockchain Start-ups and Innovation Hubs

Blockchain start-ups and innovation hubs are at the forefront of technological advancements, driving innovation in cryptocurrency and blockchain. These entities are pivotal in developing new technologies, applications, and solutions that leverage blockchain technology. Here's a closer look at blockchain start-ups and innovation hubs:

Blockchain Start-ups:

1. Definition:

> Blockchain start-ups are companies or organisations that focus on creating and developing blockchain-based solutions, products, or services.
> These start-ups often aim to address real-world problems or disrupt traditional industries by leveraging the unique capabilities of blockchain technology.

2. Diverse Focus:

> Blockchain start-ups cover various sectors and use cases, including finance, supply chain management, healthcare, identity verification, decentralised applications (dApps), and more.
> Their solutions may involve creating new cryptocurrencies, building blockchain platforms, or developing applications that enhance transparency, security, and efficiency.

3. Funding and Capital:

> Blockchain start-ups typically raise capital through various means, including initial coin offerings (ICOs), security token offerings (STOs), venture capital investments, and crowdfunding.

> Access to funding is essential for research and development, marketing, and scaling operations.

4. Innovation:

> Blockchain start-ups are known for their innovative approaches to solving complex problems. They often pioneer new consensus mechanisms, creative contract languages, and decentralised governance models.
> These innovations contribute to the overall growth and evolution of the blockchain and cryptocurrency ecosystem.

5. Ecosystem Impact:

> Blockchain start-ups can have a significant impact on the broader blockchain ecosystem. They may create partnerships, alliances, or developer communities to collaborate on projects and foster innovation.
> Some start-ups contribute to open-source blockchain projects and protocols, enhancing the technology's accessibility and functionality.

6. Challenges:

> Blockchain start-ups face various challenges, including regulatory compliance, competition, cybersecurity threats, and establishing user trust.
> Regulatory uncertainty and legal considerations can pose obstacles to growth and expansion.

Innovation Hubs:

1. Definition:

> Innovation hubs are physical or virtual spaces where entrepreneurs, developers, researchers, and experts collaborate and innovate in the blockchain and cryptocurrency domain.
> These hubs provide a conducive networking, research, and project development environment.

2. Collaboration and Networking:

> Innovation hubs serve as meeting points for individuals and organisations interested in blockchain technology. They facilitate collaboration, knowledge sharing, and networking opportunities.
> Hub members can collaborate on blockchain projects, exchange ideas, and learn from one another's experiences.

3. Education and Research:

> Many innovation hubs offer educational programs, workshops, and research resources to support blockchain start-ups and individuals interested in the technology.
> These initiatives help individuals acquire the skills and knowledge to contribute to the blockchain ecosystem.

4. Incubation and Acceleration:

> Some innovation hubs provide incubation and acceleration programs for blockchain start-ups. These programs offer mentorship, funding, office space, and access to a supportive community.
> Incubators and accelerators play a vital role in nurturing and accelerating the growth of promising blockchain projects.

5. Global Presence:

> Innovation hubs exist in various locations worldwide, with some specialising in specific blockchain use cases or industries.
> Prominent innovation hubs include Silicon Valley, London, Singapore, and Zurich.

Blockchain start-ups and innovation hubs are essential to technological progress in the blockchain and cryptocurrency. They contribute to the development of new blockchain solutions, the exploration of innovative use cases, and the advancement of the overall ecosystem. Collaboration between start-ups and innovation hubs fosters a fertile ground for ground-breaking ideas and solutions that have the potential to reshape industries and drive widespread blockchain adoption.

International Competition

International competition in cryptocurrencies and blockchain technology is a significant factor that shapes the development and regulatory landscape of the industry. Cryptocurrency projects and blockchain innovation hubs often strategically choose their operations base, headquarters, or regulatory jurisdictions to benefit from favourable conditions or regulatory arbitrage. Here's an overview of international competition in the cryptocurrency space:

1. Regulatory Arbitrage:

> Regulatory arbitrage involves selecting a jurisdiction with favourable regulations or tax treatment to conduct cryptocurrency-related activities.
> Cryptocurrency businesses may choose countries or regions with clear and accommodating regulatory frameworks to avoid legal hurdles and benefit from tax advantages.

2. Blockchain and Cryptocurrency Hubs:

> Some regions have established themselves as blockchain and cryptocurrency hubs due to their supportive regulatory environments and ecosystems.
> Prominent hubs include Switzerland (Crypto Valley), Singapore, Malta, Estonia, and Gibraltar. These hubs attract start-ups, talent, and investments, fostering innovation and economic growth.

3. Regulatory Competition:

> Countries worldwide compete to attract blockchain and cryptocurrency businesses by offering regulatory clarity and favourable conditions.
> Competition among jurisdictions has led to tailored regulatory frameworks to attract blockchain-related investments.

4. Cryptocurrency Exchanges:

> Cryptocurrency exchanges often choose their jurisdictions based on regulatory considerations. Some businesses seek out countries with well-

defined regulatory regimes, while others operate in more lenient jurisdictions.
> Regulatory competition can influence the global distribution of cryptocurrency exchanges.

5. Financial Services and Banking:

> Access to banking services is essential for cryptocurrency businesses. Some countries have embraced cryptocurrencies and offer supportive banking services, while others are more cautious.
> Fintech-friendly jurisdictions can attract businesses and start-ups seeking financial infrastructure.

6. Innovation and Talent:

> The international competition extends to attracting blockchain talent and fostering innovation. Regions with strong educational institutions, research centres, and tech communities can create environments conducive to blockchain innovation.

7. Government Initiatives:

> Governments are launching initiatives and pilot projects to explore using blockchain technology for public services, supply chain management, voting systems, and more.
> These initiatives can position countries as leaders in blockchain adoption and development.

8. Global Collaboration and Standards:

> International organisations, industry associations, and regulatory bodies collaborate on establishing global standards and best practices for blockchain technology.
> Standardisation efforts aim to promote interoperability and facilitate cross-border blockchain applications.

9. Market Access:

> Cryptocurrency projects may prioritise regions that provide access to large and diverse user bases and financial markets.
> Access to international markets and user adoption are critical factors for the success of blockchain applications and cryptocurrencies.

10. Security and Trust:

> Trust and security are paramount in the cryptocurrency space. Jurisdictions known for strong regulatory oversight and investor protection can attract businesses looking to build user trust.

International competition in the cryptocurrency and blockchain sector is dynamic and continually evolving. As blockchain technology matures and gains wider recognition, countries and regions are vying for a competitive edge in the global landscape. The outcome of this competition can influence the growth, adoption, and regulation of cryptocurrencies and blockchain technology worldwide. It also underscores the importance of regulatory clarity and cooperation in shaping the industry's future.

Financial Inclusion

Financial inclusion is a critical economic and social concept that refers to the accessibility and availability of financial services and products to all individuals and businesses, especially those in underserved or marginalised communities. It ensures everyone can access affordable and reliable financial tools like banking services, savings accounts, credit, insurance, and payment systems. Here's a detailed exploration of financial inclusion:

Key Elements of Financial Inclusion:

1. Access to Banking Services:

Financial inclusion begins with access to essential banking services, including savings accounts, checking accounts, and payment services. Traditional banks and digital banking platforms are crucial in providing these services.

2. Credit and Loans:

Access to credit and loans is vital for individuals and businesses to invest, grow, and weather financial emergencies. Inclusive lending practices consider factors beyond traditional credit scores to extend credit to underserved populations.

3. Insurance and Risk Management:

Insurance products are essential for protecting against unforeseen risks, such as health issues, natural disasters, or accidents. Inclusive insurance aims to provide affordable coverage to vulnerable populations.

4. Payment Services:

Access to secure and affordable payment systems is essential for daily financial transactions. Mobile banking, digital wallets, and electronic payment platforms have expanded access to payment services.

5. Savings and Investments:

Encouraging savings and investments helps individuals and families build financial security over time. Inclusive financial institutions offer products to promote conservation and investment among low-income and underserved groups.

6. Financial Education and Literacy:

Promoting financial literacy is a crucial aspect of financial inclusion. Education and awareness programs help individuals make informed financial decisions, understand risks, and manage their finances effectively.

Importance of Financial Inclusion:

i) Reducing Poverty: Financial inclusion can contribute to poverty reduction by providing individuals and communities with tools to save, invest, and access credit for income-generating activities.

ii) Economic Growth: Access to financial services can stimulate economic growth by fostering entrepreneurship, job creation, and investment in small and medium-sized enterprises (SMEs).

iii) Gender Equality: Financial inclusion can address gender disparities in access to financial services, empowering women to participate in the formal economy and achieve financial independence.

iv) Resilience to Shocks: Access to savings and insurance can help individuals and communities withstand financial shocks, such as health emergencies or natural disasters.

v) Social Safety Nets: Inclusive financial systems can facilitate the delivery of social welfare programs and government subsidies to those in need more efficiently and transparently.

vi) Fostering Innovation: Financial inclusion encourages innovation in the financial sector, including developing digital payment solutions, fintech services, and blockchain-based platforms.

Barriers to Financial Inclusion:

i) Lack of Infrastructure: In remote or underserved areas, the absence of physical banking branches, internet connectivity, and digital infrastructure can hinder access to financial services.

ii) Regulatory Challenges: More than overly restrictive or complex regulations can discourage financial institutions from serving low-income or marginalised populations.

iii) Financial Literacy: Limited financial literacy and awareness can prevent individuals from effectively using financial services or understanding their rights and responsibilities.

iv) Income Inequality: Income inequality can create disparities in access to financial resources and services, making it challenging for low-income individuals to save or invest.

v) Discrimination: Discriminatory practices, including gender bias and racial discrimination, can limit access to financial services for specific groups.

Global Efforts and Initiatives:

i) United Nations Sustainable Development Goals (SDGs): The UN includes financial inclusion as one of its goals (Goal 8.10) to ensure equal access to financial services for all.

ii) Financial Inclusion Initiatives: Governments, NGOs, and international organisations have launched initiatives to promote financial inclusion, such as providing microloans, improving financial literacy, and expanding access to banking services.

iii) Fintech and Mobile Banking: Technological innovations like mobile banking and digital payment platforms have expanded financial inclusion by reaching underserved populations.

iv) Blockchain and Cryptocurrency: Blockchain technology and cryptocurrencies have the potential to enhance financial inclusion by providing secure and accessible financial services to unbanked and underbanked individuals.

Financial inclusion is a critical component of economic development and poverty reduction efforts. It seeks to create a more inclusive and equitable financial system that benefits individuals and communities across the socioeconomic spectrum, fostering economic growth and social progress.

LEGAL IMPLICATIONS OF CRYPTOCURRENCY REGULATION

Analysis of the legal challenges and considerations in regulating cryptocurrencies

The legal challenges and considerations in regulating cryptocurrencies are multifaceted and complex due to digital assets' unique characteristics and global nature. Here's a detailed analysis of the key legal challenges and considerations in regulating cryptocurrencies:

1. Classification and Definition:

i) Challenge: Cryptocurrencies come in various forms and functions, making it challenging to classify them uniformly. Depending on their use case and characteristics, some may be considered commodities, securities, or currencies. Consistent definitions can lead to regulatory clarity and certainty.

ii) Consideration: Regulators must develop clear and precise definitions for cryptocurrencies and tokens. These definitions should consider their technological features, use cases, and economic functions. A well-defined classification system ensures that appropriate regulations can be applied.

2. Cross-Border Nature:

i) Challenge: Cryptocurrencies operate on a global scale, transcending national borders. This raises questions about which jurisdiction's regulations should apply to cross-border transactions and activities, leading to potential conflicts and regulatory gaps.

ii) Consideration: International cooperation is essential to address the borderless nature of cryptocurrencies. Regulators should collaborate to harmonise regulations, establish cross-border enforcement mechanisms, and share information to combat illegal activities effectively.

3. Consumer Protection:

i)Challenge: Cryptocurrency markets are known for their volatility and susceptibility to scams and fraud. Investors can be exposed to significant risks, including pump-and-dump schemes, Ponzi schemes, and fake initial coin offerings (ICOs)

ii) Consideration: Regulators should implement measures to protect consumers, such as requiring clear disclosure of risks, monitoring and reporting fraudulent activities, and educating investors about the risks associated with cryptocurrencies. Enforcement actions against fraudulent actors can also enhance investor protection.

4. AML and KYC Compliance:

i) Challenge: Balancing AML and KYC requirements with the privacy features of cryptocurrencies is a complex task. Some cryptocurrencies are designed to provide enhanced privacy and anonymity, posing challenges for regulators seeking to prevent money laundering and terrorist financing.

ii) Consideration: Regulators should adopt a risk-based approach to AML and KYC compliance. They can work with the industry to develop innovative solutions enabling compliance without compromising user privacy. Enhanced due diligence for privacy coins may also be necessary.

5. Taxation:

i) Challenge: Taxation of cryptocurrency transactions and holdings varies widely across jurisdictions. Determining tax liability, reporting requirements, and tax enforcement can be complex for individuals and businesses, leading to potential non-compliance and tax evasion.

ii) Consideration: Tax authorities should provide clear and comprehensive guidance on cryptocurrency taxation. Taxation rules should consider the different ways cryptocurrencies are used, such as investments, income, and transactions. Transparent reporting mechanisms can facilitate tax compliance.

6. Regulatory Arbitrage:

i) Challenge: Cryptocurrency businesses may seek jurisdictions with lax regulations or favourable tax treatment, potentially bypassing stricter rules in other countries. This can create regulatory gaps and challenges for enforcement.

ii) Consideration: Regulators should strive for consistency in regulations across borders to discourage regulatory arbitrage. International collaboration and adherence to common standards can help prevent businesses from evading necessary laws.

7. Smart Contracts and Legal Enforceability:

i) Challenge: Smart contracts, which self-execute based on predefined code, raise questions about their legal enforceability and liability in case of disputes. Traditional legal frameworks may need to address these unique digital agreements adequately.

ii) Consideration: Legal systems should adapt to accommodate intelligent contracts and establish mechanisms for dispute resolution in the context of blockchain-based agreements. This may involve creating specialised legal frameworks for recognising and enforcing smart contracts.

8. Privacy-Enhancing Cryptocurrencies:

i) Challenge: Privacy-focused cryptocurrencies, such as Monero and Zcash, provide enhanced privacy features that can be used for legitimate purposes and illicit activities, including money laundering and tax evasion.

ii) Consideration: Regulators should strike a balance between user privacy and regulatory requirements. They can explore privacy-preserving regulation approaches, such as requiring cryptocurrency exchanges to adhere to privacy coin transaction reporting requirements.

9. Technological Understanding:

i) Challenge: Cryptocurrencies and blockchain technology are complex and rapidly evolving. Regulators may need help to keep pace with technological advancements and understand the intricacies of blockchain systems.

ii) Consideration: Regulators should invest in educational initiatives, engage with industry experts, and collaborate with the cryptocurrency community to comprehensively understand the technology. This knowledge will enable them to develop informed and effective regulations.

10. Legal Jurisdiction:

i) Challenge: Determining the legal jurisdiction for cryptocurrency-related disputes, especially in cross-border cases, can be challenging. Jurisdictional conflicts can lead to legal uncertainties and complications.

ii) Consideration: Regulators should establish clear rules for jurisdiction and conflict resolution mechanisms for cryptocurrency-related legal matters. International agreements and treaties may be necessary to address cross-border disputes effectively.

11. Global Coordination:

i) Challenge: Achieving global coordination among regulators is challenging due to differing priorities, legal systems, and economic interests. Harmonising regulations across jurisdictions can be a lengthy and complex process.

ii) Consideration: International bodies and forums, such as the Financial Action Task Force (FATF) and the Basel Committee on Banking Supervision, should facilitate collaboration among regulators. Developing common principles and standards for cryptocurrency regulation can help create a more cohesive global regulatory framework.

Regulating cryptocurrencies presents many legal challenges, from classification and cross-border issues to privacy considerations and technological complexities. Effective regulation requires a balanced approach that considers the unique characteristics of cryptocurrencies while prioritising consumer protection, financial integrity, and legal clarity. Collaboration among governments, regulatory bodies, industry stakeholders, and legal experts is essential to develop comprehensive and adaptable regulatory frameworks that foster innovation and mitigate risks.

Discussion of the approaches taken by different countries or regulatory bodies

Countries and regulatory bodies have taken varying approaches to regulating cryptocurrencies, reflecting their unique perspectives, priorities, and legal frameworks. Here's an overview of the courses taken by some key countries and regulatory bodies.

1. United States:

Approach: The United States has a complex regulatory landscape for cryptocurrencies. Different agencies, including the Securities and Exchange Commission (SEC), the Commodity Futures Trading Commission (CFTC), and the Financial Crimes Enforcement Network (FinCEN), oversee various aspects of the crypto space.

Securities Regulation: The SEC has focused on classifying some cryptocurrencies and ICO tokens as securities, subjecting them to securities laws. It has pursued enforcement actions against unregistered ICOs and fraudulent projects.

Commodity Regulation: The CFTC has classified cryptocurrencies like

Bitcoin as commodities, allowing it to regulate cryptocurrency derivatives and futures markets.

AML and KYC: FinCEN enforces anti-money laundering (AML) and know-your-customer (KYC) regulations for cryptocurrency exchanges and requires them to report suspicious activities.

2. European Union (EU):

Approach: The EU has taken a comprehensive approach to cryptocurrency regulation to create a unified framework across member states. The Markets in Crypto-Assets (MiCA) proposal aims to regulate digital assets and provide legal certainty for market participants.

Anti-Money Laundering Directive (AMLD5): AMLD5 extended AML regulations to cover cryptocurrency exchanges and wallet providers, requiring them to perform customer due diligence and report suspicious transactions.

Token Classification: The EU aims to classify cryptocurrencies and crypto assets into three categories: e-money tokens, asset-referenced tokens, and utility tokens, each subject to varying levels of regulation.

3. Japan:

Approach: Japan has proactively regulated cryptocurrencies to promote consumer protection and foster innovation. The Payment Services Act, enacted in 2017, introduced a licensing system for cryptocurrency exchanges.

Licensing and Regulation: Cryptocurrency exchanges must obtain licenses from the Financial Services Agency (FSA) and adhere to strict regulatory requirements, including AML and KYC procedures.

4. Switzerland (Crypto Valley):

Approach: Switzerland has adopted a blockchain-friendly policy to attract cryptocurrency and blockchain companies. It has provided a clear regulatory framework to support innovation while ensuring investor protection.

Crypto Valley: The Zug region, often called Crypto Valley, has become a hub for blockchain start-ups and crypto businesses. Switzerland's regulatory environment has been instrumental in attracting these companies.

5. China:

Approach: China has taken a strict policy on cryptocurrencies and has imposed several bans. It banned ICOs in 2017 and shut down domestic cryptocurrency exchanges.

Digital Yuan (CBDC): While cracking down on private cryptocurrencies, China has developed its digital currency, the digital yuan (CBDC), which the central bank controls.

6. Singapore:

Approach: Singapore has adopted a balanced approach, striving to provide a conducive environment for blockchain and cryptocurrency businesses while maintaining strong regulatory oversight.

Payment Services Act: Singapore introduced the Payment Services Act, which includes regulations for cryptocurrency exchanges and wallet providers and requires them to obtain licenses.

7. International Bodies (FATF):

Approach: The Financial Action Task Force (FATF), an intergovernmental body, has developed global standards for AML and counter-terrorism financing (CTF) in cryptocurrency.

Travel Rule: The FATF's Travel Rule requires cryptocurrency exchanges and firms to collect and share customer information when conducting transactions, enhancing transparency and security.

These examples illustrate the diversity of approaches to cryptocurrency regulation. Some countries prioritise investor protection and AML compliance, while others aim to foster innovation and attract cryptocurrency businesses. The global nature of cryptocurrencies makes international coordination and harmonisation of regulations essential to address cross-border challenges and ensure a coherent regulatory landscape. The regulatory landscape for cryptocurrencies is continually evolving as governments and regulatory bodies adapt to the rapidly changing crypto ecosystem.

Examination of issues such as classification of cryptocurrencies, consumer protection, anti-money laundering (AML) regulations, and taxation

Examining critical issues in cryptocurrency regulation, such as classification, consumer protection, anti-money laundering (AML) laws, and taxation, provides insights into the challenges and considerations governments and regulatory bodies face. Here's a detailed examination of these issues:

Classification of Cryptocurrencies:

1. Challenge: The challenge lies in defining and categorising cryptocurrencies appropriately because they vary significantly regarding their technology, functionality, and use cases. Different jurisdictions have adopted different approaches to classifying them, leading to regulatory inconsistency and legal ambiguity.

2. Consideration: Regulators must establish clear and precise definitions for cryptocurrencies based on their technological attributes and economic functions. This classification informs the regulatory framework applied to each category of digital assets. For example:

i) Utility Tokens: Tokens primarily designed to provide access to a specific product or service may be classified as utility tokens and subjected to a lighter regulatory touch.

ii) Security Tokens: Tokens that represent ownership in a company or an asset and have characteristics similar to traditional securities should be regulated as such.

iii) Payment Tokens: Tokens used as a medium of exchange and store of value, like Bitcoin, may be classified as payment tokens and subject to relevant payment system regulations.

3. Benefits: Clear classification helps businesses and users understand their legal obligations and rights within the cryptocurrency ecosystem. It also allows regulators to apply appropriate rules and safeguards for each category, balancing innovation with consumer protection.

Consumer Protection:

1. Challenge: Cryptocurrency markets are highly volatile and can be manipulated by bad actors. Fraudulent ICOs, Ponzi schemes, and pump-and-dump schemes have harmed unsuspecting investors.

2. Consideration: To protect consumers in the cryptocurrency space, regulators can take several measures, including:

i) Disclosure Requirements: Mandating that token sales projects provide comprehensive information about their offerings, including the team, project roadmap, technology, risks, and terms and conditions.
ii) Investor Education: Promoting financial literacy and educating potential investors about the unique risks associated with cryptocurrencies, including market volatility and the lack of regulatory protection.
iii) Fraud Detection and Enforcement: Establishing mechanisms for monitoring and identifying fraudulent activities and taking swift enforcement actions against scams and fraudulent projects. Regulatory agencies should collaborate with law enforcement to prosecute wrongdoers.

3. Benefits: Consumer protection measures help build trust in the cryptocurrency market and reduce the likelihood of investors falling victim to scams. Informed investors are better equipped to make decisions and mitigate risks.

Anti-Money Laundering (AML) Regulations:

1. Challenge: Cryptocurrencies can be misused for illegal purposes, such as money laundering and terrorist financing, due to their relative anonymity and ease of cross-border transactions.

2. Consideration: Regulators address AML challenges by implementing stringent regulations, including:

i) KYC Requirements: Requiring cryptocurrency exchanges and wallet providers to conduct robust KYC checks on users, verifying their identities to prevent anonymous use.

ii) Transaction Monitoring: Monitoring cryptocurrency transactions for suspicious activities, such as large and frequent transfers, requires cryptocurrency service providers to report any suspicious transactions to relevant authorities.

iii) Travel Rule Compliance: The FATF's Travel Rule mandates including sender and recipient information in cryptocurrency transactions, similar to traditional financial institutions.

3. Benefits: AML regulations help mitigate the risk of using cryptocurrencies for illegal activities. They enhance transparency in the cryptocurrency space and enable law enforcement agencies to track and investigate suspicious transactions effectively.

Taxation:

1. Challenge: Cryptocurrency taxation is complex due to variations in tax treatment across jurisdictions and the evolving nature of cryptocurrencies. Determining tax liability, reporting requirements, and tax enforcement is challenging.

2. Consideration: Regulators address taxation challenges through various measures, such as:

i) Tax Reporting: Requiring individuals and businesses to report cryptocurrency transactions, capital gains, and mining activities to tax authorities.

ii) Taxation Clarity: Clarifying how cryptocurrencies are taxed, whether as property, income, capital gains, or a hybrid of these categories. We are providing detailed guidance on tax treatment.

iii) Tax Enforcement: Implementing mechanisms to enforce cryptocurrency taxation, which may include blockchain analysis tools to track transactions and collaborations with cryptocurrency exchanges for tax collection.

3. Benefits: Clear and consistent tax regulations provide legal certainty for cryptocurrency users and businesses. They ensure that individuals and entities comply with their tax obligations, reducing the risk of tax evasion and creating a level playing field.

Each of these considerations plays a critical role in shaping the regulatory framework for cryptocurrencies. Achieving a balance between fostering innovation and protecting investors and the financial system remains a crucial challenge for regulators as they navigate the evolving landscape of digital assets. Collaboration between regulators, industry stakeholders, and legal experts is vital to developing comprehensive and adaptable regulations.

ECONOMIC IMPLICATIONS OF CRYPTOCURRENCY REGULATION

Analysis of the effects on market stability, liquidity, and volatility

Analysing the effects of cryptocurrency regulation on market stability, liquidity, and volatility is crucial for understanding the broader economic impact of regulatory actions. Here's a detailed analysis of these effects:

Market Stability:

1. Positive Effects:

i) Investor Confidence: Clear and compelling regulations can instil confidence in investors and users. They provide security, reducing the fear of losing assets due to fraud or market manipulation.

ii) Long-Term Investment: Regulatory stability encourages long-term investment strategies. Investors are more likely to hold their assets when they trust the regulatory environment, leading to reduced panic selling during market downturns.

iii) Institutional Participation: Institutional investors often require regulatory clarity before entering the cryptocurrency market. Regulatory frameworks that address their concerns can attract institutional participation, contributing to market stability.

2. Negative Effects:

i) Uncertainty: Inconsistent or evolving regulations can create tension, leading to hesitancy among market participants. Sudden changes in regulatory direction can result in market disruptions.

ii) Market Reactions: Announcements of new regulations or enforcement actions can trigger abrupt reactions. Cryptocurrency prices may experience significant swings in response to regulatory news.

Market Liquidity:

1. Positive Effects:

i) Transparency: Regulations that promote transparency and fair trading practices can attract more participants to the market. Traders and investors are more likely to engage in markets they perceive as trustworthy.

ii) Lower Risk: Robust regulatory frameworks can reduce counterparty risks for traders and investors. This can lead to increased trading activity and liquidity.

2. Negative Effects:

i) Compliance Costs: Overly complex or stringent regulations can burden cryptocurrency businesses with compliance costs. These costs may be passed on to users through higher fees or reduced services.

ii) Market Fragmentation: Inconsistent regulations across jurisdictions can lead to market fragmentation. Some participants may prefer unregulated or lightly regulated platforms, reducing market liquidity.

Volatility:

1. Positive Effects:

i) Reduced Speculation: Regulatory measures discouraging speculative trading or pump-and-dump schemes can mitigate short-term volatility. This can make cryptocurrencies more appealing for stable value storage.
ii) Market Maturity: Over time, well-regulated markets tend to mature, attracting more responsible and informed traders. Mature markets typically experience lower levels of extreme volatility.

2. Negative Effects:

i) Regulatory Uncertainty: Lack of clarity or frequent regulation changes can create uncertainty, exacerbating short-term price volatility as traders react to regulatory news.
ii) Market Reaction to Enforcement: Regulatory enforcement actions can trigger abrupt price movements. For example, news of a significant exchange facing legal action can lead to a sharp sell-off.

Regulatory Certainty:

1. Positive Effects:

i) Business Development: Clarity and consistency in regulations provide a conducive environment for cryptocurrency businesses to plan, invest, and expand. Regulatory certainty can attract new businesses to the ecosystem.
ii) User Adoption: When users have confidence in the regulatory framework, they are more likely to adopt cryptocurrencies for various purposes, including payments and investments.

2. Negative Effects:

i) Innovation Hesitation: Uncertainty or overly restrictive regulations can deter innovative projects and start-ups. Businesses may only be able to enter the market if they know the regulatory landscape.
ii) Investment Delay: Investment decisions by individuals and institutions

may be delayed without clear regulatory guidance. This can impede the growth of virtual economies.

The impact of cryptocurrency regulation on market stability, liquidity, and volatility is a delicate balance. Well-designed and balanced rules can contribute to a stable, liquid market with reduced short-term fluctuations. However, regulatory uncertainty, excessive complexity, or inconsistency across jurisdictions can adversely affect market development and deter participants. Achieving effective regulation that promotes market integrity and innovation remains a complex challenge for regulators in cryptocurrency.

Examination of the relationship between regulatory measures and investor behaviour

The relationship between regulatory measures and investor behaviour in cryptocurrency is complex and multifaceted. Regulatory actions can significantly influence how investors perceive and interact with cryptocurrencies. Here's an examination of this relationship:

Impact on Investor Confidence:

i) Positive Regulatory Measures: Clear and investor-friendly regulations can enhance investor confidence. Investors are more likely to enter the market and hold assets when they feel regulatory safeguards protect their investments.

ii) Negative or Uncertain Regulatory Measures: Uncertainty or perceived negative actions, such as bans or harsh enforcement, can erode investor confidence. This can lead to reduced participation or even panic selling as investors seek to exit the market.

Influence on Investment Decisions:

i) Clarity and Predictability: Well-defined regulations provide a predictable environment for investors. Investors are more likely to make long-term investment decisions when they understand the regulatory framework.

ii) Innovative Investment Strategies: Regulatory support for new financial instruments, such as cryptocurrency exchange-traded funds

(ETFs) or tokenised assets, can encourage innovative investment strategies and products.

Behaviour during Regulatory Changes:

i) **Market Reaction to Announcements**: Investors react quickly to regulatory announcements or news. Positive regulatory developments, such as legal recognition or institutional involvement, can increase buying activity.

ii) **Sensitivity to Enforcement Actions**: High-profile regulatory actions, such as investigations into exchanges or ICO fraud, can trigger panic selling and market downturns.

Role of Institutional Investors:

i) **Attracting Institutional Investors**: Institutional investors, such as hedge funds and asset managers, often require clear regulations and custodial solutions before entering the cryptocurrency market. Regulatory support can attract these investors.

ii) **Influence on Market Behaviour**: Institutional investors often have a stabilising effect on markets. Their presence can reduce extreme volatility and promote liquidity.

Risk Tolerance and Compliance:

i) **Risk Tolerance Varies**: Investor behaviour in the cryptocurrency market varies widely based on risk tolerance. Some investors are more risk-averse and cautious, while others are more speculative.

ii) **Compliance with Regulations**: Regulations often require investors to undergo KYC and AML procedures. Some investors may prefer platforms with strong adherence, while others prioritise privacy and anonymity.

Innovation and Investment Trends:

i) **Impact on Investment Trends**: Regulatory measures can influence investment trends in the cryptocurrency space. For example, stricter regulations on ICOs can shift investment focus towards security tokens or decentralised finance (DeFi) projects.

Long-Term vs. Short-Term Investment:

i) Regulatory Impact on Investment Horizon: Clarity and stability in the regulatory environment can encourage long-term investment strategies. Conversely, regulatory uncertainty or frequent changes may lead to shorter investment horizons and trading-oriented behaviour.

Cross-Border Effects:

i) Global Nature of Cryptocurrencies: Cryptocurrencies are global assets, and regulatory measures in one country can affect investors worldwide. Investors may seek exchanges and jurisdictions with favourable regulations.

Education and Awareness:

i) Influence of Regulatory Information: Investors' understanding of regulatory developments can shape their behaviour. Education and awareness initiatives by regulators can help investors make informed decisions.

The relationship between regulatory measures and investor behaviour in cryptocurrency is interconnected and dynamic. Regulatory actions and the overall regulatory environment influence investors' confidence, risk tolerance, investment horizon, and choices. Clear and supportive regulations can attract investors and promote responsible behaviour, while regulatory uncertainty or hostile measures can deter investment and trigger market reactions. As the cryptocurrency market evolves, regulatory developments will play a significant role in shaping investor behaviour.

Evaluation of the potential for economic growth and innovation in regulated virtual economies

Evaluating the potential for economic growth and innovation in regulated virtual economies requires considering how regulatory measures can foster or hinder these key factors. Here's an assessment of this potential:

Economic Growth:

1. Fostering Economic Growth:

i) Investor Confidence: Clear and well-implemented regulations can boost investor confidence. This, in turn, attracts capital investment, leading to economic growth within virtual economies.

ii) Institutional Participation: Institutional investors often require regulatory certainty before entering cryptocurrency. Their involvement can significantly increase market capitalisation and liquidity.

iii) Job Creation: The growth of regulated virtual economies can lead to job creation in various sectors, including blockchain development, legal and compliance services, and financial technology.

iv) Tax Revenue: Regulatory oversight allows governments to collect taxes from cryptocurrency-related activities, contributing to public budgets.

2. Barriers to Growth:

i) Overregulation: Excessive or overly complex regulations can stifle innovation and drive businesses away. It may result in regulatory arbitrage, where companies relocate to jurisdictions with more favourable regulatory environments.

ii) Regulatory Uncertainty: Frequent regulation changes or a lack of clear guidance can create uncertainty, discouraging investment and business development.

iii) Market Fragmentation: Inconsistent regulations across jurisdictions can lead to market fragmentation, complicating cross-border operations and potentially limiting growth.

Innovation:

1. Promoting Innovation:

i) Regulatory Sandboxes: Some regulators establish regulatory sandboxes to allow blockchain start-ups to test innovative products and services with reduced regulatory constraints.

ii) Support for Tokenization: Regulatory frameworks that support the tokenisation of assets, such as real estate or art, can unlock new possibilities for asset management and trading.

iii) Legal Clarity: Clear regulations can provide legal certainty, reducing risks for innovators and encouraging them to explore novel use cases.

2. Challenges to Innovation:

i) Compliance Costs: Heavy compliance burdens can divert resources away from innovation. Start-ups may need help to allocate sufficient funds and personnel for compliance.

ii) Privacy Concerns: Regulations addressing privacy and security may limit the development of privacy-focused solutions or decentralised applications prioritising user anonymity.

iii) Institutional Inertia: Legacy financial institutions may slow the adoption of blockchain technology and require regulatory pressure or incentives to innovate.

Balance Between Regulation and Innovation:

i) Regulatory Agility: Effective regulation should balance investor protection and innovation. Regulators must be agile and capable of adapting to the evolving cryptocurrency landscape.

ii) Collaboration: Collaboration between regulators, industry stakeholders, and innovators is essential to ensure that regulations evolve to encourage responsible innovation while addressing potential risks.

iii) Educational Initiatives: Regulators can promote innovation by offering educational programs, guidelines, and resources to help businesses navigate the regulatory landscape and comply with relevant rules.

International Competition:

i) Global Race for Innovation: Countries establishing innovation-friendly regulatory environments can gain a competitive advantage in attracting blockchain start-ups and talent.

ii) Harmonisation and Collaboration: International collaboration and harmonisation of regulations can reduce regulatory arbitrage and create a more consistent global framework for innovation.

The potential for economic growth and innovation in regulated virtual economies is significant, but it hinges on the regulatory approach taken by governments and regulatory bodies. Clear, supportive, and adaptive regulations can create an environment where businesses thrive, investors participate confidently, and innovation flourishes. However, striking the right balance between regulation and innovation is challenging, and regulatory measures should evolve in tandem with the dynamic nature of the cryptocurrency and blockchain space. Collaborative efforts among stakeholders are crucial in maximising the benefits of regulation while minimising potential drawbacks.

Discussion of the challenges faced in regulating cryptocurrencies in virtual economies.

Regulating cryptocurrencies in virtual economies presents several challenges, primarily due to the unique characteristics of these digital assets and the evolving nature of the technology. Here's a discussion of the critical challenges faced in regulating cryptocurrencies:

Technological Complexity:

i) Challenge: Cryptocurrencies and blockchain technology are complex and rapidly evolving. Regulators often need help to keep pace with technological developments, leading to gaps in understanding and regulation.

ii) Impact: This complexity can result in outdated or misaligned regulations with the current state of the technology. It may also hinder regulators' ability to detect and prevent emerging risks.

Lack of Global Consensus:

i) Challenge: Cryptocurrencies operate across borders, making it difficult for any jurisdiction to regulate them effectively. There needs to be more global consensus on how to approach cryptocurrency regulation.

ii) Impact: Inconsistent international regulations can lead to regulatory arbitrage, where businesses migrate to countries with more favourable regulatory environments, creating challenges for enforcement and ensuring fair competition.

Regulatory Uncertainty:

i) Challenge: Cryptocurrency regulations in many jurisdictions are still in their infancy. Regulatory clarity is often lacking, leaving businesses and investors uncertain about their legal obligations.

ii) Impact: This uncertainty can deter investment and innovation. Startups may hesitate to enter the market, and investors may fear regulatory backlash, leading to market volatility and stagnation.

Balancing Innovation and Investor Protection:

i) Challenge: Regulators must strike a delicate balance between fostering innovation and protecting investors. Stricter regulations can provide more investor protection but may stifle innovation, while lighter rules can encourage innovation but expose investors to risks.

ii) Impact: Striking the right balance is challenging. Overregulation can drive innovation away, while underregulation can expose investors to fraudulent schemes.

AML and KYC Compliance:

i) Challenge: Anti-money laundering (AML) and know-your-customer (KYC) regulations are essential for preventing illicit activities involving cryptocurrencies. However, enforcing these regulations on decentralised platforms can be challenging.

ii) Impact: Ensuring AML and KYC compliance in cryptocurrency can be difficult due to the pseudonymous nature of transactions. Regulators need practical tools to trace and identify users while respecting privacy.

Cross-Border Transactions:

i) Challenge: Cryptocurrencies facilitate cross-border transactions with ease. Regulators need help in monitoring and regulating transactions that transcend national borders.

ii) Impact: Cross-border transactions can make it challenging to enforce tax laws, combat money laundering, and regulate cryptocurrency exchanges and businesses effectively.

Lack of Consumer Protection:

i) **Challenge**: Cryptocurrency markets are susceptible to scams, fraud, and hacking due to their relative lack of consumer protection mechanisms compared to traditional financial markets.
ii) **Impact**: Investors and users may risk losing their assets in unregulated or poorly regulated virtual economies. Lack of recourse can erode trust and deter mainstream adoption.

Evolving Use Cases:

i) **Challenge**: Cryptocurrencies are continually evolving, with new use cases such as decentralised finance (DeFi), non-fungible tokens (NFTs), and blockchain-based gaming emerging. Regulators must adapt to regulate these diverse applications effectively.
ii) **Impact**: Failure to adapt regulations can result in gaps in oversight or unintended consequences. Regulators must assess how existing rules apply to new technologies and use cases.

Technological Anonymity:

i) **Challenge**: Privacy-focused cryptocurrencies, like Monero or Zcash, offer enhanced anonymity, making it challenging for regulators to trace transactions and identify users involved in potentially illegal activities.
ii) **Impact**: Enhanced privacy features can facilitate illicit activities and hinder law enforcement efforts. Regulators need to find ways to balance privacy and security.

Lack of Enforcement Mechanisms:

i) **Challenge**: Enforcing cryptocurrency regulations can be challenging, mainly when businesses or users operate pseudonymously or through decentralised platforms.
ii) **Impact**: Weak enforcement can create an environment where bad actors thrive. Regulators must develop effective enforcement mechanisms and collaborate with international counterparts.

The challenges of regulating cryptocurrencies in virtual economies stem from the technology's complexity, global nature, and the need to balance innovation with investor protection. Addressing these challenges requires international collaboration, regulatory adaptation, and a nuanced understanding of the cryptocurrency ecosystem. Regulatory approaches should evolve in parallel with the rapid developments in the blockchain and cryptocurrency.

IDENTIFICATION OF POTENTIAL GAPS IN EXISTING REGULATIONS

Lack of Clear Definitions:

i) Challenge: Many regulatory frameworks need more precise and consistent definitions of vital cryptocurrency-related terms. For instance, different jurisdictions may define "virtual currency" or "digital asset" differently.

ii) Impact: Ambiguous definitions can lead to regulatory uncertainty, making it challenging for businesses and investors to understand their legal obligations. This can hinder compliance efforts and create a barrier to market entry for new participants.

Regulatory Fragmentation:

i) Challenge: Cryptocurrency regulations vary significantly from one country or region to another. Some jurisdictions have comprehensive regulatory frameworks, while others have adopted a more hands-off approach.

ii) Impact: Regulatory fragmentation can create confusion for businesses operating across borders. It also opens the door to regulatory arbitrage, where companies choose jurisdictions with less stringent regulations, potentially undermining investor protection and market integrity.

Regulatory Gaps for New Technologies:

i) Challenge: Emerging technologies like decentralised finance (DeFi) and non-fungible tokens (NFTs) may need to fit neatly within existing regulatory frameworks.

ii) Impact: Lack of specific regulations for these technologies can lead to legal uncertainties, hindering innovation and potentially exposing users to risks associated with unregulated activities.

Lack of Enforcement Tools:

i) **Challenge**: Regulatory authorities may need more tools and resources to enforce cryptocurrency regulations effectively, mainly when dealing with cross-border transactions and decentralised platforms.
ii) **Impact**: Inadequate enforcement capabilities can create opportunities for illicit activities, including money laundering, fraud, and tax evasion, as regulatory bodies may struggle to detect and prevent such activities effectively.

Inconsistent AML/KYC Requirements:

i) **Challenge**: AML and KYC requirements vary widely among cryptocurrency service providers and jurisdictions. Some platforms may have more stringent customer verification processes than others.
ii) **Impact**: Inconsistent AML/KYC practices can create gaps in detecting and preventing illicit financial activities, making it easier for bad actors to exploit these differences and engage in money laundering or other illegal activities.

Lack of Investor Protections:

i) **Challenge**: In some regions, investor protections for cryptocurrency users may be limited. Users may need access to insurance or compensation schemes typical in traditional financial markets.
ii) **Impact**: Inadequate investor protections can leave cryptocurrency users vulnerable to significant financial losses in the event of security breaches, scams, or platform failures, potentially eroding trust in virtual economies.

Unregulated Decentralized Platforms:

i) **Challenge**: Decentralized exchanges and platforms, which operate without intermediaries, may fall outside the scope of traditional regulatory frameworks, leading to potential gaps in oversight.

ii) Impact: These platforms may lack the safeguards and consumer protections found in centralised exchanges, exposing users to higher risks, including the potential for hacks or exit scams.

Regulatory Gaps in Cross-Border Transactions:

i) Challenge: Cryptocurrencies enable cross-border transactions, but regulations often need help to keep up with the complexities of international commerce.
ii) Impact: Regulatory gaps in cross-border transactions can hinder efforts to combat money laundering, terrorist financing, and other illicit activities that exploit the global nature of cryptocurrencies.

Privacy and Anonymity Challenges:

i) Challenge: Regulations may need to adequately address privacy-focused cryptocurrencies or the use of mixing services and privacy-enhancing technologies to obscure transaction trails.
ii) Impact: These regulatory gaps can create opportunities for individuals and entities engaging in illicit activities, such as money laundering, tax evasion, or the circumvention of sanctions.

Token Classification:

i) Challenge: Classifying tokens as securities, commodities, or currencies may need more clarity, making it difficult to determine which regulations apply.
ii) Impact: Misclassification can result in regulatory non-compliance and legal uncertainty for businesses and investors.

Addressing these regulatory gaps requires coordination among international regulators, industry stakeholders, and legal experts. The development of straightforward and adaptable regulatory frameworks that consider the unique characteristics of cryptocurrencies and emerging technologies is essential to address these challenges effectively while promoting innovation, investor protection, and market integrity.

EXPLORATION OF EMERGING TRENDS AND PROSPECTS FOR CRYPTOCURRENCY REGULATION

Exploring emerging trends and prospects for cryptocurrency regulation is essential as the cryptocurrency landscape continues to evolve. Here are some key trends and opportunities to consider:

Global Regulatory Convergence:

i) Trend: There is a growing recognition of the need for international cooperation and regulatory harmonisation in cryptocurrency. Regulators from different countries are increasingly working together to establish common standards.

ii) Prospect: In the future, we may see more efforts to create a consistent global regulatory framework for cryptocurrencies. This can help reduce regulatory arbitrage and enhance investor protection.

DeFi and NFT Regulations:

i) Trend: Decentralized finance (DeFi) and non-fungible tokens (NFTs) have gained significant popularity and attention. Regulators are starting to address potential risks and challenges associated with these emerging sectors.

ii) Prospect: Future regulation of DeFi and NFTs may focus on issues such as AML/KYC compliance, consumer protection, and taxation. Striking a balance between fostering innovation and mitigating risks will be crucial.

Central Bank Digital Currencies (CBDCs):

i) Trend: Several countries actively explore or pilot central bank digital currencies (CBDCs). These digital versions of fiat currencies could have significant regulatory implications.

ii) Prospect: CBDCs may lead to new regulatory considerations, including ensuring interoperability with private cryptocurrencies, privacy protection, and cross-border regulatory coordination.

Enhanced AML/KYC Requirements:

i) Trend: Regulators increasingly focus on strengthening anti-money laundering (AML) and know-your-customer (KYC) requirements for cryptocurrency businesses. This includes extending these requirements to DeFi platforms.

ii) Prospect: Expect stricter AML/KYC regulations in cryptocurrency and enhanced enforcement efforts to combat illicit activities.

Stablecoin Regulation:

i) Trend: Stablecoins, which are often pegged to traditional currencies, have gained widespread adoption. Regulators are concerned about their potential impact on monetary stability and financial systems.

ii) Prospect: We can anticipate increased scrutiny and regulation of stablecoins, including potential reserve requirements, audits, and regular reporting to ensure their stability.

Increased Privacy Regulation:

i) Trend: Privacy-focused cryptocurrencies, like Monero and Zcash, pose challenges for regulators as they can facilitate anonymous transactions.

ii) Prospect: Regulatory efforts may focus on balancing user privacy with the need for transaction traceability. We may see discussions on the regulation of privacy-enhancing technologies and cryptocurrencies.

Tokenisation of Traditional Assets:

i) Trend: The tokenisation of traditional assets, such as real estate, stocks, and art, is gaining traction. Regulators are examining how to apply existing securities and property laws to these tokenised assets.

ii) Prospect: Future regulations may provide more precise guidelines for tokenised assets, including legal recognition and rules for trading and custody.

Regulatory Technology (Regtech):

i) Trend: Adopting regtech solutions, such as blockchain analytics and monitoring tools, is rising. Regulators are leveraging technology to enhance their oversight capabilities.

ii) Prospect: Regulators will likely continue to invest in regtech to improve surveillance and enforcement in the cryptocurrency market.

Enhanced Consumer Protection:

i) Trend: Consumer protection remains a priority for regulators. Increased disclosures, education, and safeguards are expected to be implemented to protect retail investors.

ii) Prospect: Regulations may mandate more transparent risk disclosures, require investor education initiatives, and set limits on risky investment products.

The future of cryptocurrency regulation will likely be shaped by ongoing technological advancements, international cooperation, and a focus on striking a balance between innovation and risk mitigation. The regulatory landscape will continue to evolve to address emerging trends and challenges in cryptocurrency, with a strong emphasis on investor protection and financial stability. It will be essential for regulators to remain adaptable and engage with industry stakeholders to create practical and forward-looking regulatory frameworks.

CHAPTER VII

Data Privacy and Security in Virtual Environments: Balancing Legal Frameworks and Economic Realities

INTRODUCTION

In the contemporary era of rapid digital advancements, virtual worlds have evolved as dynamic venues that significantly alter how individuals engage in social interactions, acquire knowledge, engage in professional activities, and seek entertainment. The advent of immersive realms, which include virtual reality (VR), augmented reality (AR), and other advanced technologies, has propelled us into a novel epoch characterised by the progressive dissolution of distinctions between physical and digital facts. The potential for transformation is closely intertwined with a range of complex issues, with none being more crucial than maintaining a careful equilibrium between safeguarding data privacy and security while navigating the economic dynamics intrinsic to these virtual environments.

The complex relationship between legal frameworks and economic factors in data privacy and security in virtual environments. In the course of our exploration, we will examine the fundamental elements of legislation about data protection, the essential security measures required to strengthen digital environments against evolving risks, and the intricate balance that must be achieved to ensure both compliance with data privacy regulations and the long-term viability of flourishing online businesses. Furthermore, an analysis will be conducted on the crucial significance of user awareness and education in this context, alongside the intricate challenges of managing data across international boundaries.

It becomes increasingly apparent that the intersection of data privacy and security in virtual environments extends beyond technological and legal obstacles, including a more comprehensive societal necessity. The attainment of equilibrium in these dimensions is crucial for harnessing the limitless potential of virtual technologies and safeguarding individuals' rights and personal information. This statement highlights the pursuit of integrating the virtual and physical realms in a balanced manner, emphasising the coexistence of innovation and accountability and prioritising preserving data integrity within the constantly changing digital environment.

The prominence of data privacy and security concerns has escalated in virtual settings, encompassing virtual reality (VR), augmented reality (AR), and other immersive technologies. The problems above encompass a wide range of topics, illustrating the intricate relationship between the transformative capabilities of virtual environments and the imperative to protect individuals' personal information.

One of the foremost considerations pertains to the collection of data and the practice of profiling. Virtual environments frequently collect substantial user data, encompassing biometric information and behavioural patterns. Nevertheless, using this data for profiling and tracking raises ethical and privacy concerns without users' informed consent.

The concept of informed consent holds significant importance in safeguarding data privacy, particularly in virtual settings, where its attainment can present some difficulties. It is imperative to establish transparent consent processes as users may need a comprehensive understanding of the extent to which their data is gathered and utilised.

Data breaches pose a substantial risk within virtual environments. Cybersecurity vulnerabilities can expose sensitive user information, increasing the risk of identity theft and other criminal behaviours. Therefore, it is crucial to implement robust security protocols and promptly address any security breaches.

Achieving a delicate equilibrium between personalised experiences and user privacy presents a multifaceted and intricate problem. Incorporating personalisation features in virtual settings has positively impacted user engagement. However, this practice also gives rise to apprehensions around the potential exposure of user identities and behaviours within these digital spaces.

The practice of exchanging user data with third-party groups, such as advertising, is prevalent in virtual environments. The establishment of transparency regarding procedures around data sharing and the provision of user autonomy in determining the fate of their data are fundamental components of data privacy.

Geolocation privacy is relevant, especially in augmented reality (AR) applications that necessitate actual location information. The improper utilisation of this data for stalking or unlawful tracking can result in substantial infringements upon an individual's privacy.

Determining data ownership and portability within virtual environments is a multifaceted issue. Provision of user autonomy in managing and transferring their data between virtual platforms is desirable. However, establishing unambiguous ownership and portability rights in this context might present significant difficulties.

Data protection requirements, such as the General Data Protection Regulation (GDPR) and the California Consumer Privacy Act (CCPA), introduce an additional level of intricacy, particularly when virtual environments span many jurisdictions. The perpetual challenge lies in achieving a harmonious equilibrium between adherence to regulatory requirements and fostering innovation.

Using artificial intelligence (AI) and machine learning algorithms within virtual environments raises ethical problems. These technologies are responsible for driving content suggestions and customisation. However, addressing ethical concerns about prejudice and fairness is imperative.

Insufficient education and awareness among users are standard in virtual worlds. Many users need more understanding of the potential data privacy and security hazards. Promoting education and awareness is pivotal in empowering individuals to safeguard their data adequately.

Data movement across national borders poses significant issues due to diverse data protection laws and regulations across countries. The challenge of facilitating secure and lawful data transmission across national boundaries is a multifaceted endeavour that necessitates meticulous deliberation.

Acknowledging and tackling the complex issues surrounding data privacy and security in virtual environments is essential to promote responsible advancement and utilisation of these revolutionary technologies. Achieving a harmonious equilibrium between technological innovators, regulatory bodies, and individuals is vital to effectively navigate the delicate interplay between advancing technology and protecting personal data.

DATA PRIVACY IN VIRTUAL ENVIRONMENTS

Data privacy safeguards personal or sensitive information from individuals or organisations to prevent unlawful access, use, disclosure, or misuse. Data governance includes the regulation of data accessibility and utilisation. The following are a few essential aspects to comprehend regarding data privacy:

1. Data Categories:

Data privacy encompasses various data types, including personally identifiable information (PII), financial records, health records, biometric data, and location data. These categories of data may have different levels of sensitivity and require different levels of protection.

2. Data Processing:

Data privacy also involves how data is processed. This includes data collection, storage, use, sharing, and disposal. Each stage in the data processing lifecycle should adhere to privacy principles and legal requirements.

3. Data Privacy Principles:

Several fundamental principles underpin data privacy:

i) Consent: Individuals should provide informed support for their data to be collected and used.

ii) Purpose Limitation: Data should only be used for the specific purposes for which it was collected.

iii) Data Minimization: Only collect the necessary data for the intended purpose.

iv) Accuracy: Ensure that data is accurate and up-to-date.

v) Storage Limitation: Data should only be kept for as long as necessary.

vi) Security: Implement safeguards to protect data from breaches and unauthorised access.

4. Data Privacy Regulations:

Data privacy regulations vary by country and region. Prominent examples include:

i) GDPR (General Data Protection Regulation): Enforced in the European Union, GDPR is known for its strict requirements regarding consent, data protection officers, and heavy penalties for non-compliance.

ii) CCPA (California Consumer Privacy Act): This California law gives consumers more control over the personal information held by businesses.

iii) HIPAA (Health Insurance Portability and Accountability Act): In the United States, HIPAA sets standards for protecting health information.

iv) Privacy Shield: An agreement between the EU and the U.S. that governed the transfer of personal data between these regions until it was invalidated.

5. Data Breaches:

Data breaches often exacerbate data privacy concerns. A data breach occurs when sensitive data is accessed, disclosed, or acquired. Organisations must have protocols to respond to data breaches promptly and transparently.

6. Data Privacy Officers (DPOs):

Many organisations must appoint Data Protection Officers responsible for ensuring data privacy compliance. DPOs monitor data processing activities, advise on privacy matters, and serve as a point of contact for data subjects.

7. Data Privacy and Technology:

Technology plays a dual role in data privacy. It can pose risks (e.g., cyberattacks) and provide solutions (e.g., encryption and secure communication) to safeguard data.

8. Cross-Border Data Transfer:

Transferring personal data across borders can be complex due to varying data protection laws. Organisations must comply with legal requirements when data crosses international boundaries.

9. Data Ethics:

Beyond legal obligations, ethical considerations are vital. Organisations and individuals should consider the ethical implications of data collection, use, and sharing. Ethical data practices build trust with users and customers.

10. Data Privacy Awareness:

Education and awareness-raising efforts are crucial in promoting data privacy. Individuals must understand their rights, and organisations must train employees to handle data responsibly.

Data privacy is a multifaceted and evolving field that encompasses the protection of sensitive information, adherence to legal regulations, ethical considerations, and the responsible use of data in an increasingly digital world. Organisations and individuals have a role to play in upholding data privacy principles and safeguarding personal information.

Data Collection in Virtual Environments:

Virtual environments, such as online platforms, virtual reality (VR), augmented reality (AR), and online games, often collect various types of data to enhance user experiences, provide personalised content, and support business models. Here's a comprehensive exploration of data collection in these settings:

Types of Data Collected:

> Behavioural Data includes information about users' actions, interactions, and movements within the virtual environment. For example, they track how users navigate a VR space or interact with objects.
> Biometric Data: Some virtual environments may capture biometric data like heart rate, eye movement, or facial expressions to assess emotional responses and tailor experiences.
> Location Data: In AR applications, location data may be collected to overlay digital information onto the physical world based on a user's GPS coordinates
> User Profile Information: Virtual environments often request basic user information, such as usernames, email addresses, and, in some cases, demographic details.
> Communication Data: Data collected from in-game or in-platform chats, messages, or voice communications can be used for various purposes, including moderation and analysis.
> User-Generated Content: Virtual environments may collect and store user-generated content, such as avatars, custom maps, or virtual goods.

Purpose of Data Collection:

> Enhancing User Experience: Data is often collected to personalise the user experience. For example, tracking a user's preferences can help recommend relevant content or customise virtual spaces.
> Targeted Advertising: Many virtual environments use data to serve targeted ads, making advertising more relevant to individual users.
> Product Improvement: Developers often use data to analyse how users interact with their environments, identifying areas for improvement and innovation.

> Security and Moderation: behavioural and communication data can be used for security purposes, such as identifying and preventing abusive or harmful behaviour.
> Monetisation: Some virtual environments generate revenue by selling user data to third parties or using it for their marketing efforts.

Data Privacy Concerns:

> Data collection in virtual environments raises significant privacy concerns. Users may only sometimes be fully aware of the extent of data being collected or how it will be used.
> Privacy breaches or unauthorised access to this data can lead to severe consequences, including identity theft, harassment, or exposure to sensitive information.

Regulatory Frameworks:

> Data protection regulations, such as the GDPR in Europe or the CCPA in California, impose strict requirements on virtual environment providers. They include obtaining informed consent, transparent data practices, and the right to data deletion upon user request.

User Consent and Control:

> Ethical data collection in virtual environments involves obtaining explicit and informed consent from users regarding what data is collected and for what purposes.
> Users should be able to control their data, including opting out of certain data collection practices.

Security Measures:

> Virtual environments must implement robust security measures to protect the data they collect. This includes encryption, access controls, regular security audits, and powerful data storage practices.

Data collection in virtual environments is a complex and multifaceted process involving various data types for multiple purposes. Balancing the benefits of data-driven personalisation and business models with user privacy and data security is a crucial challenge in these digital spaces. It requires adherence to privacy regulations, ethical practices, and transparent communication with users to build trust and ensure responsible data handling in virtual environments.

RISKS AND CONCERNS

Privacy Invasion

Privacy invasion is the unauthorised or unwarranted intrusion into an individual's personal life or private affairs, often violating their privacy rights. This invasion can take various forms in the physical and digital realms. Here's a more elaborate exploration of privacy invasion:

1. Types of Privacy Invasion:

i) Physical Intrusion: This involves the unauthorised entry into an individual's physical space, such as their home or personal property, without their consent. It can include activities like trespassing, spying, or eavesdropping.

ii) Digital Intrusion: In the digital age, privacy invasion often occurs through unauthorised access to or collection of personal data and online activities. Examples include hacking, data breaches, and surveillance.

iii) Surveillance: Government agencies, corporations, or individuals may engage in surveillance activities to monitor and record people's actions, communications, or movements, often without their knowledge or consent.

iv) Peeping Tom Behaviour: This refers to spying on someone, typically for voyeuristic purposes, such as looking into someone's window or using hidden cameras to invade their privacy.

2. Privacy Invasion Scenarios:

i) Data Breaches: When organisations or individuals gain unauthorised access to databases containing personal information, it can lead to data breaches. This compromises the privacy of those whose data is exposed.

ii) Social Media Monitoring: Employers, marketers, or individuals may

monitor someone's social media accounts without their consent, which can reveal personal details, opinions, and activities
iii) Unwanted Surveillance: Government surveillance programs or cameras in public spaces can be seen as invasions of privacy, as individuals are often unaware they are being monitored.
iv) Invasive Technology: Using invasive technologies like spyware, keyloggers, or location-tracking smartphone apps can lead to the unauthorised collection of personal data.

3. Legal and Ethical Implications:

i) Privacy invasion often raises serious legal and ethical concerns. Laws and regulations vary by jurisdiction but typically protect individuals from unwarranted intrusion into their private lives.
ii) Ethical considerations include violating an individual's autonomy, trust, and personal boundaries, which can result in emotional distress and damage one's reputation.

4. Consequences:

i) Privacy invasion can have far-reaching consequences, including identity theft, fraud, harassment, emotional distress, and damage to personal relationships.
ii) In the digital context, data breaches can lead to financial losses and the misuse of personal information for malicious purposes.

5. Mitigation and Prevention:

i) Protecting privacy often involves safeguarding personal information, using encryption and strong passwords, and being cautious about sharing sensitive data online.
ii) Legal and regulatory frameworks, such as data protection laws and privacy policies, aim to deter privacy invasion and provide recourse for victims.

Privacy invasion is a serious concern in both physical and digital realms, as it violates an individual's right to privacy and personal boundaries. Protecting privacy requires a combination of legal protections, ethical considerations, and individual vigilance to prevent unwarranted intrusion and the potential harm that can result from such invasions.

USER TRACKING AND PROFILING

User tracking and profiling are practices employed by various entities, such as websites, apps, and businesses, to collect and analyse user data for multiple purposes. While they can provide benefits like personalised experiences and targeted advertising, they also raise significant privacy and ethical concerns. Here's a detailed exploration of user tracking and profiling:

User Tracking:

1. Definition: User tracking involves monitoring and recording users' online activities and behaviours as they interact with digital platforms, websites, or applications.

Methods of User Tracking:

i) Cookies: Websites often use cookies and small text files to track users' browsing history and preferences.
ii) Device Fingerprinting: Unique attributes of a device, such as its IP address and browser settings, can be used to track users.
iii) Analytics Tools: Web analytics tools, like Google Analytics, can track user interactions with a website.
iv) GPS and Location Data: Mobile apps may track users' physical locations using GPS data.
v) Behavioural Data: User actions within an app or website, such as clicks, searches, and navigation paths, are recorded.

2. Purpose of User Tracking:

i) Personalisation: Tracking allows platforms to tailor content and recommendations to individual user preferences.
ii) Performance Improvement: Analytics data can help organisations optimise their websites or apps for better user experiences.
iii) Ad Targeting: Tracking data is often used for targeted advertising to

show users ads relevant to their interests and behaviour.

3. User Profiling:

Definition: User profiling is the creation of detailed profiles of individual users based on their collected data. These profiles can include demographic information, interests, behaviour patterns, and more.

4. Methods of User Profiling:

i) Data Aggregation: Information from various sources, including browsing history, social media interactions, and purchase history, is aggregated to create comprehensive profiles.
ii) Machine Learning: Advanced algorithms and machine learning techniques can analyse data to identify patterns and preferences, contributing to more accurate user profiles.

5. Purpose of User Profiling:

i) Targeted Content: Profiling helps platforms offer personalised content, product recommendations, and user experiences.
ii) Advertising Efficiency: Advertisers can use user profiles to deliver more relevant and effective advertising campaigns.
iii) User Insights: Profiling can provide organisations valuable insights into their user base, enabling better decision-making and product development.

6. Concerns and Risks:

i) Privacy: Users may feel that their privacy is invaded when their online activities are extensively tracked and used to create detailed profiles without explicit consent.
ii) Transparency: Lack of clarity about data collection and profiling practices can erode user trust. Users often need more visibility into how their data is used.
iii) Data Security: Profiling relies on vast amounts of data, making it a lucrative target for hackers. Data breaches can expose sensitive user information.

iv) Discrimination and Bias: User profiling can lead to biased outcomes, as algorithms may make assumptions or predictions based on historical data that contains biases.

v) Regulatory Frameworks:

vi) Data protection regulations, such as GDPR (in Europe) and CCPA (in California), require organisations to inform users about data collection and profiling practices and obtain their consent.

7. Mitigation and Protection:

i) Users can protect their privacy by using ad blockers, clearing cookies, and being cautious about sharing personal information online.

ii) Organisations can adopt transparent data practices, obtain informed consent, and implement robust data security measures to protect user data.

User tracking and profiling are standard practices in the digital age but have significant privacy and ethical considerations. Balancing the benefits of personalisation and targeted content with user privacy and data security is an ongoing challenge that involves legal compliance, ethical considerations, and responsible data handling practices.

Consent And Transparency

Consent and transparency are fundamental principles in data privacy and personal information handling. They are crucial in ensuring individuals control how their data is collected, used, and shared. Let's explore these concepts in more detail:

A. Consent:

1. Definition: Consent refers to an individual's voluntary and informed agreement to allow personal data to be collected, processed, or used by an organisation or entity. It is a cornerstone of data privacy regulations like the GDPR.

2. Critical Elements of Consent:

i) Voluntary: Consent must be given freely without coercion or pressure.
ii) Informed: Individuals must clearly understand what they consent to, including the purposes for data collection and how their data will be used.
iii) Specific: Consent should be explicit to the intended data processing activities.
iv) Revocable: Individuals should have the right to withdraw their consent at anytime.
v) Obtainable: Organizations must make it easy for individuals to provide or withdraw consent.

3. Importance of Consent:

i) It empowers individuals by giving them control over their data.
ii) It promotes transparency and trust between individuals and organisations.
iii) It helps organisations comply with data protection laws and regulations.

B. Transparency:

1. Definition: Transparency in data privacy refers to the openness and clarity with which organisations communicate their data practices to individuals. It involves providing clear and accessible information about data collection, processing, and usage.

2. Critical Aspects of Transparency:

i) Privacy Policies: Organizations should have clear and easily accessible privacy policies that detail their data handling practices.
ii) Data Collection Notices: Individuals should be informed about data collection at the point of data collection. For example, a website should educate users about the use of cookies.
iii) Data Use Notifications: Individuals should be notified about how their data will be used, especially for purposes beyond what was initially disclosed.
iv) Data Breach Notifications: Organizations are often required to notify

individuals in the event of a data breach that may compromise their data.

3. Importance of Transparency:

i) It builds trust between individuals and organisations, as individuals are more likely to consent when they understand how their data will be used.
ii) It helps individuals make informed decisions about whether or not to engage with a particular service or platform.
iii) It is a legal requirement in many data protection regulations to ensure organisations are accountable for their data practices.

4. Challenges and Considerations:

i) Complexity: Privacy policies and data notices can be lengthy and complicated to understand, making it challenging for individuals to comprehend how their data is used.
ii) Dynamic Data Ecosystem: In the digital age, data flows across platforms and services can be complex, making maintaining transparency throughout the data lifecycle brutal.
iii) Third-Party Data Sharing: Organizations often share data with third parties, creating transparency challenges, as individuals may need to be aware of these data-sharing arrangements.
iv) Consent Fatigue: In an environment where individuals are bombarded with consent requests, there's a risk of consent fatigue, where people may pay less attention to consent requests than they should.

Consent and transparency are essential principles in data privacy. Individuals should be informed about how their data is being collected and used, and they should be able to provide or withdraw consent as they see fit. Organisations, in turn, are responsible for being transparent and open about their data practices to establish trust and ensure compliance with data protection laws. Balancing these principles with the complexity of the digital data landscape remains a challenge in the ongoing pursuit of protecting individual privacy.

Data Security

Data security is a critical aspect of information technology and management that protects data from unauthorised access, disclosure, alteration, or destruction. It encompasses various strategies, technologies, and best practices to ensure data confidentiality, integrity, and availability. Let's explore data security in more detail:

1. Data Security Goals:

> Confidentiality: Ensuring that data is only accessible to authorised individuals or entities and is not disclosed to unauthorised users.
> Integrity: Ensuring the accuracy and reliability of data by protecting it from unauthorised alterations or tampering.
> Availability: Ensuring data is accessible to authorised users when needed, without disruptions.

2. Data Security Components:

> Access Control: Implementing access control mechanisms to limit who can access specific data and what actions they can perform. This often involves authentication (verifying user identities) and authorisation (determining user permissions).
> Encryption: Encrypting data in transit (when it's being transmitted) and at rest (when it's stored) to protect it from unauthorised interception or theft. Encryption ensures that even if data is accessed, it cannot be read without the encryption key.
> Firewalls and Intrusion Detection/Prevention Systems (IDS/IPS): Using firewalls to control network traffic and IDS/IPS to detect and prevent unauthorised access or attacks on data and systems.
> Security Policies and Procedures: Establishing clear security policies and procedures for data handling, user access, incident response, and more. This includes defining password policies, data classification, and incident response plans.
> Data Backups and Disaster Recovery: Regularly backing up data and implementing disaster recovery plans to ensure data can be restored in case of data loss or system failures.
> Security Awareness and Training: Educating employees and users about data security best practices, including how to recognise and respond to security threats such as phishing attacks.
> Security Updates and Patch Management: Keeping software and systems

up to date with security patches to address known vulnerabilities.

3. Data Security Threats and Challenges:

> Cyberattacks: Data is often targeted by cybercriminals who use various attack methods like malware, ransomware, and phishing to gain unauthorised access to sensitive information.
> Insider Threats: Data breaches can also result from employees or individuals with insider access intentionally or accidentally compromising data security.
> Data Theft: Theft of physical devices like laptops or external drives can result in data breaches if the stored data is not adequately protected.
> Data Governance: Managing data security across complex data ecosystems, including cloud services and third-party vendors, can be challenging.

> Compliance: Meeting data security and privacy regulations, such as GDPR or HIPAA, can be demanding, and non-compliance may result in legal consequences.

4. Data Security Best Practices:

> Regularly update and patch software and systems.
> Use strong, unique passwords and implement multi-factor authentication.
> Conduct regular security audits and vulnerability assessments.
> Limit data access to only those who need it for their roles (the principle of least privilege).
> Encrypt sensitive data both in transit and at rest.
> Establish an incident response plan for data breaches.

5. Data Security Regulations:

> Various countries and regions have enacted data protection laws and regulations that require organisations to implement specific data security measures and protect individuals' privacy rights.

Data security is critical to modern information technology and data management. Organisations and individuals alike must take proactive steps to safeguard data from the ever-evolving threats in the digital age. This involves implementing security measures, educating users, and staying compliant with data protection regulations.

Legal And Regulatory Risks

Legal and regulatory risks refer to the potential legal consequences individuals or organisations may face due to non-compliance with relevant laws and regulations. These risks are particularly significant in data privacy and security, as governments worldwide have enacted stringent laws to protect individuals' data. Here, we'll explore the legal and regulatory risks associated with data privacy and security:

1. Data Protection Laws and Regulations:

i) GDPR (General Data Protection Regulation): Enforced in the European Union, GDPR imposes strict requirements on organisations that collect, process, or store personal data of EU residents. Non-compliance can result in substantial fines, as high as 4% of a company's global annual revenue.
ii) CCPA (California Consumer Privacy Act): This California law gives consumers more control over the personal information held by businesses. Failure to comply can lead to statutory damages and regulatory actions.
iii) HIPAA (Health Insurance Portability and Accountability Act): In the United States, HIPAA sets standards for protecting health information. Violations can lead to civil and criminal penalties.
iv) Other National and Regional Regulations: Many countries have their own data protection laws; even within countries, there can be state or provincial regulations. Violations of these laws can result in penalties and legal actions.

2. Legal and Regulatory Risks in Data Privacy and Security:

i) Fines and Penalties: Regulatory authorities can impose significant fines for non-compliance with data protection laws. The penalties can vary widely depending on the nature of the violation, the number of affected individuals, and the organisation's size.

ii) Legal Action by Data Subjects: Individuals whose data is mishandled may have the right to take legal action against organisations for damages caused by data breaches or privacy violations.

iii) Reputation Damage: Non-compliance can lead to reputational damage for organisations. News of data breaches or privacy violations can erode trust and lead to losing customers and business partners.

iv) Class Action Lawsuits: In some cases, data breaches can result in class-action lawsuits where multiple affected individuals join together to seek damages from the organisation responsible.

v) Criminal Liability: In cases of severe negligence or intentional wrongdoing, individuals within organisations may face criminal charges related to data breaches or privacy violations.

3. Mitigating Legal and Regulatory Risks:

i) Compliance Programs: Organizations should establish comprehensive data protection compliance programs encompassing policies, procedures, and training to ensure adherence to data protection laws.

ii) Data Protection Officers (DPOs): Appointing DPOs, as GDPR requires, can help organisations manage data protection compliance effectively.

iii) Data Breach Response Plans: Organizations should have well-defined data breach response plans to minimise the impact of breaches and comply with breach notification requirements.

iv) Regular Audits and Assessments: Regular internal audits and assessments can help identify and rectify compliance gaps.

v) Legal Counsel: Engaging legal counsel with expertise in data protection laws can guide compliance and risk mitigation.

Legal and regulatory data privacy and security risks are significant and can have far-reaching consequences for organisations and individuals. Organisations must proactively ensure compliance with relevant laws, protect personal data, and respond effectively to data breaches to mitigate these risks. Compliance is a legal requirement and crucial for maintaining trust and reputation in an era where data protection is a priority for individuals and authorities.

Ethical Concerns

Ethical concerns in data privacy and security arise from the moral implications of how personal data is collected, used, and protected. As technology advances and data plays an increasingly central role, these concerns become more pronounced. Here are some key ethical considerations related to data privacy and security:

1. Informed Consent:

Users should be fully informed about how their data will be collected and used. Obtaining genuine, informed consent is an ethical imperative. Concerns arise when organisations bury consent in lengthy terms and conditions or use dark patterns to manipulate users into consenting.

2. Data Minimization:

Collecting only the data necessary for a specific purpose, known as data minimisation, is ethical. Collecting excessive data without a clear need can be seen as invasive.

3. Transparency:

Organisations have an ethical responsibility to be transparent about their data practices. This includes communicating what data is collected, how it's used, and with whom it's shared.

4. User Control:

Ethical data practices involve giving users control over their data. Users should be able to access, correct, and delete their data. They should also be able to opt out of certain data processing activities.

5. Security:

Ensuring the security of user data is an ethical obligation. Failing to protect data can lead to data breaches and harm individuals. Ethical considerations include implementing robust security measures and promptly notifying users in case of violations.

6. Data Use for Manipulation:

Using personal data to manipulate user behaviour, such as targeted advertising or personalised content that reinforces biases, raises ethical concerns. It can be seen as exploiting users for financial gain.

7. Algorithmic Bias:

Machine learning algorithms that rely on historical data may perpetuate bias and discrimination. Addressing algorithmic bias is an ethical imperative to ensure fairness and equity.

8. Data Ownership and Property:

The question of who owns and controls personal data is an ethical issue. Users often have a sense of ownership over their data, and organisations must respect this ownership.

9. Data Sharing and Sale:

Ethical concerns arise when organisations profit from selling or sharing user data without explicit and informed consent.

10. Digital Well-Being:

Ethical considerations include the impact of technology on individuals' well-being, including concerns about addiction, mental health, and the erosion of privacy in the digital age.

11. Children's Privacy:

Special ethical considerations apply to children's data privacy. Collecting data from minors without parental consent can be ethically problematic.

12. Data Retention:

Ethical data practices involve only retaining data for as long as necessary and securely disposing it when it's no longer needed.

13. Ethics in Artificial Intelligence:

AI systems that make data-based decisions should be designed to uphold ethical principles and avoid causing harm or discrimination.

14. Corporate Responsibility:

Organisations have an ethical duty to prioritise data privacy and security, not just for legal compliance but as part of their commitment to corporate responsibility and ethical business practices.

Addressing these ethical concerns requires a combination of legal regulations, industry standards, corporate responsibility, and individual awareness. Ethical data practices are essential for building user trust and fostering a responsible digital ecosystem that respects individual privacy and values ethical decision-making in handling personal data.

Discrimination And Bias

Discrimination and bias in data privacy and security refer to the unfair or discriminatory treatment of individuals or groups based on their characteristics or attributes, which may be inferred from data. These issues can have significant ethical and social implications. Let's explore discrimination and bias in more detail:

1. Types of Discrimination and Bias:

i) Algorithmic Bias: Machine learning algorithms may exhibit bias if the training data used to develop them reflects historical discrimination. This can result in unfair or discriminatory outcomes in decision-making processes, such as hiring, lending, or criminal justice.
ii) Data Bias: Bias can be present in the data itself. For example, biased sampling or underrepresentation of certain groups in data can lead to

limited results when used for analysis or decision-making.

iii) Privacy Discrimination: Discrimination can occur when sensitive personal information is used to profile or target individuals unfairly. This can lead to discriminatory pricing, marketing, or denial of opportunities.

2. Ethical Concerns:

i) Fairness and Equity: Discrimination and bias undermine the principles of justice and equity. It's ethically wrong to intentionally or inadvertently mistreat individuals based on personal characteristics.

ii) Social Consequences: Discrimination and bias can perpetuate existing societal inequalities and injustices. For example, biased AI systems in hiring can exacerbate gender or racial disparities in employment.

iii) Loss of Trust: When individuals become aware of discrimination or bias in data-driven systems, it erodes trust in those systems and the organisations behind them.

3. Examples:

i) Job Recruitment: AI-powered hiring tools that inadvertently favour specific demographics may discriminate against candidates from underrepresented groups.

ii) Financial Services: Biased algorithms in financial services can result in discriminatory lending or insurance practices that disproportionately affect minority communities.

iii) Criminal Justice: Predictive policing algorithms may over-police specific neighbourhoods, leading to a bias in arrests and law enforcement actions.

4. Mitigating Discrimination and Bias:

i) Diverse Data: Ensuring that the data used to train algorithms is diverse and representative of different demographics can help mitigate bias.

ii) Bias Detection and Mitigation: Employing bias audits and fairness-aware machine learning can help identify and reduce algorithm bias.

iii) Transparency: Organizations should be transparent about how algorithms make decisions and what data is used. This transparency can help users and stakeholders assess the fairness of the system.

iv) Regular Audits: Regularly auditing algorithms and data for bias can help identify and correct issues over time.

v) Ethical AI Design: Designing AI and machine learning systems with ethical principles, including fairness and equity, is essential.

vi) Regulation: Governments and regulatory bodies can play a role in setting standards and rules to ensure fairness and non-discrimination in data-driven systems.

5. Legal Frameworks:

i) Legal frameworks such as anti-discrimination laws may apply to discriminatory practices, even if they occur in the context of data-driven decision-making.

Addressing discrimination and bias in data privacy and security is a multifaceted challenge with significant ethical and social implications. Ensuring fairness and equity in data-driven systems requires a combination of technical measures, transparency, ethical considerations, and, in some cases, regulatory intervention. Creating a more equitable and just digital environment for all individuals and groups is an ongoing effort.

Data Monetization And Commercialization

Data monetisation and commercialisation refer to generating revenue by leveraging data assets. In this process, organisations collect, process, and sell or license data to other entities for various purposes. While data monetisation can offer significant financial benefits, it raises important ethical and privacy considerations. Here's a detailed exploration of data monetisation and commercialisation:

1. Data Monetization Models:

i) Selling Raw Data: Organizations may sell raw data, such as user behaviour or sensor data, to other companies, often for market research or analytics.

ii) Data Licensing: Organisations may license data to other businesses instead of selling it outright, allowing them to use it under specific terms and conditions.

iii) Data-Driven Products and Services: Some companies build and monetise products or services around data, such as data analytics platforms.

iv) Personalised Advertising: Online platforms and social media companies monetise user data by providing targeted advertising based on user behaviour and preferences.

v) Data Marketplaces: Data marketplaces serve as intermediaries, allowing organisations to buy and sell data from and to other entities.

2. Ethical Concerns:

i) Privacy: Data monetisation often involves collecting and sharing personal data, raising concerns about user privacy. Users may only sometimes be aware of how their data is used or may have yet to grant informed consent.

ii) Consent: The issue of informed consent is critical. Users should have the choice to opt in or opt out of data collection and monetisation practices.

iii) Data Security: The handling and storage of data for monetisation purposes must adhere to robust security practices to prevent data breaches and unauthorised access.

iv) Transparency: Organizations must be transparent about their data practices, including who they share data with and for what purposes.

v) Algorithmic Bias: Data-driven decision-making processes can perpetuate bias if not properly designed and monitored, leading to discriminatory outcomes.

vi) Monetisation vs. User Benefit: Balancing the financial interests of organisations with the benefits to users can be ethically challenging. Users may question whether their data is used primarily for their benefit or profit.

3. Regulatory Landscape:

i) GDPR (General Data Protection Regulation): In Europe, GDPR imposes strict data handling and sharing requirements. Organisations must obtain informed consent, disclose data usage, and allow users to request the deletion of their data.

ii) CCPA (California Consumer Privacy Act): CCPA in California gives consumers more control over their personal information and requires transparency about data collection and sharing.

iii) Other National and Regional Regulations: Many countries have enacted data protection laws and regulations that impact data monetisation and commercialisation practices.

4. Mitigation Strategies:

i) Consent and Transparency: Organizations should prioritise informed consent and transparent communication regarding data handling practices with users.

ii) Data Security: Implement robust data security measures to protect the data being monetised and prevent data breaches.

iii) Ethical Data Use: Develop ethical guidelines and practices for data use, ensuring fairness, privacy, and non-discrimination.

iv) Data Governance: Establish strong data quality, security, and regulation compliance practices.

v) User Control: Provide users with control over their data, including opting out of data monetisation practices.

vi) Algorithmic Fairness: Monitor and address algorithmic bias to ensure that data-driven decisions are fair and equitable.

Data monetisation and commercialisation can be financially lucrative for organisations, but they have significant ethical and regulatory responsibilities. Balancing the potential for profit with ethical considerations, user privacy, and data security is essential for maintaining trust and ensuring responsible data handling practices in the digital age.

Lack Of Data Control

The lack of data control refers to a situation in which individuals have limited or no control over their data once organisations or entities have collected it. This lack of control can raise significant privacy and security concerns. Here's a more detailed exploration of the issue:

What is the Lack of Data Control?

Definition: Lack of data control occurs when individuals have limited authority or ability to manage, access, modify, or delete their data collected and held by organisations, platforms, or third parties.

Causes of Lack of Data Control:

i) Data Collection Practices: Organizations may collect extensive data without explicit user consent or with overly broad consent, limiting user control over what data is collected.

ii) Data Sharing and Sales: When organisations share or sell user data to third parties, users often have little or no say in how their data is subsequently used or by whom.

iii) Data Retention Policies: Some organisations retain user data for extended periods, making it challenging for individuals to have their data deleted or anonymised.

iv) Complex Ecosystems: In the digital age, data flows across various platforms, services, and third-party applications, making it difficult for users to track and control their data's journey.

Ethical Concerns:

i) Privacy: Lack of data control can result in privacy violations, as users may be unable to prevent the misuse or unauthorised access to their personal information.

ii) Autonomy: Individuals have a right to sovereignty over their data. When they lack control, this autonomy is compromised.

iii) Transparency: Lack of data control is often linked to a lack of clarity about data practices, leading to distrust among users.

iv) Data Security: Users may have concerns about the security of their data when they lack control over who has access to it.

Consequences of Lack of Data Control:

i) Privacy Violations: Users' personal information may be used for purposes they did not consent to or shared with third parties without their knowledge.

ii) Data Breaches: Inadequate data control measures can lead to data breaches, exposing sensitive information to unauthorised access and potential misuse.

iii) Loss of Trust: When users perceive a lack of control over their data, it can erode trust in the organisations and platforms collecting that data.

Mitigation Strategies:

i) Data Protection Laws: Data protection regulations like GDPR and CCPA require organisations to provide individuals with control over their data and the ability to access, modify, or delete it.

ii) User-Friendly Controls: Organizations should offer user-friendly interfaces and tools that enable users to manage their data preferences easily.

iii) Transparency: Clear and concise privacy policies and data handling practices should be provided to users so that they understand how their data is collected and used.

iv) Data Portability: Users should be able to quickly move their data from one service to another, promoting competition and user choice.

v) Consent Mechanisms: Implement transparent and granular consent mechanisms that allow users to choose what data they are willing to share and for what purposes.

The lack of data control is a significant concern in the digital age, as it can result in privacy violations, erode trust, and compromise individual autonomy. Addressing this issue requires a combination of legal frameworks, user-friendly tools, transparency, and responsible data-handling practices to ensure that individuals have meaningful control over their data.

User Trust And Reputation

User trust and reputation are essential in the digital age, particularly in data privacy and security. These factors play a significant role in shaping how individuals and organisations interact with technology and one another. Here's a detailed exploration of user trust and reputation:

A. User Trust:

1. Definition: User trust refers to the confidence and belief that individuals have in the reliability, security, and ethical behaviour of organisations, platforms, or technology. It is the foundation of positive user experiences and interactions.

2. Factors Influencing Trust:

> Privacy: Trust is closely tied to data privacy. Users trust organisations that commit to protecting their personal information and respecting their privacy rights.
> Security: Trust is built when users believe that their data and online interactions are secure from unauthorised access, breaches, or cyberattacks.
> Transparency: Organizations that are transparent about their data practices, policies, and intentions tend to earn higher trust.
> Consistency: Consistent behaviour and adherence to stated principles and policies help maintain trust over time.
> Accountability: Trust is bolstered when organisations take responsibility for their actions, especially in data breaches or mishandling of user data.

3. User Reputation:

Definition: User reputation refers to an individual's or organisation's perceived trustworthiness and credibility based on past actions, behaviours, and interactions. It can be a critical factor in building trust with others.

4. Factors Influencing Reputation:

> Data Handling: How an organisation or individual handles user data can significantly impact their reputation. Responsible data practices enhance reputation, while data breaches or misuse can damage it.
> Ethical Behaviour: Consistently ethical behaviour, including fair business practices and responsible data use, can build a positive reputation.
> Customer Reviews and Feedback: User reviews and feedback play a vital role in shaping an organisation's reputation. Positive reviews can enhance trust, while negative reviews can erode trust.
> Transparency and Communication: Open and transparent communication with users, especially during times of crisis or incidents,

can help maintain a positive reputation.

5. The Relationship Between Trust and Reputation:

> Trust and reputation are closely interlinked. A positive reputation can enhance confidence, as individuals are likelier to trust entities with a good track record.
> Conversely, trust-building actions contribute to a positive reputation. When organisations demonstrate trustworthiness through responsible data handling, security measures, and ethical behaviour, they enhance their reputation.

6. Importance of User Trust and Reputation:

> Business Success: User trust and a positive reputation are essential for business success. Customers are more likely to engage with and purchase from trustworthy organisations.
> Data Sharing and Collaboration: Trust is essential for individuals and organisations to share data and collaborate effectively. In research, partnerships, and data-sharing initiatives, trust facilitates cooperation.
> User Engagement: Users are more likely to engage with digital platforms and services if they trust their data and interactions are secure and private.
> Brand Loyalty: Trust and a positive reputation contribute to brand loyalty. Customers who trust a brand are likelier to remain loyal and recommend it to others.

7. Building and Maintaining Trust and Reputation:

> Prioritise data privacy and security through robust data protection measures.
> Be transparent about data practices and privacy policies.
> Communicate openly and honestly with users, especially during data incidents.
> Act ethically and responsibly in all interactions, including data handling.
> Encourage and address user feedback and reviews to improve reputation.

User trust and reputation are vital in the digital landscape, particularly in data privacy and security. Building and maintaining trust through responsible data practices, transparency, and ethical behaviour is essential for businesses, organisations, and individuals to thrive in the digital age. Reputation, once damaged, can be challenging to rebuild, making trust and reputation management a top priority for all stakeholders.

Regulatory Landscape

The regulatory landscape in data privacy and security is a complex and evolving framework of laws and regulations governing how organisations collect, use, store, and protect personal data. Both national and international rules shape this landscape, and they play a critical role in safeguarding individuals' privacy and data security. Here's an overview of the regulatory landscape:

1. Key Data Privacy and Security Regulations:

>GDPR (General Data Protection Regulation): Enforced in the European Union (EU), GDPR is one of the most comprehensive data protection regulations globally. It governs the processing of personal data and imposes strict requirements on organisations, including the need for informed consent, data breach notification, and the appointment of Data Protection Officers (DPOs).
> CCPA (California Consumer Privacy Act): CCPA, enacted in California, provides privacy rights and protections to California residents. It grants consumers more control over businesses' personal information and imposes transparency and data access requirements
> HIPAA (Health Insurance Portability and Accountability Act): HIPAA sets standards for protecting health information in the United States. It applies to healthcare providers, insurers, and related entities to safeguard the privacy and security of patient data.
> PIPEDA (Personal Information Protection and Electronic Documents Act): PIPEDA is Canada's federal privacy law, which regulates how private-sector organisations handle personal information. It requires consent and mandates data breach reporting.
> Other National and Regional Regulations: Many countries and regions have data protection laws, such as the UK's Data Protection Act 2018,

Brazil's LGPD (Lei Geral de Proteção de Dados), and India's Personal Data Protection Bill.

2. International Frameworks:

> Privacy Shield: Privacy Shield was a framework that allowed the transfer of personal data between the EU and the United States while complying with EU data protection standards. It was invalidated by the European Court of Justice in 2020.
> APEC CBPR (Asia-Pacific Economic Cooperation Cross-Border Privacy Rules): APEC CBPR is a voluntary framework for data protection and cross-border data flows among APEC member economies.
> Convention 108: Convention 108 is an international treaty protecting individuals about the automatic processing of personal data. Several countries have ratified it.

3. Regulatory Focus Areas:

> Data Protection: Regulations emphasise personal data protection, requiring organisations to implement appropriate safeguards and security measures.
> Consent: Many regulations require informed and explicit permission from individuals to process their data, emphasising the right to withdraw consent.
> Data Subject Rights: Individuals can access, rectify, delete, and port their data. Regulations require organisations to facilitate these rights.
> Data Breach Notification: Regulations often mandate prompt reporting of data breaches to authorities and affected individuals.
> Accountability: Organizations are required to demonstrate responsibility in data processing through data protection impact assessments and appointing DPOs.
> Cross-Border Data Transfer: Regulations provide mechanisms for legally transferring personal data across borders, such as Standard Contractual Clauses (SCCs).

4. Evolving and Emerging Regulations:

The regulatory landscape continues to evolve, with new laws being proposed and enacted in various regions, including data sovereignty laws, AI regulations, and cybersecurity standards.

5. Compliance Challenges:

> Organisations need help navigating the complex regulatory landscape, mainly if they operate globally.
> Balancing data privacy with innovation and data-driven business models is a continuous challenge.
> Ensuring compliance with data protection laws while using third-party services and cloud platforms adds complexity.

The regulatory landscape for data privacy and security is dynamic and essential for protecting individuals' rights and personal data. Organisations must stay informed about these regulations, implement necessary compliance measures, and adapt to changes in the legal framework to ensure responsible and ethical data-handling practices. Non-compliance can lead to significant legal and financial consequences.

SECURITY CHALLENGES IN VIRTUAL ENVIRONMENTS

Cybersecurity Threats

Cybersecurity threats are malicious activities and risks that target digital systems, networks, and data. These threats can lead to unauthorised access, data breaches, disruption of services, financial losses, and other adverse consequences. Understanding these threats is crucial for implementing effective cybersecurity measures. Here are some common cybersecurity threats:

1. Malware:

Malware is malicious software designed to damage, disrupt, or gain unauthorised access to computer systems. Types of malware include viruses, worms, Trojans, ransomware, spyware, and adware.

2. Phishing Attacks:

Phishing involves deceptive emails, messages, or websites that trick individuals into revealing sensitive information like passwords, credit card numbers, or login credentials.

3. Social Engineering:

Social engineering attacks manipulate human psychology to deceive individuals into revealing confidential information. This can include impersonating trusted entities, like tech support or colleagues, to gain access to systems.

4.Ransomware:

Ransomware encrypts a victim's data and demands a ransom for the decryption key. Paying the ransom does not guarantee data recovery, and it encourages cybercriminals.

5. Distributed Denial of Service (DDoS) Attacks:

DDoS attacks overwhelm a system, network, or website with a flood of traffic, making it inaccessible to legitimate users.

6. Insider Threats:

Insider threats come from within an organisation and can be malicious or unintentional. Employees, contractors, or business partners may misuse their access to systems or data.

7. Zero-Day Exploits:

Zero-day vulnerabilities are security flaws that are not yet known to the software vendor. Cybercriminals can exploit these vulnerabilities before patches or updates are available.

8. Brute Force Attacks:

Brute force attacks involve trying all possible combinations of passwords or encryption keys to gain unauthorised access to a system.

9. Man-in-the-Middle (MitM) Attacks:

In MitM attacks, an attacker intercepts and potentially alters communications between two parties without their knowledge.

10. SQL Injection:

SQL injection attacks target web applications by injecting malicious SQL code into input fields to manipulate databases and gain access to sensitive data.

11. IoT Vulnerabilities:

Internet of Things (IoT) devices often lack strong security measures, making them susceptible to attacks compromising personal data and privacy.

12. Credential Stuffing:

Cybercriminals use lists of stolen usernames and passwords from one breach to try and gain access to multiple accounts where users have reused credentials.

13. Data Exfiltration:

Attackers steal sensitive data from organisations for financial gain or to sell on the dark web. Data breaches can be highly damaging to organisations and individuals.

14. Fileless Malware:

Fileless malware does not rely on traditional files and can reside in memory, making it difficult to detect and remove.

15. Supply Chain Attacks:

Cybercriminals target the software or hardware supply chain, inserting malware or vulnerabilities into products before they reach end-users.

16. Cryptojacking:

Cryptojacking involves the unauthorised use of a victim's computer or device to mine cryptocurrencies, consuming system resources and potentially damaging hardware.

17. AI and Machine Learning Threats:

As AI and machine learning become more prevalent, there is a risk that cybercriminals can use them to create more sophisticated attacks.

18. State-Sponsored Attacks:

Some cybersecurity threats are orchestrated by nation-states or state-sponsored actors, often for espionage, disruption, or intellectual property theft.

To defend against these threats, organisations and individuals must implement robust cybersecurity practices, including regular software updates, strong password policies, employee training, network monitoring, and security technologies such as firewalls, antivirus software, and intrusion detection systems. Additionally, staying informed about emerging threats and security best practices is essential in today's constantly evolving cybersecurity landscape.

Vulnerabilities In Virtual Systems

Virtual systems, including virtual machines (VMs) and virtualised environments, offer many flexibility and resource utilisation benefits. However, they also introduce unique vulnerabilities and security challenges. Here are some common vulnerabilities in virtual systems:

1. Hypervisor Vulnerabilities:

> The hypervisor is the software that manages multiple virtual machines on a physical host. Vulnerabilities in the hypervisor can allow attackers to gain control over all hosted VMs.
> Unauthorised access or privilege escalation within the hypervisor can lead to significant security breaches.

2. VM Escape:

> VM escape is an attack where an attacker compromises a VM and then breaks out of it to gain access to the underlying hypervisor or other VMs on the same host.
> This can occur due to vulnerabilities in the VM's guest OS, virtualisation software, or misconfigurations.

3. Insecure VM Snapshots:

> Snapshots are used to capture the state of a VM at a specific point in time. If images are not correctly secured, they can expose sensitive information if accessed by an attacker.

4. Inter-VM Communication Risks:

> VMs on the same host can communicate, which attackers can exploit to move laterally within the virtual environment.
> Misconfigured network settings can lead to unauthorised access or data leakage between VMs.

5. Resource Exhaustion Attacks:

> Attackers can launch resource exhaustion attacks within a virtualised environment, such as overloading a host system with VMs or consuming excessive CPU or memory resources.

6. Misconfigured VM Permissions:

> Misconfigurations, such as overly permissive permissions or inadequate

isolation between VMs, can lead to unauthorised access and data breaches.

7. Inadequate VM Patching and Updating:

> VMs require regular patching and updating to address security vulnerabilities in the guest OS and software applications. Neglecting this can result in VMs becoming vulnerable to known exploits.

8. Orphaned VMs and Unused Templates:

> VMs that are no longer in use but need to be appropriately decommissioned can be forgotten and left unpatched, posing security risks.
> Only used VM templates may contain known vulnerabilities if updated regularly.

9. Snapshot Sprawl:

> Accumulating too many snapshots without proper management can lead to performance issues and security risks.

10. Insufficient Logging and Monitoring:

> Inadequate logging and monitoring of virtual environments can make detecting and responding to security incidents challenging.

11. Shared Storage Vulnerabilities:

> VMs often share storage resources, and vulnerabilities in shared storage systems can expose VMs to data breaches or unauthorised access.

12. Third-Party VM Images and Appliances:

> Using third-party VM images or appliances without proper vetting can introduce security risks, as these may contain malicious code or vulnerabilities.

To mitigate these vulnerabilities in virtual systems, organisations should implement the following best practices:

i) Regularly patch and update VMs and the virtualisation software.
ii) Enforce proper network segmentation and firewall rules between VMs.
iii) Apply the principle of least privilege for VM permissions.
iv) Implement strong access controls for the hypervisor.
v) Monitor VMs and the virtual environment for suspicious activities.
vi) Maintain an inventory of VMs and decommission unused or orphaned VMs.
vii) Secure shared storage resources and use encryption where applicable.
viii) Educate staff and users about virtualisation security best practices.

By proactively addressing these vulnerabilities and adopting sound security practices, organisations can maximise the benefits of virtualisation while minimising the associated risks.

Protecting Virtual Environment Security

Protecting the security of virtual environments is critical for maintaining the integrity and confidentiality of your data and applications. Virtualisation introduces unique security challenges, but you can mitigate these risks effectively with proper measures. Here are steps to protect your virtual environment security:

1. Patch and Update Regularly:

Keep all virtualisation software, hypervisors, and guest OSes updated with the latest security patches and updates. This helps close known vulnerabilities.

2. Hypervisor Security:

Secure the hypervisor by applying strong access controls, configuring secure boot options, and isolating it from the management network.

3. Network Segmentation:

Segment your virtual network to limit communication between VMs. Use firewalls and network access controls to restrict traffic to only necessary connections.

4. Access Control:

Implement strong access controls for managing and accessing VMs. Use role-based access control (RBAC) to ensure only authorised personnel can make changes.

5. Regular Audits and Monitoring:

Continuously monitor your virtual environment for suspicious activities and unusual access patterns. Set up alerts for security events.

6. Encryption:

Use encryption to protect data at rest and in transit within the virtual environment. This includes encrypting VMs and data stores and using secure communication protocols.

7. Backup and Disaster Recovery:

Implement regular backups of VMs and ensure disaster recovery plans are in place. This helps in case of data loss or a security incident.

8. Virtual Machine Security:

Configure VMs securely by removing unnecessary services, minimising attack surfaces, and keeping guest OS and software up to date.

9. Security Tools:

Utilise security tools specifically designed for virtual environments, such as intrusion detection and prevention systems (IDS/IPS) and security information and event management (SIEM) systems.

10. User Training:

Educate users and administrators on best practices for virtual environment security, including recognising phishing attacks and following secure password policies.

11. Vulnerability Scanning and Penetration Testing:

Regularly scan your virtual environment for vulnerabilities and conduct penetration testing to identify weaknesses that may be exploited.

12. Inventory and Asset Management:

Maintain an up-to-date inventory of all VMs and virtual assets. Remove or decommission VMs that are no longer in use.

13. Security Policies and Procedures:

Develop and enforce security policies and procedures specifically tailored to your virtual environment. Ensure that these policies are regularly reviewed and updated.

14. Vendor and Third-Party Security:

If using third-party VM images or templates, ensure they come from reputable sources and have been vetted for security.

15. Incident Response Plan:

Have a well-defined incident response plan to address security breaches or incidents promptly. This plan should include communication protocols, investigation procedures, and steps for containment and recovery.

16. Compliance and Regulations:

Ensure your virtual environment complies with relevant industry regulations and applicable data protection laws, such as GDPR, HIPAA, or

PCI DSS.

17. Regular Security Training:

Keep IT and security staff updated with training on the latest security threats and best practices in virtualisation security.

By implementing these security measures and maintaining a proactive and vigilant stance toward virtual environment security, you can significantly reduce the risks associated with virtualisation and protect your organisation's sensitive data and resources.

LEGAL FRAMEWORKS AND REGULATIONS

GDPR and Its Implications

The General Data Protection Regulation (GDPR) is a comprehensive data protection and privacy regulation enacted by the European Union (EU) in 2018. GDPR has far-reaching implications for organisations that process the personal data of individuals residing in the EU, regardless of where the organisation is based. Here are some critical impacts of GDPR:

1. Extraterritorial Scope:

GDPR applies to organisations worldwide if they process the personal data of EU residents. Even non-EU organisations must comply with GDPR if they handle EU citizens' data.

2. Consent and Data Subject Rights:

GDPR emphasises obtaining explicit and informed consent for data processing activities. Individuals have the right to know how their data is used and can request access, correction, erasure, and portability.

3. Data Protection Officer (DPO):

Specific organisations are required to appoint a Data Protection Officer (DPO) responsible for ensuring GDPR compliance. DPOs are a crucial point of contact for data protection authorities.

4. Data Breach Notification:

GDPR mandates reporting data breaches to supervisory authorities and, in some instances, to affected individuals. This helps ensure transparency and timely responses to violations.

5. Privacy by Design and Default:

GDPR encourages the integration of data protection into the design and operation of systems and services. Privacy should be considered from the outset of any data processing activity.

6. Data Impact Assessments (DPIAs):

Organisations must conduct Data Protection Impact Assessments (DPIAs) for high-risk data processing activities to identify and mitigate potential privacy risks.

7. Data Transfer Restrictions:

GDPR imposes strict controls on transferring personal data outside the EU, particularly to countries without adequate data protection laws.

8. Penalties and Fines:

GDPR introduces significant fines for non-compliance, with penalties that can reach up to €20 million or 4% of a company's global annual revenue, whichever is higher.

9. Accountability and Documentation:

Organisations must demonstrate compliance through documentation, including records of data processing activities, data protection policies, and evidence of consent.

10. Data Protection Impact on Marketing and Profiling:

GDPR impacts marketing practices, requiring explicit email marketing consent and limiting automated profiling and decision-making based on personal data.

11. Data Minimization and Storage Limitation:

GDPR promotes the principles of data minimisation and storage limitation, encouraging organisations to collect only the data necessary for the intended purpose and retain it for no longer than necessary.

12. Cross-Border Enforcement:

GDPR enables data protection authorities in different EU member states to cooperate and enforce the regulation across borders. This ensures consistent application of data protection rules.

13. Enhanced Rights for Data Subjects:

GDPR gives individuals enhanced rights over their data, including the right to be forgotten (data erasure), data portability, and objecting to specific data processing activities.

14. Third-Party Processor Accountability:

Organisations that use third-party processors (e.g., cloud service providers) must ensure that these processors also comply with GDPR and take appropriate security measures.

15. Data Localization:

Some organisations have had to reevaluate where they store and process data to ensure compliance with GDPR's data transfer rules.

16. Data Protection Impact on Innovation:

Organisations must balance data protection and innovation, ensuring that new technologies and data-driven initiatives comply with GDPR.

17. Data Protection Authorities (DPAs):

DPAs are responsible for enforcing GDPR at the national level. Organisations may need to engage with DPAs on data protection matters.

GDPR has profound implications for organisations worldwide, transforming how personal data is handled, protected, and managed. Compliance with GDPR requires a holistic approach encompassing data governance, security, privacy practices, and organisational culture. Non-compliance can result in severe financial penalties and reputational damage, making GDPR compliance a top priority for businesses operating within its scope.

CCPA AND U.S. DATA PRIVACY LAWS

The California Consumer Privacy Act (CCPA) and various U.S. state data privacy laws are designed to protect consumer privacy and data rights within the United States. While these laws share common objectives, they have unique provisions and requirements. Here's an overview of CCPA and some notable U.S. data privacy laws:

California Consumer Privacy Act (CCPA):

1. Scope: CCPA applies to businesses that collect and process the personal information of California residents, including companies located outside of California.

2. Key Provisions:

> Right to Know: Consumers have the right to know what personal information is collected and how it's used.
> Right to Delete: Consumers can request the deletion of their personal information.
> Right to Opt-Out: Consumers can opt out of selling their personal information.
> Non-Discrimination: Businesses cannot discriminate against consumers

who exercise their privacy rights.
> Enforcement and Penalties: The California Attorney General can enforce CCPA violations with fines of up to $7,500 per intentional violation.
> Data Protection Impact: CCPA has had a significant impact on businesses, requiring them to update privacy policies, implement mechanisms for handling consumer data requests, and provide clear privacy notices.

Virginia Consumer Data Protection Act (CDPA):

1. Scope: CDPA applies to businesses that process the personal data of Virginia residents and meet specific criteria. It went into effect on January 1, 2023.

2. Key Provisions:

> Right to Know and Delete: Consumers have the right to know what personal data is collected and processed and request the deletion of their data.
> Data Minimization: Businesses are required to minimise data collection to what is necessary for the disclosed purpose.
> Sensitive Data: Special requirements apply to processing sensitive data, including opt-In consent.
> Enforcement and Penalties: CDPA is enforced by the Virginia Attorney General, with penalties of up to $7,500 per violation.

New York Privacy Act (NYPA):

1. Scope: NYPA applies to businesses that collect and process personal information of New York residents and have a minimum annual revenue threshold.

2. Key Provisions:

> Right to Know and Delete: Consumers can access and delete their data.
> Data Minimization: Businesses must limit data collection to what is necessary for the disclosed purpose.

> Data Protection Assessments: Businesses must conduct regular assessments of data processing activities.

> Enforcement and Penalties: NYPA includes civil penalties and a private right of action, allowing consumers to sue companies for data breaches.

Other State Laws:

> Nevada: Nevada has data privacy laws requiring businesses to allow consumers to opt out of selling their personal information.

> Colorado: Colorado passed the Colorado Privacy Act (CPA), which will become effective in July 2023 and includes rights similar to CCPA.

> Washington: Washington has a comprehensive data privacy law, the Washington Privacy Act (WPA), awaiting final approval.

> Other States: Several states, including Florida, Texas, and Illinois, are considering or have introduced data privacy legislation.

CCPA and various state data privacy laws in the United States aim to protect consumers' privacy rights and personal data. While they share some common principles, such as the right to know and the right to delete, there are differences in scope, requirements, and enforcement mechanisms. Organisations operating in the U.S. must be aware of and compliant with relevant state-specific privacy laws that apply to their operations. Additionally, the potential for future federal data privacy legislation adds complexity to the regulatory landscape.

COMPLIANCE AND ENFORCEMENT

Compliance and enforcement are essential to data privacy and security regulations like GDPR, CCPA, and other state and national laws. Ensuring compliance and enforcing these regulations helps protect individuals' rights and personal data, maintain trust, and deter non-compliance. Here's an overview of compliance and enforcement mechanisms:

Compliance:

1. Data Protection Principles: Regulations, such as GDPR, often outline specific principles organisations must adhere to. These principles include data minimisation, purpose limitation, accuracy, storage limitation, and security.

2. Data Subject Rights: Compliance requires organisations to respect and uphold data subject rights, such as the right to access, rectify, delete, or port their data. Organisations must have mechanisms in place to facilitate these rights.

3. Consent: If processing personal data requires approval, organisations must obtain explicit and informed consent from individuals. Consent mechanisms must be transparent and easy to understand.

4. Data Protection Impact Assessments (DPIAs): Organizations may need to conduct DPIAs for high-risk data processing activities to assess and mitigate potential privacy risks.

5. Security Measures: Compliance mandates implementing robust security measures to protect personal data from breaches and unauthorised access. This includes encryption, access controls, and regular security assessments.

6. Documentation: Maintaining records of data processing activities, privacy policies, and consent records is vital to compliance. These records demonstrate accountability.

7. Data Transfer Mechanisms: Regulations often impose restrictions on cross-border data transfers. Organisations must use approved mechanisms, such as Standard Contractual Clauses (SCCs), to ensure lawful data transfers.

8. Privacy by Design and Default: Organizations must integrate data protection into the design and operation of systems and services, considering privacy from the outset.

Enforcement:

1. Regulatory Authorities:

Most data privacy regulations designate a regulatory authority responsible for enforcement, such as the Information Commissioner's Office (ICO) for GDPR or the California Attorney General for CCPA.

2. Investigations:

Regulatory authorities can conduct investigations into suspected violations. These investigations may include audits, inquiries, or assessments of an organisation's data practices.

3. Penalties and Fines:

Non-compliance can lead to penalties and fines. The severity of penalties varies depending on the regulation. For example, GDPR allows fines of up to €20 million or 4% of global annual turnover, whichever is higher.

4. Corrective Measures:

Authorities may order organisations to take corrective actions to bring them into compliance. This could include mandating changes in data handling practices or policies.

5. Data Breach Notifications:

Many regulations require organisations to report data breaches to authorities promptly and affected individuals. Failure to do so can result in penalties.

6. Civil Lawsuits:

Some regulations allow individuals to file civil lawsuits against organisations for data breaches or violations. This can result in financial damages and legal costs for the organisation.

7. Injunctions:

Authorities can issue injunctions to stop or prevent specific data processing activities that are non-compliant.

8. Reputation Damage:

Non-compliance can result in significant reputational damage, which can have long-lasting consequences for an organisation.

9. International Cooperation:

Regulatory authorities may cooperate across borders to enforce data privacy laws, ensuring consistent enforcement in cases involving data transfers between countries.

10. Private Right of Action:

Some laws, like the CCPA, grant consumers a private right of action, allowing them to sue organisations for certain data breaches, which can lead to significant legal liabilities.

Compliance and enforcement mechanisms ensure that organisations follow data privacy and security regulations. Organisations should invest in robust data protection practices, including compliance programs, privacy policies, security measures, and staff training, to mitigate risks and avoid non-compliance's legal and reputational consequences.

BALANCING DATA PRIVACY AND ECONOMIC REALITIES

Economic Benefits of Virtual Environments

Virtual environments, including virtualisation and cloud computing, offer numerous economic benefits to organisations of all sizes and industries. These benefits can lead to cost savings, increased efficiency, and improved agility. Here are some of the critical economic advantages of virtual environments:

1. Cost Reduction:

i) Hardware Savings: Virtualization allows multiple virtual machines (VMs) to run on a single physical server. This reduces the need to purchase and maintain various physical servers, leading to significant cost savings for hardware.

ii) Energy Efficiency: Fewer physical servers mean reduced energy consumption and lower electricity bills. Virtual environments contribute to sustainability efforts by reducing an organisation's carbon footprint.

iii) Space Savings: Virtualization reduces the physical footprint of data centres, freeing up valuable office space or reducing the need for additional real estate.

2. Optimised Resource Utilization:

i) Resource Scaling: Virtual environments enable organisations to allocate resources dynamically based on workload demands. This ensures that computing resources are used efficiently, reducing underutilisation.

ii) Improved Server Consolidation: Organizations can consolidate workloads on fewer physical servers, achieving higher server utilisation rates and better resource allocation.

3. Reduced Maintenance Costs:

i) Centralised Management: Virtualization allows for centralised management of VMs, making it easier to apply updates, patches, and security measures. This reduces the time and effort required for maintenance.

ii) More accessible Backup and Recovery: Virtual environments offer efficient backup and recovery solutions, reducing the cost and complexity associated with traditional backup methods.

4. Scalability and Flexibility:

i) Elastic Scaling: Cloud-based virtual environments provide scalability, allowing organisations to quickly adjust resources up or down as needed. This flexibility reduces the need for upfront capital investments.

ii) Faster Deployment: Virtual environments enable rapid provisioning of new servers and resources, accelerating application deployment and reducing time-to-market.

5. Business Continuity and Disaster Recovery:

i) Improved Resilience: Virtualization and cloud environments offer redundancy and failover capabilities, enhancing business continuity and reducing the economic impact of downtime.
ii) Cost-Effective DR: Virtualization can simplify and lower the cost of disaster recovery (DR) planning and implementation.

6. Improved Security:

i) Isolation: Virtual environments allow for isolation between VMs, reducing the risk of security breaches and data leaks.
ii) Enhanced Security Tools: Many virtualisation platforms offer advanced security features, such as micro-segmentation and threat detection, which can reduce the cost of cybersecurity incidents.

7. IT Staff Productivity:

i) Automation: Virtual environments can automate routine IT tasks, freeing IT staff to focus on more strategic and value-added activities.
ii) Resource Optimization: IT personnel can optimise resource allocation, improving overall system performance and reducing operational costs.

8. Reduced Licensing Costs:

i) Software Licensing: Virtualization often allows for more efficient use of software licenses, potentially reducing the required permissions.
ii) Open Source Alternatives: Virtual environments can run on open-source software, reducing software licensing costs.

9. Global Accessibility:

Remote Work: Virtual environments facilitate remote work by providing secure access to applications and data from anywhere with an internet connection. This can reduce the need for physical office space and associated costs.

10. Competitive Advantage:

Organisations that leverage virtual environments are often more agile and responsive to market changes, giving them a competitive edge.

11. Testing and Development Savings:

Virtual environments are ideal for testing and development, reducing the need for physical hardware and streamlining the development process.

Virtual environments offer substantial economic benefits by reducing costs, optimising resource utilisation, improving scalability and flexibility, enhancing security, and increasing IT staff productivity. These advantages make virtualisation and cloud computing essential components of modern IT strategies, allowing organisations to operate more efficiently and competitively in today's digital landscape.

THE COST OF DATA PRIVACY COMPLIANCE

Data privacy compliance comes with costs that organisations must bear to protect individuals' personal information and avoid legal and financial repercussions for non-compliance. While the specific prices vary based on factors like the organisation's size, industry, and existing infrastructure, here are some of the ordinary expenses associated with data privacy compliance:

1. Personnel Costs:

> Data Protection Officer (DPO): In some cases, organisations must appoint a DPO responsible for data privacy matters. This role may be a full-time or part-time position.
> Legal and Compliance Team: Organizations may need to hire or allocate legal and compliance professionals to ensure ongoing compliance with data privacy regulations.

2. Compliance Software and Tools:

> Data Management Tools: Organizations may invest in data management and data protection tools to help manage and secure personal data effectively.
> Privacy Impact Assessment (PIA) Tools: Tools for conducting PIAs and ensuring that data processing activities comply with regulations.
> Privacy Management Platforms: Comprehensive platforms for managing data privacy compliance, including consent management and data subject request processing.

3. Training and Awareness:

> Employee Training: Organizations must invest in training programs to educate employees about data privacy best practices and regulatory requirements.
> Awareness Campaigns: Initiatives to raise awareness among employees and stakeholders about the importance of data privacy.

4. Security Measures:

> Data Encryption: Implementing encryption technologies to protect data in transit and at rest.
> Access Controls: Enhancing access controls ensures that only authorised individuals can access and process personal data.
> Security Audits and Assessments: Regular security assessments and audits to identify and address vulnerabilities.

5. Compliance Assessments:

> Data Protection Impact Assessments (DPIAs): The cost of conducting DPIAs for high-risk data processing activities.
> Audits and Assessments: Costs associated with third-party audits or assessments to verify compliance.

6. Legal and Consulting Fees:

> They engage legal counsel or data privacy consultants to guide

compliance requirements and legal implications.

7. Privacy Policies and Documentation:

> Costs related to drafting, updating, and publishing privacy policies, notices, and consent forms.

8. Data Subject Request Handling:

> We are developing and implementing processes and systems for handling data subject requests, including access, deletion, and rectification requests.

9. Incident Response and Data Breach Costs:

> Costs associated with preparing for and responding to data breaches, including notifying affected individuals and regulatory authorities.

10. Record-Keeping and Documentation:

> Costs related to maintaining records of data processing activities, consent records, and compliance documentation.

11. Regulatory Fines and Penalties:

> Non-compliance can result in significant fines and penalties imposed by data protection authorities, which can be a substantial cost.

12. Data Privacy Impact on Technology:

> They are adapting existing technology systems and infrastructure to comply with data privacy requirements, which may include software updates or replacements.

13. Data Subject Compensation:

> Sometimes, organisations may need to compensate individuals for data breaches or non-compliance.

14. Insurance Premiums:

> Some organisations opt for cyber liability insurance to help mitigate the financial impact of data breaches and compliance violations.

15. Data Localization:

> Costs associated with storing data in compliance with data localisation requirements in some regions.

It's important to note that while data privacy compliance comes with costs, non-compliance's potential financial and reputational damage can be far more significant. Therefore, many organisations view data privacy compliance as an essential investment in protecting their brand and maintaining the trust of customers and stakeholders. Additionally, implementing effective data privacy practices can improve data management and enhance security, providing long-term benefits beyond mere compliance.

CASE STUDIES: BALANCING ACT

A. The Data Privacy Challenges Faced by Facebook:

Undoubtedly, Facebook has encountered many data privacy difficulties during its existence. The Cambridge Analytica controversy stands out as a particularly noteworthy event.

The Cambridge Analytica scandal is a controversial incident involving the British political consulting firm Cambridge Analytica.

The events unfolded in 2018 when it came to light that Cambridge Analytica, a British political consulting business, had illegally acquired data from around 87 million users of the social media platform Facebook. The data above was utilised for political profiling and targeting in electoral contexts, notably during the 2016 United States presidential election.

In this circumstance, Facebook encountered a substantial challenge in maintaining a delicate equilibrium. On the one hand, the company possessed a vested economic interest in acquiring and disseminating user data to external developers and advertisers, thereby bolstering its advertising enterprise. However, it was their responsibility to safeguard the confidentiality of their users.

The issue engendered widespread public anger and prompted demands for more stringent legislation about data protection. Facebook has introduced more rigorous privacy safeguards and modified its data-sharing policy. Additionally, they encountered regulatory fines and underwent probes in other nations.

The occurrence above brought attention to the imperative for technology businesses to effectively oversee user data and strike a harmonious equilibrium between economic pursuits and safeguarding user privacy. Furthermore, it played a significant part in the broader international discourse surrounding data privacy and the responsibilities of technology corporations in protecting user data.

The Cambridge Analytica incident exemplifies the difficulties significant technology corporations like Facebook encounter in striking a delicate equilibrium between their financial objectives and user privacy protection. The statement emphasises the significance of implementing strong data privacy rules and adopting responsible data management practices in the era of digitalisation.

B. The Position of Apple Inc. Regarding Privacy:

In recent years, Apple has adopted a prominent position regarding privacy, positioning itself as a corporation dedicated to safeguarding customer data. This paper provides a comprehensive analysis of Apple Inc.'s position on privacy.

App Tracking Transparency (ATT) refers to a feature introduced by Apple that allows users to have more control over the tracking of their activities and data by mobile applications.

In April 2021, Apple unveiled the "App Tracking Transparency" (ATT) feature. To monitor user data across several applications and websites for advertising reasons, applications must get explicit agreement from the users.

Apple's strategic decision regarding ATT clearly illustrates the delicate equilibrium between safeguarding user privacy and pursuing business objectives. Implementing this measure limits advertisers' capacity to monitor users for personalised advertising, which may affect the financial gains of application developers and the advertising sector.

The prioritisation of user privacy above targeted advertising by Apple has garnered commendation and critique. The decision was met with approval from specific users and privacy activists. However, advertisers expressed worries and sure app developers about the potential economic consequences.

End-to-end encryption is a cryptographic communication protocol that ensures the confidentiality and integrity of data transmitted between two parties. This method ensures Apple has successfully integrated end-to-end encryption into its communications services, such as iMessage. This implies that the content of communications can only be accessed by the sender and recipient, with Apple unable to retrieve the messages.

The action above exemplifies a robust dedication to safeguarding user privacy through the preservation of the confidentiality of user communications. Nevertheless, the implementation of encryption technology has encountered opposition from law enforcement organisations, who contend that its use can impede the progress of criminal investigations.

The outcome of this situation is that Apple has consistently upheld its position on end-to-end encryption, placing significant emphasis on safeguarding customer privacy. This occurrence has established a standard for communications systems that prioritise privacy.

C. The Importance Of Privacy Labels And Transparency In The Digital Age

Apple has implemented privacy labels within its App Store, which provide customers with comprehensive details regarding the data collection and utilisation practices of various applications. Transparency enables users to make well-informed decisions regarding the applications they utilise.

Apple's efforts to promote openness effectively contribute to safeguarding consumer privacy. Nevertheless, it can influence users' decision-making processes regarding the selection and installation of applications, potentially affecting the economic viability and prosperity of specific applications.

The implementation of Apple's privacy labels has resulted in an increased level of consciousness regarding data practices among both app developers and consumers. This has consequently fostered discussions surrounding data privacy and app data gathering.

Apple's position on privacy is indicative of its commitment to prioritise the safeguarding of customer data. While these initiatives protect user privacy, they also raise inquiries regarding their potential economic ramifications on the advertising and app development sectors. The strategy above has established Apple as a frontrunner in the discourse on data privacy and technology corporations' obligations.

D. The sharing of healthcare data:

The exchange of healthcare data is essential to contemporary healthcare, necessitating a careful equilibrium between providing high-quality patient care, advancing medical research, and protecting patient privacy. This paper presents an overview of the problems and complexities associated with healthcare data sharing, highlighting the delicate balancing act required in this process.

CHALLENGES AND THE ART OF BALANCING

The Dilemma of Balancing Patient Privacy and Data Sharing for

Treatment Purposes To deliver optimal care, healthcare providers must access patient data. Nevertheless, it is imperative to acknowledge that individuals seeking medical care possess an inherent entitlement to maintain their privacy, necessitating the acquisition of informed consent before utilising their data for treatment-related objectives.

Implementing regulations such as the Health Insurance Portability and Accountability Act (HIPAA) in the United States establishes guidelines and criteria to safeguard patients' confidentiality and privacy. These regulations balance protecting sensitive healthcare information and enabling authorised entities to share relevant data to provide appropriate medical treatment.

The Dilemma of Balancing Data Sharing for Research Purposes and Protecting Identifiability The sharing of medical data for research purposes is paramount in facilitating medical breakthroughs. Nevertheless, the act of disclosing data that has the potential to reduce the identification of patients presents inherent privacy concerns.

Techniques such as de-identification and data anonymisation are employed to safeguard the confidentiality of patient identities while facilitating the exchange of data for research objectives.

The juxtaposition between economic interests and patient privacy presents a delicate equilibrium. Entities operating within the healthcare sector, including pharmaceutical corporations, possess financial motivations to get access to healthcare data for research and development. It is crucial to strike a balance between these interests and the preservation of patient privacy.

The European General Data Protection Regulation (GDPR) and other regulatory frameworks have significant consequences for corporations' healthcare data management, as they prioritise protecting patient privacy.

Interoperability and Data Access: Striking a Balance: Healthcare data sharing frequently necessitates establishing interoperable systems, enabling diverse institutions to access and exchange data. Nevertheless, preserving data security and privacy inside these interconnected systems poses a substantial difficulty.

Several initiatives and regulations, such as the 21st Century Cures Act in the United States, aim to enhance the compatibility of systems and stimulate the exchange of information while upholding established data privacy and security standards.

The Importance of Patient Consent and Autonomy: Striking Balance patients must be granted autonomy in managing their data and are provided with comprehensive information to make educated decisions regarding its utilisation. The persistent issue lies in balancing patient liberty and the imperative of data exchange.

Permission management platforms and portals have empowered patients to exercise control over their data and explicitly grant consent for its utilisation in many scenarios.

In essence, sharing healthcare data entails navigating a multifaceted array of problems. Achieving an optimal equilibrium is imperative to deliver high-quality healthcare to patients, promote the progress of medical investigations, and safeguard the confidentiality and protection of delicate medical data. Effective management of data sharing and patient privacy difficulties necessitates implementing regulatory frameworks and technology solutions, which are crucial in maintaining a balance between these two aspects.

The Intersection of Intelligent Urban Environments and Monitoring Systems

Intelligent cities utilise technological advancements to enhance the quality of urban life. Yet, they also raise concerns regarding the delicate equilibrium between innovation and protecting individual privacy, particularly regarding surveillance. This paper comprehensively analyses the obstacles and fragile equilibrium in implementing intelligent cities and surveillance systems.

THE CHALLENGES AND BALANCING ACT: A CRITICAL EXAMINATION

The issue of public safety vs privacy presents a delicate equilibrium in the context of brilliant city efforts, wherein the incorporation of surveillance technologies such as cameras and sensors is intended to augment the overall level of public safety. Nevertheless, this practice could violate individuals' private rights.

The establishment of explicit regulations and procedures for monitoring is imperative for urban areas to ensure that the advantages of public safety surpass any potential apprehensions over privacy. The importance of transparency in data collection and utilisation cannot be overstated.

The topic at hand is the delicate balance between data collection and privacy in the context of smart cities, where a significant volume of data is gathered from various sources such as sensors, gadgets, and cameras. It is essential to balance the advantages of data-driven decision-making and safeguarding privacy.

Privacy protection can be enhanced by employing techniques such as anonymisation and data aggregation, adopting robust data encryption measures, and ensuring that personal data is not misused. These measures facilitate data utilisation for driving advancements while maintaining the confidentiality of individuals' information.

The Comparison between Public Services and Data Sharing: Striking a Balance: Sharing data with public and private entities can enhance services. However, it also gives rise to concerns over data accessibility and governance.

Establishing data exchange protocols, permission processes, and stringent access restrictions is crucial for savvy city planners to mitigate the risk of unlawful utilisation of sensitive data.

Community engagement and privacy juxtapose present a delicate equilibrium in clever city design and governance. Nevertheless, this involvement may necessitate gathering personal information and raising privacy concerns.

The importance is in establishing transparent communication with the community on data usage, actively seeking public input, and implementing stringent privacy protection procedures.

The topic concerns the delicate balance between technology innovation and privacy safeguards, explicitly focusing on intelligent cities aspiring to advance technologically. Nevertheless, the expeditious integration of novel technology may surpass the progress in establishing adequate privacy protections.

The imperative for intelligent cities lies in their proactive approach towards addressing privacy problems, conducting privacy effect assessments, and continuously updating rules in response to the ever-evolving nature of technology.

The advancement of intelligent cities necessitates a nuanced equilibrium between leveraging technological advantages to enhance urban conditions and protecting citizens' privacy and civil freedoms. To properly strike a balance and assure the realisation of the benefits of smart cities without compromising individual privacy, it is crucial to establish unambiguous rules, adopt privacy-conscious policies, actively engage the public, and implement responsible data management procedures.

ETHICAL CONSIDERATIONS IN VIRTUAL DATA PRIVACY

User Expectations and Trust

User expectations and trust are critical factors in data privacy and information security. Here's how these aspects are interlinked and what organisations can do to build and maintain trust by meeting user expectations:

User Expectations:

i) Transparency: Users expect clear and understandable privacy policies. They want to know how their data is collected, used, and shared.

ii) Consent: Users expect to give informed consent for data collection and processing. They should have the ability to control their data.

iii) Data Security: Users expect their data to be kept secure from breaches and unauthorised access. They trust organisations to protect their information.

iv) Data Accuracy: Users expect that their data is accurate and up-to-date. They want to know that organisations will take steps to correct inaccurate information.

v) Data Retention: Users expect organisations to retain their data only as long as necessary for the intended purpose.

vi) Non-Discrimination: Users expect their data won't be used to discriminate against them, such as in employment or housing.

Building and Maintaining Trust:

i) Clear Privacy Policies: Organizations must create and communicate clear and concise privacy policies that align with user expectations. Transparency is key.

ii) Consent Mechanisms: Implement robust consent mechanisms, allowing users to make informed choices about their data. Make it easy for users to adjust their preferences.

iii) Data Security: Invest in robust data security measures, including encryption, regular security audits, and prompt response to data breaches.

iv) Data Accuracy: Ensure data accuracy by providing users with mechanisms to update and correct their information.

v) Data Minimization: Only collect and retain data strictly necessary for the intended purpose.

vi) Data Retention Policies: Have clear data retention policies and delete no longer needed data.

vii) Non-Discrimination: Avoid using data for discriminatory practices and ensure fair treatment of individuals.

viii) User Education: Educate users about privacy risks, best practices, and rights. Empowered users are more likely to trust your organisation.

ix) Compliance with Regulations: Stay up-to-date with privacy regulations and ensure compliance with regional and international standards.

x) Accountability: Establish clear accountability for data handling, including assigning responsibility for data privacy within your organisation.

xi) Response to Incidents: Develop and communicate an incident response plan to promptly address data breaches and other privacy incidents.

xii) User Feedback: Encourage and act on user feedback regarding data privacy concerns and use it to improve your practices.

xiii) Social Responsibility: Recognize the broader social impact of your data handling decisions and discuss ethical data use.

Meeting user expectations and building trust in data privacy isn't a one-time effort but an ongoing commitment. Organisations that prioritise user privacy, communicate transparently, and take concrete steps to safeguard data can earn and maintain the trust of their users, which is invaluable in today's digital landscape.

Ethical Data Handling Practices

Ethical data handling practices are essential for organisations that collect, process, and store data. These practices are grounded in principles of respect, responsibility, and transparency. Here are some critical ethical data-handling practices:

i) **Transparency**: Be transparent and honest about how data is collected, used, and shared. Ensure that privacy policies and terms of service are easily accessible and written in plain language so that individuals can understand how their data is treated.

ii) **Informed Consent**: Obtain informed and explicit consent from individuals before collecting and using their data. Communicate the purposes for which the data will be used and allow individuals to opt in or out of data collection and processing.

iii) **Data Minimization**: Collect and retain only the data necessary for the intended purpose. Avoid collecting excessive or irrelevant information that could infringe on individuals' privacy.

iv) **Data Security**: Implement robust security measures to protect data from breaches and unauthorised access. Encrypt sensitive data, conduct regular security audits, and have an incident response plan.

v) **Data Accuracy**: Take steps to ensure that the data you hold is accurate and up to date. Provide individuals with the means to review and correct their information when necessary.

vi) Data Retention Policies: Develop clear policies that specify how long data will be stored. Delete data that is no longer needed for its original purpose.

vii) Non-Discrimination: Do not use data to discriminate against individuals in areas such as employment, housing, or access to services. Ensure that data-driven decisions are fair and unbiased.

viii) User Control: Empower individuals to control their data. Offer user-friendly options for managing privacy settings, accessing their data, and deleting their accounts if desired.

ix) Accountability: Assign responsibility for data handling within your organisation and conduct regular assessments to ensure compliance with ethical data practices.

x) Training and Education: Train employees and staff on ethical data handling and privacy practices. Ensure they understand their roles in safeguarding data.

xi) Consistency with Regulations: Stay informed about relevant data protection regulations, such as GDPR, CCPA, or HIPAA, and ensure compliance with applicable laws in your region.

xii) Privacy by Design: Integrate privacy considerations into the design of products and services from the outset. Consider the impact on privacy at every stage of development.

xiii) Data Impact Assessments: Conduct privacy impact assessments to evaluate data processing activities' potential risks and ethical implications.

xiv) Data Anonymization: Whenever possible, use data anonymisation techniques to protect individuals' identities while gaining insights from the data.

xv) User Education: Educate individuals about their rights regarding data privacy and provide resources for them to learn about best practices and potential risks

xvi) Ethical Data Sharing: If you share data with third parties, ensure they adhere to the same honest data handling practices and have clear agreements.

Ethical data handling practices are crucial for maintaining trust with individuals, ensuring compliance with data protection regulations, and promoting a culture of responsible data management within your organisation. They are committed to respecting individuals' rights and privacy in an increasingly data-driven world.

SOCIAL RESPONSIBILITY

Social responsibility, often referred to as corporate social responsibility (CSR) when applied to businesses, is a concept that emphasises an organisation's duty to operate in a manner that benefits society as a whole. It goes beyond profit generation and focuses on contributing positively to the well-being of communities, the environment, and various stakeholders. Here are vital aspects and practices related to social responsibility:

1. Environmental Sustainability:

i) Balancing Act: Organizations must find ways to conduct their operations while minimising their environmental impact.
ii) Outcome: This includes reducing waste, conserving energy, using sustainable materials, and adopting eco-friendly practices.

2. Community Engagement:

i) Balancing Act: Engaging with and supporting local communities is an ethical responsibility.
ii) Outcome: Organizations may sponsor local events, contribute to community projects, and invest in community development.

3. Ethical Labour Practices:

i) Balancing Act: Treating employees fairly, providing safe working conditions, and avoiding exploitative labour practices is essential.
ii) Outcome: This includes fair wages, opportunities for professional growth, and a commitment to diversity and inclusion.

4. Philanthropy:

i) Balancing Act: Supporting charitable causes and initiatives is part of social responsibility.
ii) Outcome: Companies may donate to non-profits, establish foundations, or participate in volunteer programs to give back to society.

5. Ethical Supply Chain Management:

i) Balancing Act: Ensuring suppliers follow ethical and sustainable practices is essential to CSR.
ii) Outcome: This includes scrutinising suppliers for labour conditions, environmental practices, and product safety.

6. Ethical Marketing and Advertising:

i) Balancing Act: Promoting products and services honestly and ethically is crucial.
ii) Outcome: Avoid deceptive advertising and marketing that misleads consumers, and respect consumers' privacy in data-driven advertising.

7. Transparency and Accountability:

i) Balancing Act: Maintaining transparency in business practices and being accountable for mistakes or ethical breaches is fundamental.
ii) Outcome: This includes disclosing financial information, ethical audits, and prompt responses to ethical issues.

8. Public Policy Engagement:

i) Balancing Act: Organizations may engage with public policy and advocate for regulations that support societal well-being.
ii) Outcome: They may participate in discussions on climate change, healthcare, and social justice issues.

9. Ethical Data Handling:

i) Balancing Act: Respecting individuals' data privacy and handling data ethically is a modern aspect of CSR.
ii) Outcome: Organizations should protect data, be transparent about data practices, and use data to benefit individuals and society.

10. Social Initiatives and Impact Investing:

i) Balancing Act: Investing in projects or businesses with a social or environmental impact is a way to fulfil CSR goals.
ii) Outcome: Organizations can allocate resources to initiatives that tackle pressing societal issues.

Social responsibility extends beyond businesses and applies to various organisations, including governments, non-profits, and individuals. It emphasises that organisations should consider their broader impact on society and strive to make that impact positive. Ultimately, social responsibility is about acting in ways that contribute to the common good and improve the well-being of people and the planet.

USER AWARENESS AND CONSENT

Transparency in Data Practices

Transparency in data practices is a fundamental aspect of ethical data handling and privacy protection. It involves clear and open communication with individuals about how their data is collected, used, and shared. Here are vital considerations for ensuring transparency in data practices:

1. Transparent and Accessible Privacy Policies:

Privacy policies should be easily accessible and written in plain language so that individuals can understand how their data is treated.

2. Data Collection Notice:

Notify individuals when their data is collected, even for analytics or service improvement. Transparency means keeping users informed about data collection.

3. Data Usage Explanation:

Clearly explain how collected data will be used, whether it's for improving services, personalisation, or any other purpose. Users should know why their data is being processed.

4. Data Sharing Disclosures:

Inform users if their data is shared with third parties, and specify the reasons for sharing. Transparency includes clarifying if data is sold or exchanged with external entities.

5. Data Retention Information:

Disclose how long data will be retained and the reasons for data retention periods. Users should have a clear understanding of when their data will be deleted.

6. Data Security Measures:

Explain the security measures to protect data from breaches and unauthorised access. Transparency in this area builds trust in data handling practices.

7. User Control and Consent:

Communicate how users can control their data, adjust privacy settings, and give or withdraw consent for data processing. Transparency includes explaining how users can exercise their rights.

8. Third-Party Services and Data:

Notify users if third-party services or applications are integrated into the platform and explain how these external entities handle data. Users should be aware of any data flows beyond the leading organisation.

9. Updates and Changes:

Inform users about changes in data handling practices, policies, or terms of service. Transparency means keeping users updated about any alterations that may affect their data.

10. Data Breach Notifications:

In the event of a data breach, promptly and transparently notify affected individuals about the breach and its potential impact.

11. User Education:

Provide resources and educational materials to help users understand data privacy issues, their rights, and best practices for safeguarding their data.

12. Privacy Audits and Compliance Reports:

For organisations, conducting privacy audits and making compliance reports available to the public can demonstrate a commitment to transparent data practices.

Transparency in data practices is crucial for building and maintaining trust with users. Organisations can demonstrate their commitment to ethical data handling and responsible data management by providing clear information and respecting user privacy.

OBTAINING INFORMED CONSENT

Obtaining informed consent is critical in ethical data handling and respecting individual privacy. Informed consent ensures that individuals know how their data will be used and willingly agree. Here are the fundamental principles and steps for obtaining informed consent:

Principles of Informed Consent:

> Voluntary Agreement: Consent should be given freely, without coercion or pressure. Individuals must have the option to refuse consent without adverse consequences.
> Informed and Comprehensible: Individuals must be provided with clear and understandable data collection and processing information. Avoid jargon or complex legal terms.
> Specific and Purpose-Limited: Consent should be for particular

purposes, and individuals should know exactly what their data will be used for. Avoid obtaining broad or vague consent.

> Revocable: Individuals should have the right to withdraw their consent at any time, and it should be easy to do so.

> Consent for Minors: When dealing with minors' data, obtain consent from their legal guardians or parents.

Steps for Obtaining Informed Consent:

i) Clear Communication:

Clearly explain the purpose of data collection, how data will be used, and any third parties that will have access to the data.

ii) Plain Language:

Use simple and plain language to ensure that individuals understand their agreement.

iii) Consent Forms:

Use written consent forms or digital consent mechanisms that individuals can read, understand, and sign electronically.

iv) Opt-In vs. Opt-Out:

In an opt-in model, individuals must actively agree to data collection. In an opt-out model, data is collected by default unless individuals decline.

v) Granular Consent:

Provide options for granular consent, allowing individuals to choose which specific data processing activities they agree to.

vi) Consent for Sensitive Data:

Be especially careful when obtaining consent for sensitive data, such as health or biometric data. Provide additional information about how this data will be used and protected.

vii) Consent for Third Parties:

If data will be shared with third parties, make it clear to individuals and obtain separate consent.

viii) Consent Management:

Implement a consent management system to keep track of individuals' preferences and to allow them to update their consent choices easily.

ix) Documentation:

Maintain records of consent, including when and how it was obtained, the information provided, and any changes to consent status.

x) Regular Review:

Periodically review and refresh consent to ensure it remains valid and aligned with individuals' preferences.

Obtaining informed consent is a cornerstone of ethical data handling and privacy protection. It empowers individuals to make informed choices about how their data is used and fosters trust between organisations and their users.

USER EDUCATION AND AWARENESS

User education and awareness are crucial for responsible data handling and maintaining privacy in today's digital age. Educating users about data privacy, their rights, and best practices empowers them to protect their personal information and make informed choices. Here are vital considerations for promoting user education and awareness:

1. Privacy Information:

Provide clear and accessible information about your data handling practices, including how data is collected, used, and protected.

2. Privacy Policies:

Publish easy-to-understand privacy policies and terms of service that outline your organisation's data practices. Make these policies readily available to users.

3. Consent Mechanisms:

Explain the consent process and how users can control their data. Teach users how to adjust their privacy settings and provide options for granular consent.

4. Data Security Awareness:

Educate users about the importance of strong passwords, multi-factor authentication, and secure online behaviours to protect their accounts.

5. Data Breach Notification:

Inform users about your procedures for data breach notifications. Let them know how they will be informed if a breach occurs.

6. Data Retention and Deletion:

Explain data retention policies and how long data is stored. Inform users about their right to request data deletion.

7. User Rights:

Educate users about their rights under data protection regulations, such as access to data, correct inaccuracies, and object to data processing.

8. Security Best Practices:

Share tips and best practices for online security, such as recognising phishing attempts and securing personal devices.

9. Children's Privacy:

If your service may involve children, provide specific educational materials and guidelines for parents and guardians to protect children's privacy.

10. Transparency in Data Collection:

Make users aware of when data is collected to ensure complete transparency, even for purposes like analytics.

11. Regular Updates:

Keep users informed about any changes in your data handling practices, policies, or terms of service.

12. User Support:

Offer responsive customer support channels for users to seek clarifications, report issues, and ask questions regarding privacy and data handling.

13. Resource Library:

Create a resource library with articles, FAQs, and guides about data privacy and online security that users can refer to.

14. Social Responsibility:

Communicate your organisation's commitment to social responsibility and ethical data handling, emphasising the importance of user privacy.

15. User Feedback:

Encourage users to provide feedback on privacy concerns and incorporate user suggestions into your privacy practices.

User education and awareness are essential for creating a privacy-conscious user base. Organisations can foster trust and collaboration with their user communities by equipping users with the knowledge and tools to protect their data and privacy.

IMPLEMENTING ROBUST SECURITY MEASURES

Implementing robust security measures is crucial to protect sensitive data and systems from unauthorised access, breaches, and cyberattacks. Here are vital steps and practices for enhancing security:

1. Access Control:

Implement stringent access controls to restrict access to sensitive data and systems. Use role-based access control (RBAC) and the principle of least privilege to ensure that users only need access.

2. Strong Authentication:

Enforce robust authentication methods, such as multi-factor authentication (MFA), to verify users' identities.

3. Data Encryption:

Encrypt data both in transit and at rest. Use robust encryption algorithms to protect data from interception and unauthorised access.

4. Regular Patch Management:

Keep all software, including operating systems and applications, updated with security patches and updates to address vulnerabilities.

5. Network Security:

Implement firewalls, intrusion detection and prevention systems, and network segmentation to protect your network from external threats.

6. Security Auditing and Monitoring:

Conduct regular security audits and monitor systems and networks for suspicious activities. Employ security information and event management (SIEM) solutions for real-time monitoring.

7. Incident Response Plan:

Develop and regularly update an incident response plan to outline the steps to take during a data breach or security incident.

8. Security Training:

Train employees and staff on security best practices. Educate them about recognising and mitigating security threats, including phishing attacks.

9. Secure Development Practices:

Follow secure coding practices when developing applications and systems to prevent common vulnerabilities like SQL injection and cross-site scripting.

10. Vendor Security Assessment:

Assess the security practices of third-party vendors and service providers that have access to your data. Ensure they meet your security standards.

11. Data Backups and Recovery:

Regularly back up data and ensure reliable recovery processes are in place to mitigate data loss in a disaster or cyberattack.

12. Physical Security:

Protect physical access to data storage facilities, servers, and hardware to prevent unauthorised material breaches.

13. Endpoint Security:

Implement robust endpoint security measures, including antivirus and anti-malware solutions, to protect individual devices connected to your network.

14. Regular Vulnerability Assessments:

Conduct regular vulnerability assessments and penetration testing to identify and remediate weaknesses in your systems.

15. Secure Remote Work Practices:

Implement security measures for remote work, including secure VPNs, endpoint security, and user training on remote work security.

16. Security Policies and Procedures:

Develop and document security policies and procedures and ensure all staff members know and follow them.

17. Privacy Impact Assessments:

Conduct privacy impact assessments to evaluate data processing activities' potential risks and ethical implications.

18. Security Culture:

Foster a security-aware culture within your organisation. Encourage employees to report security concerns and maintain vigilance.

19. Regulatory Compliance:

Ensure that your security measures align with regulatory requirements specific to your industry and region.

20. Cybersecurity Training and Awareness:

Provide ongoing training and awareness programs to educate employees and users about cybersecurity best practices.

Robust security measures are essential for protecting your organisation's digital assets and sensitive data. Adopting a proactive approach to security and regularly updating and improving your security protocols can significantly reduce the risk of security breaches and data loss.

STRATEGIES FOR COMPLIANCE

Compliance with data privacy and security regulations is a crucial responsibility for organisations. Failing to comply with these regulations can result in legal consequences, data breaches, and damage to your organisation's reputation. Here are strategies to ensure compliance:

1. Regulatory Awareness:

Stay informed about data privacy and security regulations in your industry and region to ensure your organisation's practices align with legal requirements. Key regulations include GDPR (General Data Protection Regulation), CCPA (California Consumer Privacy Act), HIPAA (Health Insurance Portability and Accountability Act), and more.

2. Dedicated Compliance Officer:

Appoint a compliance officer or team responsible for overseeing compliance measures. They should have the expertise to monitor, implement, and enforce compliance practices.

3. Audit and Risk Assessment:

Conduct regular audits and risk assessments to identify non-compliance areas and vulnerabilities. This helps you proactively address issues.

4. Compliance Policies and Procedures:

Develop clear and comprehensive data privacy and security policies and procedures that align with regulatory requirements. Ensure that employees are well-trained on these policies.

5. Data Mapping and Inventory:

Create an inventory of all data your organisation collects and processes. Understand where it's stored, who accesses it, and how it's used to identify potential privacy risks.

6. Consent Management:

Implement consent management systems to ensure that you have explicit and documented consent for data processing. It allows you to demonstrate that data subjects willingly agree to data use.

7. Data Security Measures:

Use data encryption, access controls, and intrusion detection systems to safeguard sensitive data from unauthorised access, breaches, and cyberattacks.

8. Data Retention and Deletion:

Define and enforce data retention and deletion policies. Ensure that data is retained only for the necessary duration, which reduces data-related risks.

9. Incident Response Plan:

Develop an incident response plan and regularly test it to address data breaches and security incidents in compliance with regulatory notification requirements.

10. Third-Party Assessments:

Evaluate the security and privacy practices of third-party vendors and service providers that handle your data. Ensure they meet your security standards.

11. Data Subject Rights:

Provide mechanisms for data subjects to exercise their rights, such as the right to access, correct, and delete their data, as required by regulations.

12. Regular Employee Training:

Offer ongoing training to employees to ensure they understand their roles in maintaining compliance, identifying security threats, and responding effectively.

13. Privacy Impact Assessments:

Conduct privacy impact assessments to evaluate data processing activities' potential risks and ethical implications, helping you proactively address privacy concerns.

14. Documentation and Record-keeping:

Maintain records of data processing activities, consent, data breaches, and compliance efforts as regulations require. This documentation provides evidence of compliance.

15. Legal Counsel and Consultation:

Consult legal experts specialising in data privacy and security to ensure your practices and policies align with regulations, reducing legal risks.

16. Compliance Monitoring:

Continuously monitor compliance to promptly identify and address any non-compliance issues, which helps you maintain regulatory adherence.

17. Transparent Communication:

Communicate your data practices to data subjects, including how their data is collected and used and how they can exercise their rights. Transparency builds trust.

18. Regulatory Reporting:

Ensure that your organisation complies with requirements for reporting data breaches and security incidents to relevant authorities and data subjects. This demonstrates accountability.

19. Privacy by Design:

Integrate privacy considerations into the design of products and services from the outset, reducing the risk of privacy violations.

20. Data Ethics:

Foster a culture of ethical data handling and social responsibility throughout your organisation, ensuring data is used ethically and responsibly.

By implementing these strategies, organisations can navigate the complex landscape of data privacy and security regulations while protecting data and respecting individuals' privacy.

FOSTERING A PRIVACY-CENTRIC CULTURE

Fostering a privacy-centric culture within your organisation is essential for protecting sensitive data and compliance with data privacy regulations. Here are strategies and steps to create a culture that prioritises privacy:

1. Leadership Commitment:

Demonstrate a commitment to privacy from the top down. Leadership should set an example by adhering to privacy principles and policies.

2. Privacy Policies and Guidelines:

Develop clear and comprehensive privacy policies and guidelines that are communicated to all employees. Ensure that these policies align with relevant regulations.

3. Privacy Training:

Provide regular privacy training for employees at all levels. Make sure they understand data privacy principles, regulations, and their responsibilities.

4. Privacy Champions:

Identify and train privacy champions or advocates within the organisation. These individuals can help promote privacy awareness and compliance among their peers.

5. Transparent Communication:

Communicate privacy principles and practices to all employees. Make sure they understand why privacy is important and how their actions can impact it.

6. Data Classification:

Educate employees about data classification and sensitivity levels. Ensure they know how to handle different types of data appropriately.

7. Data Minimization:

Encourage the practice of data minimisation, which means collecting and retaining only the data that is necessary for the intended purpose.

8. User Consent and Control:

Promote the importance of obtaining informed user consent and controlling users' data. Encourage employees to respect user preferences.

9. Security Awareness:

Combine privacy training with security awareness training. Help employees understand how privacy and security are interrelated.

10. Privacy by Design:

Incorporate privacy considerations into the design and development of products and services from the outset. Encourage teams to think about privacy implications.

11. Incident Response Preparation:

Educate employees about the organisation's incident response plan and their roles in case of a data breach. Promote a culture of prompt reporting and response.

12. Regular Audits and Monitoring:

Conduct regular privacy audits and monitoring to ensure compliance and identify improvement areas.

13. Ethical Data Handling:

Stress the importance of ethical data handling and responsible use of data. Avoid practices that may compromise individuals' privacy.

14. Incentivize Privacy Compliance:

Consider offering incentives or recognition for employees who consistently demonstrate a commitment to privacy and data protection.

15. Privacy Impact Assessments:

Encourage teams to conduct privacy impact assessments when implementing new projects or processes that involve data processing.

16. Privacy Reporting Channels:

Establish clear channels for reporting privacy concerns or potential violations. Ensure that employees feel comfortable writing issues without fear of retaliation.

17. Regular Updates and Training:

Keep employees updated on changes in privacy regulations and best practices. Provide ongoing training to keep privacy knowledge current.

18. Privacy Culture Assessments:

Periodically assess the organisation's privacy culture through surveys or feedback to identify areas for improvement.

19. Privacy Metrics and KPIs:

Define key performance indicators (KPIs) related to privacy and regularly measure the organisation's performance.

20. Celebrate Privacy Successes:

Celebrate privacy successes and recognise employees and teams contributing to a strong privacy culture.

Fostering a privacy-centric culture is an ongoing process that requires commitment and vigilance. By creating a work environment where privacy is valued, respected, and practised, you can significantly reduce the risk of data breaches and violations of data privacy regulations.

CHAPTER VIII

Virtual Advertising and Marketing: Regulatory Frameworks and Economic Impacts

OVERVIEW OF VIRTUAL ADVERTISING AND MARKETING

Virtual advertising and marketing represent a contemporary approach to reaching and engaging audiences in digital and virtual spaces. This innovative field uses digital technologies to promote products, services, or brands in novel and interactive ways. Let's break down the definition and the context:

Definition:

Virtual advertising and marketing involve the strategic use of digital and virtual environments to create, distribute, and interact with promotional content. This field encompasses diverse practices, techniques, and technologies, each aimed at engaging consumers in innovative ways. It can be broken down into various components:

i) Augmented Reality (AR) Marketing: AR overlays digital content onto the real world, typically through smartphones, tablets, or smart glasses. This technology enhances real-world experiences with digital elements. For example, furniture retailers can allow customers to visualise how a couch might look in their living room using an AR app.

ii) Virtual Reality (VR) Advertising: VR immerses users in entirely digital environments. It is often experienced through VR headsets or goggles, providing a 360-degree view of a virtual world. Within VR, businesses can place virtual billboards, create immersive product demos, or host virtual events and expos.

iii) In-Game Advertising: Video games have evolved into an advertising platform. Brands can integrate their products or services into the gameplay, from featuring branded billboards and vehicles within the game environment to incorporating virtual storefronts and interactive ads.

iv) Social Media and Virtual Worlds: Virtual advertising extends to social media platforms and virtual worlds like Second Life or digital conferences and expos. Companies set up virtual storefronts or spaces to interact with customers, showcase products, or sponsor events.

v) Immersive Content Marketing: This entails creating highly engaging and interactive digital content. For instance, 360-degree videos, interactive storytelling, or virtual tours allow users to explore products or experiences dynamically and effectively.

Context:

Understanding the context of virtual advertising and marketing requires considering various factors:

i) Technological Advancements: The evolution of technology is a driving force. Advanced AR and VR devices and high-performance gaming platforms have made it possible to create immersive digital experiences and interact with consumers in new ways.

ii) Changing Consumer Behaviour: Consumers are increasingly spending time in digital environments. Whether gaming, social media, or online shopping, these platforms offer opportunities for advertisers to engage with their target audience.

iii) Data and Targeting: Advertisers have access to abundant data in the digital space. They can leverage this data to target their campaigns precisely, ensuring they reach the right audience at the right time with tailored content.

iv) Economic Implications: Virtual advertising is not only about engagement but also about generating revenue. It can be cost-effective due to precise targeting, and it can influence consumer behaviour, leading to increased sales and revenue for businesses.

v) Challenges and Opportunities: The rise of virtual advertising brings exciting possibilities and challenges. Advertisers must navigate the complex issues of data privacy, consumer consent, and maintaining a balance between engaging users and respecting their boundaries.

HISTORICAL EVOLUTION

The historical evolution of virtual advertising and marketing is a journey through technology integration into the advertising and marketing landscape. While the concept of advertising has deep historical roots, the virtual aspect of it is a more recent development. Here's a chronological overview of the historical evolution of virtual advertising and marketing:

1. Early Digital Advertising (1990s-2000s):

The 1990s marked the advent of the World Wide Web, and with it came early digital advertising. Basic banner ads and pop-up ads began to appear on websites, representing the initial transition from traditional print and broadcast advertising to the digital realm. These early forms of digital advertising were relatively static, lacking the interactivity and engagement that virtual advertising offers today.

2. Introduction of Virtual Worlds (Early 2000s):

In the early 2000s, virtual worlds like Second Life gained popularity. These virtual spaces allowed users to create avatars and interact in a digital environment. Marketers and businesses recognised the potential to establish a presence within these spaces. Brands started to set up virtual storefronts and hold events within these virtual realms. This marked one of the first instances of virtual advertising, where brands could engage with users in a digital, immersive setting.

3. Augmented Reality (AR) and Mobile Marketing (Late 2000s-2010s):

The late 2000s and the 2010s saw the proliferation of smartphones and the rise of mobile apps. This development introduced new opportunities for virtual advertising, particularly with the growth of AR technology. AR overlays digital content onto the natural world through mobile devices. It allowed for interactive marketing campaigns. For instance, AR apps enabled users to scan product images with their mobile devices, leading to interactive experiences or access to additional product information.

4. Gaming and In-Game Advertising (2000s-Present):

Video games became a central platform for advertising during the 2000s and continue to be significant. Advertisers recognised the potential of reaching a highly engaged and often youthful audience. In-game advertising includes placing billboards, featuring branded in-game items, or integrating ads seamlessly into the gameplay. This approach offers a unique way to promote products and engage gamers.

5. Virtual Reality (VR) and Immersive Advertising (2010s-Present):

The development of VR technology and VR headsets ushered in a new era of immersive advertising. Brands can create VR content, allowing users to explore products or experiences in 360 degrees. This level of immersion has found applications in various industries, such as real estate (virtual property tours), travel (virtual destination experiences), and entertainment (VR movie trailers).

6. Social Media and Virtual Marketing (2010s-Present):

Social media platforms have evolved into virtual marketing hubs. Brands set up virtual storefronts, run campaigns within these platforms and engage users creatively. Virtual events and digital conferences are now daily in these spaces, offering unique opportunities for businesses to reach and interact with their target audience.

7. Advanced-Data Analytics (2010s-Present):

Data analytics play a pivotal role in the modern era of virtual advertising and marketing. The wealth of data available within digital and virtual spaces has transformed how advertisers operate. Advanced data analytics enable advertisers to target campaigns precisely, ensuring their content reaches the right audience at the right time. This data-driven approach has become a critical element of virtual marketing.

8. Future of Virtual Advertising (Ongoing):

The future of virtual advertising is characterised by ongoing innovation.

Concepts like the Metaverse, a collective virtual shared space, present new immersive advertising and marketing opportunities. As technology advances, artificial intelligence and augmented reality are expected to shape the evolving landscape of virtual advertising further.

The historical evolution of virtual advertising and marketing demonstrates how businesses have adapted to the changing technological and consumer landscape. From static banner ads on the early web to the immersive virtual experiences of today, this evolution underscores the flexibility of advertising and marketing in engaging consumers through digital and virtual means.

REGULATORY FRAMEWORKS IN VIRTUAL ADVERTISING

Regulatory frameworks in virtual advertising are essential to ensure consumer protection, data privacy, and fair business practices. These frameworks vary by country and region, and they continue to evolve to address the unique challenges posed by advertising in digital and virtual environments. Here's an overview of some key aspects of regulatory frameworks in virtual advertising:

1. Data Protection and Privacy Regulations:

Data protection is paramount in virtual advertising. Regulations like the GDPR in the European Union and the CCPA in California set clear rules for collecting and processing personal data. Advertisers must obtain explicit consent from users to manage their data for advertising purposes. They are also required to allow users to opt out of data collection and usage.

2. Truth in Advertising:

Truth in advertising is a foundational principle in marketing. Regulatory bodies, such as the U.S. Federal Trade Commission (FTC), have stringent guidelines to ensure that advertisements are honest, accurate, and not misleading. In virtual advertising, marketers should refrain from making false claims about their products or services and be transparent about their promotional intentions.

3. Product Placement and Disclosure:

In virtual environments, product placement can be integrated seamlessly into the content, making it sometimes challenging for users to differentiate between advertising and the core experience. Regulations often require clear and conspicuous disclosure when promoting products or services. This ensures that users can identify when they are encountering advertising content.

4. Age-Appropriate Advertising:

Advertising in virtual environments must consider the target audience's age. For instance, in the context of video games, regulatory bodies may require that advertising content is suitable for the age group of the players. This is especially important when advertising in spaces where minors are present.

5. In-Game Purchases and Microtransactions:

The use of in-game purchases and microtransactions, which often involve real money, has raised concerns, especially in the context of children's games. Regulatory authorities have examined the transparency and fairness of such practices. Some countries have implemented restrictions on the use of microtransactions to protect consumers, particularly minors.

6. Advertising to Vulnerable Audiences:

Regulations often prohibit advertising practices that exploit vulnerable audiences. For example, targeting elderly individuals with deceptive advertising or promoting products that could potentially harm individuals with cognitive impairments is unethical and often illegal.

7. Native Advertising and Influencer Marketing:

Native advertising involves blending promotional content seamlessly with non-promotional content, making it less recognisable as advertising. Influencer marketing relies on the endorsements of social media influencers. Regulatory frameworks often require clear and conspicuous disclosure in these practices to prevent deceiving consumers. This ensures that users can distinguish between unbiased content and paid endorsements.

8. Platform-Specific Regulations:

Various virtual platforms may have their specific advertising policies and guidelines. For instance, social media platforms, search engines, and online marketplaces often have rules that advertisers must follow when promoting products or services within those platforms. Advertisers must be aware of and comply with these platform-specific regulations.

9. Geographical Variations:

It's important to note that regulatory frameworks can vary significantly from one region to another. Advertisers operating globally must be aware of and comply with the specific regulations in each country or jurisdiction where they work. This can involve adapting advertising strategies to meet the legal requirements of different markets.

10. Enforcement and Penalties:

Regulatory agencies can enforce these regulations and penalise advertisers who fail to comply. Penalties can range from fines to legal action. In some cases, regulators can even request the removal of advertising content that violates the rules.

Understanding and adhering to these regulatory frameworks is essential for virtual advertisers. Violating these regulations exposes businesses to legal consequences and can damage their brand reputation. Staying informed about the evolving landscape of virtual advertising regulations is crucial to ensure compliance and maintain ethical advertising practices in a digital and virtual world.

Economic Impacts of Virtual Advertising

Virtual advertising can have profound economic implications for businesses, offering opportunities and challenges. Here, we'll explore the economic impacts in more detail:

1. Revenue Generation:

Virtual advertising creates new revenue streams for businesses. Companies can reach a broad and often highly engaged audience by promoting their products or services in virtual environments. This can lead to increased sales and revenue. For instance, placing virtual billboards in popular video games or creating immersive showrooms for products can boost sales.

2. Cost-Effectiveness:

Virtual advertising can be more cost-effective than traditional advertising methods. Advertisers can precisely target specific demographics, reducing ad spend on audiences who are unlikely to convert. Digital campaigns are often more affordable and measurable, allowing for efficient allocation of resources.

3. Consumer Behavior Influence:

Virtual advertising can significantly impact consumer behaviour. In virtual or augmented reality experiences, users can engage with products or services in an immersive manner. This interaction can influence purchasing decisions. For example, a virtual try-on feature for clothing can increase confidence in an online purchase.

4. Data-Driven Marketing:

The data-rich nature of virtual advertising allows for data-driven marketing strategies. Advertisers can collect vast amounts of data on user interactions, preferences, and behaviours. This data can be analysed to refine advertising campaigns, tailor content, and make data-informed decisions to maximise returns on investment.

5. Measurable ROI:

Virtual advertising provides detailed metrics and analytics. Advertisers can precisely track key performance indicators (KPIs) such as click-through rates, conversion rates, and return on investment (ROI). This transparency allows businesses to evaluate the effectiveness of their campaigns and make adjustments accordingly.

6. Diversification of Marketing Channels:

Virtual advertising offers an opportunity to diversify marketing channels. Businesses can explore advertising in virtual reality, social media, video games, and augmented reality, ensuring they reach their audience across various platforms.

7. Global Reach:

Virtual advertising has the potential to reach a global audience. With digital and virtual platforms accessible worldwide, businesses can extend their market reach far beyond local or regional boundaries.

8. Challenges in Monetization Models:

While virtual advertising presents revenue opportunities, it also introduces challenges in developing monetisation models. Businesses must carefully consider the best methods for generating revenue, such as in-game purchases, ad-supported content, or sponsored experiences.

9. Ad Blockers and User Resistance:

Ad blockers and user resistance are challenges in virtual advertising. Some users use ad-blocking software to avoid advertising; others may resist advertising in virtual spaces. Advertisers must address these challenges creatively and ethically.

10. Balancing User Experience and Advertising:

Achieving a balance between a positive user experience and advertising impact is crucial. Intrusive or overly frequent advertising can lead to frustration, potentially impacting brand reputation and user engagement.

The economic impacts of virtual advertising are far-reaching, with the potential to drive revenue growth, enhance consumer engagement, and offer a cost-effective marketing channel. However, they also come with challenges related to user resistance, ethical considerations, and adapting to evolving advertising landscapes. Advertisers and businesses that can navigate these dynamics effectively stand to benefit from the economic opportunities presented by virtual advertising.

Regulatory Frameworks in Virtual Advertising

1. Global Regulatory Landscape

The global regulatory landscape for virtual advertising is diverse, with various countries and regions implementing rules and guidelines to govern this dynamic and evolving field. While regulations can vary significantly, some common themes and principles emerge across different regulatory frameworks. Here's an overview of the global regulatory landscape for virtual advertising:

2. Data Privacy and Protection:

Privacy regulations are a central aspect of virtual advertising regulation worldwide. The European Union's General Data Protection Regulation (GDPR) is one of the most comprehensive and influential data privacy regulations. It applies to any business that processes the data of EU residents. The GDPR mandates explicit user consent for data collection and strict rules for data handling. Other regions, such as California with the California Consumer Privacy Act (CCPA), have introduced similar regulations, albeit with some variations.

3. Consumer Protection:

Consumer protection is a fundamental concern in most regulatory frameworks. This includes rules against deceptive advertising, ensuring that advertising content is accurate, and providing transparent information to consumers. Regulatory bodies like the U.S. Federal Trade Commission (FTC) enforce these principles to maintain trust in advertising.

4. Digital Advertising and Influencer Marketing:

Regulations often cover various forms of digital advertising, including social media marketing, influencer marketing, and native advertising. These regulations frequently require clear and conspicuous disclosure of paid endorsements or sponsored content to prevent deception.

5. Age-Appropriate Advertising:

Regulations aim to protect minors from potentially harmful advertising content. Some countries have introduced restrictions on advertising in virtual environments that target or are accessible by children, ensuring that the content is age-appropriate.

6. In-Game Advertising:

Virtual advertising within video games is subject to regulation in many regions. This includes guidelines on the placement of advertising, disclosures, and targeting specific audiences, especially in games played by children and teenagers.

7. Cross-Border Advertising:

As virtual advertising can transcend geographical borders, some regions aim to regulate cross-border advertising to ensure compliance with local rules and standards.

8. Platform-Specific Rules:

Different virtual platforms, including social media networks and online marketplaces, often have their advertising policies and guidelines. Advertisers must adhere to these rules when conducting advertising within these platforms.

9. Geo-Fencing and Location-Based Advertising:

Location-based virtual advertising can raise privacy and security concerns, especially in mobile apps and augmented reality. Regulations often stipulate clear disclosure and user consent for tracking location data.

10. Self-Regulation and Industry Standards:

Some regions promote self-regulation within the advertising industry. Industry organisations and advertising bodies may establish voluntary codes of conduct and standards to ensure ethical advertising practices.

11. Penalties and Enforcement:

Regulatory agencies can enforce these regulations and penalise advertisers who fail to comply. Penalties can range from fines to legal actions; in some cases, regulators may request the removal of non-compliant advertising content.

It's essential for businesses engaged in virtual advertising to understand and adhere to the regulatory framework in the regions where they operate. Staying informed about evolving regulations and maintaining ethical advertising practices is crucial to ensure compliance and protect brand reputation in a global advertising landscape that continues to grow.

GDPR AND DATA PRIVACY

The General Data Protection Regulation (GDPR) is a comprehensive data privacy regulation implemented by the European Union (EU) to protect the personal data of its citizens. It came into effect on May 25, 2018, and has a significant impact within the EU and globally. GDPR sets stringent rules and requirements regarding collecting, processing and protecting personal data. Here's a closer look at how GDPR impacts data privacy:

1. Scope of GDPR:

GDPR applies to any organisation that processes the personal data of individuals residing in the EU, regardless of where the organisation is located. Businesses and websites worldwide must comply with GDPR if they collect and process data from EU residents.

2. Personal Data:

GDPR defines personal data broadly, encompassing any information that can directly or indirectly identify an individual. This includes standard identifiers like names and email addresses, IP addresses, geolocation data, and genetic and biometric data.

3. Principles of Data Processing:

GDPR outlines several fundamental principles for data processing, including data minimisation (collecting only the data necessary for the intended purpose), purpose limitation (using data only for the specified purpose), and data accuracy (ensuring data is kept up to date).

4. User Consent:

GDPR mandates that organisations obtain unambiguous consent from individuals before collecting their data. Users must be informed about the purpose of data collection, how it will be used, and their rights regarding their data.

5. Data Subject Rights:

GDPR empowers data subjects (individuals) with several rights, including the right to access their data, the right to rectify inaccuracies, the right to erasure (commonly known as the "right to be forgotten"), and the right to data portability, allowing individuals to transfer their data from one service to another.

6. Data Protection Impact Assessments (DPIAs):

For high-risk data processing activities, GDPR requires organisations to conduct DPIAs. These assessments help identify and mitigate potential risks to data subjects and ensure compliance with data protection principles.

7. Data Protection Officers (DPOs):

Some organisations must appoint a Data Protection Officer who oversees data protection activities and ensures compliance with GDPR. DPOs are the point of contact for data protection authorities and data subjects.

8. Data Breach Notification:

GDPR mandates that organisations report data breaches to the relevant supervisory authority within 72 hours of becoming aware of the breach. Organisations must notify affected data subjects if the breach risks individuals' rights and freedoms.

9. International Data Transfers:

GDPR governs international data transfers by requiring organisations to protect any data transferred outside the EU. This might involve using Standard Contractual Clauses (SCCs) or other mechanisms.

10. Penalties and Enforcement:

Non-compliance with GDPR can lead to severe penalties. Organisations can face fines of up to 4% of their global annual revenue or €20 million, whichever is higher. Regulatory authorities within EU member states are responsible for enforcement.

11. Consent for Marketing and Advertising:

GDPR impacts digital advertising and marketing by requiring organisations to obtain explicit consent for data collection and processing for marketing purposes. This has led to a shift toward more transparent and opt-in-based advertising practices.

GDPR has profoundly impacted data privacy and how organisations handle personal data, including virtual advertising. To ensure compliance, businesses must implement robust data protection measures, adopt transparent data practices, and respect the rights of individuals regarding their data.

FTC GUIDELINES AND CONSUMER PROTECTION

The Federal Trade Commission (FTC) in the United States is a critical regulatory body responsible for consumer protection and enforcing laws related to deceptive and unfair business practices. It provides guidelines and regulations that impact various industries, including advertising and marketing.

Based in the United States, the FTC is a pivotal regulatory agency dedicated to safeguarding consumer interests and ensuring fair and transparent business practices. Its influence extends across various industries, including advertising and marketing. At the heart of the FTC's mission is the enforcement of "Truth in Advertising," a fundamental principle that requires advertisements to be truthful, accurate, and devoid of deception. Under this mandate, advertisers must substantiate their claims with evidence and, crucially, disclose any financial or material relationships between endorsers and advertisers. The aim is to prevent consumers from being misled by false or exaggerated advertising claims, fostering trust and integrity in the marketplace.

The FTC has formulated specific guidelines to promote transparency and honesty in endorsements and testimonials. These guidelines emphasise the imperative of disclosing any financial or material connections between endorsers and advertisers, mainly when consumers who endorse products or services are compensated in any manner. The objective is to ensure that endorsements genuinely represent the opinions and experiences of the individuals providing them. This underscores the FTC's commitment to transparency in advertising practices.

In the era of digital advertising, the FTC has adapted by issuing guidelines for online advertising and disclosure. In the digital and virtual realms, clear and conspicuous disclosure is vital. It enables users to discern the affiliations between influencers and brands, enhancing transparency in influencer marketing and other online advertising methods. These guidelines help in maintaining openness and trust in advertising across digital platforms.

Consumer privacy and data security are focal points for the FTC. The FTC sets forth rules and standards concerning data breaches to protect individuals. It mandates that organisations put in place reasonable security measures to safeguard consumer information. Additionally, the FTC addresses issues such as online tracking, data collection, and data sharing. This ensures that consumers retain control over their personal information, a crucial aspect of safeguarding privacy in an increasingly digital environment.

COPPA (Children's Online Privacy Protection Act) is another significant area of focus for the FTC. It is designed to protect the online privacy of children under 13. To achieve this, COPPA necessitates that websites and online services acquire verifiable parental consent before gathering personal information from children. Furthermore, it mandates the clear presentation of privacy policies, providing additional privacy protection for young internet users.

In telemarketing, the FTC plays a central role by regulating the industry. This involves enforcing rules like the National Do Not Call Registry, which empowers consumers to opt out of unwanted telemarketing calls. The Telemarketing Sales Rule, another FTC initiative, outlines specific disclosure requirements and outlaws deceptive practices in telemarketing, ensuring that consumers are shielded from fraudulent or coercive sales tactics.

The FTC is vested with the authority to enforce its guidelines and regulations. Violations of these rules can lead to penalties, including substantial fines, legal injunctions, or civil actions. The FTC proactively investigates and acts against businesses that engage in deceptive or unfair practices. This enforcement serves as a powerful deterrent against unethical conduct.

In addition to its enforcement role, the FTC is deeply committed to consumer education. It provides resources and guidance to empower consumers to recognise and avoid deceptive advertising and marketing practices. This educational aspect supplements its enforcement activities, equipping consumers with the knowledge and tools they need to make informed decisions and protect their interests in the marketplace.

Country-Specific Regulations

Country-specific virtual advertising and marketing regulations can vary significantly, reflecting each region's cultural, legal, and economic nuances. Here, we'll highlight a few key examples of country-specific regulations and approaches:

i) United States:

Advertising and marketing are subject to various federal and state regulations in the United States. The Federal Trade Commission (FTC) enforces truth in advertising, ensuring that advertisements are accurate and not deceptive. It also regulates endorsements, requiring clear disclosure of financial relationships between endorsers and advertisers. Additionally, the FTC enforces rules to protect children's online privacy under COPPA and oversees telemarketing practices. Data privacy laws, such as the California Consumer Privacy Act (CCPA), vary by state and add another layer of regulation, particularly in California.

ii) European Union:

The European Union's General Data Protection Regulation (GDPR) is a comprehensive data privacy regulation that sets strict data collection and processing standards. GDPR applies to all EU member states, ensuring consistent data protection rules. Each member state may also have its regulatory authorities and specific advertising regulations.

iii) Canada:

Canada's Anti-Spam Legislation (CASL) regulates electronic marketing by requiring explicit consent before sending commercial electronic messages. The Personal Information Protection and Electronic Documents Act (PIPEDA) governs data privacy and the collection of personal information, contributing to consumer protection.

iv) Australia:

Australia's Australian Privacy Principles (APPs) govern the handling of personal information, and the Australian Competition and Consumer Commission (ACCC) enforces consumer protection laws, including those about deceptive advertising.

v) China:

China's Advertising Law regulates advertising practices within the country, ensuring that advertisements are honest and compliant with local cultural norms. The Cyberspace Administration of China (CAC) oversees internet advertising practices, and specific regulations exist for online gaming and advertising to minors.

vi) India:

India's Advertising Standards Council of India (ASCI) is a self-regulatory body that oversees advertising content and practices. Data privacy is addressed through the Information Technology Act and the pending Personal Data Protection Bill.

vii) Brazil:

In Brazil, the General Data Protection Law (LGPD) regulates data privacy, ensuring that personal data is handled carefully. The Brazilian Institute of Consumer Defense (IDEC) and the National Consumer Secretariat (Senacon) work on consumer protection issues, including advertising complaints.

viii) South Africa:

South Africa's Protection of Personal Information Act (POPIA) is similar to GDPR and governs data privacy. The Advertising Standards Authority of South Africa (ASA) enforces advertising standards to ensure truthful and ethical practices.

ix) Japan:

Japan's Act on the Protection of Personal Information (APPI) addresses data privacy concerns. The Consumer Affairs Agency (CAA) is responsible for consumer protection and enforces advertising standards.

x) United Kingdom:

In the UK, adherence to data privacy regulations shifted from GDPR to the UK GDPR after Brexit. Advertising standards are enforced by the Advertising Standards Authority (ASA).

These country-specific regulations demonstrate the importance of considering cultural, legal, and economic factors when engaging in virtual advertising and marketing. Businesses operating globally or targeting international audiences must be well-informed about these regulations to ensure compliance and maintain ethical advertising practices in each region. Adhering to these rules helps with legal compliance, safeguards a brand's reputation, and fosters consumer trust.

CHALLENGES AND COMPLIANCE ISSUES

Challenges and compliance issues in virtual advertising and marketing are complex and multifaceted. Navigating this space requires a deep understanding of the evolving digital landscape and its regulations. Here are some of the critical challenges and compliance issues:

Data Privacy and Security:

i) Challenge: Gathering and managing user data in virtual advertising while adhering to data privacy regulations, such as GDPR or CCPA, is challenging. Ensuring that data is secure and used ethically is a constant concern.

ii) Explanation: Data privacy is a top priority in the digital age. Advertisers must obtain explicit and informed consent from users to collect and use their data. They must also implement robust security measures to protect this data from breaches or unauthorised access. Please do so not only violates privacy laws but can result in substantial fines and damage to a brand's reputation.

Transparency in Advertising:

i) **Challenge**: Ensuring that advertising content is transparent and not deceptive can be difficult in virtual environments, especially when seamlessly integrated with content.

ii) **Explanation**: Transparency is crucial to maintaining trust with consumers. Advertising should be distinguishable from non-commercial content. Failing to do so can mislead users and damage the credibility of the advertising and the platform on which it appears. Regulatory bodies, such as the FTC, closely monitor deceptive advertising practices.

Influencer Marketing:

i) **Challenge**: Collaborating with influencers while maintaining transparency and compliance with guidelines, like FTC endorsements, is challenging.

ii) **Explanation**: Influencer marketing has become a powerful advertising tool. However, it can present compliance challenges when influencers endorse products or services without clear disclosure of their relationships with brands. This lack of transparency can mislead consumers and lead to regulatory investigations and penalties.

Cross-Border Advertising:

i) **Challenge**: Conducting advertising campaigns across countries with varying regulations can be complex.

ii) **Explanation**: Global advertising campaigns require a deep understanding of each region's unique regulations. Advertising that complies with one country's rules may not meet the standards of another. Failure to comply with local regulations can result in legal consequences, fines, and damage to a brand's reputation.

Native Advertising:

i) **Challenge**: Balancing native advertising that seamlessly blends with content while ensuring clear disclosure is a constant challenge.

ii) Explanation: Native advertising, which integrates promotional content with non-promotional content, can be challenging regarding disclosure. Maintaining transparency is crucial so that users can distinguish advertising from regular content. Please do so to avoid consumer confusion, regulatory issues, and brand reputation damage.

Age-Appropriate Advertising:

i) Challenge: Tailoring advertising content to the audience's age is complex, particularly in virtual environments where different age groups can overlap.

ii) Explanation: Advertisers must ensure that their content is appropriate for their target age group. In virtual environments where demographics can overlap, this can be challenging. Failing to provide age-appropriate content can result in legal issues, public outrage, and a damaged brand image. Advertisers should be aware of age-specific regulations and adapt their campaigns accordingly.

Addressing these challenges and compliance issues requires a proactive approach that includes staying informed about evolving regulations, implementing robust data protection measures, maintaining transparency in advertising practices, and respecting consumer expectations. By prioritising ethical advertising practices in the digital and virtual space, businesses can protect their brand reputation, ensure legal compliance, and build trust with their audience.

ECONOMIC IMPACTS OF VIRTUAL ADVERTISING

1. Revenue Generation and New Business Models

Virtual advertising and marketing have brought about significant shifts in revenue generation and business models. These technologies have transformed how brands connect with audiences and monetise their efforts. Here are critical aspects of revenue generation and new business models in this field:

2. Programmatic Advertising:

Explanation: Programmatic advertising leverages automated technology to purchase and place ads in real time. It optimises ad targeting and placement, enhancing efficiency and cost-effectiveness. Advertisers pay for impressions and clicks, making it a dominant revenue source in the digital advertising landscape.

3. In-Game Advertising:

Explanation: In-game advertising involves integrating ads within video games or virtual environments. This model generates revenue through partnerships with game developers and ad placements within free-to-play games. It offers interactive and immersive marketing experiences, creating a valuable advertising channel.

4. Social Media Advertising:

Explanation: Social media platforms, such as Facebook, Instagram, and Twitter, offer extensive advertising opportunities. Advertisers can target specific demographics and interests, employing models like pay-per-click (PPC) and sponsored content. Social media platforms generate substantial revenue through these advertising channels.

5. Subscription-Based Models:

Explanation: Some virtual advertising and marketing platforms adopt subscription-based models. Users pay a fee to access content without ads. This model is exemplified by services like Netflix and YouTube Premium, creating an alternative revenue stream and offering ad-free experiences to subscribers.

6. Data Monetization:

Explanation: Businesses accumulate substantial user data, which can be monetised by selling to third parties like marketers. Data monetisation is prevalent in programmatic advertising, where data-driven insights enhance targeting and campaign effectiveness.

7. Virtual Reality (VR) and Augmented Reality (AR):

Explanation: VR and AR technologies are revolutionising advertising by providing immersive experiences. Brands generate revenue by developing branded VR/AR content, product placements, and interactive ad campaigns within these environments, creating new marketing channels.

8. E-Commerce and Shoppable Content:

Explanation: Integration with e-commerce allows consumers to purchase directly from ads or content. Shoppable posts on social media and interactive product placements enable direct revenue generation by facilitating immediate product sales through advertising efforts.

These revenue-generation channels in virtual advertising and marketing underscore the industry's dynamism. New business models constantly emerge, and advertisers adapt to evolving technologies and consumer behaviours. Staying abreast of these changes is essential for brands to remain competitive and drive revenue in the digital and virtual marketing landscape.

Consumer Behavior and Purchasing Decisions

Understanding consumer behaviour and purchasing decisions is pivotal for the success of virtual advertising and marketing campaigns. Virtual environments offer unique opportunities to connect with and influence consumers. Here are critical aspects of consumer behaviour and how it shapes purchasing decisions in the context of virtual advertising and marketing:

1. Digital Consumer Journey:

Explanation: Consumers often embark on a digital journey, exploring various online channels and platforms before purchasing. Advertisers must understand this journey and strategically place ads at different touchpoints, from initial awareness to the final purchase.

2. Personalisation:

Explanation: Personalized advertising leverages data and technology to create tailored ad experiences. Consumers appreciate relevant content, and personalisation can significantly impact their purchasing decisions. Advertisers must collect and analyse user data to deliver personalised ads effectively.

3. Emotional Appeal:

Explanation: Emotional engagement plays a crucial role in virtual advertising. Well-crafted storytelling and emotionally resonant content can evoke positive emotions, leading to stronger brand attachment and increased purchase likelihood.

4. User Experience (UX):

Explanation: A seamless and user-friendly experience in virtual environments is essential. If consumers encounter technical issues or poor UX, it can lead to frustration and deter them from purchasing. Brands must invest in a positive digital experience.

5. Social Proof and Reviews:

Explanation: Consumers often rely on social proof, such as reviews and testimonials, to inform purchasing decisions. In virtual advertising, showcasing positive reviews and social endorsements can boost consumer trust and confidence.

6. FOMO (Fear of Missing Out):

Explanation: Creating a sense of urgency or exclusivity can be a powerful motivator for virtual advertising. Limited-time offers exclusive access, or scarcity tactics can tap into consumers' FOMO and drive them to make quicker decisions.

7. Influencer Marketing:

Explanation: Influencers can shape purchasing decisions through their recommendations and authentic content. Collaborating with influencers who align with the brand's values and target audience can significantly impact consumer behaviour.

8. Social Media Influence:

Explanation: Social media platforms are influential in shaping consumer behaviour. The power of social media in product discovery, reviews, and user-generated content is immense. Brands that leverage these platforms effectively can drive consumer decisions.

9. Visual and Interactive Content:

Explanation: Visual content, such as videos, images, and interactive elements, can captivate consumers. Well-designed virtual ads that are visually appealing and interactive can engage users and positively influence their purchasing choices.

10. Data-Driven Insights:

Explanation: Data analytics plays a critical role in understanding consumer behaviour. By analysing user data, advertisers can gain insights into consumer preferences, behaviour patterns, and purchasing trends, allowing for data-driven decision-making in advertising campaigns.

11. In-Game Advertising:

Explanation: In-game advertising allows for immersive, interactive experiences. Brands can strategically place ads within games, influencing purchasing decisions as users engage with products or brands in the gaming environment.

12. Augmented Reality (AR) and Virtual Reality (VR):

Explanation: AR and VR technologies provide innovative ways for consumers to experience products virtually before purchasing. This immersive experience can enhance consumer confidence and lead to informed purchasing decisions.

Understanding consumer behaviour and purchasing decisions in virtual advertising and marketing is ongoing. Advertisers must adapt to the evolving digital landscape, employ data-driven strategies, and create content that resonates emotionally with consumers to drive successful campaigns and ultimately influence purchasing decisions.

COST-EFFECTIVENESS AND ROI

Cost-effectiveness and return on investment (ROI) are fundamental considerations for businesses engaged in virtual advertising and marketing campaigns. The unique nature of virtual advertising allows for innovative strategies to maximise ROI while efficiently managing resources. Here, we explore how virtual advertising achieves cost-effectiveness and delivers measurable ROI.

i) Targeted Advertising: One of the primary drivers of cost-effectiveness in virtual advertising is the ability to target specific demographics, interests, and behaviours. Advertisers can refine their audience selection, ensuring their ads reach those most likely interested in their products or services. This precision reduces ad spend wastage, as advertisers can allocate resources to get the most relevant potential customers.

ii) Performance Tracking: Virtual advertising platforms offer robust tracking and analytics tools, providing real-time insights into campaign performance. Advertisers can monitor key metrics such as click-through, conversion, and engagement. This data-driven approach empowers advertisers to make timely adjustments, optimising ad spend and ensuring the budget is allocated to the most effective channels and strategies.

iii) A/B Testing: A/B testing is a powerful tool in virtual advertising. It involves experimenting with different elements of an ad campaign to determine which combinations yield the best results. This iterative approach ensures that resources are focused on the most effective strategies, thus enhancing ROI. By continuously refining ad content, targeting, and placement, advertisers can increase their campaigns' efficiency.

iv) Data-Driven Decision Making: Data-driven decision-making is a cornerstone of cost-effective advertising. Advertisers can leverage insights from user data to make informed choices. For example, they can identify which channels, content types, or audience segments yield the best results. This enables efficient resource allocation and maximises ROI by investing in strategies that are proven to be effective.

v) Programmatic Advertising: Programmatic advertising automates ad buying, optimising ad placements for cost efficiency. Advertisers can set budgets, bid strategies, and targeting parameters to reach their audience cost-effectively. The automated nature of programmatic advertising ensures that ads are placed where they are most likely to achieve desired outcomes.

vi) Influencer Marketing Efficiency: Collaborating with influencers can be cost-effective, particularly for niche markets. Micro-influencers often offer high engagement rates at a lower cost compared to macro-influencers. Their authentic and relatable content can resonate strongly with specific audiences, resulting in efficient resource allocation and favourable ROI.

vii) Social Media Cost-Per-Click (CPC): Many social media platforms offer cost-per-click (CPC) advertising models, where advertisers pay only when users click their ads. This pay-for-performance model aligns ad spending with user engagement and actions taken. Advertisers have greater control over their budgets and can closely monitor their campaigns' efficiency.

viii) Content Repurposing: Virtual advertising campaigns often involve the creation of compelling content. The beauty of virtual content is its versatility; it can often be repurposed across different platforms and campaigns. By creatively repackaging existing content, advertisers can maximise ROI without incurring additional production costs. This recycling approach optimises the value of each piece of content.

ix) Performance-Driven Metrics: Measuring ROI is not a one-size-fits-all process. Advertisers rely on performance-driven metrics like click-through rates, conversion rates, and cost per acquisition to gauge the effectiveness of their campaigns. These metrics provide clear insights into the efficiency of advertising efforts, enabling advertisers to adjust strategies and resources accordingly.

Cost-effectiveness and ROI in virtual advertising and marketing are intricately linked. Advertisers strive to strike a balance between maximising reach and engagement while minimising costs. Leveraging data-driven strategies, employing efficient targeting, and adopting an agile approach to campaign management is essential for achieving a positive ROI in the dynamic and ever-evolving landscape of virtual advertising. With the right approach, virtual advertising can deliver cost-effective results and measurable returns on investment.

CASE STUDIES ON SUCCESSFUL VIRTUAL ADVERTISING CAMPAIGNS

A. Case Study: Burger King's "Whopper Detour"

Objective: Burger King aimed to increase foot traffic to its stores and create buzz around its brand.

Strategy: In December 2018, Burger King launched an audacious and attention-grabbing campaign called "Whopper Detour." The campaign was designed to playfully challenge the brand's biggest competitor, McDonald's. Here's how it worked:

i) Geo-Targeted Advertising: Burger King used geo-fencing technology to identify users within 600 feet of a McDonald's restaurant. When users entered this zone, the Burger King app would trigger a notification with a special offer for a Whopper for just one cent.

ii) Mobile App Integration: Users must download the Burger King app to participate. This strategic move increased app downloads and ensured users engaged directly with Burger King's digital platform.

iii) Playful Messaging: The campaign's messaging was cheeky and encouraged users to "unlock the Whopper detour." It created a sense of adventure and intrigue, driving users to visit a McDonald's to claim their Whopper for a penny.

iv) Social Media Buzz: Burger King amplified the campaign, encouraging users to share their experiences and the unbelievably low-priced Whoppers. The campaign's hashtag, #WhopperDetour, quickly gained traction.

Results: Burger King's "Whopper Detour" was a massive success:

> The app was downloaded over 1 million times within nine days of the campaign's launch.

> During the campaign, Burger King reported a remarkable 37% increase in foot traffic to its stores.

> The campaign garnered significant media attention, generating substantial free publicity.

> It showcased the power of virtual advertising to drive real-world actions, boosting sales and enhancing Burger King's brand image.

The "Whopper Detour" campaign demonstrated how innovative and playful virtual advertising, combined with geo-targeting and a clever narrative, could drive substantial foot traffic, sales, and social media engagement. It remains a classic example of a creative and effective virtual advertising campaign with a real-world impact.

B. Case Study: Nike's AR "SNKRS" App

Objective: Nike aimed to engage sneaker enthusiasts and boost sales of its exclusive and limited-edition sneaker releases.

Strategy: Nike's "SNKRS" app, launched in 2015, leveraged augmented reality (AR) to create immersive shopping experiences and connect with sneaker enthusiasts. The app's features and strategies include:

i) **AR Integration**: The SNKRS app integrated augmented reality to offer immersive and interactive features. Users could access exclusive content and experiences by scanning physical posters or real-world objects. This encouraged users to explore and engage with the app in unique ways.

ii) **Exclusive Sneaker Drops**: Nike used the app to manage and control the release of limited-edition sneakers. Users could access information and updates about upcoming sneaker releases and purchase them directly through the app—the exclusive nature of these releases generated excitement and anticipation.

iii) **AR Stickers**: The app featured an "AR Stickers" function, allowing users to superimpose AR sneaker designs onto their surroundings using their smartphone's camera. This feature engaged users and allowed them to visualise sneakers in their environment, enhancing the shopping experience.

iv) **Gamification**: The app incorporated gamification elements, such as gamified challenges and quizzes related to sneaker culture. These elements encouraged user participation and added an element of fun to the app.

Results: Nike's SNKRS app achieved remarkable success and became a favourite among sneaker enthusiasts.

> The app created a strong sense of exclusivity and interactivity, driving high user engagement.
> Sneakerheads eagerly anticipated new releases and queued up virtually to secure limited-edition sneakers.
> The app fostered a loyal community of users who actively participated in challenges and shared their AR experiences on social media.
> The app's success led to increased sales of Nike's exclusive sneaker releases and helped create a culture around sneaker collecting.

The "SNKRS" app exemplifies how augmented reality can create interactive and exclusive shopping experiences. Nike effectively harnessed AR to engage its audience, build a dedicated community, and drive sales of limited-edition products. The app showcases how innovative virtual advertising can connect with passionate audiences and boost brand engagement and sales.

QUANTIFYING ECONOMIC IMPACTS

Quantifying the economic impacts of virtual advertising and marketing is a complex but essential task. Understanding the financial outcomes and benefits of these strategies is crucial for businesses. Here are vital factors to consider when quantifying the economic impacts:

i) Revenue Growth: Assess how virtual advertising contributes to revenue growth. Compare sales and revenue figures before and after the implementation of virtual advertising campaigns. Identify specific products or services that experienced increased sales due to these campaigns.

ii) Return on Investment (ROI): Calculate the ROI of virtual advertising campaigns. This involves comparing the cost of running campaigns to the revenue generated. ROI can be calculated per campaign or over a specified period.

iii) Customer Acquisition and Retention: Measure how virtual advertising contributes to customer acquisition and retention. Analyse the cost of acquiring new customers through virtual advertising and compare it to the lifetime value of those customers. Retention rates can also be monitored to gauge the effectiveness of marketing efforts.

iv) Conversion Rates: Analyze conversion rates from virtual advertising efforts. Track the percentage of users who take desired actions, such as purchasing, signing up for a newsletter, or filling out a contact form. Improving conversion rates can significantly impact economic outcomes.

v) Cost Per Acquisition (CPA): Calculate the CPA, which represents the cost of acquiring a new customer. Understanding the cost of each new customer gained through virtual advertising helps optimise campaign efficiency.

vi) Traffic and Engagement Metrics: Analyze website traffic, click-through rates, and other engagement metrics generated by virtual advertising. These metrics help assess the effectiveness of ad campaigns and their economic impact on website traffic and user engagement.

vii) Customer Lifetime Value (CLV): Calculate the CLV to understand the long-term economic impact of virtual advertising efforts. This metric considers the total revenue a customer is expected to generate over their entire relationship with the business.

viii) Customer Segmentation: Segment the customer base to assess how different groups respond to virtual advertising. Understanding which segments yield the most revenue and profits can guide targeted advertising efforts.

ix) Cost Savings: Consider cost savings in terms of reduced marketing costs. Virtual advertising can be more cost-effective than traditional advertising channels, leading to savings in ad spend.

x) Market Expansion: Analyze the impact of virtual advertising on market expansion. Assess whether virtual campaigns have facilitated entry into new markets or increased market share.

xi) Competitive Advantage: Evaluate the competitive advantage gained through virtual advertising. If virtual campaigns outperform competitors or allow for innovative approaches, this can lead to economic benefits.

xii) Data Analytics: Leverage data analytics to gain insights into user behaviour and preferences. This information can guide advertising strategies to align with consumer demands, thereby increasing economic benefits.

xiii) Social Media Metrics: Monitor social media metrics such as likes, shares, comments, and social reach. Engaging content in virtual advertising can substantially impact brand visibility and customer engagement, leading to economic benefits.

xiv) Customer Feedback and Surveys: Collect customer feedback and conduct surveys to understand the economic impact of virtual advertising on customer satisfaction and brand loyalty.

xv) Sales Funnel Analysis: Map the customer journey from initial awareness to sales funnel. Assess how virtual advertising campaigns influence each funnel stage, from awareness and consideration to conversion.

Quantifying economic impacts requires a multifaceted approach considering various metrics and their interplay. Data analysis, ROI calculations, and the careful examination of customer behaviour are essential for businesses to gauge the economic effectiveness of virtual advertising and marketing efforts.

Interplay Between Regulation and Economic Impacts

The relationship between regulation and economic impacts in virtual advertising and marketing is intricate and multifaceted. Regulations influence how businesses conduct advertising campaigns and can have positive and negative economic effects. Here's an overview of the interplay between these factors:

1. Compliance Costs:

Regulatory Impact: Regulations often require businesses to invest in compliance measures, such as data protection, transparency, and consumer protection. These measures can increase operational costs.

Economic Impact: Compliance costs may reduce short-term profitability for businesses. However, these costs can also lead to better data security, consumer trust, and reduced legal risks, which can benefit businesses in the long term.

2. Consumer Trust and Confidence:

Regulatory Impact: Regulations protecting consumers can enhance trust and confidence in virtual advertising. For example, data privacy regulations like GDPR promote user data protection.

Economic Impact: Building consumer trust can increase brand loyalty and repeat business, ultimately driving economic benefits. Consumers are more likely to engage with businesses they trust.

3. Levelling the Playing Field:

Regulatory Impact: Regulations can level the playing field by ensuring all businesses adhere to the same advertising standards. This can help prevent unfair competitive advantages.

Economic Impact: A level playing field encourages healthy competition, leading to innovation, better products, and competitive pricing—all of which can benefit consumers and the overall economy.

4. Adaptation and Innovation:

Regulatory Impact: Some regulations may push businesses to innovate and find new, compliant advertising strategies. For example, stricter advertising standards can lead to more creative and informative campaigns.

Economic Impact: Innovation can drive economic growth. Businesses that adapt to regulatory changes by creating more effective and ethical advertising campaigns may experience increased revenue and market share.

5. Consumer Protection and Satisfaction:

Regulatory Impact: Regulations that protect consumers from deceptive advertising practices enhance consumer satisfaction.

Economic Impact: Satisfied consumers are likelier to repeat purchases and recommend a brand to others. This can contribute to long-term financial success.

6. Market Entry Barriers:

Regulatory Impact: Stringent regulations can create barriers to entry for new businesses, notably smaller startups. Compliance with complex regulations may require substantial resources.

Economic Impact: Barriers to entry can limit competition, potentially leading to reduced innovation and higher prices. Striking a balance between regulation and fostering a competitive market is crucial for economic health.

7. Global Expansion:

Regulatory Impact: Regulations vary across countries and regions. Expanding into international markets may require businesses to navigate different regulatory landscapes.

Economic Impact: Successful global expansion can lead to increased revenue and profitability. Adhering to diverse regulatory requirements is essential for international growth.

8. Enforcement and Penalties:

Regulatory Impact: Strict enforcement of regulations with significant penalties for non-compliance can act as a deterrent against unethical or unlawful advertising practices.

Economic Impact: Businesses may incur financial losses from penalties for non-compliance. However, effective enforcement can create a fair and trustworthy advertising environment that benefits compliant businesses in the long run.

9. Innovation in Compliance Solutions:

Regulatory Impact: The need for compliance has spurred innovation in compliance solutions, including data protection technologies and ad-tracking tools.

Economic Impact: Companies that develop and offer compliance solutions can generate revenue while helping other businesses adhere to regulations.

10. Adaptive Marketing Strategies:

Regulatory Impact: Businesses often adapt their marketing strategies to align with regulations, which can lead to more ethical and transparent advertising.
Economic Impact: Ethical advertising can build a more substantial brand reputation and consumer trust, contributing to economic growth through increased sales and loyalty.

The interplay between regulation and economic impacts in virtual advertising and marketing is dynamic and influenced by various factors. Balancing compliance with the financial interests of businesses requires careful consideration of the specific regulatory environment and its implications for each organisation. Businesses navigating this interplay effectively will likely achieve sustainable economic success in the virtual advertising landscape.

CHAPTER IX

Virtual Dispute Resolution: Challenges and Opportunities in Resolving Metaverse Conflicts

INTRODUCTION

Virtual dispute resolution is essential in the digital age, particularly in virtual environments like the metaverse. One of the key reasons for its importance lies in its accessibility and inclusivity. Unlike traditional legal proceedings, virtual dispute resolution offers an accessible and inclusive way to address conflicts, enabling individuals from different locations to resolve conflict without needing physical presence. This accessibility reduces barriers to entry, ensuring that individuals, regardless of their location, can seek resolution for their conflicts.

Another critical aspect is the speed of conflict resolution. Issues can escalate rapidly in the fast-paced digital world, and traditional legal proceedings can be time-consuming. Virtual dispute resolution processes can be quicker and more efficient, providing a timely response to conflicts, which is crucial in preventing the escalation of disputes.

Moreover, the cost-efficiency of virtual dispute resolution cannot be understated. Traditional legal proceedings often involve substantial legal fees, court costs, and travel expenses. In contrast, virtual dispute resolution can be a more cost-effective alternative, saving parties time and money and making it an attractive option for individuals and organisations.

The global reach of virtual dispute resolution is another crucial advantage. The metaverse and virtual environments transcend national borders, making resolving conflicts involving individuals from different countries and legal systems possible. This global accessibility is vital for addressing the international nature of disputes that can arise in the metaverse.

Anonymity and privacy are also significant factors. In virtual dispute resolution, parties can resolve conflict while maintaining anonymity and privacy, which can be crucial for individuals concerned about public exposure. This sense of security encourages individuals to come forward and address their concerns.

Additionally, virtual dispute resolution processes can adapt to the unique norms and rules within virtual spaces, respecting the characteristics of the environment. Conflicts can be addressed effectively by aligning conflict resolution mechanisms with these virtual norms, ensuring a more harmonious virtual environment.

Furthermore, virtual dispute resolution plays a role in preventing offline harm. Conflicts originating in the metaverse can sometimes have real-world repercussions. Effective resolution of virtual disputes can help prevent real-world harm or legal issues, making it a proactive approach to maintaining overall safety and order.

Preservation and authentication of digital evidence are also integral components of virtual dispute resolution. These processes ensure that digital evidence is protected and maintained, essential for addressing conflicts in the digital realm where evidence often takes the form of text logs, videos, or digital artefacts.

In the larger context, virtual dispute resolution can drive the evolution of legal and regulatory frameworks to better align with the digital age, adapting to virtual environments' unique challenges and nuances.

Virtual dispute resolution can contribute to community building within virtual spaces. When users know that conflicts can be resolved fairly and efficiently, it promotes a sense of trust and community. Users are more likely to engage in virtual activities and build relationships, ultimately contributing to the growth and development of the metaverse and digital communities.

Existing approaches to virtual dispute resolution

Online Dispute Resolution (ODR) is a widely adopted method for settling problems in digital contexts. Online Dispute Resolution (ODR) is a method that harnesses the capabilities of technology and the internet to enable the resolution of disputes inside a digital environment. These platforms offer a neutral virtual environment where parties can present their arguments, share information, and potentially participate in mediation or arbitration without physical presence. Online Dispute Resolution (ODR) offers significant advantages in resolving low-value conflicts that frequently arise in online markets, e-commerce platforms, and social media environments. The platform provides rapidity, ease of access, and the advantage of resolving conflicts without requiring expensive and time-consuming conventional legal procedures. Furthermore, ODR frequently incorporates functionalities such as encrypted communication, file exchange, and case monitoring, rendering it a complete settlement approach for conflicts in the digital era.

Smart contracts leveraging blockchain technology embody a pioneering methodology for virtual conflict resolution. Smart contracts are agreements capable of executing themselves, with predetermined conditions that initiate automated steps in the event of disagreements. Smart contracts have the potential to significantly contribute to resolving issues about financial transactions, ownership of virtual assets, and decentralised apps (DApps) within virtual environments. These contracts obviate the necessity of intermediaries, as the terms and activities are included inside the contract itself. In a dispute, the smart contract can independently carry out predetermined resolutions, guaranteeing that the parties obtain the outcomes they have mutually agreed upon. This approach's decentralised and automated methodology results in time efficiency and mitigates the possibility of biased or fallible human involvement. Consequently, it provides a transparent and reliable mechanism for resolving disputes inside ecosystems based on blockchain technology.

The prevalence of community-driven conflict resolution processes is increasing in virtual environments. Numerous virtual communities, spanning multiplayer games, social platforms, and virtual worlds, have autonomously developed distinct norms, principles, and codes of conduct. In instances of conflict, community members can notify authorised community moderators or administrators regarding disputes or infractions of established rules. These persons frequently assume the role of mediators, evaluating the information offered and determining suitable resolutions, which may encompass issuing warnings, imposing temporary suspensions, or even implementing permanent bans. This strategy is based on the distinct norms and values seen within each virtual community, facilitating a form of self-governance, and enabling users to uphold the desired order and culture inside their selected digital environment. The practice promotes a robust feeling of communal ownership and governance in resolving conflicts.

Artificial Intelligence (AI) and data analytics are becoming more prevalent in virtual conflict resolution. Artificial intelligence algorithms can analyse extensive volumes of data to discern patterns of conflict and prospective disagreements inside virtual worlds. These systems can identify and address harmful behaviours, such as harassment, fraud, or abuse, by offering timely intervention. In addition, they can propose suitable courses of action or interventions that align with the characteristics and magnitude of the dispute. The utilisation of AI-driven dispute resolution not only facilitates the prompt management of conflicts but also contributes to the cultivation of a more secure and cohesive digital milieu. With the ongoing expansion of virtual environments, the involvement of artificial intelligence (AI) in conflict analysis and resolution is expected to increase, leading to improved management of disputes and enhanced user experiences.

The intricacy of virtual dispute resolution has prompted the emergence of global collaboration and cross-border initiatives. With the increasing transcendence of virtual spaces over national boundaries, problems arising from the interactions between users from many countries and legal systems have become increasingly prevalent. Global activities are focused on establishing a comprehensive framework for addressing conflicts inside the metaverse, considering its users' many cultural backgrounds and legal standards. These endeavours aim to assemble a consortium of legal scholars, technologists, and relevant parties from several nations to formulate universally accepted norms and recommendations for resolving conflicts in the digital domain. These initiatives aim to provide uniform and equitable ways worldwide, offering users dependable and impartial mechanisms to resolve problems beyond national boundaries. The authors discuss the issue of jurisdictional uncertainty and the obstacles it poses in the resolution of cross-border conflicts inside virtual environments.

The strategies above for virtual dispute resolution, namely Online Dispute Resolution (ODR), blockchain-based smart contracts, community-driven mechanisms, AI-driven conflict analysis, and global collaborative initiatives, exemplify novel and productive methods for resolving conflicts within the metaverse and other digital contexts. Each solution possesses distinct strengths and applications tailored to address the specific difficulties and requirements of the virtual domain.

VIRTUAL DISPUTE RESOLUTION: CHALLENGES IN THE METAVERSE

Lack of established legal frameworks

The need for established legal frameworks for virtual dispute resolution is a significant challenge in the digital age, particularly in virtual environments like the metaverse. Traditional legal systems, rooted in the physical world, often struggle to adapt to the unique dynamics of virtual spaces. Here, we will delve into this challenge in more detail.

Virtual environments, such as online games, social media platforms, and virtual worlds, pose challenges that traditional legal systems need to be equipped to address. These digital spaces operate beyond the boundaries of physical jurisdictions, often without a clear geographical presence. As a result, conflicts within the metaverse may involve users from different countries, each governed by its own set of laws and regulations. This jurisdictional ambiguity can make determining which legal framework applies challenging, leading to clarity and consistency in resolving disputes.

Moreover, virtual environments often lack clear legal definitions and precedents in the physical world. Concepts like property rights, digital assets, and the boundaries of freedom of expression in virtual spaces must be better defined in traditional law. This legal void can create uncertainty and disputes, mainly when issues related to virtual property ownership, digital theft, or defamation arise.

The enforcement of legal decisions in virtual spaces is another intricate problem. Traditional legal systems have physical means of enforcement, such as court orders, bailiffs, and police. These mechanisms often need to be more present in the metaverse, as digital assets and online interactions must conform to physical realities. As a result, even when a legal decision is reached, ensuring compliance or restitution can be highly challenging.

To address this challenge, there is a growing need to develop new legal frameworks and regulations tailored to the unique characteristics of virtual environments. These frameworks should provide clear guidelines on intellectual property rights, data privacy, contract enforcement, and dispute resolution within the metaverse. International collaboration and the creation of global standards are essential to ensure consistency and fairness in resolving conflicts that transcend national borders.

Legal experts, policymakers, and stakeholders must work together to bridge the gap between traditional legal systems and the digital landscape. This involves considering the principles of digital rights, the preservation of digital evidence, and mechanisms for cross-border cooperation in resolving disputes. By establishing comprehensive legal frameworks that reflect the nature of virtual environments, we can create a more predictable, just, and orderly legal environment for all participants in the metaverse. These efforts are crucial to ensuring that virtual dispute resolution can effectively address the challenges and opportunities of the digital age.

Jurisdictional issues

Jurisdictional issues are complex legal matters that revolve around determining which legal authority or court has the right to hear a particular case or enforce the law in a specific geographical area. These issues can arise in various contexts, including civil, criminal, and administrative proceedings. Understanding jurisdictional issues is essential in the legal field, as they can significantly impact the outcome of legal disputes. In this explanation, I'll elaborate on the various aspects of jurisdictional issues.

1. Types of Jurisdiction: Jurisdiction can be broadly categorised into several types, including:

i) Personal Jurisdiction: Personal jurisdiction is a fundamental concept in the legal field that pertains to a court's authority over the parties involved in a legal case. It determines whether a court can hear a case and make binding decisions on individuals or entities. Personal jurisdiction is crucial because it ensures that defendants have a fair opportunity to defend themselves in a court that is both reasonable and convenient. To explain personal jurisdiction in maximum detail, we'll explore its various aspects:

ii) Basis for Personal Jurisdiction: Personal jurisdiction is typically based on a defendant's connection to the jurisdiction in which the court is located. There are several grounds for establishing personal jurisdiction, including:

iii) Residency: A defendant is subject to the court's jurisdiction if they reside or have a domicile within the jurisdiction.

iv) Consent: A defendant can consent to the jurisdiction of a particular court through explicit agreement, such as a forum selection clause in a contract.

v) Minimum Contacts: The famous "minimum contacts" principle, established by the U.S. Supreme Court in the case of International Shoe Co. v. Washington, requires a defendant to have sufficient connections with the jurisdiction, such as doing business within the state, to be subject to personal jurisdiction.

vi) Long-Arm Statutes: Many jurisdictions have "long-arm" statutes that expand personal jurisdiction to out-of-state defendants with specific contacts with the state, like causing harm or entering into contracts.

2. Specific vs General Jurisdiction: Personal jurisdiction can be further categorised into specific and general jurisdiction:

i) Specific Jurisdiction: This type of jurisdiction applies when a defendant's activities within the jurisdiction give rise to the lawsuit. It is limited to the particular claims related to those activities.

ii) General Jurisdiction: General jurisdiction exists when a defendant's contacts with the jurisdiction are so extensive that they can be sued for any claim, even those unrelated to their activities in that jurisdiction. This is a higher threshold to meet.

3. Challenges to Personal Jurisdiction: Parties can challenge personal jurisdiction, and the court must address these challenges before proceeding with the case. Common challenges include:

i) Lack of Sufficient Contacts: A defendant may argue that they lack the minimum contacts with the jurisdiction and, therefore, should not be subject to personal jurisdiction.

ii) Due Process Concerns: A defendant may claim that being haled into the court would violate their due process rights under the Constitution, especially if the court's exercise of jurisdiction is unreasonable or unfair.

iii) Venue vs. Personal Jurisdiction: It's essential to distinguish between personal jurisdiction and venue. Personal jurisdiction focuses on whether a court has the power to hear a case based on the defendant's connections to the jurisdiction. At the same time, the venue determines the most appropriate location within a jurisdiction for the case to be heard. Both concepts are interrelated but distinct.

iv) International Personal Jurisdiction: In international cases, establishing personal jurisdiction can be particularly complex. Various treaties and principles, such as the Hague Convention on the Service Abroad of Judicial and Extrajudicial Documents, help manage jurisdictional issues when parties are in different countries.

Enforcement of Judgments: Once a court establishes personal jurisdiction and issues a judgment, enforcing that judgment in another jurisdiction can be challenging. This may involve recognising and enforcing foreign judgments through the legal process known as comity.

Subject Matter Jurisdiction: Subject matter jurisdiction, often called the court's authority to hear a particular type of case, is a fundamental concept in the legal system. It defines the scope of cases that a court can adjudicate based on the subject matter or the type of legal issues involved. Understanding subject matter jurisdiction is crucial because it ensures that cases are heard by the appropriate court, whether a federal, state, or specialised tribunal. Here, we'll explore subject matter jurisdiction in maximum detail:

Federal vs. State Subject Matter Jurisdiction:

Federal Jurisdiction: Federal subject matter jurisdiction is defined by the United States Constitution and federal laws. Federal courts have authority over cases that involve federal questions, diversity of citizenship, and cases against the United States or its officers. National questions refer to cases involving federal law or constitutional issues.

State Jurisdiction: State subject matter jurisdiction is generally broader, encompassing all cases not specifically within federal jurisdiction. State courts hear cases involving state law issues, such as family law, contracts, and property disputes.

Exclusive vs. Concurrent Jurisdiction:

i) Exclusive Jurisdiction: In some cases, subject matter jurisdiction is exclusive to one court system. For example, certain cases involving patents and copyrights fall under exclusive federal jurisdiction.

ii) Concurrent Jurisdiction: In other cases, state and federal courts may have concurrent jurisdiction, allowing the plaintiff to choose where to file the case. However, concurrent jurisdiction can lead to strategic decisions about which court to use based on case law, jury pools, and the nature of the claims.

iii) Specialised Tribunals: Besides general state and federal courts, there are specialised tribunals, such as bankruptcy courts, tax courts, and immigration courts. These tribunals have subject matter jurisdiction over specific types of cases or disputes. For example, the U.S. Tax Court deals exclusively with tax-related matters.

iv) Determining Subject Matter Jurisdiction: The court's jurisdiction is typically determined at the outset of a case. To establish subject matter jurisdiction, the plaintiff must show a "cause of action" or legal claim within the court's authority. This requires analysing the legal issues involved in the case and selecting the appropriate court system.

v) Jurisdictional Amount: In some cases, subject matter jurisdiction may also depend on the amount in controversy. For example, some federal courts only have jurisdiction if the amount in controversy exceeds a certain threshold. This is often seen in diversity jurisdiction cases.

vi) Jurisdictional Challenges: If a party believes that a court lacks subject matter jurisdiction over a case, they can challenge it through a motion to dismiss or other legal means. If the court determines that it does not have the requisite subject matter jurisdiction, the case will be ignored or transferred to the proper court.

vii) Implications for Legal Outcomes: The choice of court with the appropriate subject matter jurisdiction can have significant implications for the outcome of a case. Different courts may have other legal standards, procedures, and traditions that can influence the case's resolution.

viii) Removal and Remand: In cases where there is a dispute over whether a case should be in state or federal court, a process known as removal and remand can occur. A defendant may seek to remove a case from state court to federal court, and the parties may then litigate the issue of subject matter jurisdiction.

Territorial Jurisdiction: Territorial jurisdiction, also known as territorial scope or geographical jurisdiction, is a concept in the legal system that defines the geographic boundaries within which a court or legal authority can exercise its authority. It dictates where a lawsuit or legal proceeding should be filed based on the location of the events, parties involved, or property. Territorial jurisdiction is essential to ensure that cases are heard in the appropriate geographic area. Here, we'll delve into the details of territorial jurisdiction:

i) Territorial Boundaries: Territorial jurisdiction establishes the geographic boundaries within which a court can operate. Different types of courts have varying territorial boundaries. For example, local or municipal courts have jurisdiction within a specific city or town, while state courts have jurisdiction throughout their respective states. Federal courts, on the other hand, have jurisdiction across the entire nation.

Venue vs. Territorial Jurisdiction: It's important to distinguish between venue and territorial jurisdiction. Venue refers to the specific geographic location within a jurisdiction where a case should be filed for convenience. Territorial jurisdiction determines which court system should hear the case based on the location of the events or parties involved.

State vs. Federal Territorial Jurisdiction:

i) State Territorial Jurisdiction: State courts have territorial jurisdiction over matters that involve state law or disputes occurring within the state's boundaries. For instance, a state court in California would have territorial jurisdiction over a contract dispute between parties located within California.

ii) Federal Territorial Jurisdiction: Federal courts have territorial jurisdiction over specific federal law matters that apply nationwide. These may include cases involving federal crimes, bankruptcy, patents, and diversity jurisdiction, where parties are from different states.

iii) International Territorial Jurisdiction: Territorial jurisdiction can also apply in international contexts. In such cases, the issue becomes determining which country's courts have jurisdiction over disputes involving parties in different countries. International conventions and principles help address these conflicts.

Jurisdictional Challenges: Challenges to territorial jurisdiction can arise when parties dispute whether a particular court within a jurisdiction is the appropriate venue. Parties may file motions to change venue if they believe the chosen court is not the proper location for the case.

i) Implications for Legal Proceedings: Territorial jurisdiction has significant implications for legal proceedings. It dictates the legal standards, rules, and procedures that apply to a case. Different jurisdictions may have distinct laws and traditions that can influence the case's outcome.

ii) Long-Arm Statutes: Some jurisdictions have "long-arm" statutes that extend territorial jurisdiction beyond their geographic boundaries. These statutes allow the court to exercise jurisdiction over out-of-state parties or events that have a sufficient connection to the jurisdiction.

iii) Forum Non-Conveniens: In cases where a court has territorial jurisdiction but parties believe another jurisdiction is more suitable for the litigation, the doctrine of forum non conveniens may be invoked. This allows a court to dismiss the case in favour of another jurisdiction more conveniently for the parties and witnesses.

Challenges to Jurisdiction: Parties involved in a legal dispute may challenge the court's jurisdiction for various reasons. Common challenges include:

i) **Lack of Personal Jurisdiction**: If a defendant argues that they do not have sufficient contact with the jurisdiction, they may seek to dismiss the case based on a lack of personal jurisdiction.

ii) **Lack of Subject Matter Jurisdiction**: Parties can challenge a court's authority to hear a particular type of case. For instance, a state court cannot adjudicate disputes involving federal patents.

iii) **Forum Non-Conveniens**: This doctrine allows a court to dismiss a case if it believes another jurisdiction is more suitable for the litigation. This is often used in international cases.

Jurisdiction in International Cases: In cases involving parties from different countries, jurisdictional issues can be even more intricate. Several principles come into play, such as:

i) **Forum Selection Clauses**: These are contractual agreements in which parties specify the jurisdiction where any disputes arising from the contract will be resolved.

ii) **Choice of Law**: Determining which jurisdiction's laws apply in a cross-border dispute can be contentious. Courts consider factors like where the contract was formed, the parties' location, and the dispute's subject matter.

iii) **Extraterritorial Jurisdiction**: Some cases involve the assertion of jurisdiction by one country over activities outside its borders, which can lead to conflicts and legal challenges.

Resolution of Jurisdictional Issues: When jurisdictional issues arise, they must be resolved before the substantive legal matters can be addressed. This can involve extensive legal proceedings, including:

i) **Motion to Dismiss**: Parties may file motions to dismiss a case for lack of jurisdiction, which the court must consider and rule on.

ii) **Jurisdictional Discovery**: In complex cases, parties may conduct discovery to gather evidence related to jurisdictional issues.

iii) Interlocutory Appeals: Sometimes, jurisdictional issues can be appealed before the case proceeds to trial.

iv) Impact on Legal Outcomes: The outcome of a case often depends on jurisdiction. Jurisdictions may have different laws, procedures, and biases that can affect the ultimate judgment. Parties may choose where to file their cases based on perceived advantages in a particular jurisdiction.

AUTHENTICATION AND IDENTITY VERIFICATION CHALLENGES

Authentication and identity verification challenges are significant issues in today's digital age, where many transactions and interactions occur online. These challenges revolve around ensuring the authenticity and identity of individuals in various contexts, such as online banking, e-commerce, social media, and government services. In this explanation, I'll elaborate on the complexities and methods related to authentication and identity verification:

Authentication Methods

Authentication methods are essential in verifying the identity of users and ensuring secure access to various systems and services, especially in the digital realm. Several authentication methods are available, each with its strengths and weaknesses. Below, I'll elaborate on different authentication methods:

A. Password-Based Authentication:

i) Description: This is the most common authentication method, where users enter a password or a personal identification number (PIN) to access their accounts.

ii) Strengths: Familiar, easy to implement, and low cost.

iii)Weaknesses: Vulnerable to password theft hacking and often requires complex, hard-to-remember passwords.

B. Two-Factor Authentication (2FA):

i) Description: 2FA combines something the user knows (password) with something the user has (e.g., a mobile device that generates one-time codes).

ii) Strengths: Provides an additional layer of security, even if the password is compromised.

iii) Weaknesses: Users may find it cumbersome, and some 2FA methods can be vulnerable to interception (e.g., SMS-based codes).

C. Biometric Authentication:

i) Description: This method uses unique physical or behavioural characteristics, such as fingerprints, facial recognition, or voice patterns, to verify a user's identity.

ii) Strengths: Difficult to forge, convenient, and user-friendly.

iii) Weaknesses: Can be subject to biometric spoofing privacy concerns and only sometimes readily available on all devices.

D. Smart Cards and Tokens:

i) Description: Users possess physical cards or tokens (hardware devices) that store authentication data or generate one-time codes.

ii) Strengths: Offers strong security, especially in corporate settings.

iii) Weaknesses: It may be costly to implement, and users can lose or forget their devices.

E. Knowledge-Based Authentication (KBA):

i) Description: Users answer specific questions they should only know, such as "What is your mother's maiden name?" or "Where did you go to elementary school?"

ii) Strengths: Provides an additional layer of security.

iii) Weaknesses: Answers may be guessable, especially with public data available on social media.

F. Certificate-Based Authentication:

i) Description: Users possess a digital certificate issued by a trusted authority that is used to authenticate them.

ii) Strengths: Highly secure and commonly used in corporate and government settings.

iii) Weaknesses: Complex to implement and manage, and may need to be more practical for everyday consumer use.

G. Behavioural Authentication:

i) Description: Analyzes user behaviour patterns, such as typing speed and mouse movements, to confirm their identity.

ii) Strengths: Non-intrusive and can provide continuous authentication.

iii) Weaknesses: It may have false positives or negatives, and user behaviour can change over time.

H. Location-Based Authentication:

i) Description: Verifies a user's identity based on their physical location, often through GPS or IP address data.

ii) Strengths: Can enhance security, especially for mobile devices.

iii) Weaknesses: It may only be precise and available in some situations and can be spoofed with VPNs.

I. Social Authentication:

i) Description: Users verify their identity through their social media profiles or connections.

ii) Strengths: Convenient and can sometimes be used for single sign-on (SSO).

iii) Weaknesses: It may raise privacy concerns and be vulnerable to social engineering attacks.

J. Time-Based Authentication:

i) Description: Users have a limited time window to complete the authentication process, typically by entering a time-based code.

ii) Strengths: Provides a level of security, especially for remote access.

iii) Weaknesses: Users must synchronise their devices with the correct time source.

The choice of authentication method depends on the specific use case, the level of security required, and the user experience. Many modern systems combine these methods to create a multi-layered security approach, often called multi-factor authentication (MFA). MFA enhances security by requiring users to pass through multiple authentication layers, making it more challenging for attackers to gain unauthorised access.

IDENTITY VERIFICATION METHODS

Identity verification methods are employed to confirm the identity of individuals in various contexts, both in physical and digital domains. These methods are crucial in enhancing security, preventing fraud, and ensuring compliance with legal and regulatory requirements. Below, I'll elaborate on different identity verification methods.

A. Document Verification:

i) **Description**: This method involves verifying an individual's identity by examining official documents, such as driver's licenses, passports, or government-issued IDs.
ii) **Strengths**: Provides tangible proof of identity, widely accepted, and challenging to forge high-quality documents.
iii) **Weaknesses**: Vulnerable to counterfeit documents and not entirely foolproof.

B. Biometric Verification:

i) **Description**: Biometric verification uses unique physical or behavioural characteristics to verify identity. Common biometric modalities include fingerprints, facial recognition, iris scans, voice recognition, and hand geometry.
ii) **Strengths**: Difficult to forge or impersonate, user-friendly, and often provides high accuracy.
iii) **Weaknesses**: This can be subject to biometric spoofing (e.g., using a photo for facial recognition) and may raise privacy concerns.

C. Knowledge-Based Verification (KBA):

i) **Description**: KBA involves asking individuals questions that only they should know the answers to, such as details about their past addresses, relatives, or financial history.

ii) Strengths: Provides an additional layer of security, especially for online account recovery.

iii) Weaknesses: Answers may be guessable, especially with access to public records or social media.

D. Social Verification:

i) Description: Social verification involves verifying identity through a user's social network connections or online presence. It can include confirming a person's identity through friends, connections, or online profiles.

ii) Strengths: It can provide an extra layer of trust in specific scenarios, such as online marketplaces.

iii) Weaknesses: It may need to be sufficiently secure or privacy-compliant and can be manipulated through fake social profiles.

E. Credit Checks:

i) Description: Some organisations use credit reports to verify a person's identity. A credit check confirms that the individual's information matches their credit report.

ii) Strengths: Offers an additional layer of verification, especially in financial and lending contexts.

iii) Weaknesses: Not suitable for all identity verification needs and may raise privacy concerns.

F. Behavioural Biometrics:

i) Description: This method analyses an individual's behaviour patterns, such as typing speed, keystrokes, or mouse movements, to continuously verify their identity.

ii) Strengths: Provides ongoing authentication without the need for additional user actions.

iii) Weaknesses: It may have false positives or negatives, and user behaviour can change over time.

G. Blockchain-Based Verification:

i) Description: Leveraging blockchain technology for identity verification can provide a secure, tamper-resistant way to confirm identity. Users control their identity information and can selectively disclose it when needed.

ii) Strengths: Offers a decentralised and secure method of identity verification, providing users with greater control over their data.

iii) Weaknesses: It is still emerging, and the adoption and standards are evolving.

H. Government-Backed ID Verification:

i) Description: In some regions, government-issued identity verification methods are used. This can include digital national IDs or e-residency programs.

ii) Strengths: Provides a highly trusted and government-backed means of verification.

iii) Weaknesses: Availability may be limited to specific regions, and adoption can be challenging.

I. Third-Party Verification Services:

i) Description: Organizations can leverage third-party services that specialise in identity verification. To confirm identity, these services often combine various methods, such as document verification, biometrics, and data analysis.

ii) Strengths: Provides a comprehensive approach to identity verification and can adapt to specific needs.

iii) Weaknesses: Costs may be associated with using third-party services and may not be accessible to all businesses.

The choice of identity verification method depends on factors such as the level of security required, the specific use case, and the regulatory environment. In many cases, a combination of methods is employed to create a robust identity verification process, ensuring the authenticity of individuals while maintaining user convenience and privacy.

CHALLENGES IN AUTHENTICATION AND IDENTITY VERIFICATION

Authentication and identity verification are critical processes in the digital age, but they come with various challenges that can impact security, user experience, and compliance. Below, I'll elaborate on some of the key challenges in these areas:

A. Identity Theft and Fraud:

i) **Challenge**: Cybercriminals continuously develop new tactics to steal personal information and commit identity fraud. This can include phishing attacks, social engineering, and data breaches.
ii) **Impact**: Unauthorized access to accounts, financial losses, and reputational damage for individuals and organisations.

B. Weak Passwords:

i) **Challenge**: Many users still use weak passwords that are easy to guess or crack. Additionally, they may reuse passwords across multiple accounts.
ii) **Impact**: Vulnerability to brute-force attacks, account takeovers, and unauthorised access to sensitive information.

C. Biometric Spoofing:

i) **Challenge**: Despite advancements in biometric authentication, techniques to spoof or replicate biometric data (e.g., fingerprints, facial features) exist.
ii) **Impact**: Reduced effectiveness of biometric verification, especially in high-security environments.

D. Privacy Concerns:

i) **Challenge**: Collecting and storing personal data for identity verification can raise privacy concerns and potential misuse of this data.
ii) **Impact**: Erosion of privacy rights, potential data breaches, and user mistrust.

E. Phishing and Social Engineering:

i) Challenge: Cybercriminals use deceptive tactics to trick individuals into revealing their personal information, including usernames and passwords.
ii) Impact: Unauthorized access, data breaches, and financial losses.

F. Complex User Experience:

i) Challenge: Implementing robust authentication and identity verification methods can sometimes create a complex and cumbersome user experience.
ii) Impact: Frustration among users, lower adoption rates, and increased organisation support costs.

G. Regulatory Compliance:

i) Challenge: Organizations, especially in sectors like finance and healthcare, must adhere to strict regulatory requirements (e.g., KYC, AML, GDPR) related to identity verification.
ii) Impact: Non-compliance can lead to legal consequences, fines, and reputational damage.

H. False Positives and Negatives:

i) Challenge: Some verification methods, primarily behavioural and biometric authentication, can produce false positives (incorrectly granting access to unauthorised users) or false negatives (erroneously denying access to legitimate users).
ii) Impact: Security vulnerabilities or user frustration, depending on the type of error.

I. Cross-Channel Authentication:

i) Challenge: Users engage with organisations through various channels (web, mobile apps, call centres), and ensuring consistent and secure authentication across all channels can be challenging.
ii) Impact: Inconsistent security practices can lead to vulnerabilities in specific channels.

J. International Transactions:

i) Challenge: Identity verification can be more complex in cross-border transactions, as different countries have varying requirements and processes for identity confirmation.
ii) Impact: Delays, added costs, and complexities in global business operations.

K. User Education:

i) Challenge: Many users need to gain awareness of the importance of strong authentication and identity verification practices.
ii) Impact: Increased vulnerability to cyberattacks, fraud, and misuse of personal information.

L. Emerging Technologies and Threats:

i) Challenge: As technology evolves, new authentication and identity verification challenges arise, such as quantum computing's potential impact on encryption and AI-driven attacks.
ii) Impact: Rapidly evolving threats may outpace current security measures.

To address these challenges, organisations and individuals must remain vigilant, implement multi-layered security approaches, keep software and systems updated, and continuously educate users on best authentication and identity verification practices. Developing new technologies, like blockchain and advanced biometrics, also offers potential solutions to these challenges.

Legal And Regulatory Compliance

Legal and regulatory compliance is crucial to conducting business and ensuring the security and privacy of individuals' data, especially in the digital age. Adhering to relevant laws and regulations is essential to avoid legal consequences, fines, and damage to an organisation's reputation. Here, I'll elaborate on the concept of legal and regulatory compliance in a variety of contexts:

A. Data Protection and Privacy:

i) Challenges: Numerous data protection laws, such as the European Union's General Data Protection Regulation (GDPR) and the California Consumer Privacy Act (CCPA), require organisations to handle personal data responsibly, obtain consent, and provide data subjects with rights over their data.
ii) Impact: Non-compliance can result in substantial fines, legal actions, and reputational harm.

B. Know Your Customer (KYC) and Anti-Money Laundering (AML):

i) Challenges: Regulations in the financial sector, like the Bank Secrecy Act (BSA) in the U.S., require financial institutions to verify the identity of customers, report suspicious activities, and prevent money laundering.
ii) Impact: Non-compliance can lead to financial penalties, loss of banking licenses, and criminal investigations.

C. Healthcare Compliance:

i) Challenges: The Health Insurance Portability and Accountability Act (HIPAA) in the U.S. mandates strict privacy and security standards for healthcare providers and organisations that handle health data.
ii) Impact: Violations can result in substantial fines and legal liabilities.

D. Consumer Protection:

i) Challenges: Consumer protection laws, such as the U.S. Federal Trade Commission (FTC) Act, require companies to provide accurate information, protect consumers from deceptive practices, and secure personal information.
ii) Impact: Fines, lawsuits, and reputation damage can result from non-compliance.

E. Cybersecurity Regulations:

i) Challenges: Various industries and regions have specific cybersecurity regulations that mandate measures to protect data from breaches. For example, the New York Department of Financial Services (NYDFS) cybersecurity regulations require financial institutions to implement robust cybersecurity programs.

ii) Impact: Non-compliance can lead to penalties and legal actions, and data breaches can also result in severe consequences.

F. Intellectual Property and Copyrights:

i) Challenges: Intellectual property laws protect inventions, trademarks, copyrights, and trade secrets. Organisations must respect these rights to avoid infringement.

ii) Impact: Lawsuits and damages for intellectual property violations can be costly.

G. Environmental Compliance:

i) Challenges: Environmental regulations vary by region and industry, requiring organisations to adhere to specific standards for emissions, waste disposal, and resource conservation.

ii) Impact: Non-compliance can result in fines, legal actions, and environmental damage.

H. International Regulations:

i) Challenges: International transactions and operations may be subject to a complex web of regulations, including import/export controls, trade sanctions, and international privacy laws.

ii) Impact: Violations can result in penalties, sanctions, and legal actions, as well as damage to international relations.

I. Labor and Employment Laws:

i) Challenges: Labor and employment laws govern workplace practices, including minimum wage, working hours, discrimination, and safety.

ii) Impact: Non-compliance can lead to lawsuits, penalties, and reputational damage.

J. Antitrust and Competition Laws:

i) Challenges: Antitrust and competition laws aim to prevent anti-competitive practices, such as monopolies and price-fixing.
ii) Impact: Violations can result in substantial fines and legal actions.

Organisations must stay informed about relevant laws and regulations, implement appropriate policies and procedures, and conduct regular compliance audits to ensure legal and regulatory compliance. They should also seek legal counsel and invest in technology and processes to support compliance efforts. Non-compliance leads to legal and financial consequences and damages an organisation's reputation and stakeholder trust.

Advanced Technologies

Advanced technologies continually shape our world, from how we live and work to how businesses operate and innovate. These technologies are often at the forefront of scientific and engineering advancements and profoundly impact society. Here, I'll discuss several advanced technologies that are driving change and innovation in various fields:

A. Artificial Intelligence (AI):

i) Description: AI involves the development of computer systems that can perform tasks that typically require human intelligence, such as problem-solving, natural language understanding, and decision-making.
ii) Applications: AI is used in various applications, including machine learning, natural language processing, computer vision, and robotics.

B. Machine Learning:

i) Description: Machine learning is a subset of AI that focuses on creating algorithms and models that allow computers to improve their performance on a specific task through experience.

ii) Applications: Machine learning is used in predictive analytics, recommendation systems, autonomous vehicles, and fraud detection.

C. Blockchain:

i) Description: Blockchain is a distributed ledger technology that enables secure, transparent, and immutable record-keeping of transactions.
ii) Applications: Beyond cryptocurrencies like Bitcoin, blockchain is used for supply chain management, smart contracts, and securing sensitive data.

D. Quantum Computing:

i) Description: Quantum computing leverages the principles of quantum mechanics to perform complex calculations at speeds unimaginable with classical computers.
iii) Applications: Quantum computing has the potential to revolutionise fields like cryptography, drug discovery, and optimisation problems.

E. 5G Technology:

i) Description: 5G is the fifth generation of wireless communication technology, providing significantly faster data speeds, lower latency, and increased connectivity.
ii) Applications: It enables IoT, augmented and virtual reality experiences, and high-speed mobile communication.

F. Internet of Things (IoT):

i) Description: IoT connects physical objects and devices to the internet, allowing them to collect and exchange data, leading to more intelligent and automated systems.
ii) Applications: IoT is used in smart homes, industrial automation, healthcare monitoring, and environmental sensing.

G. Biotechnology:

i) Description: Biotechnology combines biology, genetics, and technology to develop products and technologies that improve human health and the environment.

ii) **Applications**: Biotech is used in gene editing, personalised medicine, and the development of biofuels.

H. Augmented Reality (AR) and Virtual Reality (VR):

i) **Description**: AR overlays digital information in the real world, while VR creates immersive virtual environments.

ii) **Applications**: AR is used in gaming, navigation, and education, while VR is applied in gaming, training, and therapy.

I. Renewable Energy Technologies:

i) **Description**: These technologies harness energy from sustainable sources, such as solar, wind, and hydropower.

ii) **Applications**: They provide clean energy solutions for electricity generation, transportation, and heating.

J. Advanced Materials:

i) **Description**: Advanced materials include innovative substances engineered for exceptional properties or improved performance.

ii) **Applications**: They are used in aerospace, electronics, construction, and healthcare.

K. Cognitive Computing:

i) **Description**: Cognitive computing systems use AI and machine learning to simulate human thought processes, enhancing problem-solving and data analysis.

ii) **Applications**: Cognitive computing is employed in data analytics, healthcare diagnostics, and customer service chatbots.

L. Robotics:

i) **Description**: Robotics involves designing and constructing autonomous or semi-autonomous machines capable of performing tasks in various domains.

ii) Applications: Robotics is used in manufacturing, healthcare, agriculture, and space exploration.

M. Biomedical Engineering:

i) Description: Biomedical engineering combines engineering principles with biology and medicine to develop technologies and devices for healthcare applications.

ii) Applications: It includes the design of medical devices, tissue engineering, and drug delivery systems.

These advanced technologies continually evolve, pushing the boundaries of what is possible and transforming industries, economies, and our daily lives. They offer significant opportunities for innovation and have the potential to address some of the world's most pressing challenges. However, they also raise ethical, legal, and security concerns that must be carefully managed.

1. User Experience: Balancing security with user convenience is a challenge. Overly complex authentication processes can frustrate users, leading to poor adoption, while too lax security can expose systems to fraud.

2. Multi-Channel Authentication: As users interact with businesses and services through various channels (web, mobile apps, call centres, etc.), ensuring consistent and secure authentication across these channels is challenging.

3. Cross-Border Transactions: Identity verification can be more complex for cross-border transactions, as different countries may have varying requirements and processes for identity confirmation.

In conclusion, authentication and identity verification are critical in a world where digital interactions are the norm. These processes are essential for security, fraud prevention, and regulatory compliance. While technological advancements have provided new and more secure methods, the challenges in this field, including privacy concerns, fraud, and legal compliance, continue to evolve and require ongoing attention and innovation.

Technical Limitations and Infrastructure Requirements

Technical limitations and infrastructure requirements are critical considerations when implementing advanced technologies. These factors can impact technology initiatives' effectiveness, scalability, and success. Here, I'll delve into the challenges and concerns related to technical limitations and infrastructure requirements:

Technical Limitations:

A. Processing Power:

i) Challenge: Advanced technologies like artificial intelligence and quantum computing demand substantial processing power. There may need to be more than existing hardware for complex tasks.
ii) Impact: Limited capabilities can slow down or hinder the adoption of these technologies.

B. Data Quality and Quantity:

i) Challenge: Many advanced technologies, especially in AI and machine learning, require vast amounts of high-quality data to train models effectively.
ii) Impact: Inadequate data can result in models with poor accuracy and performance.

C. Energy Consumption:

i) Challenge: Some advanced technologies, such as data centres or high-performance computing, consume large amounts of energy.
ii) Impact: This can lead to increased operational costs and environmental concerns.

D. Interoperability:

i) Challenge: Ensuring that different technologies and systems work together seamlessly can be challenging, especially when dealing with legacy systems.

ii) Impact: Lack of interoperability can result in inefficiencies and data silos.

E. Software Limitations:

i) Challenge: Software constraints, such as software bugs, compatibility issues, or limitations in available software tools, can hinder technology adoption.

ii) Impact: These issues can lead to reduced functionality and potential security vulnerabilities.

F. Security Concerns:

i) Challenge: Ensuring the security of advanced technologies, particularly in IoT and cloud computing, is a complex task that requires constant vigilance.

ii) Impact: Security breaches can result in data leaks, financial losses, and damage to reputation.

G. Regulatory Compliance:

i) Challenge: Staying compliant with evolving regulations related to advanced technologies, like data privacy laws, can be complex and resource-intensive.

ii) Impact: Non-compliance can lead to legal and financial consequences.

Infrastructure Requirements:

A. Network Infrastructure:

i) Consideration: High-speed, reliable network infrastructure is essential for technologies like 5G, IoT, and cloud computing.

ii) Impact: Inadequate network infrastructure can result in slow performance and disruptions.

B. Data Storage:

i) Consideration: Advanced technologies generate and require vast amounts of data. Adequate data storage solutions are crucial.
ii) Impact: Insufficient storage can lead to data loss and limit the scalability of systems.

C. Data Centers:

i) Consideration: Data centres are critical for operating cloud-based services and data-intensive applications.
ii) Impact: Inadequate data centre facilities can lead to service interruptions and performance issues.

D. Power and Cooling:

i) Consideration: Data centres and high-performance computing facilities require robust power and cooling systems to operate efficiently.
ii) Impact: Inadequate power and cooling can result in system failures and downtime.

E. Edge Computing Infrastructure:

i) Consideration: Edge computing relies on localised infrastructure for processing data closer to the source. This is crucial for real-time applications.
ii) Impact: Inadequate edge computing infrastructure can lead to delays and latency.

F. Scalability and Redundancy:

i) Consideration: Building infrastructure that can scale with technology demands and includes redundancy for failover is vital.
ii) Impact: Inflexible or non-redundant infrastructure can result in downtime and data loss.

G. Security Infrastructure:

i) Consideration: Robust security infrastructure, including firewalls, intrusion detection systems, and encryption mechanisms, is necessary to protect against cyber threats.

ii) Impact: Inadequate security infrastructure can result in data breaches and compromised systems.

Addressing technical limitations and infrastructure requirements is essential for successfully deploying and utilising advanced technologies. Organisations must invest in hardware and software solutions that can meet the demands of these technologies while remaining adaptable to future changes and compliance with relevant regulations. Planning for scalability, redundancy, and security is critical to ensure reliable and secure technology operations.

Cultural And Ethical Considerations

Cultural and ethical considerations are significant in developing, adopting, and using advanced technologies. These considerations ensure that technology aligns with societal values, respects individual rights, and avoids unintended negative consequences. Let's explore the critical cultural and ethical aspects:

Cultural Considerations:

A. Cultural Sensitivity:

i) Consideration: Different cultures have diverse norms, values, and beliefs. Technologies should be designed with cultural sensitivity in mind to avoid causing offence or discomfort.

ii) Impact: Insensitivity to culture can result in backlash, reduced adoption, or even legal consequences.

B. Language and Localization:

i) Consideration: Language barriers can hinder the accessibility and usability of technology. Localisation is vital, including translation and adaptation to local languages and customs.

ii) **Impact**: Please address language and localisation issues to ensure the reach of technology.

C. Digital Inclusion:

i) **Consideration**: Bridging the digital divide is crucial. Access to advanced technologies should be equitable, ensuring that all segments of society can benefit.

ii) **Impact**: Lack of digital inclusion can exacerbate inequalities and exclude specific populations from opportunities.

D. Cultural Appropriation:

i) **Consideration**: Using cultural elements in technology or marketing should be respectful and avoid cultural appropriation.

ii) **Impact**: Cultural appropriation can lead to public outrage, harm a brand's reputation, and create legal and ethical challenges.

E. Customisation and Personalization:

i) **Consideration**: Technology customisation features allow users to adapt their experiences to align with their cultural preferences and values.

ii) **Impact**: Failing to provide customisation options can alienate users.

Ethical Considerations:

A. Privacy and Data Ethics:

i) **Consideration**: Respecting individuals' privacy rights and handling data ethically are paramount. Technology companies must be transparent about data usage and obtain informed consent.

ii) **Impact**: Privacy violations can lead to legal penalties and a loss of trust.

B. Bias and Fairness:

i) **Consideration**: Ensuring that technology is free from bias and provides

equitable outcomes is crucial, particularly in AI and machine learning applications.
ii) Impact: Biased technology can perpetuate discrimination and unfairness.

C. Algorithm Transparency:

i) Consideration: Understanding and mitigating biases requires transparency in algorithms and AI decision-making processes.
ii) Impact: Lack of transparency can lead to distrust and uncertainty about decisions.

D. AI in Decision-Making:

i) Consideration: Using AI in essential decision-making processes, such as hiring, lending, and law enforcement, requires ethical considerations to avoid discrimination and bias.
ii) Impact: Biased AI can lead to legal liabilities and social unrest.

E. Digital Responsibility:

i) Consideration: Technology companies must take responsibility for the ethical use of their products and address their societal impact.
ii) Impact: Failing to act responsibly can result in public outrage and legal consequences.

F. Ethical AI Development:

i) Consideration: Ethical AI development principles, such as fairness, accountability, and transparency (FAT), should guide the design and deployment of AI systems.
ii) Impact: Unethical AI development can lead to ethical dilemmas and negative consequences.

G. Disinformation and Fake News:

i) Consideration: Combatting disinformation and fake news is an ethical responsibility for technology platforms and social media companies.

ii) Impact: Spreading false information can have real-world consequences, including inciting violence and undermining trust.

H. Ethical Autonomous Systems:

i) Consideration: Autonomous systems, like self-driving cars and drones, must adhere to ethical standards, including safety, accountability, and decision-making ethics.
ii) Impact: Ethical lapses in autonomous systems can lead to accidents and harm to individuals.

Addressing cultural and ethical considerations in developing and deploying advanced technologies is essential for building trust, ensuring fairness, and minimising negative societal impact. Organisations should adopt ethical frameworks, engage with diverse stakeholders, and incorporate cultural perspectives into technology design and implementation. Moreover, vigilance and accountability are vital to navigating the evolving cultural and ethical concerns landscape.

OPPORTUNITIES FOR EFFECTIVE DISPUTE RESOLUTION IN THE METAVERSE

Mediation and arbitration in virtual environments

Mediation and arbitration are widely used methods for resolving disputes, and in today's digital age, they have adapted to virtual environments. These alternative dispute resolution (ADR) techniques provide efficient and cost-effective ways to settle conflicts without going to court. Let's explore how mediation and arbitration work in virtual environments:

Mediation in Virtual Environments:

Mediation involves a neutral third party, the mediator, who assists disputing parties in reaching a mutually acceptable agreement. In virtual environments, mediation takes place through online platforms or video conferencing. Here's how it works:

> **Online Mediation Platforms**: Dedicated online mediation platforms

provide secure virtual meeting spaces where participants can communicate and collaborate with the mediator.

> **Scheduling and Preparation**: Parties and the mediator agree on a suitable time for the mediation session. They may also exchange relevant documents and information electronically.

> **Virtual Mediation Session**: During the session, participants join the virtual meeting and present their perspectives, concerns, and proposed solutions. The mediator facilitates communication and helps explore options for resolution.

> **Private Caucuses**: The mediator can conduct private caucuses with each party separately within the virtual environment to discuss sensitive issues or gather additional information.

> **Agreement and Documentation**: If an agreement is reached, it can be drafted and signed electronically. The mediator may also assist in clarifying the terms of the agreement.

Arbitration in Virtual Environments:

Arbitration involves a neutral third party, the arbitrator, who acts like a judge and makes a binding decision on the dispute. Virtual arbitration offers an efficient and accessible way to resolve conflicts:

> **Choice of Virtual Arbitration Platform**: Parties and arbitrators can select a virtual arbitration platform that provides the necessary tools and security for conducting the arbitration proceedings.

> **Virtual Hearings**: Arbitration hearings can occur via video conferencing, where parties and witnesses present their evidence and arguments. The arbitrator oversees the proceedings.

> **Evidence Submission**: Parties can submit documents, exhibits, and other evidence electronically. The arbitrator reviews this material within the virtual environment.

> **Witness Testimony**: Witnesses can testify via video conference, and cross-examination can occur virtually.

> **Arbitral Award**: The arbitrator delivers a legally binding award once the arbitration proceedings are complete. This award can be shared electronically.

Advantages of Virtual Mediation and Arbitration:

> **Accessibility**: Virtual ADR allows parties and participants from different locations to resolve disputes without physical presence.
> **Cost-Efficiency**: Virtual ADR can be more cost-effective by reducing travel and logistical expenses.
> **Speed and Efficiency**: Proceedings in virtual environments can often be scheduled and conducted more efficiently, reducing the time required for resolution.
> **Document Management**: Electronic document submission and management simplify the exchange of evidence and information.
> **Confidentiality**: Virtual platforms can provide secure, confidential discussion spaces, preserving the parties' privacy.

Challenges and Considerations:

> **Technology Issues**: Parties should have access to reliable technology and internet connections to participate effectively.
> **Privacy and Security**: Virtual environments must ensure the confidentiality and security of the proceedings and data.
> **Digital Divide**: Not all individuals or communities may have equal access to virtual ADR, which could result in disparities in participation.
> **Cultural and Language Differences**: Virtual ADR should consider participants' cultural and language needs.
> **Enforcement of Awards**: In some cases, enforcing arbitral awards may still require traditional legal procedures.

Virtual mediation and arbitration have become increasingly prevalent, especially in response to the COVID-19 pandemic, which limited in-person interactions. They offer a practical and effective means of dispute resolution while leveraging digital tools to streamline the process. However, like any ADR method, they require careful planning, adherence to ethical standards, and consideration of the specific needs and dynamics of the dispute.

Blockchain Technology for Secure And Transparent Dispute Resolution

Blockchain technology has gained attention for its potential to revolutionise dispute resolution by offering a fast and transparent platform for recording and managing disputes. Here's an exploration of how blockchain can be used for quick and satisfactory dispute resolution:

Blockchain in Dispute Resolution:

> **Smart Contracts:** Blockchain allows for creation of intelligent contracts and self-executing agreements with predefined rules and conditions. These contracts can automate various aspects of dispute resolution, such as payment releases or triggering predefined actions upon contract breaches.

> **Immutable Record:** Data recorded on a blockchain is tamper-resistant and immutable. This ensures that the information is securely stored and cannot be altered once a dispute is registered, providing an auditable trail of events.

> **Transparency:** Blockchains are inherently transparent. Dispute-related information, including agreements, evidence, and actions taken, can be accessible to authorised parties, increasing transparency in the dispute resolution process.

> **Decentralisation:** Blockchain operates on a decentralised network, reducing the reliance on a central authority. This can make the dispute resolution process less biased and more objective.

> **Security:** Blockchain's cryptographic features enhance security. Data is encrypted and stored across multiple nodes, making it difficult for unauthorised parties to manipulate or access the information.

> **Consensus Mechanism:** Dispute resolution can involve multiple parties and arbitrators. Blockchain's consensus mechanism ensures that all relevant parties reach an agreement, reducing the potential for disputes and disagreements in the resolution process.

Using Blockchain for Secure and Transparent Dispute Resolution:

> **Smart Dispute Resolution Contracts:** Parties involved in a contract can create smart dispute resolution contracts that automatically trigger predefined actions in the event of a dispute, such as initiating mediation or arbitration.

> **Evidence and Document Storage:** Blockchain can securely store evidence and documents related to a dispute. Timestamps and encryption

ensure the integrity and authenticity of these records.

> **Arbitration and Mediation Records**: Arbitration and mediation proceedings, including decisions and communications, can be recorded on a blockchain. These records are secure, transparent, and accessible by the relevant parties.

> **Automated Payments**: In cases where dispute resolution involves financial compensation, intelligent contracts can automate payment processes upon resolving a dispute, ensuring a fair and transparent disbursement of funds.

> **Blockchain-Based Dispute Resolution Platforms**: Several platforms have emerged to provide blockchain-based dispute resolution services. These platforms use blockchain to record and manage disputes, often incorporating arbitration and mediation services.

Challenges and Considerations:

> **Adoption**: Widespread adoption of blockchain technology for dispute resolution requires buy-in from multiple stakeholders, including legal professionals, organisations, and governments.

> **Legal Recognition**: Blockchain-based dispute resolution processes' legal status and recognition may vary by jurisdiction. Legal frameworks must adapt to accommodate these innovative approaches.

> **Scalability**: Blockchain networks like Bitcoin and Ethereum have faced scalability challenges. The technology must scale to handle a potentially large volume of disputes efficiently.

> **Privacy**: While blockchain is transparent, privacy concerns may arise in dispute resolution, especially when sensitive personal or commercial information is involved. Balancing transparency with privacy is crucial.

> **Education and Training**: Users and professionals involved in dispute resolution may require training to understand and utilise blockchain-based tools effectively.

Blockchain technology has the potential to make dispute resolution more secure and transparent, offering parties involved in disputes greater confidence in the process and its outcomes. As the technology continues to evolve and gain broader acceptance, it may become a more prominent feature of the dispute resolution landscape. However, like any innovation, it should be implemented with a thorough understanding of its capabilities and limitations while considering legal and privacy implications.

AI And Machine Learning for Automated Dispute Resolution

AI and machine learning are transformative technologies that enhance and automate dispute resolution processes. These technologies can provide efficient, data-driven, and fair methods for resolving disputes by leveraging data analysis, natural language processing, and predictive algorithms. Here's an exploration of AI and machine learning for automated dispute resolution:

AI and Machine Learning in Dispute Resolution:

> **Data Analysis and Prediction**: AI and machine learning algorithms can analyse historical dispute data, identifying patterns and trends to predict likely outcomes and potential resolutions. This predictive capability assists in assessing a dispute's strengths and weaknesses early.

> **Natural Language Processing (NLP)**: NLP enables the automated analysis of textual data, such as case documents, emails, or chat logs, to extract relevant information and sentiments. This aids in understanding the arguments and emotions of the parties involved.

> **Chatbots and Virtual Assistants**: Chatbots equipped with AI and machine learning can provide initial support to parties in dispute, answer common questions, and guide them through the initial stages of the resolution process.

> **Decision Support**: Machine learning models can provide decision support by analysing legal precedents and historical case outcomes, offering insights to lawyers, arbitrators, or mediators.

> **Negotiation and Mediation**: AI can facilitate negotiation and mediation by suggesting potential compromise solutions based on the parties' stated preferences and the likelihood of success.

> **Document Automation**: AI-powered systems can automate the creation of legal documents, making the process faster and more accurate. This can include contract generation and settlement agreements.

> **Case Prioritization**: Machine learning can help prioritise cases based on urgency, complexity, and potential impact, allowing dispute resolution professionals to allocate their resources more effectively.

Using AI and Machine Learning for Automated Dispute Resolution:

> **Automated Triage**: AI can automatically classify and prioritise incoming disputes, ensuring that the most critical cases receive immediate attention.
> **Early Case Assessment**: Machine learning can assist in assessing the merits of a dispute early in the process, helping parties make informed decisions about pursuing or settling the case.
> **Predictive Analytics**: AI-driven models can predict the probable outcome of a dispute based on historical data, assisting parties in evaluating their position.
> **Automated Mediation and Negotiation Platforms**: These platforms can facilitate online mediation and negotiation, guiding parties through structured processes and suggesting potential resolutions.
> **Virtual Judges and Arbitrators**: AI-powered virtual judges or arbitrators can resolve less complex disputes swiftly and cost-effectively.

Challenges and Considerations:

> **Quality of Data**: The effectiveness of AI and machine learning models heavily depends on the quality and quantity of available data. Biased or incomplete data can lead to inaccurate predictions and recommendations.
> **Ethical and Legal Considerations**: There are ethical concerns around using AI in dispute resolution, particularly regarding fairness, transparency, and accountability. Legal standards for AI-driven decisions need to be established.
> **Privacy and Security**: Handling sensitive legal information and personal data requires robust data protection and security measures to prevent unauthorised access or breaches.
> **User Acceptance**: Parties in a dispute may be hesitant to fully embrace automated dispute resolution processes, fearing a lack of human judgment or emotional understanding.
> **Regulatory Compliance**: AI and machine learning in dispute resolution must adhere to legal and regulatory standards, such as data protection and privacy laws.
> **Complex Cases**: Highly complex or novel cases may require human intervention and judgment that AI and machine learning cannot provide.

AI and machine learning offer the potential to significantly streamline and automate dispute resolution processes, making them more efficient and accessible. However, it's crucial to strike a balance between automation and the preservation of fairness, accountability, and ethical considerations. As these technologies continue to advance, their integration into the dispute-resolution field should be done thoughtfully and in alignment with legal and ethical standards.

Virtual Courts and Legal Systems

Virtual courts and legal systems are rapidly evolving in response to technological advancements, offering innovative ways to conduct legal proceedings, access justice, and administer the rule of law. Here's an exploration of the concept of virtual courts and their various aspects:

Virtual Courts and Legal Systems:

> **Online Case Filing**: Parties can file legal documents, complaints, and evidence electronically through web-based portals, reducing the need for physical paperwork and in-person courthouse visits.

> **Virtual Hearings**: Legal proceedings, including hearings, trials, and arbitrations, can be conducted through video conferencing, allowing participants to join remotely from anywhere with an internet connection.

> **Digital Evidence Presentation**: Parties can submit, access, and present evidence electronically, streamlining the process and enabling efficient sharing of documents and multimedia materials.

> **Remote Legal Consultations**: Lawyers and clients can communicate and hold consultations through virtual platforms, making legal services more accessible, especially in remote or underserved areas.

> **Online Dispute Resolution (ODR)**: Specialized ODR platforms offer digital solutions for resolving disputes outside traditional court settings, including e-negotiation and e-mediation services.

> **Virtual Legal Research and Databases**: Access to legal research, statutes, case law, and legal databases can be done online, facilitating legal research and making legal information more widely available.

> **Electronic Filing and Case Management**: Courts can use electronic filing systems and case management software to track and manage cases, improving the efficiency and organisation of the judicial process.

> **Remote Jury Selection**: Jury selection can be conducted online, and jurors can participate in trials from their homes, reducing the need for large in-person gatherings.
> **Court Reporting and Transcription**: Virtual court reporters and transcription services can capture and document legal proceedings for the record.

Advantages of Virtual Courts and Legal Systems:

> **Accessibility**: Virtual courts make legal proceedings and services more accessible to individuals facing physical or geographical barriers.
> **Cost Savings**: Reduced travel and administrative costs for legal professionals, parties, and the court system.
> **Efficiency**: Virtual court processes can be more efficient, with fewer delays due to scheduling conflicts or logistical issues.
> **Safety and Health**: Virtual proceedings became crucial during the COVID-19 pandemic as they allowed legal processes to continue while reducing health risks.
> **Environmental Impact**: Reduced travel to and from court can positively impact the environment by lowering carbon emissions.

Challenges and Considerations:

> **Technology Access**: Not all parties or participants may have access to the necessary technology or reliable internet connections, potentially leading to disparities in access to justice.
> **Privacy and Security**: Protecting sensitive legal information and ensuring the security of virtual court proceedings is paramount.
> **Digital Divide**: Bridging the digital divide is essential to ensure equal access to justice for all, regardless of technological proficiency.
> **Ensuring Due Process**: Virtual courts must uphold due process, including the right to be heard, present evidence, and receive a fair trial.
> **Cultural and Language Considerations**: Addressing language and cultural differences is crucial to ensuring that virtual courts are accessible and fair for diverse populations.
> **Legal and Regulatory Frameworks**: Virtual courts must operate within the existing legal and regulatory frameworks, which may require updates and adaptations to accommodate virtual proceedings.

Virtual courts and legal systems offer numerous advantages, particularly regarding accessibility, cost savings, and efficiency. They have proven invaluable during times of crisis and can provide long-term benefits for the legal system. However, addressing the challenges, such as technology access, privacy, and cultural considerations, is essential to ensure that virtual courts remain a fair and effective means of accessing justice. As technology evolves, the legal profession must adapt and embrace these innovations while preserving fundamental justice and due process principles.

COLLABORATIVE PLATFORMS AND COMMUNITY-BASED RESOLUTIONS

Collaborative platforms and community-based resolutions are innovative approaches to dispute resolution that leverage technology to foster cooperation, communication, and consensus among parties involved in conflicts. These methods encourage dialogue and cooperation to find mutually satisfactory solutions. Here's an exploration of these concepts.

Collaborative Platforms and Community-Based Resolutions:

> **Online Collaboration Tools**: Collaborative platforms provide digital spaces where parties can discuss, share information, and work together to resolve disputes. These tools can include messaging apps, video conferencing, and shared document repositories.
> **Community Mediation**: Community-based resolutions involve local mediators facilitating discussions between parties in a neighbourhood, workplace, or other community settings. These mediators help parties find common ground and reach mutually acceptable solutions.
> **Online Dispute Resolution (ODR)**: ODR platforms facilitate the resolution of conflicts through online processes. They can include negotiation, mediation, and arbitration services conducted virtually.
> **Collaborative Decision-Making**: These platforms enable collective decision-making by allowing parties to contribute to solutions collaboratively. This can be applied to disputes within organisations or communities.
> **Crowdsourcing Solutions**: Crowdsourcing platforms gather input and

suggestions from a community or a large group of individuals to help find innovative resolutions to problems or disputes.

Advantages of Collaborative Platforms and Community-Based Resolutions:

> **Empowerment**: These approaches empower parties to resolve their disputes actively, fostering a sense of ownership and responsibility.

> **Effective Communication**: Collaborative platforms facilitate open and transparent communication among parties, leading to better understanding and cooperation.

> **Consensus Building**: These methods emphasise consensus and collaboration, which can result in more enduring and mutually satisfactory solutions.

> **Community Engagement**: Community-based resolutions strengthen social bonds and encourage individuals to participate in the resolution of local issues.

> **Cost-Efficiency**: These approaches can often be more cost-effective than traditional legal proceedings.

Challenges and Considerations:

> **Cultural Sensitivity**: Cultural differences and sensitivities must be considered, especially in community-based resolutions, to ensure inclusivity and fairness.

> **Mediation and Facilitation Skills**: Effective mediators and facilitators are essential to guide the resolution process and ensure that parties are treated fairly.

> **Conflict of Interest**: In community-based resolutions, conflicts of interest may arise if mediators or facilitators have personal or professional relationships with the parties involved.

> **Digital Divide**: Access to collaborative platforms can be limited by the digital divide, where not all parties have the necessary technology or internet access.

> **Privacy and Security**: Protecting the privacy and security of parties involved in online processes is crucial to maintaining trust.

> **Enforcement**: While collaborative solutions may be reached, there may be challenges in enforcing agreements, especially in community-based

resolutions.

Collaborative platforms and community-based resolutions offer innovative, participatory, and cost-effective approaches to dispute resolution. They emphasise open communication, consensus building, and empowering parties to engage in the resolution process actively. While they have many advantages, addressing challenges such as cultural sensitivity and privacy and ensuring the effectiveness of mediators and facilitators are essential to making these methods successful. They are particularly relevant for disputes where relationships, community cohesion, and active engagement are crucial.

CHAPTER X

Charting the Metaverse: Blockchain, Smart Contracts, and Challenges

INTRODUCTION

Blockchain technology is a decentralised and distributed ledger system that is the foundational infrastructure for numerous cryptocurrencies, such as Bitcoin. The technology offers a reliable and easily verifiable method for documenting transactions and data in a manner that ensures security and transparency. This introduction examines the core concepts of blockchain technology, including its historical background, essential constituents, and diverse applications that extend beyond the realm of cryptocurrencies.

The inception of blockchain technology occurred in 2008 when an unidentified individual named Satoshi Nakamoto announced it as the foundational technology underpinning Bitcoin. The primary objective of its design was to tackle the issue of double-spending, which pertains to the potential for a digital currency to be utilised for multiple transactions. With the implementation of blockchain technology, Bitcoin effectively addressed this problem and brought about a paradigm shift in digital banking.

Fundamentally, a blockchain can be defined as a sequential arrangement of blocks whereby each block encompasses a compilation of transactions. The blocks are interconnected, forming a cohesive chain. The distinguishing characteristic of blockchain lies in its decentralised nature. Instead of being dependent on a centralised entity such as a financial institution or governmental body, it operates on a decentralised network of computers, known as nodes, responsible for verifying and documenting transactions. The process of decentralisation offers enhanced levels of security and transparency.

The immutability of blockchain technology is regarded as one of its fundamental characteristics. Once a transaction has been recorded on the blockchain, it becomes highly challenging to modify or remove. The state of being unchangeable is attained by employing cryptographic hashing and consensus processes, which will be further explored in subsequent sections of this discourse.

The utilisation of blockchain extends beyond cryptocurrencies, encompassing other domains like supply chain management, voting systems, healthcare, and other sectors. The technology possesses the capacity to revolutionise diverse sectors through the augmentation of operational effectiveness, mitigation of fraudulent activities, and amplification of transparency. This introductory section provides a fundamental basis for comprehending the underlying mechanisms of blockchain technology and its diverse applications.

Distributed ledger and consensus mechanisms

Distributed ledger technology and consensus mechanisms are fundamental components of blockchain systems.

Distributed Ledger Technology (DLT):

i) Decentralisation: In a distributed ledger, data is not stored on a single server but spread across multiple network nodes. This decentralisation reduces the risk of a single point of failure. If one node fails, the network can continue functioning because other nodes maintain a copy of the ledger.
ii) Transparency: DLTs are designed to be highly transparent. All participants in the network have access to the same ledger, and they can view and verify the data and transactions. This transparency promotes trust and accountability as participants can independently verify the information on the ledger.
iii) Immutability: Once data is recorded on a distributed ledger, it becomes challenging to alter or delete. This immutability is ensured through cryptographic hashing and consensus mechanisms. Each block in the chain contains a reference to the previous block, creating a secure and

irreversible history of transactions.

Consensus Mechanisms:

i) Proof of Work (PoW): PoW is the consensus mechanism used by Bitcoin. Miners compete to solve complex mathematical puzzles, which require significant computational power. The first miner to solve the puzzle gets the right to add a new block to the blockchain. PoW is energy-intensive but highly secure because altering the blockchain's history is costly and time-consuming.

ii) Proof of Stake (PoS): PoS is a consensus mechanism where validators are chosen to create new blocks based on the number of cryptocurrency coins they hold and are willing to "stake" as collateral. Validators with more coins have a higher chance of being selected. PoS is considered more energy-efficient than PoW, requiring less computational work.

iii) Delegated Proof of Stake (DPoS): DPoS is a variation of PoS. Instead of all validators competing to create new blocks, the community elects a few delegates to validate transactions. DPoS is known for its speed and efficiency, as decision-making is concentrated among a few chosen nodes.

iv) Proof of Authority (PoA): PoA relies on approved validators who take turns adding blocks to the blockchain. Validators are trusted entities, often in private or consortium blockchains. PoA provides control and security, as only reputable validators participate.

v) Proof of Space and Time (PoST): PoST is a consensus mechanism that uses the available storage space on a participant's device for mining or validating transactions. It's energy-efficient and eco-friendly because it doesn't rely on computational power but on storage capacity and time.

These consensus mechanisms ensure that only valid transactions are added to the blockchain and that all network participants agree on the ledger's state. They contribute to the security and reliability of blockchain systems by making it highly challenging for malicious actors to manipulate the ledger. In combination with these consensus mechanisms, distributed ledger technology forms the backbone of blockchain networks, enabling them to achieve trust, transparency, and security in a decentralised environment.

Key features and benefits of blockchain for the Metaverse

Blockchain technology offers several key features and benefits that can significantly enhance the development and functioning of the Metaverse. Let's explore these in more detail:

Key Features of Blockchain for the Metaverse:

1. Decentralisation: Blockchain operates on a decentralised network of nodes. This aligns with the decentralised nature of the Metaverse, where there's no single controlling entity. This decentralisation ensures that no single entity has absolute control over the virtual world, promoting fairness and inclusivity.

2. Immutable and Transparent Ledger: The immutability of blockchain data ensures that it cannot be altered once transactions or ownership records are recorded. This feature is crucial in the Metaverse to guarantee the ownership of digital assets, such as virtual real estate, avatars, or in-game items. Users can trust that their virtual property rights are secure.

3. Digital Scarcity: Blockchain can enable the creation of scarce digital assets and tokens. This scarcity can be applied to digital collectables, in-game items, or virtual real estate. Users can have confidence in the uniqueness and value of their virtual possessions.

4. Interoperability: Blockchain can facilitate interoperability among different Metaverse platforms and virtual worlds. Users can transfer assets and identities seamlessly between other virtual spaces, promoting a unified Metaverse experience.

5. Smart Contracts: Smart contracts, self-executing code on the blockchain, can automate various processes in the Metaverse. For example, they can facilitate automatic in-game item trading, ensure revenue sharing among content creators, or govern virtual land rental agreements.

6. Digital Identity: Blockchain can provide users with secure and portable digital identities. This is essential in the Metaverse, where individuals may want to maintain consistent identities across different virtual spaces while retaining control over their personal information.

Benefits of Blockchain for the Metaverse:

1. Ownership and Authenticity: Blockchain ensures actual ownership of virtual assets and verifies their authenticity. This is particularly important for creators and collectors in the Metaverse, as it prevents counterfeiting and fraud.

2. Security: Blockchain's cryptographic techniques enhance the security of digital assets and data. Users can be confident that their assets and personal information are protected from hacks and unauthorised access.

3. Economic Ecosystem: Blockchain enables the creation of virtual economies within the Metaverse. Users can earn, spend, and trade digital assets and content creators can monetise their work through digital currencies and tokens.

4. User Control: Blockchain gives users greater control over their data and digital assets. They can decide who accesses their information and how it's used, increasing privacy and data sovereignty.

5. Cross-Platform Integration: Blockchain facilitates cross-platform interactions within the Metaverse, enabling seamless movement of assets and identities between different virtual worlds, games, and experiences.

6. Reduced Transaction Costs: Blockchain can reduce transaction costs associated with asset trading and microtransactions within the Metaverse, making it economically viable for users and creators.

7. Community Governance: Decentralized autonomous organisations (DAOs) built on blockchain can enable community-driven governance in the Metaverse, allowing users to have a say in the rules and policies of the virtual world they inhabit.

Blockchain technology offers a robust set of features and benefits that align well with the requirements of the Metaverse. These include decentralisation, immutability, digital scarcity, interoperability, smart contracts, and enhanced security. These features, coupled with the benefits of ownership, security, economic ecosystems, user control, cross-platform integration, reduced transaction costs, and community governance, make blockchain a valuable enabler for the future of the Metaverse.

Challenges and limitations of blockchain in the Metaverse context

While blockchain technology has many advantages for the Metaverse, it also faces several challenges and limitations. Let's explore these in more detail:

Challenges of Blockchain in the Metaverse:

1. Scalability: Blockchain networks, particularly public ones like Bitcoin and Ethereum, often need help with scalability. The Metaverse will require massive transaction throughput to support real-time interactions, in-game transactions, and the movement of assets. Scaling solutions are necessary to meet these demands.

2. Latency: The Metaverse requires low latency to provide a seamless, immersive experience. Blockchain networks can introduce delays due to the time it takes to reach a consensus on transactions. This can impact real-time interactions and gameplay.

3. Energy Consumption: Proof of Work (PoW) consensus mechanisms, used by some significant blockchains, are energy-intensive. Given the ecological concerns surrounding energy consumption, this is a considerable challenge in the context of the Metaverse, where large-scale adoption can exacerbate environmental issues.

4. User-Friendly Interfaces: Many blockchain applications still need to be more user-friendly. To make the Metaverse accessible to a broad audience, user interfaces and interactions with blockchain systems must be intuitive and straightforward.

5. Regulatory Challenges: The Metaverse may face regulatory hurdles related to blockchain technology. Digital asset taxation, identity verification, and legal jurisdiction can be complex in a decentralised, global virtual environment.

6. Data Privacy: Blockchain's transparency can conflict with the privacy expectations of Metaverse users. Striking a balance between transparency and user privacy is challenging, especially when handling sensitive personal information in virtual worlds.

Limitations of Blockchain in the Metaverse:

1. Storage and Bandwidth: Storing and transmitting vast amounts of virtual world data on a blockchain can be expensive and slow. While specific blockchain solutions aim to address this, it remains a limitation.

2. Interoperability: While blockchain can promote interoperability, achieving a seamless exchange of assets and identities between different virtual worlds is a complex task. Standards and protocols need to be established to ensure effective interoperability.

3. On-Chain Governance: Decentralized governance on the blockchain can sometimes be slow and inefficient when quick decisions are needed, which is common in dynamic Metaverse environments.

4. Security Risks: While blockchain is secure, the Metaverse introduces new security risks. Hacks and attacks can target virtual assets and personal information. Users must be educated on security practices, and robust security measures are essential.

5. Market Fragmentation: Multiple blockchains with different features and capabilities may lead to fragmentation in the Metaverse. Users might need to navigate multiple blockchain ecosystems, which can be confusing and hinder a unified experience.

6. Economic Disparities: Blockchain-based assets and economies can create economic disparities in the Metaverse. Early adopters and those with significant resources can gain an advantage, potentially excluding others from participation.

7. Legal Challenges: Determining legal ownership and rights in the Metaverse can be complex, and blockchain's immutability can pose challenges if disputes arise. Legal frameworks need to adapt to this new virtual reality.

Blockchain holds promise for the Metaverse but has challenges and limitations. Among the challenges are scalability, latency, energy consumption, regulatory issues, and user-friendliness. The limitations include storage and bandwidth constraints, interoperability hurdles, on-chain governance issues, security risks, market fragmentation, economic disparities, and legal complexities. Overcoming these challenges and addressing these limitations will be critical for successfully integrating blockchain technology in the Metaverse.

SMART CONTRACTS IN THE METAVERSE

Definition And Characteristics of Smart Contracts

Definition of Smart Contracts:

Smart contracts are autonomous agreements in which the contractual terms and conditions are encoded directly into computer code, enabling them to execute themselves without human intervention. The contracts are implemented on blockchain platforms and autonomously carry out, enforce, or facilitate the terms of the agreement upon the fulfilment of predetermined criteria or triggers. Smart contracts can eliminate the necessity of intermediaries in executing conventional contracts, diminishing the likelihood of conflicts, errors, and dependence on centralised authority. Smart contracts are an essential element of blockchain technology, facilitating the secure and trustless execution of various transactions and processes.

The attributes of smart contracts include:

Characteristics of Smart Contracts:

> Self-execution: Smart contracts automatically execute when the specified conditions are met, ensuring that contractual agreements are enforced without manual intervention.
> Automation: They automate complex processes and transactions, reducing the risk of human error and streamlining workflows.
> Immutable: Once deployed on a blockchain, smart contracts are typically firm, meaning their code and execution cannot be altered or tampered with, enhancing trust and security.
> Trust and Transparency: Smart contracts operate on a blockchain, which is a transparent and tamper-resistant ledger. This transparency builds trust among parties as contract execution can be independently verified.
> Decentralisation: Smart contracts run on decentralised blockchain networks, reducing the reliance on centralised authorities or intermediaries, which can lead to more trust and autonomy for participants.

> Cost Efficiency: By removing intermediaries, smart contracts can reduce transaction costs associated with traditional contract execution, making them economically efficient.

> Conditional Logic: Smart contracts rely on conditional statements, often using "if-then" logic to determine when and how actions should be executed based on predefined conditions.

> Cryptographic Security: Security is maintained through cryptographic methods. Participants in the network use digital signatures to authenticate their identity and ensure the integrity of the contract.

> Global Reach: Smart contracts are not bound by geographical limitations. They can be accessed and executed by parties worldwide, making them ideal for international transactions.

> Real-time Updates: Smart contracts can incorporate real-time data, enabling dynamic adjustments based on changing conditions, particularly useful in financial applications.

> Integration: Smart contracts can be integrated with other applications, services, or smart devices, expanding their utility in various industries beyond finance, such as supply chain management, insurance, and healthcare.

> Permissioned or Permissionless: Depending on the blockchain platform, smart contracts can be either open for anyone to use (permissionless) or restricted to specific participants (permissioned).

> Auditable: The blockchain's ledger records all transactions and contract executions, making it easy to audit and verify the history of the contract.

Smart contracts are automated, self-executing agreements that operate on blockchain networks. They are characterised by their immutability, trust, transparency, decentralisation, cost efficiency, cryptographic security, conditional logic, and adaptability to various applications. These characteristics make intelligent contracts a promising technology for revolutionising contract execution and automating multiple processes across different industries.

Role of Smart Contracts in the Metaverse

Intelligent contracts are of the utmost importance in constructing and functioning the Metaverse, an immersive, interconnected, and virtual environment. Their function can be briefly outlined in various pivotal facets:

Intelligent contracts are crucial in developing and operating the Metaverse, a virtual, interconnected, and immersive digital world. Their role can be summarised in several key aspects:

1. Digital Ownership and Property Rights: Smart contracts in the Metaverse enable the creation and enforcement of digital property rights. Users can have verifiable ownership of virtual assets, including virtual real estate, avatars, in-game items, and digital collectables. These assets can be bought, sold, or transferred with the assurance that the ownership is secure and transparent.

2. Virtual Economies: Smart contracts underpin virtual economies within the Metaverse. Users can trade digital assets, participate in in-game transactions, and conduct financial interactions using blockchain-based tokens and cryptocurrencies. This economic ecosystem allows for the exchange of value within the virtual world.

3. Asset Interoperability: Smart contracts promote interoperability between virtual spaces and Metaverse platforms. They enable seamless digital assets and identities to be transferred across various virtual worlds and games, creating a unified and interconnected user experience.

4. Decentralized Governance: Decentralized autonomous organisations (DAOs) built on blockchain can govern Metaverse's rules and policies. Users can collectively make decisions, vote on changes, and participate in virtual world governance through clever contract-based voting mechanisms.

5. In-World Services: Smart contracts facilitate the provision of in-world services and utilities. For example, they can govern virtual land rental agreements, automate in-game item trading, and ensure revenue sharing among content creators. This reduces the need for centralised intermediaries and enhances the efficiency of virtual service delivery.

6. Digital Identities: Smart contracts can provide users with secure and portable digital identities. Users can maintain consistent identities across various virtual spaces while retaining control over their personal information, ensuring privacy and security in the Metaverse.

7. Trust and Security: The transparent and immutable nature of blockchain-based intelligent contracts builds trust among Metaverse participants. Users can be confident in the fairness of digital transactions and the security of their virtual property.

8. Real-time Updates: Smart contracts can incorporate real-time data and environmental variables, allowing for dynamic adjustments and interactions within the Metaverse. This is particularly valuable in scenarios where virtual experiences change in response to user actions or external events.

9. Content Monetization: Content creators in the Metaverse can use intelligent contracts to monetise their work. They can receive payments, royalties, and tips in cryptocurrencies or blockchain-based tokens directly from users, reducing reliance on traditional payment methods and intermediaries.

10. Legal Frameworks: Smart contracts can automate and streamline legal processes and contract execution in the Metaverse. However, they also pose new legal challenges related to digital property rights, dispute resolution, and jurisdiction, requiring the development of legal frameworks to address these issues.

In essence, smart contracts in the Metaverse enhance digital ownership, foster virtual economies, ensure asset interoperability, support decentralised governance, enable in-world services, provide digital identities, establish trust and security, offer real-time updates, empower content creators, and drive the development of legal frameworks. They are an essential technology that underpins the seamless, secure, and decentralised operation of the Metaverse, offering users new levels of control and economic opportunities within this digital realm.

Use cases and applications of smart contracts in the Metaverse.

Smart contracts in the Metaverse have many use cases and applications, revolutionising how transactions and interactions occur within this digital, interconnected world. Here are some notable use cases and applications of smart contracts in the Metaverse:

i) Virtual Real Estate Transactions: Smart contracts can automate virtual real estate purchases, sales, and rentals within the Metaverse. Users can secure ownership of digital properties, and transactions are executed automatically when payment is confirmed.

ii) Digital Collectibles: Smart contracts enable the creation and trade of digital collectables, such as virtual trading cards, art, or unique in-game items. Users can have verifiable ownership and value transfer of these digital assets.

iii) Virtual Currency and Microtransactions: Smart contracts facilitate using virtual currencies and microtransactions within the Metaverse. Users can make small, frequent payments for in-game purchases, virtual services, or access to premium content.

iv) Content Creation and Monetization: Content creators can use intelligent contracts to monetise their work. They can receive payments, royalties, and donations directly from users, ensuring fair compensation for their contributions to the Metaverse.

v) Virtual Identity and Avatars: Smart contracts allow users to create and manage digital identities and avatars. These identities can be used consistently across different virtual worlds and experiences, enhancing personalisation and recognition.

vi) Decentralised Autonomous Organizations (DAOs): Smart contracts enable the creation of DAOs within the Metaverse. Users can participate in the governance of virtual communities, voting on rules, policies, and content curation.

vii) Secure Escrow Services: Smart contracts can provide escrow services for Metaverse transactions. They hold assets or funds in trust until predefined conditions are met, ensuring safe and fair exchanges.

viii) Virtual Events and Ticketing: Smart contracts can manage virtual events and ticket sales. They can issue, validate, and enforce digital tickets to access concerts, conferences, and other virtual gatherings.

ix) Real-time Dynamic Gameplay: Smart contracts can adjust in-game conditions and interactions based on real-time data and user actions. This can create immersive and ever-changing gaming experiences.

x) Virtual Land and Property Management: Smart contracts automate virtual land and property management, including land registration, taxation, and rental agreements. Users can securely trade or rent virtual land parcels within the Metaverse.

xi) Gamified Incentives: Smart contracts can implement gamified incentives and rewards for users, encouraging participation and engagement within the virtual world. These incentives can be programmed to distribute rewards automatically.

xii) Decentralised Marketplaces: Smart contracts can power decentralised marketplaces within the Metaverse. Users can buy and sell virtual assets, services, or experiences directly without relying on centralised intermediaries.

xiii) Cross-Platform Asset Transfer: Smart contracts promote the interoperability of digital assets and identities between different virtual platforms and worlds, enabling seamless transitions and experiences.

xiv) Secure and Private Messaging: Smart contracts can enhance messaging systems by providing fast and private communication channels, ensuring user privacy and data security.

xv) Virtual Legal Agreements: Smart contracts can automate legal agreements and contract execution within the Metaverse. They can be used for dispute resolution, property rights, and other legal interactions.

These use cases illustrate how intelligent contracts are integral to the development of the Metaverse, providing the infrastructure for secure and automated transactions, content creation, governance, and the establishment of trust and ownership in this digital universe. As the Metaverse continues to evolve, the applications of smart contracts are likely to expand and diversify even further.

Benefits And Challenges of Implementing Smart Contracts In The Metaverse

Implementing smart contracts in the Metaverse offers various benefits and, at the same time, presents unique challenges. Here's an in-depth exploration of both aspects.

Benefits of Implementing Smart Contracts in the Metaverse:

> Trust and Security: Smart contracts provide high trust and security in the Metaverse. Transactions and agreements are executed automatically, and the immutable nature of the blockchain ensures that once a contract is deployed, its terms cannot be altered or tampered with.

> Efficiency: Smart contracts automate many processes in the Metaverse, reducing the need for intermediaries and manual interventions. This increases efficiency in handling transactions, content distribution, and digital asset ownership.

> Transparency: Transactions and contract execution are recorded on the blockchain, providing complete transparency. Users can verify every

action taken, fostering trust in the system.

> Decentralisation: Smart contracts are executed on decentralised blockchain networks, reducing the risk of centralised control or manipulation. This aligns with the principles of the Metaverse, where decentralisation is a core feature.

> Interoperability: Smart contracts can be designed to operate across various virtual worlds and Metaverse platforms, allowing for seamless asset transfers and experiences as users move between different digital environments.

> Digital Ownership: Smart contracts enable users to have verifiable and secure ownership of virtual assets, digital content, and virtual real estate within the Metaverse.

> Economic Opportunities: Content creators, artists, developers, and users can monetise their activities and creations through intelligent contracts. This opens up new economic opportunities within the Metaverse.

> Customisation: Smart contracts can be tailored to suit different virtual communities' specific needs and rules, providing flexibility in the Metaverse's governance and operations.

Challenges of Implementing Smart Contracts in the Metaverse:

> Technical Complexity: Developing and deploying smart contracts requires a deep understanding of blockchain technology, which can be a barrier for some users and developers.

> Security Risks: While smart contracts offer security, they are not immune to vulnerabilities. Bugs or coding errors in smart contracts can lead to exploits and losses of digital assets.

> Legal and Regulatory Issues: The legality of smart contracts in various jurisdictions and their enforcement in case of disputes is a complex issue that requires legal frameworks to evolve and adapt to the Metaverse.

> Scalability: As the Metaverse grows, the demand for smart contracts increases, potentially leading to scalability issues on some blockchain networks. This can result in slower transaction speeds and higher fees.

> Privacy Concerns: While blockchain provides transparency, it may also expose user data. Balancing privacy and transparency is challenging, especially for sensitive information in the Metaverse.

> User Education: Users need to understand how smart contracts work and how to interact with them. This education process can be time-

consuming and may deter some from fully participating in the Metaverse.
> Interoperability Challenges: While interoperability is a benefit, it also presents challenges in ensuring smart contracts work seamlessly across different Metaverse platforms, given their varying technological infrastructures.
> Content Management: Ensuring digital content, especially user-generated content, adheres to copyright, licensing, and content moderation rules can be challenging within decentralised environments.
> Decentralised Governance: While DAOs and smart contracts enable decentralised governance, decision-making processes may be slow, and disputes may be challenging to resolve.

Implementing smart contracts in the Metaverse offers numerous advantages, including trust, efficiency, transparency, and economic opportunities. However, challenges such as technical complexity, security risks, legal considerations, and the need for user education must be addressed to fully realise the potential of smart contracts in this emerging digital frontier.

LEGAL IMPLICATIONS IN THE METAVERSE

Overview Of Legal Issues in The Metaverse

Legal issues in the Metaverse are complex and multifaceted, spanning many areas. As this virtual realm expands and gains prominence, legal frameworks are evolving to address its unique challenges. Here's an overview of the critical legal issues in the Metaverse.

1. **Digital Property Rights:** Determining ownership and property rights in the Metaverse is challenging. Users and creators own virtual assets, digital real estate, and in-game items, but these rights' legal recognition and protection can be uncertain.
2. **Intellectual Property:** The Metaverse hosts a large amount of user-generated content, including virtual art, music, and 3D models. Enforcing copyright, trademark, and intellectual property rights in the virtual world is complex.
3. **Jurisdiction and Governance:** Determining which legal jurisdiction governs activities and disputes in the Metaverse is a significant challenge.

Virtual communities often need more centralised governance, making it easier to enforce traditional legal standards.

4. Privacy and Data Protection: Privacy concerns arise in the Metaverse as users interact with others and share personal information. Ensuring data protection and privacy rights while maintaining transparency is a delicate balance.

5. Smart Contracts and Legal Enforceability: Smart contracts play a vital role in the Metaverse but raise questions about their enforceability in a legal context. Parties may need legal recourse when smart contract disputes arise.

6. Virtual Crime and Cybersecurity: Virtual spaces are not immune to cybercrimes such as hacking, fraud, and identity theft. Law enforcement faces challenges in pursuing criminals who operate within decentralised virtual environments.

7. Digital Identity and Authentication: Verifying the identity of users in the Metaverse is a legal and security concern. Digital identity theft and fraudulent activities pose risks that need to be addressed.

8. Child Protection and Age Verification: Protecting minors in the Metaverse is a priority. Implementing age verification mechanisms and ensuring that age-appropriate content is accessible are legal issues to consider.

9. Virtual Economies and Taxation: Taxation in virtual economies and the Metaverse is a growing concern. Defining tax policies for digital transactions and assets poses a challenge for governments.

10. Virtual Harassment and Cyberbullying: Ensuring a safe and respectful environment in the Metaverse is essential. Addressing issues of harassment, bullying, and harmful behaviour is a legal and community challenge.

11. Regulatory Compliance: Various industries, such as gaming, finance, and entertainment, are integrating with the Metaverse. Regulatory compliance is essential in ensuring businesses operating in this space adhere to applicable laws and standards.

12. Liability and Accountability: Determining liability for accidents, disputes, and damages within the Metaverse can be complex, especially when multiple parties are involved.

13. Real-World Consequences: Actions in the Metaverse can have real-world consequences. For instance, virtual theft or property disputes may lead to legal action in the physical world.

14. Content Moderation: Balancing free expression with content moderation is challenging. Communities in the Metaverse must address harmful content, misinformation, and extremism while respecting users' rights.

15. Cross-Metaverse Disputes: As users navigate between different Metaverse platforms, resolving disputes that transcend platforms and ecosystems is a legal and technical challenge.

16. Ethical and Moral Dilemmas: The Metaverse raises ethical and moral dilemmas, such as questions about the digital representation of people, the creation and use of AI, and the impact of virtual reality on society.

The legal issues in the Metaverse are diverse and evolving. Addressing these challenges requires collaboration between legal experts, technology developers, policymakers, and the Metaverse community to develop appropriate legal frameworks that protect users' rights and ensure the responsible growth of this digital frontier.

Intellectual property rights and ownership in the Metaverse

The intricate and multifaceted nature of intellectual property rights and ownership in the Metaverse reflects the complex interplay between legal frameworks, technology, and creativity in this emergent digital landscape. In the ever-changing landscape, many intellectual property forms—such as copyright, trademarks, patents, and the comparatively recent classification of Non-Fungible Tokens (NFTs)—remain significant.

Copyright is one of the most pervasive forms of intellectual property protection in the Metaverse. It applies to digital content, including written works, virtual artwork, music, 3D models, and videos. Copyright protection is typically reserved for original content creators in the Metaverse. Consequently, unauthorised reproduction, distribution, or performance of such works is strictly prohibited. Particularly evident is the difficulty in safeguarding these rights, given the ease with which content can be duplicated and distributed on digital platforms.

In the Metaverse, trademarks serve an essential function by safeguarding corporations, logos, and symbols. Virtual businesses and organisations must protect their trademarks against infringement by other entities or users within the digital realm. Although the Metaverse is a domain of ingenuity and novelty, it must uphold established trademarks and intellectual property rights.

While patents are less prevalent in the Metaverse than copyrights and trademarks, they remain significant. Patent protection may be extended to innovations in virtual technologies, virtual reality hardware, or software functionalities. These patents serve to acknowledge and safeguard technological advancements within the Metaverse.

In the Metaverse, Non-Fungible Tokens (NFTs) constitute a distinct type of intellectual property. They signify digital assets and can comprise various materials, including virtual real estate and digital artwork. When NFTs are sold, their owners frequently retain certain privileges associated with the underlying asset. Smart contracts, fundamental components of the Metaverse, encapsulate licensing terms that delineate the permissions and restrictions for using the content. These concepts can include copyright attributions and resale restrictions, thereby adding a new dimension to the administration of intellectual property.

Virtual real estate is an essential component of the Metaverse, wherein participants obtain virtual land and property rights that resemble ownership of property in the physical world. Users can construct and expand virtual spaces and frequently assert legal rights to these digital assets. Legal validation and safeguarding of virtual property rights are of the utmost importance in this decentralised setting to ensure enforceable and secure ownership.

Digital personas representing Metaverse users are also susceptible to intellectual property rights. Individuals can claim proprietorship over their avatars' visual and conceptual aspects; any unauthorised reproduction or utilisation of these depictions may violate their intellectual property rights.

Constantly balancing the notion of fair use in the Metaverse presents a challenge. Although fair use permits the unrestricted utilisation of copyrighted material for critical, informative, or scholarly purposes without requiring permission, its implementation in the digital realm can be intricate. The task of ascertaining fair use in the Metaverse, a dynamic and creative environment, necessitates meticulous deliberation.

As a cross-platform ecosystem, the Metaverse consists of numerous virtual realms, each with its regulations and legal frameworks. The consistent recognition and enforcement of intellectual property rights and ownership across these heterogeneous platforms present a formidable legal and logistical obstacle.

Intellectual property rights and ownership play a crucial role in the Metaverse by promoting innovation and creativity while upholding the rights of content creators and rights holders. In an ever-evolving digital landscape, governments, creators, users, and platforms must work together to establish a legal framework that effectively safeguards intellectual property rights and fosters a prosperous virtual environment.

Digital Assets and Virtual Property Rights

Digital assets and virtual property rights are core components of the Metaverse, where users and businesses invest in and own various forms of virtual property and assets. Here's a detailed exploration of digital assets and virtual property rights in the context of the Metaverse:

1. **Virtual Real Estate:** In the Metaverse, virtual real estate consists of digital lands, buildings, and spaces that users can own and develop. These properties can serve as social interactions, events, businesses, and entertainment locations. Blockchain technology and NFTs often secure ownership, providing users with verifiable property rights.

2. **Non-Fungible Tokens (NFTs):** NFTs are digital tokens that represent ownership of unique virtual assets, whether it's virtual art, collectables, in-game items, or virtual real estate. NFTs provide a means of asserting ownership over digital assets in the Metaverse and are often linked to smart contracts that define their characteristics and ownership rules.

3. **In-Game Items and Virtual Currency:** Many Metaverse environments feature in-game items and virtual currency, which users can acquire, trade, or purchase. Digital property rights are crucial here, as users invest real money in these items, and clear ownership and transfer mechanisms are needed.

4. User-Generated Content: Users in the Metaverse generate content, including 3D models, virtual fashion, virtual art, and music. Virtual property rights pertain to these creations, allowing creators to control and monetise their content and define how others can use or remix it.

5. Avatar and Identity Customization: Customization of avatars and digital identities is a fundamental aspect of the Metaverse. Users may assert ownership over the designs and appearances of their avatars, potentially extending to custom clothing and accessories.

6. Intellectual Property and Content Licensing: Users often license their content and virtual property through intelligent contracts, specifying how others can use, purchase, or experience their creations. These licenses can encompass terms for royalties, resale rights, and copyright protections.

7. Digital Collectibles: Collectibles in the Metaverse, like virtual trading cards, digital pets, and limited edition items, are subject to digital property rights. Collectors purchase, trade, and collect these virtual assets, with NFTs representing ownership.

8. Virtual Pet Ownership: Some Metaverse platforms offer virtual pets for users to raise and care for. These virtual pets have unique characteristics; users can assert ownership rights over them.

9. Smart Contracts and Ownership Verification: Intelligent contracts often confirm ownership of digital assets and virtual property. These contracts define the ownership rules, verify authenticity, and provide a transparent record of ownership changes.

10. Digital Theft and Security: Protecting digital assets and virtual property from theft, fraud, or hacking is a critical concern. Blockchain technology, cryptographic security measures, and decentralised storage solutions help safeguard these assets.

11. Legal and Regulatory Considerations: As the Metaverse matures, legal and regulatory frameworks are evolving to address virtual property rights. Governments and legal authorities are exploring how to apply existing property laws and intellectual property rights to digital assets and virtual property.

12. Cross-Metaverse Property: As users traverse different Metaverse platforms, ensuring consistent property rights and asset ownership standards is challenging. Interoperability and standards for digital property rights are areas of ongoing development.

In the Metaverse, digital assets and virtual property rights are fundamental to the user experience and economic activities. Ownership and control over these assets are managed through blockchain technology, NFTs, and smart contracts, ensuring that users can invest in, create, and enjoy the unique virtual world while asserting their rights as digital property owners.

Jurisdictional Challenges and Regulatory Considerations

Jurisdictional challenges and regulatory considerations are pivotal aspects of the Metaverse as it operates across borders and challenges traditional legal frameworks. Navigating these challenges is essential for ensuring legal compliance and a safe user environment. Here's an in-depth exploration of jurisdictional challenges and regulatory considerations in the Metaverse:

i) Legal Frameworks: Existing legal frameworks may need to adequately address the novel aspects of the Metaverse, such as virtual property rights, digital assets, and smart contracts. Policymakers and legal experts must adapt or create new regulations to address these unique challenges.

ii) Intellectual Property and Copyright: Protecting intellectual property in the Metaverse, where users create and trade digital assets, is complex. Copyright laws need to be adapted to cover virtual content and user-generated creations.

iii) Privacy and Data Protection: Privacy laws vary globally, and the Metaverse collects and handles user data. Adhering to diverse data protection regulations while maintaining transparency can be challenging.

iv) Age Restrictions and Child Protection: A priority is to protect minors from inappropriate content and interactions in the Metaverse. Implementing age verification mechanisms and compliance with child protection laws are necessary.

v) Cybersecurity and Digital Theft: The Metaverse is susceptible to cybercrimes, including hacking, fraud, and identity theft. Legal authorities need to address these crimes and enforce cybercrime laws in a virtual context.

vi) Virtual Property and Real-World Consequences: Virtual property and digital asset disputes in the Metaverse can have real-world consequences, requiring legal mechanisms to address real-world remedies, compensation, and liability.

vii) Content Moderation and Community Guidelines: Ensuring user-generated content complies with regulations, including content moderation and adherence to community guidelines, is essential for maintaining a safe and respectful environment.

viii) Taxation and Virtual Economies: The Metaverse has complex financial transactions and virtual economies. Governments must establish clear tax policies for digital transactions and assets and enforce tax compliance.

ix) International Cooperation: The global nature of the Metaverse necessitates international cooperation in addressing jurisdictional challenges. Agreements and standards are needed to harmonise regulations and establish a framework for cross-border activities.

x) Legal Disputes and Resolution: There must be precise mechanisms for legal resolution when disputes arise in the Metaverse. These mechanisms might involve traditional legal proceedings, arbitration, or decentralised autonomous organisations (DAOs) for dispute resolution.

xi) Blockchain and Smart Contracts: Legal recognition and enforcement of smart contracts and blockchain transactions must be clarified. The application of existing contract law to these technologies is an evolving area.

xii) Ethical and Moral Considerations: The Metaverse raises ethical and moral questions related to digital identity, AI, and the impact of virtual reality on society. Policymakers must consider these aspects while creating regulations.

xiii) Regulatory Framework for Businesses: Various industries, such as gaming, finance, and entertainment, are integrating with the Metaverse. Regulatory compliance for businesses operating in this space is crucial.

xiv) Standardisation and Interoperability: Establishing standards and protocols for interoperability and cross-platform compatibility is vital to creating a cohesive and user-friendly Metaverse.

Jurisdictional challenges and regulatory considerations are pivotal in shaping the legal landscape of the Metaverse. Addressing these challenges involves international cooperation, adapting legal frameworks, and the establishment of clear guidelines for users and businesses. Legal experts, policymakers, and the Metaverse community must collaborate to ensure a safe, compliant, innovative digital realm.

The concept of decentralisation in the Metaverse presents unique jurisdictional challenges, as it disrupts traditional legal frameworks and makes it difficult to determine the appropriate legal jurisdiction for activities and disputes. Here, we delve into the complexities surrounding decentralisation and jurisdiction in the context of the Metaverse:

Decentralisation in the Metaverse:

Decentralisation is a core feature of the Metaverse, where power and control are distributed among network participants rather than concentrated in a central authority. This decentralisation is achieved through blockchain technology and smart contracts, which operate autonomously without intermediaries. In the Metaverse, decentralisation is evident in various aspects:

i) Virtual Property Ownership: Users can own and trade virtual property and assets through blockchain technology, eliminating the need for intermediaries like real estate agents or brokers.

ii) Digital Identity: Users can control their digital identities and avatars without relying on centralised identity verification systems. This enhances privacy and user control.

iii) Transactions: Financial transactions in the Metaverse are conducted directly between users through smart contracts, reducing the need for banks or payment processors.

iv) Content Distribution: User-generated content can be monetised without reliance on centralised platforms, giving creators greater autonomy.

Jurisdictional Challenges:

i) Determining Legal Jurisdiction: The decentralised nature of the Metaverse complicates the determination of the legal jurisdiction under which disputes and activities fall. Users may engage with the Metaverse from different parts of the world, and their digital actions may not have a physical location.

ii) Legal Recognition: Traditional legal systems may need help recognising and enforcing contracts, property rights, and transactions conducted in the Metaverse. This raises questions about the enforceability of smart contracts in a decentralised context.

iii) International Legal Cooperation: Jurisdictional disputes that span multiple countries require international cooperation. Harmonising legal standards and cross-border collaboration are essential to address these complex cases.

iv) Data Privacy: Data privacy and protection becomes challenging when user data is stored and processed across a decentralised network. Balancing the rights of individuals with regulatory requirements poses a legal problem.

v) Regulatory Compliance: Businesses operating within the Metaverse must navigate complex and often ambiguous regulatory environments. Compliance with local, national, and international regulations is a significant challenge.

vi) Legal Disputes: When disputes arise in the Metaverse, it may need to be clarified where they should be prosecuted. Traditional legal mechanisms like courts may not easily fit within the decentralised context.

vii) Virtual Property Rights: Determining and enforcing property rights in virtual real estate and digital assets involve unique legal challenges. Ownership claims in a decentralised environment may be disputed.

viii) Taxation: Taxation within a decentralised system poses a challenge. Governments need to adapt tax policies to digital transactions and ensure compliance.

ix) Content Moderation: Traditional content moderation laws may not align with the decentralised nature of the Metaverse. Defining and enforcing content standards are complex tasks.

In the Metaverse, decentralisation offers users autonomy and control but necessitates evaluating existing legal systems to address jurisdictional challenges. Policymakers, legal experts, and international organisations must collaborate to create legal frameworks that adapt to this decentralised digital frontier while preserving user rights and safety. Finding solutions that balance decentralisation with legal accountability is an ongoing endeavour.

ECONOMIC INNOVATIONS IN THE METAVERSE

Tokenisation and virtual currencies in the Metaverse

Tokenisation and virtual currencies play a significant role in the Metaverse, enabling digital economies, ownership, and interactions. These concepts provide the foundation for various financial activities and decentralised systems within the Metaverse. Here, we delve into the details of tokenisation and virtual currencies in the Metaverse:

Tokenisation:

i) Digital Assets as Tokens: Tokenization refers to representing real or virtual assets as digital tokens on blockchain networks. In the Metaverse, assets like virtual real estate, digital art, collectables, and real-world assets can be tokenised, allowing for fractional ownership and transferability.

ii) Non-Fungible Tokens (NFTs): NFTs are a specialised form of tokenisation used to represent unique and indivisible assets. They have gained immense popularity in the Metaverse for trading digital art, virtual property, and in-game items.

iii) Fungible Tokens: Fungible tokens, like cryptocurrencies (e.g., Ethereum, Bitcoin), are also used in the Metaverse for transactions, virtual economies, and financial activities. These interchangeable tokens can be used for various purposes, including purchases, investments, and trading.

iv) Smart Contracts: Smart contracts, powered by blockchain technology, enable the automation of tokenised asset transactions. They define the rules and conditions of the transactions, such as ownership transfers, royalties, and usage rights.

v) Ownership and Provenance: Tokenization provides a clear record of ownership and provenance for digital assets in the Metaverse. Users can verify the authenticity and history of assets through blockchain records.

Virtual Currencies:

i) Metaverse Currencies: Some virtual worlds and platforms within the Metaverse have their native digital currencies. These currencies are used for in-world transactions, trading, and economic activities. Examples include Decentraland's MANA and The Sandbox's SAND.

ii) Cryptocurrencies: Cryptocurrencies like Bitcoin and Ethereum are widely used as virtual currencies in the Metaverse. They facilitate cross-platform transactions and are often the primary means of exchange for digital assets and services.

iii) Microtransactions: Virtual currencies enable microtransactions, allowing users to make small, frequent payments for content, virtual items, and services in the Metaverse. This microtransaction model is integral to various Metaverse business models.

iv) Interoperability: Virtual currencies can often be used across Metaverse platforms, enhancing interoperability. Users can carry their assets and virtual currencies across various worlds and experiences.

v) Monetisation and Earnings: Virtual currencies are essential for monetising content, services, and experiences in the Metaverse. Creators and developers can earn virtual currencies through sales, subscriptions, and in-world activities.

vi) Digital Economies: Virtual currencies underpin the digital economies of the Metaverse, where users can buy, sell, and trade virtual assets, virtual real estate, and in-game items.

vii) Exchanges and Marketplaces: Cryptocurrency exchanges and virtual marketplaces have emerged in the Metaverse, facilitating the buying and selling virtual assets and currencies. These platforms provide liquidity and price discovery mechanisms.

viii) Decentralised Finance (DeFi): Some elements of decentralised finance, such as lending, borrowing, and yield farming, are beginning to integrate into the Metaverse, offering new financial opportunities to users.

Challenges and Considerations:

i) Regulatory Compliance: Using virtual currencies and tokenised assets in the Metaverse has raised regulatory concerns in various jurisdictions. Ensuring compliance with local and international financial regulations is a critical challenge.

ii) Security and Fraud: As virtual currencies and tokenised assets become more valuable, the Metaverse faces security threats, including hacking and fraud. Security measures are essential to protect users and their digital wealth.

iii) Privacy and Data Protection: Handling financial transactions and user data within the Metaverse raises privacy concerns. Striking the right balance between privacy and transparency is a challenge.

iv) Scalability: The growing popularity of the Metaverse places demands on blockchain networks, leading to scalability challenges. Ensuring efficient and low-cost transactions is an ongoing concern.

Tokenisation and virtual currencies are the backbone of the Metaverse's digital economies, enabling ownership, trade, and financial activities. These concepts are central to the vision of a decentralised and immersive digital reality. However, addressing regulatory, security, and scalability challenges is essential for their continued growth and integration into the Metaverse.

Decentralised finance (DeFi) applications in the Metaverse

Decentralised Finance (DeFi) applications increasingly find their place in the Metaverse, offering innovative financial services, investment opportunities, and economic activities. DeFi leverages blockchain technology and smart contracts to provide trustless and decentralised financial solutions. Here's an exploration of DeFi applications in the Metaverse:

Digital Asset Trading: - DeFi platforms enable users to trade virtual assets and currencies within the Metaverse. This includes buying, selling, and exchanging non-fungible tokens (NFTs), virtual real estate, and in-game items.

Virtual Currency Lending and Borrowing: - DeFi lending and borrowing protocols are extended to virtual currencies used in the Metaverse. Users can lend their virtual currencies in exchange for interest or borrow assets for various purposes, including buying virtual real estate or in-game items.

Yield Farming and Staking: - Yield farming and staking mechanisms are integrated into the Metaverse's digital economies. Users can earn rewards by providing liquidity to decentralised exchanges, participating in governance activities, or staking virtual assets.

Cross-Platform Asset Swaps: - DeFi applications facilitate cross-platform asset swaps, allowing users to exchange virtual assets and currencies across Metaverse platforms. This interoperability enhances the fluidity of the virtual economy.

Tokenization of Virtual Assets: - DeFi solutions enable the tokenisation of virtual assets, such as virtual real estate and digital art. This tokenisation allows users to fractionalise ownership and trade these assets on decentralised exchanges.

Decentralized Autonomous Organizations (DAOs): - DAOs are integrated into the Metaverse to manage governance, decision-making, and investment strategies. Users can participate in Metaverse-specific DAOs to influence the direction of virtual communities and economies.

Asset Management and Yield Optimization: - DeFi platforms in the Metaverse offer asset management services, allowing users to entrust their digital wealth to decentralised protocols, optimising yield and returns.

Liquidity Pools for Virtual Currencies: - Decentralised liquidity pools are established for virtual currencies used in the Metaverse. Users can provide liquidity to these pools and earn rewards through interest or tokens.

Virtual Currency Insurance: - DeFi-based insurance protocols cover virtual assets and virtual currencies in the Metaverse. Users can protect themselves against potential losses due to hacks, theft, or other unforeseen events.

Predictive Markets and Derivatives: - DeFi-based predictive markets and derivatives are integrated into the Metaverse, enabling users to speculate on virtual asset prices and participate in complex financial instruments.

Governance and Community Tokens: - Many Metaverse platforms issue governance tokens, allowing users to participate in decision-making and community governance. These tokens may also have utility within the Metaverse ecosystem.

Cross-Chain and Cross-Metaverse Integration: - DeFi bridges and solutions are developed to facilitate cross-chain and cross-Metaverse interactions, allowing assets and tokens to move seamlessly between different virtual environments.

Challenges and Considerations:

> Security: DeFi applications in the Metaverse must address security vulnerabilities and protect users' digital assets from hacks and vulnerabilities.
> Regulatory Compliance: Regulatory concerns, especially regarding virtual currencies and financial activities, must be addressed to ensure legal compliance in the Metaverse.
> Scalability: As DeFi activities in the Metaverse grow, scalability challenges arise, and efficient solutions are required to handle the increased demand.
> User Education: Users need to understand the complexities of DeFi and its applications in the Metaverse to make informed financial decisions and protect their assets.
> Interoperability: Ensuring seamless interoperability between various Metaverse platforms and DeFi protocols is essential for a cohesive and integrated virtual economy.

DeFi applications are reshaping the financial landscape in the Metaverse, offering new opportunities and challenges. These applications can create a decentralised and user-centric financial ecosystem within the digital realm, enhancing the economic experiences and possibilities in the Metaverse.

Virtual Economies and Marketplaces

Virtual economies and marketplaces are fundamental components of the Metaverse, as they provide the infrastructure for buying, selling, and trading digital assets, virtual currencies, and services within this immersive digital realm. Here, we explore the dynamics of virtual economies and marketplaces in the Metaverse:

1. Digital Asset Trading: - Virtual marketplaces in the Metaverse facilitate the buying and selling digital assets, including virtual real estate, digital art, NFTs, and in-game items. Users can trade these assets with others, often utilising cryptocurrencies and virtual currencies.

2. Virtual Currency Exchanges: - Digital exchanges within the Metaverse allow users to convert between virtual currencies and cryptocurrencies. These platforms offer liquidity and price discovery for the digital economy.

3. Auctions and Bidding: - Some virtual marketplaces host auctions and bidding mechanisms for rare or high-value digital assets. This format is commonly used for unique NFTs and collectables.

4. Decentralized Marketplaces: - Decentralised marketplaces powered by blockchain technology and smart contracts enable users to trade digital assets without intermediaries. These platforms provide trustless and transparent transactions.

5. Virtual Real Estate Transactions: - Virtual real estate marketplaces allow users to buy, sell, and lease virtual land and properties. These transactions often involve intelligent contracts to govern ownership and usage rights.

6. In-Game Marketplaces: - Many virtual worlds and gaming platforms within the Metaverse have in-game marketplaces where users can trade in-game items, virtual currencies, and other digital assets. These items can be used within the game or traded externally.

7. Content Marketplaces: - Through specialised content marketplaces, creators can monetise their digital content, such as 3D models, virtual fashion, and music. Users purchase and use these creations in their virtual experiences.

8. Service Marketplaces: - Virtual service marketplaces connect users with providers offering various services within the Metaverse, from virtual design and development to event planning.

9. Cross-Platform Trading: - Some virtual marketplaces facilitate cross-platform trading, allowing users to buy and sell assets that can be used across different Metaverse platforms and ecosystems.

10. Integration with DeFi: - Virtual marketplaces are increasingly integrating with decentralised finance (DeFi) applications, allowing users to earn, borrow, and lend virtual currencies while participating in the virtual economy.

11. Virtual Economies and Jobs: - Virtual economies within the Metaverse are creating opportunities for users to earn virtual currencies and assets through various activities, including content creation, virtual real estate development, and gaming.

12. Market Data and Analytics: - Marketplaces often provide users with data and analytics to make informed trading decisions, including historical asset prices, trading volumes, and user activity.

13. User-Generated Markets: - Many Metaverse platforms allow users to create virtual marketplaces, fostering a peer-to-peer economy where users can sell, trade, or auction their creations and assets.

Challenges and Considerations:

i) Security and Trust: Ensuring secure and trustworthy transactions is crucial in virtual marketplaces. Security measures and mechanisms are necessary to prevent fraud and scams.

ii) Regulatory Compliance: The operation of virtual economies and marketplaces may involve regulatory considerations related to financial transactions, taxation, and legal compliance.

iii) Monetisation: Creators and service providers in the Metaverse need to explore monetisation strategies and pricing models to generate income from their virtual assets and services.

iv) Market Volatility: The value of virtual assets and currencies in the Metaverse can be volatile, posing risks for traders and investors. Users need to be aware of market fluctuations.

v) User Education: Understanding the dynamics of virtual economies and marketplaces is essential for users to participate effectively and make informed decisions.

vi) Interoperability: Ensuring interoperability and cross-platform compatibility between virtual marketplaces is essential to create a cohesive digital economy in the Metaverse.

Virtual economies and marketplaces are central to the Metaverse's vision, enabling users to engage in commerce, create value, and participate in an immersive digital economy. The development and expansion of these markets contribute to the evolving landscape of the Metaverse.

Impact Of Economic Innovations on The Metaverse Ecosystem

Economic innovations profoundly shape the Metaverse ecosystem, usher in new possibilities, redefine value creation, and enhance user experiences in this digital realm. These innovations are integral to the evolution of the Metaverse. Let's explore the impact of economic innovations on the Metaverse ecosystem:

1. Virtual Property Ownership and Monetization:

Economic innovations have enabled users to own, trade, and monetise virtual properties. Virtual real estate, in particular, has become a significant asset class within the Metaverse. Users can purchase and develop land and generate income through businesses, events, and rent.

2. Digital Collectibles and NFTs:

The rise of non-fungible tokens (NFTs) has revolutionised the concept of digital ownership. Users can buy, sell, and trade unique digital collectables, art, and assets. These innovations have empowered artists and creators, providing new revenue streams.

3. Virtual Economies and In-World Jobs:

Economic innovations have given rise to virtual economies where users can earn virtual currencies and assets through various activities. Content creators, designers, developers, and event planners can find employment and generate income within the Metaverse.

4. Decentralized Finance (DeFi) Integration:

DeFi applications are integrated into the Metaverse, offering financial services, lending, borrowing, and yield farming opportunities. Users can leverage DeFi protocols to optimise their virtual wealth and participate in decentralised economic activities.

5. Virtual Currency and Microtransactions:

Microtransactions are a cornerstone of the Metaverse, allowing users to make small, frequent payments for content, services, and in-game items. Innovations in microtransactions drive revenue for content creators and provide affordable options for users.

6. Tokenization of Virtual Assets:

Users can tokenise their virtual assets, including digital art, fashion, and in-game items. This tokenisation allows for fractional ownership, trading, and investment, unlocking new value propositions.

7. Digital Asset Marketplaces and Auctions:

Economic innovations in the form of digital asset marketplaces and auctions provide a vibrant ecosystem for users to trade, invest, and discover rare and unique digital assets. These platforms create liquidity and price discovery mechanisms.

8. Cross-Metaverse and Cross-Platform Integration:

The Metaverse is becoming increasingly interconnected, allowing users to carry their assets and virtual identities across different Metaverse platforms. This interoperability enhances the user experience and expands economic opportunities.

9. Virtual Reality and Augmented Reality Commerce:

Integrating virtual and augmented reality technologies into the Metaverse ecosystem enables immersive shopping experiences, product visualisation, and virtual showrooms. Users can shop and interact with products in virtual spaces.

Challenges and Considerations:

i) Security and Trust: With the rise of virtual assets and currencies, ensuring the security and trustworthiness of transactions is paramount. Security measures and protection against fraud are essential.

ii) Regulatory Landscape: Navigating the regulatory environment, particularly in areas related to virtual currencies, taxation, and financial transactions, remains a challenge.

iii) Market Volatility: The value of virtual assets and currencies in the Metaverse can be volatile, necessitating risk management strategies for users.

iv) User Education: Enhancing user understanding of economic innovations and financial literacy in the Metaverse is vital for users to make informed decisions and protect their assets.

v) Privacy and Data Protection: Managing user data and privacy within the Metaverse is an ongoing challenge, especially as economic activities involve personal information and transactions.

INTEGRATION OF BLOCKCHAIN AND SMART CONTRACTS IN THE METAVERSE

Opportunities And Challenges of Integrating Blockchain and Smart Contracts

Integrating blockchain technology and smart contracts into the Metaverse offers a range of opportunities and challenges that significantly impact the development and operation of this digital realm. Here, we explore both the possibilities and challenges of integrating blockchain and smart contracts in the Metaverse:

Opportunities:

i) Trust and Security: Blockchain's decentralised and immutable ledger enhances trust and security within the Metaverse. It provides a transparent and tamper-proof record of all transactions and asset ownership.

ii) Ownership and Provenance: Blockchain enables users to have clear ownership of virtual assets, including NFTs, virtual real estate, and digital art. Users can verify the provenance and authenticity of these assets.

iii) Decentralisation: Blockchain removes the need for transaction intermediaries, reducing fees and increasing user autonomy. Smart contracts execute predefined actions automatically, further decentralising processes.

iv) Cross-Platform Interoperability: Blockchain standards and protocols enhance cross-platform interoperability, allowing users to carry their assets and identities across Metaverse environments.

v) The tokenisation of Virtual Assets: Users can tokenise virtual assets, allowing for fractional ownership, trading, and investment. This innovation unlocks liquidity and investment opportunities for virtual property and collectables.

vi) Decentralised Finance (DeFi) Integration: DeFi applications integrated with blockchain enable users to lend, borrow, and earn interest on virtual currencies. This expands financial opportunities within the Metaverse.

vii) Transparent and Efficient Transactions: Blockchain technology streamlines transactions by reducing settlement times and transaction costs. It offers transparency and auditability for virtual economies and marketplaces.

viii) Smart Contracts for Automation: Smart contracts automate various processes, from virtual property rental agreements to revenue-sharing arrangements for creators. These self-executing contracts provide efficiency and reduce the need for intermediaries.

ix) User Control and Privacy: Blockchain allows users greater control over their digital identities and data privacy. Users can maintain sovereignty over their virtual personas.

Challenges:

i) Scalability: Scalability challenges persist within blockchain networks, leading to congestion and high transaction fees. Scaling solutions are essential to support the growing user base in the Metaverse.

ii) Regulatory Compliance: Navigating the regulatory landscape is a complex challenge in the Metaverse, especially concerning virtual currencies, smart contracts, and digital asset ownership.

iii) User Experience: The complexity of blockchain and innovative contract interactions can be intimidating for non-technical users. Ensuring a seamless and user-friendly experience is essential.

iv) Security Risks: While blockchain technology is secure, smart contracts are susceptible to vulnerabilities and exploits. Ensuring the security of these contracts and protecting user assets is paramount.

v) Legal Recognition: Achieving legal recognition of blockchain transactions and smart contracts in various jurisdictions is a significant challenge. Many existing laws were designed for something other than these decentralised technologies.

vi) Privacy Concerns: Balancing transparency and privacy in blockchain transactions is challenging, especially in a virtual environment where user data is essential for personalisation and security.

vii) Interoperability: Achieving seamless interoperability across diverse blockchains and Metaverse platforms is an ongoing challenge. Efforts to standardise protocols are essential.

viii) User Education: Users need to understand the intricacies of blockchain technology, smart contracts, and virtual currencies to make informed decisions and protect their assets.

ix) Environmental Impact: Some blockchain networks, particularly those relying on proof-of-work consensus, have faced criticism for their environmental impact. Addressing sustainability concerns is essential.

x) Market Volatility: The Metaverse's virtual currencies can be highly volatile, posing risks to users who may experience fluctuations in the value of their assets.

Integrating blockchain technology and smart contracts into the Metaverse offers numerous opportunities, including enhanced security, decentralisation, and innovative financial services. However, these opportunities come with significant challenges, including scalability, regulatory complexities, and user education, which must be addressed to fully realise the potential of this integration in the digital realm.

Technical considerations and interoperability

Technical considerations and interoperability are critical to building a successful and cohesive Metaverse. Ensuring that different components of the Metaverse can work together seamlessly and efficiently while addressing technical challenges is essential. Here, we delve into the technical considerations and interoperability within the Metaverse:

Technical Considerations:

i) Scalability: The Metaverse is expected to have a vast and growing user base. Ensuring the underlying infrastructure, including blockchain networks, can scale to accommodate the demand is crucial. Scalability solutions like layer-2 solutions and sharding are being explored.

ii) Consensus Mechanisms: Different Metaverse platforms may use varying consensus mechanisms, such as proof of stake or proof of work. Compatibility and integration between these mechanisms must be considered for cross-platform interactions.

iii) Interoperable Protocols: Standardization of protocols is essential for cross-platform compatibility. Creating protocols that can be implemented uniformly across the Metaverse ensures that different components can communicate effectively.

iv) Virtual Reality and Augmented Reality Integration: Integrating virtual reality (VR) and augmented reality (AR) technologies with the Metaverse introduces technical challenges related to rendering, latency, and hardware compatibility. Ensuring a smooth and immersive user experience is a top priority.

v) Data Handling and Storage: Storing and processing user data, including virtual assets and avatars, requires robust and scalable data handling solutions. Blockchain, distributed databases, and cloud computing technologies are considered.

vi) Security and Privacy: Protecting user data and assets in the Metaverse is paramount. Implementing robust security measures, including encryption, authentication, and access controls, is necessary to prevent data breaches and theft.

vii) Content Distribution: Distributing and streaming content, such as 3D models, music, and virtual worlds, poses technical challenges regarding bandwidth, latency, and load balancing. Content delivery networks and edge computing may be employed.

viii) Cross-Platform Integration: Different Metaverse platforms may be built on varying technologies and programming languages. Ensuring cross-platform integration requires comprehensive APIs and development frameworks.

Interoperability:

i) Cross-Platform Compatibility: Interoperability ensures users can carry their virtual assets, identities, and currencies across Metaverse platforms. This allows for a seamless experience as users explore various virtual environments.

ii) Cross-Game Interaction: Gamers often move between different games within the Metaverse. Interoperability enables users to use in-game items, currency, and assets across multiple gaming experiences.

iii) Blockchain Interoperability: Different blockchain networks underpin various Metaverse platforms. Interoperability solutions like cross-chain bridges and asset transfer protocols enable assets to move seamlessly between blockchains.

iv) Decentralised Identity: Solution solutions allow users to maintain their virtual identities and avatars across Metaverse platforms. This interoperability is vital for a consistent user experience.

v) Smart Contract Standardization: Standardizing intelligent contract protocols and languages helps ensure that these self-executing contracts can work consistently across various Metaverse platforms.

vi) Content and Asset Sharing: Users often create content and assets in one virtual world and want to share or sell them to others. Interoperability solutions enable content sharing and cross-platform asset trading.

vii) Marketplace Compatibility: Virtual marketplaces in the Metaverse should support interoperability, allowing users to trade virtual assets and currencies regardless of the platform they originate from.

viii) Cross-Reality Integration: As virtual and augmented reality become more integrated with the Metaverse, ensuring that these technologies can work together seamlessly is a technical challenge that must be addressed.

Challenges:

i) Technical Heterogeneity: Metaverse platforms may differ in their underlying technologies and architecture. Achieving interoperability between such heterogeneous systems is complex.

ii) Standardisation Delays: Standardizing protocols and technologies across the Metaverse can take time, delaying achieving full interoperability.

iii) Scalability and Performance: Ensuring that interoperable solutions can scale and perform efficiently is a technical challenge, especially when dealing with a large and diverse user base.

iv) Privacy and Security: Handling user data and assets in an interoperable environment requires robust privacy and security measures to prevent breaches or misuse.

v) User Experience: The technical complexity of achieving interoperability should be manageable for the user experience. Ensuring a seamless and user-friendly experience is essential.

Technical considerations and interoperability are vital for creating a cohesive and user-friendly Metaverse. Standardisation, cross-platform compatibility, and the ability to seamlessly move assets and identities across the Metaverse are essential objectives that require ongoing development and innovation in this rapidly evolving digital realm.

Scalability And Performance Issues

Scalability and performance issues are significant challenges that must be addressed in developing the Metaverse. As this digital realm continues to expand and accommodate a growing user base, the ability to provide efficient and seamless experiences becomes paramount. Here, we explore the scalability and performance issues in the Metaverse:

Scalability Issues:

i) Growing User Base: The Metaverse is attracting an ever-increasing number of users. As the user base expands, scalability challenges emerge. Virtual worlds and platforms must handle a high volume of concurrent users without degrading the user experience.

ii) Blockchain Scalability: Many Metaverse platforms rely on blockchain technology for asset ownership and transactions. As demand increases, blockchain networks face scalability issues, such as slow transaction times and high fees. This hampers the efficiency of virtual economies.

iii) Data Processing: The Metaverse generates vast amounts of data, including user-generated content, interactions, and virtual property information. Efficiently processing and storing this data while maintaining low latency is a scalability concern.

iv) Content Delivery: Virtual environments often require 3D models, textures, and other content streaming. Scalability challenges arise when multiple users access the same content simultaneously, putting strain on content delivery networks.

v) Cross-Platform Compatibility: Achieving scalability while ensuring cross-platform compatibility is a complex challenge. The Metaverse's expansion requires systems that can interact seamlessly, which can strain existing infrastructure.

Performance Issues:

Latency and Response Time: High latency can disrupt the immersive experience of the Metaverse. Real-time interactions and movements within virtual worlds demand low latency and fast response times to maintain user engagement.

i) Content Rendering: Rendering virtual environments in real-time, especially in VR and AR, can be resource-intensive. Ensuring smooth and detailed rendering without performance degradation is a performance challenge.

ii) Blockchain Congestion: Slow transaction times and high gas fees on blockchain networks impact the performance of virtual economies. Users may experience delays and increased costs when conducting transactions.

iiii) Security and Privacy: Maintaining robust security and privacy measures can affect system performance. Extensive encryption and authentication processes may introduce performance overhead.

iv) Cross-Platform Consistency: Consistency in user experiences and asset rendering across different Metaverse platforms is essential for a seamless transition between environments. Achieving this without performance disparities is challenging.

Solutions and Mitigations:

Scalability Solutions: Implement layer-2 scaling solutions, such as sidechains and state channels, to offload transactions from the main blockchain and increase throughput.

i) Optimised Data Handling: Implement efficient data processing and storage strategies to manage the large volume of user-generated data, such as content caching and distributed databases.

ii) Content Delivery Networks (CDNs): Leverage CDNs and edge computing to reduce latency and improve content delivery for virtual environments and assets.

iii) Interoperability Protocols: Develop standardised interoperability protocols to enhance cross-platform compatibility, allowing assets and data to move seamlessly between Metaverse platforms.

iv) Blockchain Optimization: Choose or develop blockchain networks optimised for the Metaverse's needs, addressing scalability and cost concerns.

v) Advanced Rendering Technologies: Utilize advanced rendering techniques and technologies, including cloud-based rendering, to enhance performance without compromising visual quality.

vi) Security and Privacy Measures: Implement security and privacy solutions that balance protection and performance, such as efficient encryption and data access controls.

vii) Load Balancing: Employ load balancing techniques to distribute server and network loads, ensuring consistent and high-performance experiences for users.

viii) User Experience Optimization: Continuously optimise the user experience to prioritise low latency, smooth interactions, and high-quality rendering while providing adequate performance.

CASE STUDIES AND EXAMPLES OF BLOCKCHAIN AND SMART CONTRACT

1. Decentraland (MANA)

Decentraland (MANA) is a prominent example of blockchain and smart contract integration in the Metaverse. It is a virtual world built on the Ethereum blockchain that allows users to buy, sell, develop, and interact within a decentralised and user-generated virtual environment. Here's an in-depth look at how Decentraland utilises blockchain and smart contracts:

2. Ownership and Virtual Real Estate:

In Decentraland, the entire virtual world is divided into parcels of virtual land, each represented by a non-fungible token (NFT). Smart contracts on the Ethereum blockchain govern the ownership and transfer of these virtual land parcels. Users can buy, sell, and trade these NFTs, giving them complete control over virtual real estate.

3. Content Creation and Monetization:

Users can create content and experiences on their virtual land parcels. This can include everything from 3D models, games, and virtual art galleries to social spaces and events. Smart contracts enable users to monetise their content, setting rules and fees for entry, usage, and transactions within their virtual spaces.

4. Currency and Transactions:

Decentraland has its native cryptocurrency, MANA, which is used for transactions and payments within the virtual world. MANA can buy virtual land, pay for services, and facilitate economic activities within Decentraland. Blockchain technology ensures secure and transparent transactions.

5. Digital Identity and Avatars:

Users have digital avatars representing them in Decentraland. These avatars are tied to blockchain-based identities, allowing for unique and persistent digital personas across the platform. Users' avatars and identities are stored on the blockchain, providing trust and security.

6. Gaming and Interactive Experiences:

The Decentraland platform hosts games and interactive experiences, often powered by smart contracts. Users can participate in activities, earn rewards, and trade in-game assets like wearables and collectables as NFTs.

7. Decentralised Autonomous Organizations (DAOs):

Decentraland has introduced DAOs that use smart contracts for governance and decision-making. MANA holders can participate in these DAOs to influence the development and direction of the virtual world.

8. Events and Festivals:

Decentraland has hosted virtual events and festivals within the platform, demonstrating the potential of blockchain technology in organising and managing large-scale events. Users can participate in these events and engage in blockchain-based transactions, such as buying virtual event tickets.

9. Art Galleries and NFT Showcases:

Many users and organisations have created virtual art galleries and showcases within Decentraland. These spaces display NFT art pieces, demonstrating how blockchain and smart contracts enable the sale and exhibition of digital art in a virtual space.

10. Virtual Real Estate Marketplaces:

Decentraland hosts virtual real estate marketplaces where users can browse, purchase, and develop virtual land. Smart contracts govern the transactions, ensuring transparent and secure ownership transfers.

11. Cross-Platform Interoperability:

Decentraland is exploring cross-platform interoperability, allowing users to carry their avatars, assets, and digital identities to other virtual worlds, contributing to the broader Metaverse ecosystem.

Decentraland exemplifies how blockchain and smart contracts can empower users to own, create, and monetise content and assets in a decentralised and user-driven virtual environment. This integration fosters a dynamic and immersive experience within the Metaverse while providing a secure and transparent framework for virtual property ownership and economic activities.

THE SANDBOX (SAND)

The Sandbox (SAND) is another prominent example of blockchain and smart contract integration in the Metaverse. It's a user-generated virtual world and game creation platform that employs blockchain technology to enable users to build, own, and monetise their virtual experiences and assets. Here's an in-depth look at how The Sandbox utilises blockchain and smart contracts:

1. Virtual Real Estate and LAND:

The primary virtual asset in The Sandbox is called LAND, which represents virtual real estate. Each LAND token is an NFT stored on the Ethereum blockchain. Users can buy, sell, and develop LAND parcels using smart contracts. These smart contracts govern ownership and development rights, offering users complete control over their virtual properties.

2. ASSET and NFT Creation:

The Sandbox allows users to create ASSETS, which can be 3D models, textures, animations, or interactive elements. These ASSETS are represented as NFTs on the blockchain. Users can monetise their creations by selling or licensing them to other users for use in their virtual experiences.

3. SAND Cryptocurrency:

The native cryptocurrency of The Sandbox is SAND, an ERC-20 token on the Ethereum blockchain. SAND is used for transactions, purchases, and interactions within the virtual world. Users can acquire SAND through various means, including gameplay and contributions to the platform.

4. Content Monetization:

Smart contracts govern the monetisation of user-generated content.

Creators can set rules and pricing for using their ASSETS and experiences. Users can pay SAND to access or experience content and services within The Sandbox.

5. Gaming and Experiences:

The Sandbox platform allows users to create and play games and interactive experiences. Smart contracts facilitate in-game transactions, item ownership, and rewards. This includes items, wearables, and other in-game assets represented as NFTs.

6. Governance through DAO:

The Sandbox has a Decentralized Autonomous Organization (DAO) that uses smart contracts for decision-making and platform governance. SAND token holders can vote on proposals and shape the platform's future.

7. Cross-Platform Compatibility:

The Sandbox aims to offer cross-platform compatibility, allowing users to carry their ASSETS and avatars to other virtual worlds and Metaverse environments. Blockchain technology underpins this interoperability.

8. Virtual Art Galleries and Events:

Users and organisations have created virtual art galleries and hosted events within The Sandbox. These events often showcase NFT art pieces, and blockchain transactions enable the sale and exhibition of digital art within the platform.

9. Partnerships and Collaborations:

The Sandbox has collaborated with well-known brands, artists, and game developers to bring recognisable and valuable content and experiences to the platform. These partnerships often involve blockchain-based assets and transactions.

The Sandbox demonstrates how blockchain and intelligent contracts empower users to own and control virtual assets and experiences while providing a platform for creativity, gaming, and economic activities within the Metaverse. Integrating blockchain technology enhances users' and content creators' transparency, security, and monetisation opportunities.

CRYPTOKITTIES

CryptoKitties is one of the early and iconic examples of blockchain and smart contract integration in the Metaverse. It's a blockchain-based game that allows users to collect, breed, and trade unique digital cats, represented as non-fungible tokens (NFTs) on the Ethereum blockchain. Here's a closer look at how CryptoKitties leverages blockchain and smart contracts:

1. Ownership and Unique Digital Cats:

Each CryptoKitty is a unique and collectable digital cat represented by an NFT on the Ethereum blockchain. These NFTs use intelligent contracts to govern each cat's ownership, attributes, and provenance. Users can buy, sell, and trade these digital cats.

2. Breeding and Generative Art:

Breeding CryptoKitties is a core gameplay mechanic. Users can mate two CryptoKitties to create a new NFT with a combination of attributes from the parent cats. This breeding process is controlled by smart contracts, which determine the offspring's attributes.

3. Marketplace and Trading:

CryptoKitties has a marketplace where users can list their cats for sale and conduct transactions. Smart contracts facilitate these peer-to-peer transactions, ensuring secure ownership transfers and the exchange of digital assets.

4. Provenance and Rarity:

Each CryptoKitty's unique characteristics, such as colour, pattern, and traits, are stored on the blockchain. This blockchain-based provenance guarantees the rarity and authenticity of each cat, making some more valuable than others.

5. Collectible and Investment Value:

CryptoKitties have gained value as collectables, with some of the rarest and most unique cats fetching high prices in the secondary market. Some users invest in these digital assets as a form of digital art and collectables.

6. Partnerships and Collaborations:

CryptoKitties has partnered with various brands and organisations to create special edition kitties and themed collections. These partnerships often involve blockchain-based NFTs and limited-edition digital cats.

7. Cross-Platform Integrations:

CryptoKitties has explored cross-platform integrations, allowing users to use their CryptoKitties in other virtual worlds and games, demonstrating the potential for interoperability in the Metaverse.

8. Community and Events:

The CryptoKitties community hosts events, contests, and showcases within the platform, highlighting the creativity and user engagement made possible by blockchain technology and NFTs.

CryptoKitties became widely recognised as an NFT pioneer and an example of blockchain technology's potential for creating unique and tradable digital assets within the Metaverse. It has also contributed to the broader understanding of blockchain-based collectables and digital scarcity in virtual environments.

SOMNIUM SPACE (CUBE)

Somnium Space is a virtual world and Metaverse platform that utilises blockchain technology and its native cryptocurrency, CUBE, to enable users to buy, sell, and develop virtual real estate and create immersive experiences. Here's a detailed overview of how Somnium Space leverages blockchain and the CUBE cryptocurrency:

1. Virtual Real Estate and Parcels:

Somnium Space divides its virtual world into parcels of virtual land. Each parcel is a non-fungible token (NFT) on the Ethereum blockchain. Intelligent contracts govern ownership and transfers of these virtual land parcels, allowing users to buy, sell, and develop their virtual properties.

2. CUBE Cryptocurrency:

CUBE is the native cryptocurrency of Somnium Space, based on the Ethereum blockchain. CUBE is used for transactions, in-world purchases, and activities within the virtual world. Users can earn CUBE through participation in the platform's economy.

3. Content Creation and Monetization:

Users can create and monetise content on their virtual land parcels, including 3D models, interactive experiences, art galleries, and social spaces. Smart contracts enable creators to set rules and pricing for their content, facilitating transactions and monetisation.

4. User-Generated Content and Experiences:

Somnium Space encourages user-generated content like games, interactive experiences, and events. Intelligent contracts play a role in managing interactions and rewards within these experiences.

5. Blockchain-Based Identity and Avatars:

Users in Somnium Space have blockchain-based identities tied to their avatars. These digital identities offer trust and security, ensuring persistent user profiles in the virtual world.

6. Virtual Reality Integration:

Somnium Space is known for its compatibility with virtual reality (VR) headsets, providing immersive VR experiences. Blockchain technology and the CUBE cryptocurrency support transactions and in-world activities in the VR environment.

7. Events and Art Galleries:

The platform hosts virtual events, art exhibitions, and showcases within the virtual world. Users can explore, purchase, and experience blockchain-based NFT art pieces in these galleries.

8. Partnerships and Collaborations:

Somnium Space has collaborated with artists, brands, and organisations to bring valuable and recognisable content and experiences to the platform. These partnerships often involve blockchain-based assets and transactions.

9. Cross-Platform and Cross-Reality Interoperability:

Somnium Space has explored cross-platform and cross-reality integration, allowing users to carry their avatars, assets, and digital identities to other virtual worlds and experiences. This interoperability demonstrates the potential for a seamless transition between different Metaverse environments.

Somnium Space exemplifies how blockchain technology and a native cryptocurrency like CUBE can empower users to own, create, and monetise content and assets in a user-driven virtual environment. This integration enhances transparency, security, and economic opportunities for users and content creators within the Metaverse.

AXIE INFINITY (AXS AND SLP)

Axie Infinity is a blockchain-based online game and virtual world that uses two cryptocurrencies, AXS and SLP, to enable users to collect, breed, and battle fantasy creatures called Axies. Here's a detailed overview of how Axie Infinity utilises blockchain technology and these two cryptocurrencies:

1. Axie NFTs:

The core assets in Axie Infinity are the Axies themselves. Each Axie is represented as a unique non-fungible token (NFT) on the Ethereum blockchain. These NFTs are created, owned, and transferred using smart contracts.

2. Axie Breeding and Genes:

Users can breed their Axies to create new NFTs with a combination of traits and genes from the parent Axies. The genetic makeup of each Axie is stored on the blockchain, ensuring transparency and uniqueness.

3. AXS Token:

AXS is the native cryptocurrency of the Axie Infinity ecosystem. It has various use cases, including governance, staking, and earning rewards within the platform. Users can earn AXS by playing the game, participating in governance, and contributing to the ecosystem.

4. SLP Token:

SLP (Smooth Love Potion) is another cryptocurrency in the Axie Infinity ecosystem. It's earned by playing the game and breeding Axies. SLP can be used for various in-game activities, such as healing and other transactions.

5. Gameplay and Battles:

Users engage in turn-based battles with their Axies. These battles have a play-to-earn model, allowing users to earn SLP and other rewards based on their performance. Smart contracts govern the outcomes of battles and the distribution of rewards.

6. Marketplace and Trading:

Axie Infinity has a marketplace where users can buy, sell, and trade Axies. Users conduct AXS and SLP transactions, and smart contracts facilitate these peer-to-peer exchanges.

7. Governance and Staking:

AXS holders have governance rights and can participate in decision-making through proposals and voting. Users can also stake their AXS tokens to earn rewards and influence the direction of the ecosystem.

8. Partnerships and Collaborations:

Axie Infinity has collaborated with brands, organisations, and artists to create special edition Axies and themed collections. These partnerships often involve blockchain-based NFTs and limited-edition Axies.

9. Community and Tournaments:

The Axie Infinity community organises tournaments and events within the platform. These events demonstrate the potential for blockchain technology to support competitive gaming and digital collectables.

10. Economic Opportunities:

Axie Infinity has created economic opportunities for users in countries with lower income levels by allowing them to earn income through playing the game and trading Axies.

Axie Infinity showcases how blockchain technology and cryptocurrencies can be integrated into an online game and virtual world to create unique and tradable digital assets while providing a play-to-earn model. The game has attracted a large and active user base, emphasising the potential for blockchain technology to transform the gaming and virtual world landscape.

THE CENTRAL AND ART WEEK FESTIVAL

The Central and Art Week Festival is a notable event in the Decentraland platform, highlighting the integration of blockchain and smart contracts in the Metaverse to host virtual art exhibitions and facilitate the sale of NFT art pieces. Here's an overview of the festival:

1. Event and Concept:

The Central and Art Week Festival was a virtual art event in the Decentraland virtual world. It aimed to showcase the potential of blockchain technology and NFTs in the art world.

2. Virtual Art Galleries:

The festival featured virtual art galleries, where artists and creators displayed their digital artwork, which had been tokenised as NFTs. These galleries allowed attendees to explore, interact with, and purchase digital art pieces.

3. Blockchain-Based NFT Art:

The art showcased during the festival consisted of blockchain-based NFTs. Each piece was a unique digital asset with provenance and ownership secured by blockchain technology and smart contracts.

4. Smart Contract Transactions:

Attendees could engage in blockchain-based transactions to purchase NFT art pieces. Smart contracts facilitated the secure and transparent buying and selling of digital art.

5. Exhibitions and Showcases:

The festival hosted a variety of exhibitions and showcases, including digital art, virtual reality experiences, and interactive installations. Attendees could immerse themselves in the Metaverse while exploring these creative displays.

6. Limited Edition and Collectible Art:

Some art pieces on display were limited edition NFTs, making them highly collectable. The festival emphasised the concept of digital scarcity, where ownership of unique digital art had value and exclusivity.

7. Art Sales and Collecting:

Attendees had the opportunity to view the art and purchase NFTs of the artwork, adding them to their digital art collections. These purchases are both an investment and a way to support the artists.

8. Community Engagement:

The festival encouraged community engagement and participation, allowing attendees to interact with artists, curators, and other art enthusiasts. Attendees could discuss the art, its creation, and the impact of blockchain technology on the art world.

9. Blockchain Technology and NFTs:

The festival demonstrated how blockchain technology, smart contracts, and NFTs are transforming the art industry by providing artists with new opportunities for monetisation and art collectors with digital art ownership and provenance.

The Central and Art Week Festival exemplifies the role of blockchain and smart contracts in facilitating art exhibitions, art sales, and the creation of a unique and immersive art experience in the Metaverse. It showcases how this technology changes how we create, exhibit, and collect art in a virtual environment.

ENS AND .ETH DOMAINS

ENS, or the Ethereum Name Service, is a blockchain-based decentralised domain name system that allows users to register and manage .eth domains on the Ethereum blockchain. Here's a detailed overview of ENS and .eth domains:

ENS (Ethereum Name Service):

ENS is a decentralised, blockchain-based naming system that enables users to assign human-readable names to their Ethereum addresses, smart contracts, and decentralised applications. ENS is built on the Ethereum blockchain and leverages intelligent contracts for domain management.

.eth Domains:

.eth domains are specific domain names registered and managed through ENS. These domains end with ".eth" and are used for various purposes within the Ethereum ecosystem and the broader blockchain space.

Key Features and Functions:

> ENS and .eth domains provide several key features and functions:
> Human-Readable Addresses: ENS allows users to associate complex Ethereum addresses, which are typically long and alphanumeric, with user-friendly domain names. This makes it easier for people to send cryptocurrency and interact with decentralised applications.
> Decentralisation: ENS is decentralised and trustless, meaning it doesn't rely on a central authority to manage domain names. Instead, it uses Ethereum smart contracts to maintain the registry.
> Ownership and Control: Users have full ownership and control over their .eth domains. They can transfer, update, or sell their domains without requiring permission from a central authority.
> Integration: .eth domains can be used in various applications, including sending and receiving cryptocurrency, accessing decentralised websites, interacting with decentralised applications, and more.
> Security and Trust: ENS enhances security by reducing the risk of human errors in cryptocurrency transactions. Users can rely on memorable domain names rather than manually entering lengthy addresses.

Registration and Management:

To register a .eth domain, users can use ENS-enabled wallets or registrars. Registration involves interacting with smart contracts on the Ethereum blockchain. Users can configure their domains to point to their Ethereum address, IPFS content, and more.

Use Cases:

.eth domains have a wide range of use cases, including:

Simplified Transactions: Users can send cryptocurrency to human-readable addresses, reducing the risk of transaction errors.

> Decentralised Websites: .eth domains can access decentralised websites hosted on IPFS or other decentralised storage systems.
> Decentralised Applications: Developers can use .eth domains to enhance the user experience when interacting with decentralised applications (dApps).
> Personal Branding: .eth domains allow individuals and businesses to create a unique online identity in the blockchain space.
> NFTs and Digital Collectibles: .eth domains can be associated with NFTs and digital collectables, adding a layer of authenticity and ownership.

Interoperability:

ENS is working on improving cross-platform and cross-chain compatibility. This means .eth domains could be used in various blockchains and virtual worlds within the Metaverse.

ENS and .eth domains are pivotal in enhancing the user experience, security, and decentralisation of the Ethereum ecosystem and the broader blockchain space. They are a prime example of how blockchain technology evolves to meet users' needs in the Metaverse and beyond.

Reference Links

1. Significant Price Impact. (2021, April). fastercapital.com. Retrieved August 30, 2023, from https://fastercapital.com/keyword/significant-price-impact.html

2. Lubogo. (2023, February). Ethical AI and Algorithmic Decision-Making in IoT. In THE INTERNET OF THINGS: CONNECTING A SMARTER WORLD - A LESSON FOR UGANDA (1st ed., Vol. 1). Jescho Publishing House.

3. Agrawal. (2023, July 28). Taxation of cryptocurrencies in India. *AKLegal.*

4. Singha, S. & Mukthar, K. P. (2024). Transitioning to Digital Merchandise: Integrating Metaverse Into Retail Offerings. In B. Singla, K. Shalender, & N. Singh (Eds.), *Creator's Economy in Metaverse Platforms: Empowering Stakeholders Through Omnichannel Approach* (pp. 71-96). IGI Global. https://doi.org/10.4018/979-8-3693-3358-7.ch005

5. Djalolov, F. S. O. (2023, May 1). ISSUES FOR IMPROVING INCENTIVE STANDARDS IN LAW. *The American Journal of Political Science Law and Criminology,* 05(05), 46–49. https://doi.org/10.37547/tajpslc/volume05issue05-09

6. Xuan, P. Y., Fahumida, M. I. F., Al Nazir Hussain, M. I., Jayathilake, N. T., Khobragade, S., Soe, H. H. K., Moe, S., & Htay, M. N. N. (2023, June 30). *Readiness Towards Artificial Intelligence Among Undergraduate Students in Malaysia.* Education in Medicine Journal, 15(2), 49–60. https://doi.org/10.21315/eimj2023.15.2.4

7. Moro-Visconti , & Cesaretti. (2023, October 20). Digital Token Valuation. *SpringerLink.*

8. Barabási, A. (2016). *Network science.* Cambridge University Press.

9. Barabási, A., & Albert, R. (2002). Statistical mechanics of complex

networks. *Reviews of Modern Physics, 74*(1), 47–97.

10. Beckström, R. (2008). *The economics of networks and cybersecurity.* https://www.slideshare.net/RodBeckstrom/economics-of-networks-beckstrom-national-cybersecurity-center-department-of-homeland-security

11. Cheng, R., Wu, N., Chen, S., & Han, B. (2022). *Will metaverse be NextG internet? Vision, hype, and reality.* https://arxiv.org/abs/2201.12894

12. Gartner Research. (2022). *Emerging technologies: Critical insights on metaverse.* https://www.gartner.com/en/documents/4010017

13. Johnson, J. (2022, February). Metaverse—statistics & facts. *Statista.*

14. JP Morgan Onyx. (2022). *Opportunities in the metaverse: How business can explore the metaverse and navigate the hype vs. reality.* https://www.jpmorgan.com/content/dam/jpm/treasury-services/documents/opportunities-in-the-metaverse.pdf

15. Radoff, J. (2021). *Network effects in the metaverse.* https://medium.com/building-the-metaverse/network-effects-in-the-metaverse-5c39f9b94f5a

16. Jung. (2023, August 8). The Quiet Crypto Revolution. *SpringerLink.*

17. Chavan. (2023, January 6). Blockchain Essentials. *SpringerLink.*

18. Yadav. (2023, November 30). Digital Dimensions: Unveiling the Potential of E-Design and Virtual Prototyping. *International Conference on Sustainable Development Goals.*

19. Ashish Jagdish Sharma. (2023, September 19). The Future of the Metaverse: A Paradigm Shift in Digital Experiences. *Medium.*

20. Mwangi. (2022, December 19). Distributed Solutions for Secure Healthcare Data Exchange: A Critical Review of Privacy and Regulations. *Google Scholar.*

21. Adams. (2023, July 8). CCA vs GDPR: Understanding the Key Differences and Implications. *BusinessTech*.

22. Prakash. (2023, July 12). Data Privacy and Compliance Guide for Data Engineers: GDPR, CCPA, and Emerging Regulations. *Airbyte*.

23. Berlau. (2021, June 21). Deep Dive Episode 185 – SEC v. Ripple Labs: Cryptocurrency and "Regulation by Enforcement." *The Federalist Society*.

24. Ali. (2023, March). The Metaverse: The Future of Online Business. *LifeHack*.

25. (2023, July 27). Grading Criteria: Data Privacy, Cybersecurity, and Academic Integrity. *ZHENSHANGSUN*.

26. M. Asad, S. Otoum and O. Al Fandi, "Edge Computing for the Metaverse: Balancing Security and Privacy Concerns," 2023 International Conference on Intelligent Metaverse Technologies & Applications (iMETA), Tartu, Estonia, 2023, pp. 1-8, doi: 10.1109/iMETA59369.2023.10294768.

27. Campbell-Verduyn, Malcolm. (2018). Bitcoin, crypto-coins, and global anti-money laundering governance. Crime, Law and Social Change. 69. 10.1007/s10611-017-9756-5.

28. Boopathi, S. (2024). Balancing Innovation and Security in the Cloud: Navigating the Risks and Rewards of the Digital Age. In P. Goel, H. Pandey, A. Singhal, & S. Agarwal (Eds.), *Improving Security, Privacy, and Trust in Cloud Computing* (pp. 164-193). IGI Global. https://doi.org/10.4018/979-8-3693-1431-9.ch008

29. Agrawal A. V. Magulur L. P. Priya S. G. Kaur A. Singh G. Boopathi S. (2023). Smart Precision Agriculture Using IoT and WSN. In Handbook of Research on Data Science and Cybersecurity Innovations in Industry 4.0 Technologies (pp. 524–541). IGI Global. 10.4018/978-1-6684-8145-5.ch026

30. Agrawal, A. V., Pitchai, R., Senthamaraikannan, C., Balaji, N. A., Sajithra, S., & Boopathi, S. (2023). Digital Education System During the COVID-19 Pandemic. In *Using Assistive Technology for Inclusive Learning in K-12 Classrooms* (pp. 104–126). IGI Global. 10.4018/978-1-6684-6424-3.ch005

31. Agrawal, A. V., Shashibhushan, G., Pradeep, S., Padhi, S. N., Sugumar, D., & Boopathi, S. (2024). Synergizing Artificial Intelligence, 5G, and Cloud Computing for Efficient Energy Conversion Using Agricultural Waste. In *Practice, Progress, and Proficiency in Sustainability* (pp. 475–497). IGI Global. 10.4018/979-8-3693-1186-8.ch026

32. Al-Issa Y. Ottom M. A. Tamrawi A. (2019). eHealth cloud security challenges: A survey.Journal of Healthcare Engineering.31565209

33. Anitha, C., Komala, C., Vivekanand, C. V., Lalitha, S., & Boopathi, S. (2023). Artificial Intelligence driven security model for Internet of Medical Things (IoMT). IEEE Explore, (pp. 1–7). IEEE.

34. Arunprasad, R., & Boopathi, S. (2019). Chapter-4 Alternate Refrigerants for Minimization Environmental Impacts: A Review. In *Advances In Engineering Technology* (p. 75). AkiNik Publications New Delhi.

35. Awaysheh F. M. Aladwan M. N. Alazab M. Alawadi S. Cabaleiro J. C. Pena T. F. (2021). Security by design for big data frameworks over cloud computing.IEEE Transactions on Engineering Management, 69(6), 3676–3693. 10.1109/TEM.2020.3045661

36. Babu, B. S., Kamalakannan, J., Meenatchi, N., Karthik, S., & Boopathi, S. (2022). Economic impacts and reliability evaluation of battery by adopting Electric Vehicle. IEEE Explore, (pp. 1–6). IEEE.

37. Boopathi, S. (2021). *Pollution monitoring and notification: Water pollution monitoring and notification using intelligent RC boat.*

38. Boopathi S. (2023a). Internet of Things-Integrated Remote Patient

Monitoring System: Healthcare Application. In Dynamics of Swarm Intelligence Health Analysis for the Next Generation (pp. 137–161). IGI Global. 10.4018/978-1-6684-6894-4.ch008

39. Boopathi, S. (2023b). Securing Healthcare Systems Integrated With IoT: Fundamentals, Applications, and Future Trends. In Dynamics of Swarm Intelligence Health Analysis for the Next Generation (pp. 186–209). IGI Global.

40. Boopathi S. Kanike U. K. (2023). Applications of Artificial Intelligent and Machine Learning Techniques in Image Processing. In Handbook of Research on Thrust Technologies' Effect on Image Processing (pp. 151–173). IGI Global. 10.4018/978-1-6684-8618-4.ch010

41. Dotson C. (2023). Practical Cloud Security. O'Reilly Media, Inc.

42. Durairaj M. Jayakumar S. Karpagavalli V. Maheswari B. U. Boopathi S. (2023). Utilization of Digital Tools in the Indian Higher Education System During Health Crises. In Multidisciplinary Approaches to Organizational Governance During Health Crises (pp. 1–21). IGI Global. 10.4018/978-1-7998-9213-7.ch001

43. Gozman D. Willcocks L. (2019). The emerging Cloud Dilemma: Balancing innovation with cross-border privacy and outsourcing regulations.Journal of Business Research, 97, 235–256. 10.1016/j.jbusres.2018.06.006

44. Harikaran M. Boopathi S. Gokulakannan S. Poonguzhali M. (2023). Study on the Source of E-Waste Management and Disposal Methods. In Sustainable Approaches and Strategies for E-Waste Management and Utilization (pp. 39–60). IGI Global. 10.4018/978-1-6684-7573-7.ch003

45. Hema N. Krishnamoorthy N. Chavan S. M. Kumar N. Sabarimuthu M. Boopathi S. (2023). A Study on an Internet of Things (IoT)-Enabled Smart Solar Grid System. In Handbook of Research on Deep Learning Techniques for Cloud-Based Industrial IoT (pp. 290–308). IGI Global. 10.4018/978-1-6684-8098-4.ch017

46. Ingle, R. B., Senthil, T. S., Swathi, S., Muralidharan, N., Mahendran, G., & Boopathi, S. (2023). Sustainability and Optimization of Green and Lean Manufacturing Processes Using Machine Learning Techniques. In IGI Global. 10.4018/978-1-6684-8238-4.ch012

47. Jyoti A. Shrimali M. Tiwari S. Singh H. P. (2020). Cloud computing using load balancing and service broker policy for IT service: A taxonomy and survey.Journal of Ambient Intelligence and Humanized Computing, 11(11), 4785–4814. 10.1007/s12652-020-01747-z

48. Karthik, S., Hemalatha, R., Aruna, R., Deivakani, M., Reddy, R. V. K., & Boopathi, S. (2023). Study on Healthcare Security System-Integrated Internet of Things (IoT). In Perspectives and Considerations on the Evolution of Smart Systems (pp. 342–362). IGI Global.

49. Kavitha C. R. Varalatchoumy M. Mithuna H. R. Bharathi K. Geethalakshmi N. M. Boopathi S. (2023). Energy Monitoring and Control in the Smart Grid: Integrated Intelligent IoT and ANFIS. In ArshadM. (Ed.), (pp. 290–316). Advances in Bioinformatics and Biomedical Engineering. IGI Global. 10.4018/978-1-6684-6577-6.ch014

50. Koshariya A. K. Kalaiyarasi D. Jovith A. A. Sivakami T. Hasan D. S. Boopathi S. (2023). AI-Enabled IoT and WSN-Integrated Smart Agriculture System. In Artificial Intelligence Tools and Technologies for Smart Farming and Agriculture Practices (pp. 200–218). IGI Global. 10.4018/978-1-6684-8516-3.ch011

51. Koshariya A. K. Khatoon S. Marathe A. M. Suba G. M. Baral D. Boopathi S. (2023). Agricultural Waste Management Systems Using Artificial Intelligence Techniques. In AI-Enabled Social Robotics in Human Care Services (pp. 236–258). IGI Global. 10.4018/ 978-1-6684-8171-4.ch009

52. Kumar R. Goyal R. (2019). On cloud security requirements, threats, vulnerabilities and countermeasures: A survey.Computer Science Review, 33, 1–48. 10.1016/j.cosrev.2019.05.002

53. Kunduru A. R. (2023). Artificial intelligence usage in cloud application

performance improvement.Central Asian Journal of Mathematical Theory and Computer Sciences, 4(8), 42–47.

54. Maguluri, L. P., Ananth, J., Hariram, S., Geetha, C., Bhaskar, A., & Boopathi, S. (2023). Smart Vehicle-Emissions Monitoring System Using Internet of Things (IoT). In Handbook of Research on Safe Disposal Methods of Municipal Solid Wastes for a Sustainable Environment (pp. 191–211). IGI Global.

55. Maguluri L. P. Arularasan A. N. Boopathi S. (2023). Assessing Security Concerns for AI-Based Drones in Smart Cities. In KumarR.Abdul HamidA. B.Binti Ya'akubN. I. (Eds.), (pp. 27–47). Advances in Computational Intelligence and Robotics. IGI Global. 10.4018/ 978-1-6684-9151-5.ch002

56. Maheswari, B. U., Imambi, S. S., Hasan, D., Meenakshi, S., Pratheep, V., & Boopathi, S. (2023). Internet of Things and Machine Learning-Integrated Smart Robotics. In Global Perspectives on Robotics and Autonomous Systems: Development and Applications (pp. 240–258). IGI Global. 10.4018/978-1-6684-7791-5.ch010

57. Mohanty, A., Venkateswaran, N., Ranjit, P., Tripathi, M. A., & Boopathi, S. (2023). Innovative Strategy for Profitable Automobile Industries: Working Capital Management. In Handbook of Research on Designing Sustainable Supply Chains to Achieve a Circular Economy (pp. 412–428). IGI Global.

58. Pramila, P., Amudha, S., Saravanan, T., Sankar, S. R., Poongothai, E., & Boopathi, S. (2023). Design and Development of Robots for Medical Assistance: An Architectural Approach. In Contemporary Applications of Data Fusion for Advanced Healthcare Informatics (pp. 260–282). IGI Global.

59. Rahamathunnisa U. Subhashini P. Aancy H. M. Meenakshi S. Boopathi S. (2023). Solutions for Software Requirement Risks Using Artificial Intelligence Techniques. In Handbook of Research on Data Science and Cybersecurity Innovations in Industry 4.0 Technologies (pp. 45–64). IGI Global.

60. Rahamathunnisa U. Sudhakar K. Murugan T. K. Thivaharan S. Rajkumar M. Boopathi S. (2023). Cloud Computing Principles for Optimizing Robot Task Offloading Processes. In AI-Enabled Social Robotics in Human Care Services (pp. 188–211). IGI Global. 10.4018/978-1-6684-8171-4.ch007

61. Ramudu, K., Mohan, V. M., Jyothirmai, D., Prasad, D., Agrawal, R., & Boopathi, S. (2023). Machine Learning and Artificial Intelligence in Disease Prediction: Applications, Challenges, Limitations, Case Studies, and Future Directions. In Contemporary Applications of Data Fusion for Advanced Healthcare Informatics (pp. 297–318). IGI Global.

62. Rayhan R. Rayhan S. (2023). AI and Human Rights: Balancing Innovation and Privacy in the Digital Age.

63. Reddy, M. A., Gaurav, A., Ushasukhanya, S., Rao, V. C. S., Bhattacharya, S., & Boopathi, S. (2023). Bio-Medical Wastes Handling Strategies During the COVID-19 Pandemic. In Multidisciplinary Approaches to Organizational Governance During Health Crises (pp. 90–111). IGI Global. 10.4018/978-1-7998-9213-7.ch006

64. Reddy M. A. Reddy B. M. Mukund C. Venneti K. Preethi D. Boopathi S. (2023). Social Health Protection During the COVID-Pandemic Using IoT. In The COVID-19 Pandemic and the Digitalization of Diplomacy (pp. 204–235). IGI Global. 10.4018/978-1-7998-8394-4.ch009

65. R.M. , S. P., Bhattacharya, S., Maddikunta, P. K. R., Somayaji, S. R. K., Lakshmanna, K., Kaluri, R., Hussien, A., & Gadekallu, T. R. (2020). Load balancing of energy cloud using wind driven and firefly algorithms in internet of everything.Journal of Parallel and Distributed Computing, 142, 16–26. 10.1016/j.jpdc.2020.02.010

66. Sankar K. M. Booba B. Boopathi S. (2023). Smart Agriculture Irrigation Monitoring System Using Internet of Things. In Contemporary Developments in Agricultural Cyber-Physical Systems (pp. 105–121). IGI Global. 10.4018/978-1-6684-7879-0.ch006

67. Satav, S. D., Hasan, D. S., Pitchai, R., Mohanaprakash, T. A., Sultanuddin, S. J., & Boopathi, S. (2024). Next Generation of Internet of Things (NGIoT) in Healthcare Systems. In Practice, Progress, and Proficiency in Sustainability (pp. 307–330). IGI Global. 10.4018/979-8-3693-1186-8.ch017

68. Satav, S. D., & Lamani, D. G, H. K., Kumar, N. M. G., Manikandan, S., & Sampath, B. (2024). Energy and Battery Management in the Era of Cloud Computing. In Practice, Progress, and Proficiency in Sustainability (pp. 141–166). IGI Global. 10.4018/979-8-3693-1186-8.ch009

69. Schneckenberg D. Benitez J. Klos C. Velamuri V. K. Spieth P. (2021). Value creation and appropriation of software vendors: A digital innovation model for cloud computing.Information & Management, 58(4), 103463. 10.1016/j.im.2021.103463

70. Sengeni D. Padmapriya G. Imambi S. S. Suganthi D. Suri A. Boopathi S. (2023). Biomedical Waste Handling Method Using Artificial Intelligence Techniques. In Handbook of Research on Safe Disposal Methods of Municipal Solid Wastes for a Sustainable Environment (pp. 306–323). IGI Global. 10.4018/978-1-6684-8117-2.ch022

71. Shahid M. A. Islam N. Alam M. M. Su'ud M. M. Musa S. (2020). A comprehensive study of load balancing approaches in the cloud computing environment and a novel fault tolerance approach.IEEE Access : Practical Innovations, Open Solutions, 8, 130500–130526. 10.1109/ ACCESS.2020.3009184

72. Srinivas B. Maguluri L. P. Naidu K. V. Reddy L. C. S. Deivakani M. Boopathi S. (2023). Architecture and Framework for Interfacing Cloud-Enabled Robots. In Handbook of Research on Data Science and Cybersecurity Innovations in Industry 4.0 Technologies (pp. 542–560). IGI Global. 10.4018/978-1-6684-8145-5.ch027

73. Syamala M. Komala C. Pramila P. Dash S. Meenakshi S. Boopathi S. (2023). Machine Learning-Integrated IoT-Based Smart Home Energy Management System. In Handbook of Research on Deep Learning Techniques for Cloud-Based Industrial IoT (pp. 219–235). IGI Global.

10.4018/978-1-6684-8098-4.ch013

74. Ugandar R. E. Rahamathunnisa U. Sajithra S. Christiana M. B. V. Palai B. K. Boopathi S. (2023). Hospital Waste Management Using Internet of Things and Deep Learning: Enhanced Efficiency and Sustainability. In ArshadM. (Ed.), (pp. 317–343). Advances in Bioinformatics and Biomedical Engineering. IGI Global. 10.4018/978-1-6684-6577-6.ch015

75. Venkateswaran N. Kumar S. S. Diwakar G. Gnanasangeetha D. Boopathi S. (2023). Synthetic Biology for Waste Water to Energy Conversion: IoT and AI Approaches. In ArshadM. (Ed.), (pp. 360–384). Advances in Bioinformatics and Biomedical Engineering. IGI Global. 10.4018/978-1-6684-6577-6.ch017

76. Venkateswaran, N., Vidhya, K., Ayyannan, M., Chavan, S. M., Sekar, K., & Boopathi, S. (2023). A Study on Smart Energy Management Framework Using Cloud Computing. In 5G, Artificial Intelligence, and Next Generation Internet of Things: Digital Innovation for Green and Sustainable Economies (pp. 189–212). IGI Global. 10.4018/978-1-6684-8634-4.ch009

77. Andonov S, Cundeva-Blajer M (2018) Calibration for industry 4.0 metrology: touchless calibration. J Phys Conf Ser 1065(7):072019

78. Andresen SL (2002) John McCarthy: father of AI. IEEE Intell Syst 17(5):84–85

79. Arute F, Arya K, Babbush R, Bacon D, Bardin JC, Baren R, Biswas R, Boixo S, Brandao FGSL, Buell DA, Burkett B, Chen Y, Chen Z, Chiaro B, Collins R, Courtney W, Dunsworth A (2019) Quantum supremacy using a programmable superconducting processor. Nature 574:505–510

80. Aslan A, Zhang K (2021) AI technologies for education: recent research & future directions. Comput Educ Artif Intell 2:100025

81. Aswal DK (2020) Quality infrastructure of India and its importance for inclusive national growth. Mapan 35:139–150

82. Bloomberg J (2018) Digitization, digitalization, and digital transformation: confuse them at your peril. Forbes. https://www.forbes.com/sites/jasonbloomberg/2018/04/29/digitization-digitalization-and-digital-transformation-confuse-them-at-your-peril. Accessed 2023

83. Commins K (2004) Overview of current status of standards and conformity assessment systems. In: Background papers of the International Task Force on Harmonisation and Equivalence in Organic Agriculture

84. Creswell A, White T, Dumoulin V, Arulkumaran K, Sengupta B, Bharath AA (2018) Generative adversarial networks: an overview. IEEE Signal Process Mag 35(1):53

85. Government of India (2010) Guidelines for usage of digital signatures in e-Governance. [Online]. https://egovstandards.gov.in/sites/default/files/2021-07/Usage%20of%20Digital%20Signature%20in%20e-Governance%20Ver1.0.pdf

86. Gupta P (2022) Industrial internet of things in intelligent manufacturing: a review, approaches, opportunities, open challenges, and future directions. Int J Interact Des Manuf. Published by Springer Nature. https://doi.org/10.1007/s12008-022-01075-w

87. Johannes V (2020) NDE perception and emerging reality: NDE 4.0 value extraction. Mater Eval 78(7):835–851

88. Malali AB, Gopalakrishnan S (2020) Application of artificial intelligence and its powered technologies in the Indian banking and financial industry: an overview. IOSR J Humanit Soc Sci 25(4):55–60

89. Mogali S (2014) Artificial intelligence and its applications in libraries. In: Conference: bilingual international conference on information technology: yesterday, today and tomorrow. At Defence Scientific Information and Documentation Centre, Ministry of Defence, Delhi

90. Panicker RA, Kalyanakrishnan S, Natarajan S, Rao S (2018)

Opportunities and challenges for artificial intelligence in India. In: Proceedings of the 2018 AAAI/ACM conference on AI, ethics, and society

91. Runkler TA (2020) Data analytics: models and algorithms for intelligent data analysis. Springer Vieweg, Wiesbaden, pp 1–4

92. Simon HA (1995) Artificial intelligence: an empirical science. Artif Intell 77(1):95–127

93. van der Zant T, Kouw M, Schomaker L (2012) Generative artificial intelligence. In: Theory and philosophy of artificial intelligence. Springer, Berlin

94. Dr G. Nagarajan, SundharaMoorthy.V, Dr. A. Khan Mohamed, Dr.A sulthanMohideen, Dr M.Mohamed Ishaq, M.Raja Laksmi(2023). The Role Of The Metaverse In Digital Marketing.Journal for Educators, Teachers and Trainers14(5). 51-59

95. Achar S. (2021). An Overview of Environmental Scalability and Security in Hybrid Cloud Infrastructure Designs.Asia Pacific Journal of Energy and Environment, 8(2), 39–46. 10.18034/apjee.v8i2.650

96. Agrawal A. V. Magulur L. P. Priya S. G. Kaur A. Singh G. Boopathi S. (2023). Smart Precision Agriculture Using IoT and WSN. In Handbook of Research on Data Science and Cybersecurity Innovations in Industry 4.0 Technologies (pp. 524–541). IGI Global. 10.4018/ 978-1-6684-8145-5.ch026

97. Agrawal, A. V., Shashibhushan, G., Pradeep, S., Padhi, S. N., Sugumar, D., & Boopathi, S. (2024). Synergizing Artificial Intelligence, 5G, and Cloud Computing for Efficient Energy Conversion Using Agricultural Waste. In Practice, Progress, and Proficiency in Sustainability (pp. 475–497). IGI Global. 10.4018/979-8-3693-1186-8.ch026

98. Al-Issa Y. Ottom M. A. Tamrawi A. (2019). eHealth cloud security challenges: A survey.Journal of Healthcare Engineering, 2019.31565209

99. Alghofaili Y. Albattah A. Alrajeh N. Rassam M. A. Al-Rimy B. A. S. (2021). Secure cloud infrastructure: A survey on issues, current solutions, and open challenges.Applied Sciences (Basel, Switzerland), 11(19), 9005. 10.3390/app11199005

100. Anitha, C., Komala, C., Vivekanand, C. V., Lalitha, S., & Boopathi, S. (2023). Artificial Intelligence driven security model for Internet of Medical Things (IoMT). IEEE Explore, 1–7.

101. Awaysheh F. M. Aladwan M. N. Alazab M. Alawadi S. Cabaleiro J. C. Pena T. F. (2021). Security by design for big data frameworks over cloud computing.IEEE Transactions on Engineering Management, 69(6), 3676–3693. 10.1109/TEM.2020.3045661

102. Bhajantri L. B. Mujawar T. (2019). A survey of cloud computing security challenges, issues and their countermeasures.2019 Third International Conference on I-SMAC (IoT in Social, Mobile, Analytics and Cloud)(I-SMAC), (pp. 376–380). ACM. 10.1109/I-SMAC47947.2019.9032545

103. Boopathi, S. (2023). Deep Learning Techniques Applied for Automatic Sentence Generation. In Promoting Diversity, Equity, and Inclusion in Language Learning Environments (pp. 255–273). IGI Global. 10.4018/978-1-6684-3632-5.ch016

104. Dhanya, D., Kumar, S. S., Thilagavathy, A., Prasad, D., & Boopathi, S. (2023). Data Analytics and Artificial Intelligence in the Circular Economy: Case Studies. In Intelligent Engineering Applications and Applied Sciences for Sustainability (pp. 40–58). IGI Global.

105. George A. S. Sagayarajan S. (2023). Securing Cloud Application Infrastructure: Understanding the Penetration Testing Challenges of IaaS, PaaS, and SaaS Environments.Partners Universal International Research Journal, 2(1), 24–34.

106. Gnanaprakasam, C., Vankara, J., Sastry, A. S., Prajval, V., Gireesh, N., & Boopathi, S. (2023). Long-Range and Low-Power Automated Soil Irrigation System Using Internet of Things: An Experimental Study. In

Contemporary Developments in Agricultural Cyber-Physical Systems (pp. 87–104). IGI Global.

107. Gozman D. Willcocks L. (2019). The emerging Cloud Dilemma: Balancing innovation with cross-border privacy and outsourcing regulations.Journal of Business Research, 97, 235–256. 10.1016/j.jbusres.2018.06.006

108. Hema N. Krishnamoorthy N. Chavan S. M. Kumar N. Sabarimuthu M. Boopathi S. (2023). A Study on an Internet of Things (IoT)-Enabled Smart Solar Grid System. In Handbook of Research on Deep Learning Techniques for Cloud-Based Industrial IoT (pp. 290–308). IGI Global. 10.4018/978-1-6684-8098-4.ch017

109. Ingle, R. B., Senthil, T. S., Swathi, S., Muralidharan, N., Mahendran, G., & Boopathi, S. (2023). Sustainability and Optimization of Green and Lean Manufacturing Processes Using Machine Learning Techniques. IGI Global. 10.4018/978-1-6684-8238-4.ch012

110. Isharufe W. Jaafar F. Butakov S. (2020). Study of security issues in platform-as-a-service (paas) cloud model.2020 International Conference on Electrical, Communication, and Computer Engineering (ICECCE), (pp. 1–6). IEEE. 10.1109/ICECCE49384.2020.9179414

111. Jyoti A. Shrimali M. Tiwari S. Singh H. P. (2020). Cloud computing using load balancing and service broker policy for IT service: A taxonomy and survey.Journal of Ambient Intelligence and Humanized Computing, 11(11), 4785–4814. 10.1007/s12652-020-01747-z

112. Karthik, S., Hemalatha, R., Aruna, R., Deivakani, M., Reddy, R. V. K., & Boopathi, S. (2023). Study on Healthcare Security System-Integrated Internet of Things (IoT). In Perspectives and Considerations on the Evolution of Smart Systems (pp. 342–362). IGI Global.

113. Kavitha C. R. Varalatchoumy M. Mithuna H. R. Bharathi K. Geethalakshmi N. M. Boopathi S. (2023). Energy Monitoring and Control in the Smart Grid: Integrated Intelligent IoT and ANFIS. In ArshadM. (Ed.), (pp. 290–316). Advances in Bioinformatics and Biomedical

Engineering. IGI Global. 10.4018/978-1-6684-6577-6.ch014

114. Kumar P. R. Meenakshi S. Shalini S. Devi S. R. Boopathi S. (2023). Soil Quality Prediction in Context Learning Approaches Using Deep Learning and Blockchain for Smart Agriculture. In KumarR.Abdul HamidA. B.Binti Ya'akubN. I. (Eds.), (pp. 1–26). Advances in Computational Intelligence and Robotics. IGI Global. 10.4018/ 978-1-6684-9151-5.ch001

115. Kumar R. Goyal R. (2019). On cloud security requirements, threats, vulnerabilities and countermeasures: A survey.Computer Science Review, 33, 1–48. 10.1016/j.cosrev.2019.05.002

116. Maguluri L. P. Arularasan A. N. Boopathi S. (2023). Assessing Security Concerns for AI-Based Drones in Smart Cities. In KumarR.Abdul HamidA. B.Binti Ya'akubN. I. (Eds.), (pp. 27–47). Advances in Computational Intelligence and Robotics. IGI Global. 10.4018/ 978-1-6684-9151-5.ch002

117. Maheswari, B. U., Imambi, S. S., Hasan, D., Meenakshi, S., Pratheep, V., & Boopathi, S. (2023). Internet of Things and Machine Learning-Integrated Smart Robotics. In Global Perspectives on Robotics and Autonomous Systems: Development and Applications (pp. 240–258). IGI Global. 10.4018/978-1-6684 7791-5.ch010

118. Mukhopadhyay B. Bose R. Roy S. (2020). A novel approach to load balancing and cloud computing security using SSL in IaaS environment.International Journal (Toronto, Ont.), 9(2).

119. Parast F. K. Sindhav C. Nikam S. Yekta H. I. Kent K. B. Hakak S. (2022). Cloud computing security: A survey of service-based models.Computers & Security, 114, 102580. 10.1016/j.cose.2021.102580

120. Pramila, P., Amudha, S., Saravanan, T., Sankar, S. R., Poongothai, E., & Boopathi, S. (2023). Design and Development of Robots for Medical Assistance: An Architectural Approach. In Contemporary Applications of Data Fusion for Advanced Healthcare Informatics (pp. 260–282). IGI Global.

121. Rahamathunnisa U. Subhashini P. Aancy H. M. Meenakshi S. Boopathi S. (2023). Solutions for Software Requirement Risks Using Artificial Intelligence Techniques. In Handbook of Research on Data Science and Cybersecurity Innovations in Industry 4.0 Technologies (pp. 45–64). IGI Global.

122. Rahamathunnisa U. Sudhakar K. Murugan T. K. Thivaharan S. Rajkumar M. Boopathi S. (2023). Cloud Computing Principles for Optimizing Robot Task Offloading Processes. In AI-Enabled Social Robotics in Human Care Services (pp. 188–211). IGI Global. 10.4018/978-1-6684-8171-4.ch007

123. Ramudu, K., Mohan, V. M., Jyothirmai, D., Prasad, D., Agrawal, R., & Boopathi, S. (2023). Machine Learning and Artificial Intelligence in Disease Prediction: Applications, Challenges, Limitations, Case Studies, and Future Directions. In Contemporary Applications of Data Fusion for Advanced Healthcare Informatics (pp. 297–318). IGI Global.

124. Rayhan R. Rayhan S. (2023). AI and Human Rights: Balancing Innovation and Privacy in the Digital Age. DOI.

125. RM , S. P., Bhattacharya, S., Maddikunta, P. K. R., Somayaji, S. R. K., Lakshmanna, K., Kaluri, R., Hussien, A., & Gadekallu, T. R. (2020). Load balancing of energy cloud using wind driven and firefly algorithms in internet of everything.Journal of Parallel and Distributed Computing, 142, 16–26. 10.1016/j.jpdc.2020.02.010

126. Saini D. K. Kumar K. Gupta P. (2022). Security issues in IoT and cloud computing service models with suggested solutions.Security and Communication Networks, 2022, 2022. 10.1155/2022/4943225

127. Satav, S. D., & Lamani, D. G, H. K., Kumar, N. M. G., Manikandan, S., & Sampath, B. (2024). Energy and Battery Management in the Era of Cloud Computing. In Practice, Progress, and Proficiency in Sustainability (pp. 141–166). IGI Global. 10.4018/979-8-3693-1186-8.ch009

128. Shahid M. A. Islam N. Alam M. M. Su'ud M. M. Musa S. (2020).

A comprehensive study of load balancing approaches in the cloud computing environment and a novel fault tolerance approach.IEEE Access : Practical Innovations, Open Solutions, 8, 130500–130526. 10.1109/ ACCESS.2020.3009184

129. Srinivas B. Maguluri L. P. Naidu K. V. Reddy L. C. S. Deivakani M. Boopathi S. (2023). Architecture and Framework for Interfacing Cloud-Enabled Robots. In Handbook of Research on Data Science and Cybersecurity Innovations in Industry 4.0 Technologies (pp. 542–560). IGI Global. 10.4018/978-1-6684-8145-5.ch027

130. Syamala M. Komala C. Pramila P. Dash S. Meenakshi S. Boopathi S. (2023). Machine Learning-Integrated IoT-Based Smart Home Energy Management System. In Handbook of Research on Deep Learning Techniques for Cloud-Based Industrial IoT (pp. 219–235). IGI Global. 10.4018/978-1-6684-8098-4.ch013

131. Veeranjaneyulu, R., Boopathi, S., Narasimharao, J., Gupta, K. K., Reddy, R. V. K., & Ambika, R. (2023). Identification of Heart Diseases using Novel Machine Learning Method. IEEE- Explore, 1–6.

www.ingramcontent.com/pod-product-compliance
Lightning Source LLC
Chambersburg PA
CBHW021332150726
47989CB00005B/1957